Identity, Conflict, and Cooperation

Identity, Conflict, and Cooperation

Central Europeans in Cleveland, 1850–1930

Edited by

David C. Hammack,
Diane L. Grabowski,
and John J. Grabowski

The Western Reserve Historical Society

Cleveland, Ohio

Dedicated to the memory of Werner D. Mueller.

LC 2002019048
ISBN 0-911704-55-8
Manufactured in the United States of America
The Western Reserve Historical Society Publication Number 190
06 05 04 03   5 4 3 2 1

Library of Congress Cataloging-in-Publication Data
Identity, conflict, and cooperation : Central Europeans
in Cleveland, 1850–1930 / edited by David C. Hammack,
Diane L. Grabowski, and John J. Grabowski.
p. cm.
Includes bibliographical references and index.
ISBN 0-911704-55-8 (alk. paper)
1. East European Americans—Ohio—Cleveland—History. 2. East European
Americans—Ohio—Cleveland—Ethnic identity. 3. East European
Americans—Ohio—Cleveland—Social conditions. 4. Immigrants—
Ohio—Cleveland—History. 5. Immigrants—Ohio—Cleveland—
Social conditions. 6. Cleveland (Ohio)—History. 7. Cleveland (Ohio)—
Ethnic relations. 8. Cleveland (Ohio)—Social conditions.
I. Title: Central Europeans in Cleveland, 1850–1930. II. Hammack, David C.
III. Grabowski, Diane L., 1954– IV. Grabowski, John J.
F499.C69 E17 2002
977.1'32004918—dc21   2002019048

British Library Cataloging-in-Publication data are available.

Contents

Preface and Acknowledgments

In 1989 a group of group of scholars from Europe and the United States came to Cleveland, Ohio, to undertake an intensive study of the history of six immigrant communities in that city. Those six groups, Croatians, Czechs, Hungarians, Poles, Slovaks, and Slovenes, had a substantial presence in the city during the early years of the twentieth century and were pivitol to its industrial economy. Supported by a grant from the Volkswagen Foundation and directed by Professor Dirk Hoerder of the University of Bremen, the scholars sought to discover ways in which these communities interacted with one another in the years between the end of the American Civil War and the beginning of the Great Depression. The Cleveland study was envisioned as part of a larger, transnational comparative study with Láslo Katus and Gábor Gyáni reviewing the history of migrant and immigrant groups in Budapest during the late nineteenth and early twentieth centuries. The Case Western Reserve University Department of History and the Western Reserve Historical Society served in a number of ways as local hosts for the visiting scholars; the Cleveland Public Library, Cleveland State University, the Catholic Diocese of Cleveland, and other Cleveland organizations also provided resources.

Those who participated in the research in Cleveland brought important skills and viewpoints. Their linguistic abilities allowed them to fully utilize foreign-language sources in various archives in Cleveland. As Europeans, Dirk Hoerder and five of his colleagues brought a different intellectual and political perspective to a topic that had theretofore been viewed largely through parochial lenses. The two American scholars on the initial research team also had a broader view of the groups they were to study and thus provided additional perspective to the research.

The research in Cleveland took a better part of the year. Its initial product was a set of six substantial immigrant community histories and a short overview of the Cleveland setting. Each of the histories contained information that had not before been available in English. Each still represents the best available overview of the particular immigrant community for the time period of the study.

Discussions of publishing the community histories as a single unit began immediately upon completion of the research phase; Dirk Hoerder graciously arranged for a follow-up conference for this purpose in Worpswede, near Bremen. However, a number of factors served to delay that process for over a decade. The sheer length of the individual histories, added to the fact that they had been written in what amounted to seven different voices, posed an enormous editorial challenge. Equally challenging was the need to provide introductory material that would place the individual chapters into the perspective of the history of urban and economic development in Europe and in Northeast Ohio, and that would elaborate on the common themes that occurred within them.

Although the authors, working with David Hammack and John Grabowski, initially attempted to make these changes, it soon became apparent that none could devote the necessary time to the task given their duties as teachers and their needs to pursue new research. Most of the European authors lived in Hungary, Poland, Croatia, and Slovenia: the events that overtook their nations after the late 1980s made it all the more difficult to focus on this project. Funding for independent editorial work became the key to completing this work. Fortunately, Mr. Werner D. Mueller of Cleveland agreed to provide the support necessary to edit and publish the manuscript. It was to be one of many publications that he funded for the Western Reserve Historical Society. In many ways it was the one closest to his interests. Unfortunately, his death in September 2001, denied him the opportunity to see the finished product.

The essential final funding came available almost a decade after the original research. By that time the fields of immigration history and ethnic studies had seen considerable change. New issues concerning gender and race have come to the theoretical forefront of the field. More generally, the study of European immigrant communities in the United States has been eclipsed by attention to non-European peoples and to a focus on global migrant diasporas. Those changes are not fully reflected in this study. Nevertheless, this study does continue to have value for the historian, both in the way it addresses issues of conflict and cooperation, and in the data it provides on the immigrant experience in a major American city. That data hints at and provides the basis for further explorations of immigration and ethnicity in Cleveland.

Those wishing to further explore such issues should note that the six immigrant community histories presented in this volume represent abridged versions of the original manuscripts prepared in 1989. Those manuscripts are preserved in the library of the Western Reserve Historical Society where they are accessible to researchers. Additionally, several of the authors have published fuller versions of their Cleveland research elsewhere. Such publications are noted at the end of each of the chapters.

As editors of this study we owe a debt to the authors, Winston Chrislock, Ivan Čizmić, Matjaž Klemenčič, Michael Kopanic, Julianna Puskás, and Adam Walaszek, for their patience and for their valuable assistance in getting the manuscript into a final, publishable form. We owe a particular debt to Adam Walaszek for his early, voluntary work in preparing a concise form of each essay. Additional voluntary work by Loraine Hammack moved the work closer to its final format. Diane Ewart Grabowski served as the principal editor for this final version, working to insure consistency of style and a balance of content among the various essays.

Professor Dirk Hoerder, the initiator of the project, deserves commendation both for his patience and for his vision. Without his foresight and fund raising skills the histories of six immigrant communities in Cleveland, Ohio, would likely have remained only marginally known, as would the story of cooperation and conflict between them. If the publication of this study serves to catalyze further work it will be to his credit.

If we have any regrets they are that Dr. Gudrun Birnbaum who brought insight and great sophistication to the initial investigation, and Werner Mueller who supported this publication, will not see it in its final form.

From Ethnic to Interethnic History: An Introduction

DIRK HOERDER

The history of Cleveland, like that of other American cities, has frequently been written in terms of immigration and ethnic groups. Such histories have, however, often overlooked interethnic cooperation while emphasizing conflict between groups. The interaction of ethno-cultural groups is in fact more complex, for although cultural traditions differed, conditions of entry were similar, and the migration experience shared.

The continuities between old world and new expressed themselves in interethnic cooperation in the initial phase of immigration, when only a few men and women from a given cultural group had arrived, too few to build their own institutions, to find labor market niches, or to satisfy their emotional and spiritual desires. In a second stage, when group size was sufficiently large, an ethnicization of parishes, mutual-aid societies, and other associations took place. Once intellectuals—journalists, teachers, priests—arrived, they provided an additional focus for ethnic cohesion and identity, for instance by establishing newspapers. But these cultural sentries, whose incomes depended on group coherence, also expressed old world antagonisms. They jealously guarded their group against those regarded as enemies, attacking with sharp pens. In 1904 and 1911, for example, during the visits of a prominent Hungarian politician to Cleveland, spokesmen for the city's Slovaks responded to the event by raising demands for more Slovak rights in Hungarian-ruled lands. But workers on the shop floor, neighborhood merchants, and women sharing front steps could not afford old-world conflicts in their daily lives; they needed to cooperate.

Since men and women carry their cultural traditions, political opinions, and practices of resistance and accommodation as well as their emotional and spiritual values with them, scholars of the immigrant experience, or the multiple experiences, need a thorough understanding of the culture of origin and childhood socialization in it. To study the *interethnic* history of East European immigrants in Cleveland, the Labor Migration Project at the University of Bremen brought together scholars from six East Central and Southeast European societies of origin for a research project, "Conflict and Cooperation: Comparative Research on the East European Migratory Experience, 1880s–1930s."[1]

When the project was in its planning stages in the early 1980s, the "uprooted" paradigm had lost its hold on scholars of immigration, but the Chicago School's important work and Milton Gordon's oft-cited study of assimilation still informed approaches.[2] Other theoretical concepts—Chicago sociologists' work on Latin America, the context of "peasant studies" and a "folk-urban continuum," the research of the Manchester research groups on kinship networks and mobility, the studies of Everett and Helen MacGill Hughes in Montreal—were overlooked. The Cleveland-centered research team of the Labor Migration Project began its work informed by the cultures of origin in the spirit of the women social workers in turn-of-the-century Chicago and elsewhere. Jane Addams, Grace and Edith Abbott, Sophonisba Brekinridge, and other settlement house residents collected data to understand and help immigrant individuals rather than to theorize about group cultures. Robert E. Park, on the other hand, fit his valuable data on the ethnic press into preconceived notions about propaganda and Americanization.[3]

Using their life-experiences in the culture of origin to enter Cleveland's labor markets quickly, migrants, who had to earn the means for physical subsistence immediately after arrival, invalidated scholars' notions of "dislocation." Some migrants perceived a bewildering amount of difference between their old world and their new surroundings, and were terrified by, for example, the thunderous din in a factory; while others, arriving in Cleveland, focused on the developing ethnic settlement itself, happily exclaiming, "This is Tarnow!"—the old world existing in the new and yet different, the new world to be understood with the emotions, values, and experiences of the old.[4]

It was clear to the research group that no single "American" model to which immigrants might aspire existed. Cleveland's society was heterogeneous by class, gender, occupation, and other criteria. The newcomers, few of whom spoke English upon arrival, for the most part mingled with earlier immigrants. If models of acculturation were accessible, they were the experiences of those earlier immigrants. According to conventional wisdom,

ethnic children would become Americans in the school system. Socialization of the second generation would, however, therefore depend on attendance, and, as research has shown, neither official regulations nor parental
aspirations required regular presence in the classroom. Thus schools had
only a limited impact. Teaching in bicultural Montreal at McGill University
in the 1930s, the Hughes had realized early that no monocultural model of
acculturation was provided by receiving societies, whether Canadian or
American. Their cautious critique of the assimilation model, however, did
not enter scholarly discourse, not even when they taught at the University
of Chicago.[5]

In response to the new developments in migration and acculturation history, the Cleveland project's research team constituted itself in a different
way and chose a different approach. Scholars from the six cultures of origin,
Polish, Magyar, Czech, Slovak, Slovene, and Croatian (at the time divided
into four countries, Poland, Hungary, Czechoslovakia, and Yugoslavia),
developed a research agenda in cooperation with other scholars in the Labor
Migration Project and with the advice of colleagues in Cleveland.[6] The
powers-that-were did not grant exit permits to the Czech and Slovak researchers, but two American colleagues with research experience in the two
cultures of origin were able to take their places. The participating East Central and Southeast European scholars also had previous North American
research experience. Thus all had experienced bicultural lives and had to
interact across the boundaries of national or ethnic scholarly discourse. The
research was coordinated by a French-German scholar able to speak or read
several of the Central European languages involved.[7] Parallel research on
the cultures from which the migrants came was coordinated by a German
scholar and took a broadly comparative approach.[8] After a period of joint
research by the seven scholars in Cleveland, results of all these investigations
were discussed at an international symposium in 1990.[9] Other scholars in
the field provided input on immigrants and Cleveland's public libraries,[10]
on an Austrian labor activist and editor in Cleveland,[11] and on parallel migration and acculturation processes within historic Hungary to Budapest.[12]
In Cleveland, several scholars provided advice and support.[13] Thus a truly
cooperative project evolved in which linguistic capabilities, cultural experience, and differing approaches permitted a maximization of research input.[14]

On the basis of their work in the cultures of origin, the research team first
studied the social environment into which the immigrants came: Cleveland's neighborhoods, school system, cultural services to the newcomers,
and city politics. Geographic features, such as ravines and rivers, and human

constructs, most importantly transportation arteries, divided the cityscape into localized regions, or even "islands" of settlement. Industrialization and Taylorization permitted skilled agriculturalists to find unskilled factory jobs, as peasants turned proletarians. Many of the immigrant workers, however, came from the landless or marginal rural population. Their new employers, Cleveland's industrialists and commercial proprietors, came from Protestant New England stock or from earlier immigrants of different cultures. Schools provided education, but neither established city authorities nor newly arrived parents, not to mention many of the pupils themselves, took attendance seriously. Living conditions could in some instances be healthy and even provide economic benefits, as in the outlying areas where immigrants tended household vegetable patches, and sometimes entered market gardening. Other areas of settlement, in the dirty and toxic environs of transportation facilities and factories, were at best unpleasant and at worst posed serious health and safety risks. Environmental protection and conservation may have been a concern of President Theodore Roosevelt, but not of Cleveland's industrialists and city fathers.

In the second stage of research, each scholar concentrated on his/her group and its several communities. In the process archival materials were unearthed that had never been used before and that provided insights far beyond what had been expected,[15] providing material for expanded separate studies of some groups.[16] The research confirmed that with the arrival of the newcomers, the city's once mainly Protestant religious life diversified to include varieties of belief or opinion ranging from Orthodox to freethought, but with Roman Catholicism, in particular, gaining new importance and also organizational complexity. Parishes emerged from the bottom up, a community-generated activity unthinkable in Europe where hierarchies or landlords were in charge of church organization. Priests faced "flocks" of independent-minded men and women who demanded a share in the governance of the church and its parish, who through their contributions funded parish expenses (including the priest's salary), and who sometimes defied pastors and diocesan authorities by, for example, marrying outside of their designated parish. Other institutions formed by the immigrant groups included the numerous cultural, self-help, and mutual aid societies that emerged in their communities. On a more informal basis, group cohesion was reinforced by the women who met in neighborhood shops and elsewhere to discuss subjects such as childrearing and the peer-group influence on their offspring that countered parental views, and to exchange recipes and news about kin in the old world. Although some might discount this as "gossip," it must be remembered that these women held together families spread across two continents in global villages—long before pundits had arrived at the concept—and raised the next generation of Cleveland's citizens, workers, and taxpayers.

Thirdly, the research team turned to the interaction among the six ethnocultural groups as well as with Jews, Germans, and others. Poles frequently associated with Czechs, and Croats with Slovenes. Some labor market segments were the territory of a particular group; in others, workers of different cultures but similar class status competed. Interethnic conflicts as well as cooperation occurred. To enter city politics, ethnic Clevelanders on occasion had to combine their votes. On the other hand, visible occupation of public space for political purposes, for example the placement of a statue of Louis Kossuth, could cast communities with memories of old-world antagonisms into bitter strife. The Americanization of immigrant men and women took place in the parameters established by old-world political experience and resistance to exploitation. When monolingual English-speaking union leaders claimed that the newcomers were unorganizable, the problem was the leaders' own inability to communicate with them, rather than the immigrant workers' lack of experience in standing up for their interests and dignity.[17] Within the communities, middle classes also developed and acted as cultural guardians, keeping the ethnic group together and close it to outside influences, or as brokers mediating contact with the institutions and customs of the new society.

When the project's research on Cleveland began, the traditional image of East and South European migrants as uncouth villagers was already waning. The early sensitive works by Emily Balch and William Thomas and Florian Znaniecki, the research of Victor Greene, Mark Stolarik, June Alexander, and Josef Barton, as well as John Bodnar's study of kinship and protest and Ewa Morawska's fascinating portrait of life-worlds in which there was not only bread but also butter, had replaced heavily biased negative views, such as those expressed in the reports of the Dillingham Commission.[19] At the same time, research in several European countries was achieving a high level of sophistication, whether the Swedish (later Nordic) migration project, or studies of German working men and women in Chicago or of English and Italian emigration.[20] In Canada, too, research moved from ethnic group histories to interdisciplinary research on cultural interaction.[21]

Traditions of research on migration from East Central and Southeastern Europe stem from cultural roots, in the first place from the assertion of ethnic/national cultures against imperial domination by the Habsburgs and

Hohenzollerns in the west and the Romanovs and Ottomans in the east. Secondly, the concept of peoples dispersed around the world was part of the research discourse even before the emphasis on diasporas in the 1990s. This double impetus led to the foundation of "matica" centers by southeastern European groups' intellectuals, institutions that served and continue to serve cultural needs, support research on ethnicity and emigration, and provide services to returning or visiting immigrants.[22] In the north, similarly, the concept of Polonia—a Polish culture spread around the world by sojourners and emigrants—was developed and investigated.[23]

Scholars at these institutions published a large amount of research, often in the tradition of nineteenth-century national consciousness and the associated drawing of often conflicting boundaries, as "nations" claimed their "historic" lands. At the same time, emphasis on intra-regional migrations and mixed settlement patterns pointed up the existence of cultural interaction, sometimes limited to the marketplace or mediated by Jewish merchants, and often involving multilingualism (however rudimentary) among illiterate but highly articulate peasant men and women. Common people, who spoke their own vernacular, also had to deal with the language of their respective churches, of the marketplace in which Yiddish-, Greek-, Italian-, and German-speaking merchants did business, and of German, Austrian-German, and Russian imperial administrators.

All of the men and women who decided to leave Europe and to reconstitute life-courses and cultures in North America, as exemplified by the migrants from the six societies studied here who settled in Cleveland, left old world family-based economies which were being seriously challenged by technological change. They were not tradition-bound people cast adrift by "modernization," "capitalist penetration," "industrialization," or "urbanization." They were active agents of change in their own lives who devised strategies of risk diversification, hoping to accumulate savings to invest in additional land in the society of origin, or to establish a second permanent base for the family abroad. They lived transcultural lives, able to move in two different national, or, more often, regional cultures. Had at least a few of the Irish- or German-origin Roman Catholic diocesan administrators, the American-born politicians and city officials, or the union organizers chosen to learn at least one of the immigrants' languages and to understand their material, emotional, and spiritual worlds, newcomers

Croatian-language flyer promoting the services of
the Hamburg-America line, ca. 1914. WRHS

would not have appeared as alien to the receiving society. Many of the immigrants' employers, the immigration officials, social workers, and other "natives" lacked transcultural experience and were caught in a monocultural vision of American society. It is the complex process of acculturation, community-building, workplace activity, and family life to which the authors of this study turn. The life-trajectories of the immigrants and sojourners were more complex than any one-dimensional model of Americanization suggested. They constructed a wide variety of institutions, social spaces, and transoceanic networks, and in the process played a central part in determining the future course of a prototypical American city, Cleveland.

Notes

1. The project "Conflict and Cooperation: Comparative Research on the East European Migratory Experience, 1880s–1930s" was funded by the Stiftung Volkswagenwerk, Hanover, Germany, from 1987–89.

2. Oscar Handlin, *The Uprooted: The Epic Story of the Great Migrations that Made the American People* (Boston, 1951); Rudolph J. Vecoli, "The Contadini in Chicago: A Critique of the Uprooted," *Journal of American History* 51 (1964), 404–417; Fred H. Matthews, *Quest for an American Sociology: Robert E. Park and the Chicago School* (Montreal, 1977); Stow Persons, *Ethnic Studies at Chicago, 1905–45* (Urbana, IL: University of Illinois Press, 1987); Herbert Blumer, *An Appraisal of Thomas and Znaniecki's "The Polish Peasant in Europe and America,"* (New York: SSRC, 1949); Dirk Hoerder, "Immigration History and Migration Studies Since *The Polish Peasant*: International Contributions," *Journal of American Ethnic History* 16 (1996), 26–36. Parallel to the Chicago sociologists, Polish ethnographers and historians collected material on peasant and emigrant culture: *Historia Ethnografii Polski,* ed. Malgorzata Terlecka (Wroclaw: Zakland Narodowy im. Osolinskie, 1973). I am grateful to Adam Walaszek and Piotr Wroblewski for references and translations. For a social anthropologist's discussion of "little traditions," see Robert Redfield, *Peasant Society and Culture: An Anthropological Approach to Civilization* (Chicago: University of Chicago Press, 1960); Andreas Ackermann, "Ethnologische Migrationsforschung: ein Überblick," *kea. Zaetschrift für Kulturwissenschaften* 10 (1997), 1–28.

3. Robert E. Park, *The Immigrant Press and Its Control* (1922; repr. New York, 1970), a volume in the "Methods of Americanization" study funded by the Carnegie Corporation of New York; Dirk Hoerder with Christiane Harzig, eds., *The Immigrant Labor Press in North America, 1840s–1970s. An Annotated Bibliography,* 3 vols. (Westport, CT: Greenwood, 1987), esp. 1: 1–47.

4. See Adam Walaszek's study of Poles, below. Dirk Hoerder, "From Migrants to Ethnics: Acculturation in a Societal Framework," in Hoerder and Leslie P. Moch, eds., *European Migrants: Global and Local Perspectives* (Boston, 1995), 211–262.

5. Everett C. Hughes and Helen MacGill Hughes, *Where People Meet: Racial and Ethnic Frontiers* (Glencoe, IL: Free Press, 1952) and Everett C. Hughes, "The Study of Ethnic Relations," *Dalhousie Rev.* 24 (1948), 477–482; E. C. Hughes, *French Canada in Transition* (Chicago, 1943).

6. At the time of emigration the people came from the three empires of the Habsburgs, Hohenzollerns and Romanovs. In 1867, the realm of the Habsburgs had been divided into a Dual Monarchy of Austria and Hungary, with both sections incorporating many peoples.

7. The affiliations of the individuals involved are: Adam Walaszek—Polonia Research Institute, Jagiellonian University, Krakow; Winston Chrislock—Dept. of History, University of St. Thomas, St. Paul; Michael Kopanic—University of Akron; Julianna Puskas—Institute of History, Hungarian Academy of Sciences, Budapest; Matjaž Klemenčič—Dept. of History, University of Maribor; Ivan Čizmić—Matica Iseljenika Hrvatske, Institute for Migration Research, Zagreb; coordinator: Gudrun N. Birnbaum—University of Strasbourg.

8. Dirk Hoerder—University of Bremen; this research and the resulting symposium were also supported by the Stiftung Volkswagenwerk.

9. Dirk Hoerder, et al., eds., *Roots of the Transplanted*, 2 vols. (Boulder: East European Monographs, 1994).

10. Ilona Kovacs, "Contributions of the Cleveland Public Library to the Acculturation of Immigrants," (manuscript, Budapest, c. 1987).

11. *Josef N. Jodlbauer. Dreizehn Jahre in Amerika, 1910–1923* [An Autobiography], Dirk Hoerder, ed. (Wien: Böhlau, 1996).

12. Laszlo Katus with Gábor Gyáni, "Immigration and Ethnicity in a Central European City: Budapest, 1850–1914," (manuscript, Budapest, Oct. 1991); Gábor Gyáni, "Comparison of Two Metropolitan Societies in a Spatial Context," in 17th International Congress of Historical Sciences, ed., *II—Chronological Section: Methodology* (Madrid: Comité International des Sciences Historiques, 1992), 1081–85; Peter Sipos, "Migration, Labor Movement and Workers' Culture in Budapest, 1867–1914," in Hoerder, et al., *Roots of the Transplanted*, 2:155–71; Ildikó Kríza, "Ethnic Identity and National Consciousness of the Hungarian Peasantry during the Age of Dualism," ibid., 1: 175–97.

13. John J. Grabowski, Curator of Manuscripts, Western Reserve Historical Society; David C. Hammack—Dept. of History, Case Western Reserve University; Donald Tipka, Cleveland Public Library; Karl Bonutti, Cleveland State University.

14. Dirk Hoerder, "Why Did you Come"—*The Proletarian Mass Migration. Research Report 1980–1985* (Bremen: Labor Migration Project, 1986), and "Immigrants, Sojourners, Transients in the Atlantic Economies. A Progress Report of the Labor Migration Project, University of Bremen," *Ethnic Forum* 8 (1988), 106–117.

15. Some of the materials have been deposited in the Western Reserve Historical Society.

16. Adam Walaszek, *Swiaty imigrantow: Tworzenie polonijnego Cleveland, 1880–1930* [Worlds of Immigrants: The Creation of Cleveland's Polonia, 1880–1930]

(Krakow: Nomos, 1994); Matjaž Klemenčič, *Slovenes of Cleveland: The Creation of a New Nation and a New World Community* (Ljubljana: Dolenjska Zalozba, 1995).

17. See the essays by Catherine Collomp and Marianne Debouzy, James R. Barrett, Donald Avery and Bruno Ramirez, and Dirk Hoerder in the section "Working-Class Cooperation and Conflict in North America," *Roots of the Transplanted* vol. 2, 339–448.

18. Emily G. Balch, *Our Slavic Fellow Citizens* (New York, 1910); William I. Thomas and Florian Znaniecki, *The Polish Peasant in Europe and America,* 5 vols., (Chicago, Boston, 1918–1920, repr. in several different editions). Emily Greene Balch had been a student of Levasseur in Paris and of Schmoller in Berlin.

19. Victor R. Greene, *The Slavic Community on Strike. Immigrant labor in Pennsylvania Anthracite* (Notre Dame, Ind., 1968); Susan Megles and Mark Stolarik, *Slovak Americans and their Communities in Cleveland* (Cleveland: Cleveland State University, 1979); and Stolarik, *Immigration and Urbanization: The Slovak Experience, 1870–1918* (New York: AMS Press, 1989); June Alexander, *The Immigrant Church and Community: Pittsburgh's Slovak Catholics and Lutherans, 1880–1915* (Pittsburgh: University of Pittsburgh Press, 1987); Josef J. Barton, *Peasants and Strangers: Italians, Rumanians, and Slovaks in an American City, 1890–1950* (Cambridge, MA: Harvard University Press, 1985). Henry Madison Grant, *The Passing of the Great Race. Or the Racial Basis of European History* (New York, 1916); Dillingham Commission (= U.S. Senate, Immigration Commission), *Reports of the Immigration Commission,* 41 vols. (Washington, D.C., 1911–12). John Goldlust and Anthony H. Richmond, "A Multivariate Model of Immigrant Adaptation," *International Migration Review* 8 (1974), 193–225; Thomas J. Archdeacon, "Problems and Possibilities in the Study of American Immigration and Ethnic History," *International Migration Review* 19 (1985), 112–34; Ewa Morawska, "The Sociology and Historiography of Immigration," in Virginia Yans-McLaughlin, ed., *Immigration Reconsidered* (Oxford, 1990).

20. Hans Norman and Harald Runblom, *Transatlantic Connections: Nordic Migration to the New World after 1880* (Oslo, 1987), and *From Sweden to America: A History of the Migration* (Minneapolis: University of Minnesota Press, 1976), and "Migration Patterns in the Nordic Countries," in Dirk Hoerder, ed., *Labor Migration in the Atlantic Economies. The European and North American Working Classes during the Period of Industrialization* (Westport, CT: Greenwood, 1985), 35–68; Hartmut Keil and John B. Jentz, eds., *German Workers in Industrial Chicago, 1850–1910: A Comparative Perspective* (DeKalb: Northern Illinois University Press, 1983); Christiane Harzig, ed., *Peasant Maids, City Women. From the European Countryside to Chicago* (Ithaca, NY, 1997); Charlotte Erickson, *Invisible Immigrants* (Miami, 1972); Bruno Bezza, ed., *Gli Italiani fuori d'Italia. Gli emigrati Italiani nei movimenti operai dei paesi d'adozione (1880–1940)* (Milano, 1983); Donna Gabaccia, *From Sicily to Elizabeth Street: Housing and Social Change among Italian Immigrants, 1880–1930* (New York, 1984).

21. Anthony W. Rasporich, "Ethnicity in Canadian Historical Writing, 1970–1990," in J. W. Berry and J. A. Laponce, eds., *Ethnicity and Culture in Canada: The Research Landscape* (Toronto: University of Toronto Press, 1994), 153–178.

22. In Czechoslovakia, research stagnated among Czech scholars after the work of Josef Polisensky (*Zaciatky ceskej a slovenskej emigracie do USA*, 1970), while Slovak scholars at the Slovakian Matica remained active (Frantisek Bielik). In Hungary, a considerable amount of work was done at the Hungarian Academy of Sciences (Julianna Puskás) and at the University of Debrecen. In Yugoslavia, research concentrated on Croatians and Slovenes since emigration from Serbia began late, and that from Macedonia even later.

23. Celina Bobinska and Andrzej Pilch, eds., *Employment-Seeking Emigrations of the Poles World Wide, XIXc and XXc* (Krakow, 1975); Ewa Morawska, "Labor Migrations of Poles in the Atlantic World Economy, 1880–1914," *Comparative Studies in Society and History* 31 (1989), 237–72. At the Polonia Research Center of the Jagiellonian University scholars from several social sciences cooperated in comparative research on Polish migrants in Europe, North America, Brazil, and Australia. West European scholars have studied acculturation of East European immigrants in Vienna, Paris, the Ruhr district, and British cities (Monika Glettler, Nancy Green, Christoph Klessman and others). Research on Poles in the German Ruhr district has also been published by Krystyna Murzynowska, John Kulczycki, and Richard C. Murphy.

24. Dirk Hoerder and Armin Hetzer, "Linguistic Fragmentation on Multilingualism among Labor Migrants in North America," in Hoerder and Harzig, *Immigrant Labor Press*, 2:29–52.

Identity, Conflict, and Cooperation

Central Europeans in Cleveland, 1850–1930

DAVID C. HAMMACK, WITH THE
ASSISTANCE OF GUDRUN BIRNBAUM,
LÁSZLO KATUS, AND GÁBOR GYÁNI

Between 1860 and 1930 a majority of the people who came to Cleveland and the other large Great Lakes cities in the United States—Buffalo, Detroit, Chicago, Milwaukee—came from Central, Southern and Eastern Europe. Throughout those years, Cleveland was one of the most "European" of all American cities. But who were these people? What experiences and ambitions did they bring with them? In what senses were they "European" or "foreign"? How did they see themselves? What did they seek for themselves and their children? What did the newcomers find in Cleveland when they arrived? What work was there for them to do? What living conditions awaited them? How would Cleveland's churches, synagogues, labor unions, voluntary associations, political parties receive them? As Kathleen Conzen and her associates have put the question, once they arrived in Cleveland, how would they "incorporate, adapt, and amplify" their "pre-existing, communal solidarities, culture, and historical memories"? Or as Werner Sollors has put the question, how did they—and their descendants—balance the questions of "consent and descent" in shaping their lives in the United States?[1] Previous studies have paid too little attention to those who came from Europe to the Great Lakes cities: this volume seeks to redress the balance.

As the United States entered World War I in 1917 the leader of Cleveland's Protestant Federated Churches noted some of the difficulties facing Clevelanders who sought to describe recent European arrivals—and indicated some of the attitudes that faced the newcomers:

There is no city in the United States, except possibly New York and Chicago, which is more truly foreign than Cleveland. We may well apply to this city the terms "Cosmopolitan," "Polyglot," "Modern Babel," and "Melting Pot." The West Side of Cleveland is fundamentally German. . . . The German language has been given a larger place than any other foreign language in Cleveland. It has been taught in the elementary schools as well as the high schools for many years. . . . Cleveland is the third largest Bohemian center in America. . . . Accurate statistics regarding the Polish people in America are wanting for the reason that they are listed as Russians, Germans and Austrians according to the country from which they come. . . . Slavs come from Hungary but cannot be entirely distinguished from those coming from Russia or Slavonia. . . . All the people coming to us from the Russian Empire are listed in the statistical reports as Russians. After they are settled in our city these same people are known to us as Jews, Poles, Slavs, Finns, and Lithuanians.[2]

The immigrants themselves faced the question of identity in the most acute way. They had to ask themselves who they were, and often they felt strong pressure to redefine or even change their identity. Should an individual describe himself—to himself or to another person—as a "Russian," a "Ukrainian," a member of the Orthodox Church, a former peasant, a worker, a union man, a Republican, simply a man from a village near Kiev, a Russian- or Ukrainian-American, or just an American citizen? Should another individual consider herself a "Hungarian," a "Slovak," a "Slav," a Catholic, a seamstress, simply a woman from a town just north of Bratislava (or should she call it "Pressburg"), an advocate of the "cooperative commonwealth,"[3] or a Slovak- or Slavic- or Hungarian-American—or an American plain and simple?

These were complicated and difficult questions; answers to them determined who would help a person find a place to live and a job, who might become a possible marriage partner, how a person would be viewed and treated by others,[4] how a person saw his or her personal life story. Many conflicts, and many instances of cooperation, hinged on these questions of identity. In the cases of people whose families were already deeply committed to a particular identity, the answer appeared self-evident, a matter of deep inheritance and long-standing tradition. But in the mid-nineteenth-century many ethnic identities and traditions had often been invented only recently.[5] As historian Patrick J. Geary has shown, the documents that historians have used for the study of national traditions in Europe were themselves assembled for the purpose of celebrating a particular notion of German nationhood. In reality, the people often described as making up specific "national" groups in the early middle ages never represented "pure," coherent groups. National identities emerged through historical and political processes that continue to this day.[6] Some European national identities would, in fact, be refined in Cleveland and other American cities. Some identities would be imposed on immigrants despite their own ideas of themselves. Political commitments were even newer, and would come under intense discussion in Cleveland.

In the short run, migrants from Central Europe to Cleveland were concerned with their immediate chance of earning a living. But from the beginning they brought other concerns with them—concerns that were religious and political and national as well as personal. In Cleveland, they cooperated with and competed against one another for work and income. They also cooperated and competed in their efforts to define, and to create, the kind of society they saw as desirable. In the United States, they could not avoid questions of racial and ethnic identity. Like other American cities—and like cities across Europe itself—Cleveland was a theater for debates about national identity, about the civil obligations of religious commitment, about socialism, about race, about economic and social opportunity.[7]

The scores of thousands of people who came to Cleveland from Central Europe between 1850 and 1930 left a vast world caught up in revolutionary economic, political, and cultural change. They arrived in one of the world's most rapidly developing industrial regions. Neither Cleveland nor Central Europe was the same sort of place in the 1880s it had been in the 1850s, or that it would become in the 1920s. People who came in the earlier years had lived under one set of conditions: their European experiences helped them understand and respond to what they found in Cleveland, and they, in turn, changed Cleveland for those who came later. Some also sought to use the United States as a base from which to transform Europe. People who came later left a Europe that was in the throes of revolutionary change for an America, and a Cleveland, that had not existed in 1860 and that had been shaped in important ways by the ideas and efforts of previous immigrants.

Identifying European Migrants to Cleveland

We cannot simply say that a certain number of migrants to Cleveland came from Austria, Hungary, Poland, or Russia. "Poland," "Slav," and even "Hungary," were abstractions, and people disagreed about what these terms meant in practice and on the ground. We can say that over the years, people came to Cleveland from different parts of Europe, and that almost every migrant had to confront complex questions of identity both in Europe and in the

United States. In the middle years of the nineteenth century most immigrants came from the British Isles and Germany. Later, Cleveland's migrants came from southern Germany and Bohemia and Hungary in the western parts of the Austro-Hungarian empire. Later still, they came from Poland, Russia, Slovakia, Slovenia, Croatia, Serbia, the Ukraine, and southern Italy.

The immigrants had varying ideas about their own identities; American officials had other ideas. As a result, although there are extensive census and police records, we can never know exactly how many came from each European area to Cleveland and northeastern Ohio. We know even less about the size of particular communities from year to year: many immigrants moved from place to place in the United States, and many came only for a few years' work, then returned to their homelands.

Since we must work largely from records created by U.S. census takers and police officials, it is important to note that these officials brought definite assumptions to their work. Although census officials did base their analysis on statements from the immigrants themselves, the census-takers' questions shaped the immigrants' statements, and the census reports reflected American, not necessarily immigrant, concerns. As political controversy over immigration intensified after 1900, the U.S. census paid more and more attention to the questions of "nationality" and "ethnic stock." "In most cases," it explained in 1910, "mother tongue may be taken as indicative of *ethnic stock.*" Yet the census always treated the British Isles, and Germany, as special cases. Most immigrants from those areas spoke a common language. Yet among English speakers the Census carefully distinguished "four ethnically distinct peoples, namely, the English, the Irish, the Scotch, and the Welsh." In addition, the census recognized the Manx, from the tiny Isle of Man between Britain and Ireland, as a separate "ethnic" group. "In very many cases" of people from the British Isles, census-takers reported "nationality rather than mother tongue."[8] Similarly, the "Instructions to Enumerators Relating to Nativity and Parentage" for the 1870 census asked not for a general identification of people from "Germany," but for specifics: "Prussia, Baden, Bavaria, Hesse-Darmstadt."[9]

American officials who emphasized local differences in Northern Europe paid much less attention to the specific origins of people from Central and Eastern Europe. It was not until 1910 when, for the first time, the official instructions of the U.S. census directed census-takers to "write Hungary or Bohemia, rather than Austria for persons born in Hungary or Bohemia . . . ." Previously, the census included people from Bohemia and Moravia, the two Czech lands, with others from "Austria." The 1910 census instructions added that "in the case of persons speaking Polish, as Poland is not now a country, inquire whether the birthplace is what is now known as German Poland or Austrian Poland or Russian Poland."[10] The census used a special broad category, "Slavic, not specified," for people who were "reported, contrary to the instructions given to the enumerators, as "Slav," "Slavic," Slavish," or "Slavonian;" many of these would no doubt have called themselves "Slovak" or "Slovenian."

Conditions in Europe further complicated these questions: their languages were closely related, but neither Slovakia nor Slovenia had a clearly defined territory in 1910. Some aspects of identity were in fact being worked out in the United States. In Cleveland during these years, Stefan Furdek, leader of the Slovak Catholics, spent much effort persuading Peter Rovnianek, president of the Slovak National Society, that "Slovak" rather than "Slavonian" should be the English term for their group.[11] Clevelanders also used a variety of terms for "Russians:" "Little Russians," "Galicians," "Rusins," "Carpatho-Russians": in fact, most of these terms actually referred to Ukrainian-speakers from areas under the control of different national governments in Europe.[12]

A dramatic indication of the importance of changing perceptions of ethnic and national identity is found in the radical changes in the national identity of Clevelanders reported by the U.S. Census for 1900, 1910, 1920 and 1930. Big changes in the numbers reflect different ways of identifying people, at least as much as they reflect big changes in the backgrounds of the people who lived in Cleveland. The numbers also varied according to whether the Census was counting immigrants, or immigrants and their children.

These numbers obscure as much as they reveal. They do make it clear that significant numbers of people came to Cleveland from the Czech lands of Bohemia and Moravia, from Poland, Hungary, Slovakia, Slovenia, and Croatia. They also make it clear that these people were welcomed by not only by people whose families had come to Ohio from New England, New York, and Pennsylvania, but also by very large numbers of recent and established migrants from Germany and Ireland. And that many Eastern European Jews, Italians, and others came with the Catholics, Orthodox, and some Protestants who came from Central Europe.

Central Europe as a Major Source of Cleveland's People: With Some Notes on the Parallel Case of Budapest

All migrants from Central Europe to Cleveland in the late nineteenth and early twentieth century were participating in a single long-term process: the great expansion and integration of the Atlantic market. That expansion had brought Africa into the Atlantic market as a source of slave labor as early as the 1600s, and in some ways the slave plantations of the Atlantic and Caribbean islands were among the earliest examples of industrialized agriculture.

Varied U.S. Census Reports of the Identities of Cleveland's Immigrants, 1900, 1910, 1920, 1930

Language or Nationality	"Country of Origin" 1900	"Mother Tongue" 1910	"Country of Origin" 1920	"Country of Origin" 1930
English/Irish/ England	12,869	94,114	11,126	9,606
Ireland	14,043	11,316	10,983	6,842
German/Germany	45,787	132,793	102,441	22,532
Austria	5,004	42,059	124,900	6,774
Polish/Poland	8,592	35,615		32,668
Bohemian & Moravian/ Czechoslovakia	13,599	39,296		34,695
Magyar/Hungary	9,893	23,028	75,666	19,073
Slovak		12,977		
Slovenian		14,332		
Serbo-Croatian/ Yugoslavia		3,899	4,112	18,326
Russia	3,685		76,866	15,193
Yiddish & Hebrew		23,169		
Italian/Italy	3,065	17,133	35,687	23,524
Romania	39		4,112	6,672

Sources: Wellington G. Fordyce, "Immigrant Colonies in Cleveland," *Ohio Archaeological and Historical Quarterly* 47 (1936), 323; U.S. Census, "Mother Tongue of Foreign White Stock. Leading Mother Tongues of the Foreign White Stock of Selected Cities, 1910," Table 20, 989; Table 24, 1012–1014; Van David D. Tassel and John J. Grabowski, eds., *Encyclopedia of Cleveland History*, second edition (Bloomington: Indiana University Press, 1996), 558–559.

The industrial revolution that began in parts of Great Britain, Belgium, and Northeastern France in the eighteenth century intensified both expansion and integration. Over the next one hundred years and more, key elements of that revolution penetrated both the Americas and the societies of Central and then Eastern Europe. Canals and railroads and efficient ocean ports tied more and more parts of North America, South America, Africa, and Europe into an integrated international economy, opening new markets to eastern and western producers and at the same time opening eastern and western regions to new goods. Labor, free, encumbered, and slave, flowed along the new lines of trade.

As transportation cost barriers fell so did many prices. Cheap soap and cheap washable cloth came into wider use, while potatoes and other new and more nutritious foods became more and more generally available. Infectious diseases and famines became less lethal, lowering death rates: in Budapest, death rates fell sharply after the mid-1870s.[13] Cheap rail transportation encouraged eastern European landlords to specialize in cash crops and to intensify their farming practices. Central Hungary, Poland, and the Ukraine became great suppliers of grain to western European cities, even as the Great Plains of North America, as well as large areas of Argentina and Australia, were put to the plow. Peasant families grew. But many central and eastern European landlords moved to take advantage of new markets by "rationalizing" their farming practices and narrowing the range of crops they produced. Peasants found themselves confined to smaller and smaller plots, or forced off the land entirely. On occasion the new crops failed—disastrously in the potato famines of the 1840s, which affected the European continent as well as Ireland. Cholera, plague, and other diseases could follow the new lines of movement, and did, with Europe-wide epidemics in the early 1830s, the late 1840s, and the mid-1860s.

Faced with new hazards as well as old ones, young men and young women from peasant and town families moved about in search of better opportunity. As Frank Thistlethwaite put it in a classic article, Europe's people developed "a latent propensity to emigrate." "Sometimes, though by no means invariably," he added, "actual emigration [occurred], not only at times of catastrophe caused by the failure of the potato crop, but as transport and communication . . . made this possible."[14]

In one European province after another, thoroughgoing change transformed all aspects of life and fed a very rapid movement to the towns and cities. Vienna and its suburbs formed an important industrial center before the middle of the nineteenth century. From the early 1830s Vienna drew grain and other agricultural products from by steamship up the Danube from Hungary, consuming much and sending more on to other markets in Western Europe. The twin towns of Buda and Pest, across the river from one another at the northwestern end of Hungary's great central plain, provided the Hungarian pole for this trade. The famous Chain Bridge linked the two towns as early as 1849, and following a concerted government policy, railroads radiated from Budapest in the next decade. The rail link to Vienna opened in 1851, reinforcing Budapest's dominance over areas to the south and east.[15] Bohemia also industrialized quite early. Between 1869 and 1902 large mill towns, including Pilsen and Brno, grew rapidly as the labor force on Bohemia's farms plummeted from 1,189,770 to 299,446.[16] By the end of the nineteenth century, Lodz, in the foothills south of Warsaw, bristled with smokestacks as it became Poland's most striking new industrial city.

Many Central Europeans passed through Budapest (or one of the other newly large cities of the region) before coming on to Cleveland, so a look at Budapest and its people can suggest something of the concerns and ideas the migrants brought with them to the United States. Hungary emancipated its peasants from many feudal dues and obligations in 1848, setting off a thoroughgoing and difficult reorganization of the Hungarian economy. In the next twenty years some 20,000 Hungarian landowners, peasants and aristocrats alike, went bankrupt and were forced to throw their lands onto the market. Conditions were worse further east: one observer wrote in 1882 that "the misery in which most of the Romanian peasantry lives beggars all description," and the Polish- and Ukrainian-speaking peasants of Galicia (Austrian Poland) "suffered great poverty and deprivation." Emancipation from feudal dependency did not bring equality: as late as 1914 ninety-two aristocratic families still controlled about seven percent of the land in all of Hungary.[17] None of the nations of Central Europe offered universal manhood suffrage before World War I.[18]

New owners increased production for market, and by the late 1860s, more goods were passing through Budapest that through any European port except Hamburg. Grain and flour constituted half the shipments on Hungarian railroads in the 1860s, and between 1855 and 1873 Budapest merchants built the largest steam-powered flour mill in Europe, as well as very large warehouses, slaughter-houses, breweries, distilleries, beet-sugar refineries, and fruit-canning plants.[19] By 1872 eleven large mills employed 2,600 people in Budapest, and the new Kőbánya district was fast becoming Eastern Europe's largest pig market.[20]

In the early 1890s Albert Shaw, an ambitious young journalist and former secretary of the Minneapolis Chamber of Commerce, reported that Budapest was "to the Hungarian plain what Chicago is to Illinois and Iowa, or what Minneapolis is to Minnesota and Dakota." He added that "within twenty-five years the processes of flour-making throughout the world have been revolutionized by reason of certain Budapest inventions," including "the substitution of steel rollers of various sizes and patterns for the old-time millstones." The new ideas "were quickly borrowed by Minnesota millers, and by them were largely developed and improved; and Minneapolis and Budapest have grown contemporaneously as the two great milling centers of the world."[21]

Ironworks, foundries, and shops making parts for Danube steamboats, railroad cars and locomotives, and agricultural machines such as steam threshers followed—sometimes subsidized by the Austro-Hungarian government. In 1875 these industries already employed as many as 3,700 people in Budapest; as that city became a major rail and manufacturing center the numbers increased to 13,104 in 1890 and to over 33,000 in 1910.[22] Pest's Ganz company sold its patented railway wheels all over Europe, and Budapest threshing machines were finding their way into many of Hungary's largest farms. According to a contemporary account, the city's Óbuda shipyard alone employed about 2000 during the 1880s.[23] After 1900 the vast Csepel Island iron and steel works, intended in part for military purposes, grew up in one Budapest suburb, while major engineering, chemical, and electrical plants arose in the other settlements of the city's suburban industrial belt. By 1910 the city and its suburbs contained 1397 factories that employed at least twenty workers, 289 that employed more than one hundred workers, and seventeen that employed over one thousand.[24]

In many ways Budapest paralleled the rise of such American centers as Cleveland, Buffalo, Chicago, and Minneapolis. Its industry developed as part of the general trans-Atlantic economic expansion; it used and contributed to a common pool of technical knowledge. Its products competed with those of the American cities. And Budapest recruited its people from many of the same regions that sent people to the cities of the American midwest. For more than 150 years, Buda's castle hill housed the region's Hungarian rulers, while Pest was a German city, drawing its people from the territories of Austria, the Czech lands, and southern Germany, and until the mid-nineteenth century using German as the language of its shops and its local government. Until the end of the century, Pest continued to draw on southern Germany and the western parts of the Austro-Hungarian empire for German-speaking skilled craftsmen and machine workers.

Typically, people came to Budapest (and other European cities) through a series of short moves. Landless workers went first to a familiar nearby town, and then, perhaps, on to a larger but still nearby city. Workers who possessed skills or education typically started in larger places, but they, too, moved up the urban ladder seeking wider opportunities. As it grew, Budapest drew on migrants and immigrants from nearby counties dominated by Magyar- (Hungarian) speakers, from the Slovak-speaking areas to the north, and to a lesser extent from the Croatian- and Slovenian-speaking territories to the south and south-west. The more skilled and literate a person was, the more likely he or she was to move to the city. László Katus shows, in a very thorough analysis, that "the intensity of migration to Budapest from the 63 counties of Hungary was positively related to the percentage of the population living from industry and transport, to the productivity of agriculture, to the development of agricultural commodity production, and to literacy." Few people moved to Budapest from areas that practiced more traditional farming.[25] Cleveland and other American cities (including Montreal, Toronto, Buenos Aires, São Paulo, Santiago, and other cities in the Americas) also belonged to this international network. People who moved on from Hungary to an international destination such as Cleveland were likely to be more highly skilled, more literate, and often more deeply engaged in political or religious movements than many of those who did not emigrate.

Some migrants found a reasonably comfortable life in Budapest, but many struggled. Budapest's machine-building industry was exceptionally productive, and it paid the highest wages. In the first decades after the founding of the Óbuda Shipyard in the 1830s, "most of the skilled workers were from abroad, and the Hungarian element dominated only the crowd of the day-workers." Like the national railroad and a few other large industrial enterprises, the shipyard had to provide housing of a very good western European standard for the skilled workers it recruited. Lajos Allt, a skilled railway worker of German origin, for example, lived in a series of railway housing developments; in the 1890s, when he was in his fifties, he could provide his family a nicely-furnished Budapest apartment of three rooms and a kitchen.[26] Over the years, Hungarian workers acquired better skills. By the nineties most of the Óbuda Shipyard's skilled workers were Hungarians, though some Czechs and Moravians were still employed as metal workers and bricklayers, and some of the carpenters came from "Dalmatia and Istria," near the Adriatic. Slovaks and Galician Poles had largely replaced Hungarians as day-laborers.

According to an 1887 study translated by Katus, in the "village-like" district near the Óbuda Shipyard, the well-kept one-story houses often had "a few flowers in the window and embroidered curtains." Most houses presented a "friendly-looking" appearance, although they contained apartments

of just one room and a kitchen and failed to meet all "demands of public health." "Two families very often get together and rent a bigger apartment," the study concluded. "They use a common kitchen." A majority of
workers took lodgers into their small quarters: "the worker with his family
of 6–8 persons rather frequently squeezes into the kitchen to let a lodger
have the expensve room for good money . . . A separate room is a luxury and
a very few can afford it." This 1887 study added:

> As far as the food is concerned the workers of the shipyard are used to live
> well. They can not believe that some people hardly eat beef during the year
> and live on potato and bread. Every worker interviewed identified his three
> main foods as meat, bread, and wine. Many of them could not imagine a
> lunch without meat and wine. Breakfast always consists of bacon, bread,
> and a small glass of brandy. . . Lunch regularly consists of some soup, boiled
> vegetables with a slice of meat, or rarely pasta. Dinner consists of the warmed
> leftovers from noon. They often eat sausage or cheese for dinner. . . They
> mainly buy beef and rarely pork because many of them feed pigs at home.
> The Sunday lunch is very rich. There are four or five dishes, meat, fish, and
> fruits. They bake bread at home. . . Wine belongs to the main food items
> but the workers do not make ill use of it. . .[27]

All members of the family earned money, and the workers helped themselves by organizing cooperatives:

> What they buy in the cooperative stores is noted in their booklets and they
> have to pay weekly. The married workers have their wives sew their and the
> children's clothes. Most of the women are employed in the domestic indus-
> try besides the household and thus make the family's situation easier. Most
> of them work for the war material stocks. . . Usually the women are the
> leaders of the families, they keep the money . . . it is not unusual on Saturday
> afternoons that women are waiting for their husbands, and they take the
> weekly wages away from them. The women deal with the money, the hus-
> bands only get some pocket money to buy tobacco and wine."

But as historian David Landes observed, in these years Austria-Hungary—like Italy, Poland, Russia, and the Balkans—"assimilated only pieces
of modern technology, and these advances, achieved at discrete points of
the economy, were slow. . . Industry accounted for so small a fraction of
national wealth and income that even rapid gains in this sector did relatively
little at first for. . . the standard of living."[28]

Budapest offered opportunity, and it grew very rapidly in the late nineteenth century—by 35% per decade between 1870 and 1900. But employment was irregular: in bad times nearly half the employees of the Óbuda Shipyard might lose their jobs. Many residents of Budapest did have to live on potatoes and bread. Slovaks dominated Budapest's building trades and did much of the heavy labor in its factories. Rapid growth led to overcrowding, and as late as 1910 84% of the Slovak-speaking residents of Budapest lived in one-room apartments, and 20% of their apartments lacked a kitchen. Katus calculates that at any given time a third of the industrial workers were renting beds in others' (one- or two-room) flats, and that "nearly every member of the working classes in Budapest was involved in sub-letting." A mass meeting of Hungarian and Slovak brick-makers in 1897 advanced demands that must strike us as shockingly modest. "To avoid the overcrowding of lodgings, more than two families must not be placed into a particular flat," they insisted, and "males and females should be placed into separate rooms, one bed and a straw mattress should be given to each of them."[29]

In the early 1870s, ten percent of Pest's people lived in damp basements; in 1880, only a quarter of the city's houses had filtered water. Crowded conditions, in a city that only slowly introduced adequate water mains and sewers despite the creation of an important Public Works Commission in 1870,[30] made for unhealthy living. New water and sewer lines had reached about 70% by 1901, and life expectancy at birth was by then higher in Budapest than in Hungary in general, but it was only 39.5 years for males, 40.7 years for females.[31] Many people living in Hungary and the other parts of the Austro-Hungarian Empire felt pressure to follow the earlier example of Ireland and Germany, and to emigrate entirely from their home village or town, from their province, and from Europe.

Political and religious conflict reinforced the economic motives for emigration, and these conflicts greatly complicated questions of personal and ethnic identity for Southeastern Europe's emigrants. Any account of the growth of Budapest must certainly take into account the fact that Hungary was part of the Austro-Hungarian Empire. It must also consider that the provinces ruled from Budapest itself, especially after 1867, included areas in which the chief local language was Slovak (to the north), Croatian or Serbian (to the south), and Romanian (to the northeast). Budapest's small communities of Slovak and Croatian students, and of Slovak and Croatian landowners and religious leaders, sought to advance their interests with Hungarian officials. Often, students from these communities demanded too much, fell afoul of the Hungarians, and were forced to emigrate.

Hungary also included many German-speaking (sometimes, "Swabian" or "Saxon") towns, large communities of Yiddish-speaking Jews and Romance-speaking Gypsies, and smaller numbers in which the language was variously Ukrainian, Polish, Czech, etc. German and Jewish craftsmen and traders had long moved back and forth along the Danube and throughout Central and Eastern Europe, usually under the protection and encouragement of local authorities. In the nineteenth century, Hapsburg officials in Vienna encouraged these movements by granting civil rights to Jews as well as to the skilled and educated. Pest owed much of its rapid growth in the late nineteenth century to the efforts of Germans and emancipated Jews. In 1920, nearly a quarter of Budapest's population was Jewish.[32]

In all linguistic communities, many peasants simply considered themselves members of their own village. But they were also, and increasingly, exposed to both religious and nationalist claims on their identity and their loyalty. As historian Robert A. Kann noted, Austria-Hungary's nationalities had two different historical trajectories. Germans, Czechs, Hungarians, and Poles had for hundreds of years experienced "the mixed blessings of a nationally conscious nobility, gentry, and urban burgher class." Many aristocrats and intellectuals in these communities "possessed a strong national identity and consciousness."[33] There were, of course, many complexities. Aristocratic landlords often oppressed their tenants and were strongly tempted to identify and join forces with their Austrian or Hungarian counterparts in defense of aristocratic rather than national rights, especially after the French Revolution and the Terror of the early 1790s, and again after the revolutions of 1848. Other aristocrats resisted imperial Austria's efforts to protect the rights of peasants and townsmen by joining conservative but anti-Habsburg (and aristocrat-dominated) movements of Polish, Hungarian, or Czech nationalism.

Among the Slovaks, Slovenes, Serbs, Rumanians, Ruthenians, and others who had long been "deprived by foreign overlords of autonomous political development," national consciousness provided few challenges to imperial authorities until the nineteenth century. In those communities, many found themselves attracted to one or another version of pan-Slavic nationalism.[34] Some were drawn to notions of general Slavic unity under the leadership of the Russian czar and the Russian Orthodox Church. Others favored some form of unity for Slovenes and other Catholic Slavs of the west, and for a while, Austrian rulers encouraged this last tendency, in part by subsidizing certain Slovene writers. Some Slovak Protestants sought a national alliance with Slovak Catholics to make common cause against both Czechs and Austrians.[35] In Hungary, nationalists imposed a strong policy of "Magyarization" in the 1890s, increasing the pressure on residents of Budapest, in particular, to use the Hungarian language and in general to identify with the Hungarian nation.[36]

Religious conflict complicated national and ethnic history. The Hapsburgs and their officials long saw themselves as defenders of Catholicism, in western Europe as well as in the east. Their successful defense of Vienna against the Ottoman Turks in 1683 and the permanent expulsion of the Turks from Hungary by 1699 greatly enhanced their position. The Reformation had less impact in southern than in northern Europe, but significant numbers of Protestants appeared in Bohemia and Moravia, and in scattered places further east. The Hapsburg emperor's "ruthless attempts" to impose a rigorous counter-reformation had damaged "great opportunities for genuine integration of the reconquered lands."[37] On the other hand, Hapsburg officials had long relied on Jews and on German-speaking Protestants to provide the skills needed for economic development. By the end of the eighteenth century Hapsburg leaders moved toward the toleration and even the protection of Protestant and Jewish minorities. They also suppressed Catholic religious orders they viewed as excessively independent.

Economic development with its attendant population movements, urban growth, and expansion of the market, greatly intensified the impact of these national and religious forces. The growth of commerce and industry, as well as the expanded role of the national state in transportation, public health, banking, and other services, required a significant increase in literacy. Convinced of the utility and superiority of the German language, several Hapsburg leaders promoted education in German. German was indeed the language of much of Europe's most rapidly developing scientific, legal, and commercial thinking, and of a very large territory that was on the verge of significant economic growth. Knowledge of German did open many opportunities to a young person in Central Europe. But German was also the language of rulers in Vienna. Some of those who sought to resist the centralization of power and authority in Vienna supported the continued use of Latin as an official and scholarly as well as priestly language. Hungarians pressed, successfully, for the right to govern in their own Magyar tongue. Slovaks, Serbs, Croats responded by demanding official status for their languages. As schools expanded and as more and more families sought education for their children, people in every village and town from Prague to Cracow to Belgrade had to confront the question of linguistic and national identity.

The late Gudrun Birnbaum, a native of Bratislava who contributed much to this study, summed up part of the story as follows:

[The people who came from Central Europe to Cleveland] could not simply be identified with their country of birth and citizenship. The vast majority of all immigrants after 1900 came from states whose territories, principalities, provinces, kingdoms, and counties had been amassed over centuries through treaties, marriages, inheritance, wars and conquest. They existed in a particularism of regional and local entities with special political, legal, and administrative traditions and rights. As long as they were governed through special rights and customary laws from a distant center, large numbers of people could remain in a state of indifference about national or cultural identity. Once the state began to exert modernizing, centralizing, unifying pressures, as in Prussia, Austria-Hungary, Italy, and Russia in the second half of the 19th century, choices had to be made. These pressures were exerted among other things through an expanding system of public education which imposed a "national" language and thereby created resistance from those not belonging to the "Staatsvolk" [the ethnic group specially identified with the nation].[38]

In the last decades of the nineteenth century widespread movement of working-class protest based on Marxist socialism and other radical doctrines raised another big question of identity: was an individual a member of a religious community, a nationality group—or the international working class? Paul Krause has argued persuasively that many Slovak immigrants brought with them from the old country a strongly communitarian, and even collectivist, twist to their search for means to support their families.[39] In Hungary, left-wing ideas were strong enough to give rise to the short-lived communist government of Bela Kun in the immediate aftermath of World War I.

But by the 1920s more than one Central European immigrant shared the feelings of Louis Adamic, who had come to California from Slovenia. In 1926 Adamic wrote the editor of a Slovenian-language paper in Chicago, "Perhaps I should be ashamed of myself because I have no deep patriotic feeling as a Slovenian." Adamic added that he had "never heard of a single Socialist venture that ever amounted to anything." The question of the relative importance of class and national commitment had arisen in many places by the mid-1920s. Dismay at the consequences of violent national and class conflict received classic expression in Sean O'Casey's 1926 play, *The Plough and the Stars,* about the 1916 Easter Rising in Ireland.[40] But nationalist, fascist, conservative Catholic, social democratic, and communist political movements continued to defeat political liberalism in Central Europe through the 1920s and 1930s.

Cleveland as a Focus for Immigration

Migrants to Cleveland from the 1860s to the 1930s encountered a rapidly growing industrial and trading city built on a deceptively fragmented landscape. Cleveland's great advantage lay in its location at the easternmost point from which goods could be moved by water from Lake Erie to the Ohio River. The opening of the Erie Canal in 1825 gave Cleveland a direct water-level connection with New York; the 1829 Welland Canal tied Lake Erie, and Cleveland, with Lake Ontario; the Ohio & Erie Canal greatly improved Cleveland's connections with Akron in 1827 and with the Ohio River in 1832. In the 1850s Cleveland became an important railway center, with lines through Ashtabula to Buffalo (and on to Toronto and New York City); through Pittsburgh to Philadelphia; via the Baltimore and Ohio to the Chesapeake; and through Toledo to Detroit, western Michigan, and Chicago. By the 1870s most of the trade between the Great Lakes and the northwest and the East Coast passed through or around Cleveland, and the area had developed great railroad freight yards to manage the movement of goods east and west.

As early as the 1860s Cleveland employed significant numbers of people in the repair and manufacture of lake steamers, canal boats, and railroad cars; in the supply and maintenance of ships and trains; and in the construction of railway bridges and telegraph lines. Early in its history settlers made use of the limited water power available where streams fell into the valley of the Cuyahoga, and of extensive deposits of clay (for pottery) and limestone (for paving and construction). With the discovery of large deposits of iron ore on Michigan's Upper Peninsula, and then in the Iron Range of Minnesota, and with its easy access to coal and coke from the Appalachians, Cleveland became one of the world's great steel-making centers in the last third of the nineteenth century. Costs required the production of steel right where the ore boats and coal barges landed their bulky raw materials, and the Flats along the twisting Cuyahoga, as well as the Lake Erie shoreline, provided several good sites. Steel is heavy, so Cleveland's use of steel in manufacturing increased with its output of steel. By the 1920s Cleveland was one of the world's leading producers of transportation equipment, rails, construction materials, barrels, automobile engines and transmissions, valves, pumps, light bulbs, sewing machines, refrigerators, washing machines, vacuum cleaners, and office equipment.[41]

A superficial view might suggest that Cleveland, which lacks big hills and valleys, is a geographically coherent and simple area. In fact the city and its surrounding area is sharply divided by ravines, wetlands, and cliffs.

Kingsbury Run, Morgan Run, and Mill Creek on the east side, Walworth Run and Big Creek on the west, and several other small streams cut down to the Cuyahoga. Roads, canals, and rail lines follow these routes to the Cuyahoga, distributing water-level industrial sites over many miles. On the east side, Giddings Brook, Doan Brook and Euclid Creek cut through the higher ground to Lake Erie. West side streams and cliffs divide Whiskey Bend on the Cuyahoga from hilly Tremont and Brooklyn Heights, and these areas from Ohio City and the flat plains that extend along the Lake Erie shore to the Rocky River. Streams and hills also separate the East Side into many small areas. Downtown Cleveland lies above the lower Flats and the adjacent lakeside; the Hamilton Avenue industrial district sits above Lake Erie, with the Central area to the immediate south; Woodland Hill and Mt. Pleasant rise to the east; Newberg Heights, Broadway, Slavic Village, Cuyahoga Heights, and Garfield Heights stand further South. Collinwood and Euclid lie along the lakeshore yet further to the east, divided by streams and fairly steep slopes from East Cleveland and Cleveland Heights.

Until substantial and expensive bridges were built, land travel to and from these separate areas was difficult. Major industrial facilities were built all along the Cuyahoga, up Walworth Run and Big Creek to the west, and up Kingsbury Run, Mill Creek, and other waterways to the east. Other industrial areas developed along Lake Erie, notably to the immediate west and east of the Cuyahoga, along Hamilton Avenue, in Collinwood and Euclid. Even as new bridges connected the areas that natural features had separated, man-made rail lines and trolleys imposed new divisions. Factories and warehouses lined the belt railroads that circled around the central part of Cleveland from 55th Street and 79th Street down to Cuyahoga Heights and along the west side's Brook Park Road, and several railroads cut through the east and west sides. From the 1890s, electric streetcar and interurban lines made it more difficult to cross major roads.

Until well into the twentieth century, most industrial workers could only afford to walk to work. Thus crowded and geographically separated residential areas developed on the hills above Cleveland's industrial sites, served by retail districts along 25th Street and Pearl Road, and by Lorain, Detroit, Dennison, Clark, and other roads on the west side. Broadway, Kinsman, Woodland, Central, Cedar, 55th Street, St. Clair, Superior, Buckeye, 185th, and other major streets served similar purposes on the East Side. Each of these streets paralleled a major industrial area; each commercial area grew along with employment in the factories and rail yards nearby. Skilled workers and foremen who enjoyed higher incomes and greater security gradu-

ally moved into streetcar neighborhoods on the West Side, Hough and
Mount Pleasant and Glenville, East Cleveland and Cleveland Heights on the
East Side.

Industrial opportunity attracted immigrants to Cleveland, and the scale
and nature of the jobs changed dramatically over the years. The number
of people employed tripled between 1870 and 1890, more than doubled
between 1890 and 1910, then grew an additional two-thirds by 1930. Manufacturing provided many new jobs, but transportation and professional service expanded even more rapidly, especially after 1910. Those who arrived
in the 1860s or 1870s or 1880s found themselves in a middle-sized manufacturing district in which German was often the language of the shop floor,
the market, and the tavern. After 1910, new arrivals encountered one of the
largest manufacturing cities in the world—a city in which trade and professional service were rapidly equaling manufacturing as a source of employment, and a city whose population exceptionally large communities
of most groups from Central and Eastern Europe. The following table, based
on U.S. census classifications of people's statements about their occupations,
summarizes some of the changes:

Number Working in:	1870	1890	1910	1930
Manufacturing	13,874	41,186	127,845	174,832
Trade and Transport	8,212	23,642	77,958	139,322
Personal Service	6,795	32,200	26,063	45,461
Professional Service	996	4,651	15,573	32,756
All fields	30,211	102,435	248,886	394,842

By the 1890s Cleveland amounted to a sprawling collection of mill and
factory districts, warehouse areas, docks, supply dumps, and rail yards as
well as a downtown business district. Residential areas were widely scattered, and were usually mixed in with industrial and commercial activities. Arriving immigrants, familiar with the impressive royal, aristocratic,
and church buildings of Vienna, Prague, Buda, Zagreb, Lublijana, Cracow,
and Warsaw, often found Cleveland's physical conditions dismaying. In 1889
a Czech found in the Broadway neighborhood "unpaved streets full of mud,
no stone sidewalks;" there were no sewers. "I never thought that such a big
and already 60-year-old city could have such a strange appearance," wrote
a Polish journalist in 1893. "One has the impression of the Far West, where

house after house is being built, where everything is only just being delineated and remains unfinished ... [where] beautiful buildings filled with
modern objects exist side by side with unbridled jungle... Going from one
part of the city to another, we have to wade through a knee-deep gorge
cutting across the eastern part of the city, while further north there are numerous steel plants."[42]

Fifteen years later, Frederick C. Howe, a young American lawyer, noted
that Cleveland "stretched for miles along the lake front and still kept some
of the quality of a small town." Soon he found himself working with Mor-
ris Black, the grandson of Hungarian Jewish immigrants to Cleveland, to
promote the first "splendid" civic buildings in the city. Both young men had
studied in Germany and, as if responding to immigrant criticism of Cleveland's unimpressive appearance, worked to bring a European standard to
the city. "We prepared illustrated stories of the grouping of public buildings
in Vienna, Paris, Budapest, Dresden, and Munich, and printed them in the
Sunday papers" Howe recalled. They won Chamber of Commerce support
and saw the new complex of city, county, federal, school district, library, and
post office buildings rise in the years around World War I.[43]

Cleveland in the 1860s, the 1890s, and the 1920s: Three Cities

The questions of identity, conflict, and cooperation that presented themselves to those who migrated to Cleveland changed over the years. People
who traveled from the Czech lands of Bohemia and Moravia in the 1850s
and 1860s left parts of the Hapsburg Empire that contained mixed Czech-,
German-, and Slovak-speaking populations, were dominated by German-
speaking landowners and town councils, and served by mostly German-
speaking craftsmen and merchants. Migrants from Bohemia and Moravia
included Protestants, Freethinkers, and Jews as well as many Catholics, and
some of them had been affected by the stirrings of Czech nationalism. They
had been governed, usually from impressive palaces and monasteries, by
local leaders in Prague and in provincial towns as well by German-speaking imperial officials in Vienna, the great Austrian capital.

On arriving in Cleveland in 1860, migrants from the Czech lands found
a largely unpaved, wood-frame town of 43,000 that had nearly tripled (from
17,000) in ten years, and that contained about 9,000 people born in German
lands, over 5,500 immigrants of Irish heritage, nearly 500 from Scotland.
Nearby landowning farmers retained close ties to the Isle of Man; skilled
German workers had organized their own unions.[44] Protestants of New

England background had founded Cleveland and still dominated much of the surrounding country, but even in 1860 they found themselves outnumbered in the city itself. In 1860 English-speaking Protestants had a total of forty churches in the city: already there were also one African-American church, nine German-speaking Protestant churches, eight Catholic churches, and three Jewish synagogues. Michael McTighe estimated that in 1860 Cleveland's English-speaking Protestant church members amounted to less than ten percent of the city's population, whereas Catholics were thirty percent, and Jews, five percent.[45]

In 1860 Cleveland was a rapidly expanding manufacturing center, making and rolling iron and fabricating locomotives as well as rails, processing food, and producing clothing. Cleveland's manufacturing establishments were already scattered along the Cuyahoga River, the Lake Erie shoreline, at waterfalls on Mill Creek and a few other tributaries to the Cuyahoga, and at the head of the Ohio Canal. In Cleveland and in Ohio generally, public officials and judges owed their posts to the votes of white men over the age of twenty-one. In the 1850s, these men were sharply divided over the life-and-death issues that were rapidly leading to the American Civil War. Ohio would supply Ulysses S. Grant, Rutherford B. Hayes, John Sherman, William McKinley, and several other important generals to the Union cause, but it would also support one of the most effective groups of "Copperhead" anti-war Democrats. In 1860, Clevelanders saw newcomers not only as workers for their mills, but also as potential buyers of town lots and as voters who might help their side win a crucial election.

Joseph Grossman's recollections describe one experience of migration from Central Europe to Cleveland in the 1880s and 1890s:

May 28th, 1884 our family arrived from Europe. . . My older brother, Albert, was here just two years ahead of us and, as there were no streetcars running to the Depot, he thoughtfully loaded eight of us and a girl cousin on an open grocery delivery wagon for our trip to Hamilton Street in the neighborhood which is now about E. 14th. A small dwelling had been modestly furnished by him for our reception, into which we crowded very happy about it all after a strenuous voyage from the northern part of Hungary. . . Our neighbors were mostly immigrants. It was customary to receive the new "greenhorns" in a friendly spirit, as we were all struggling to get a foothold in this golden country. . .

For some reason not clear to me, the Irish of the city resented the advent of Hungarians and Slovaks and made no bones about it. I found that out as soon as my brother Albert escorted me downtown . . . and chose the corner of Bank Street (West 6th) and Superior to put me into the newspaper business. Coming from a Latin High School where I went from our village to the nearest city on a horse-drawn vehicle with a coachman, and being directed to sell papers without knowing one word of English was quite a come-down. When I found a shoe shining box on my shoulder and was told to make use of it on the public's shoes, that was almost too much. After American money trickled into my pockets, I felt as though I was a useful member of Cleveland's population. . . The Kleins came to Cleveland the same year we came. Sam Klein had spent weekends at our home in Hungary, where my father had leased one of the estates of the waning nobility.[46]

Joseph Grossman described himself as a Hungarian, reflecting the Hungarian view of Slovakia as "northern Hungary," as well as the fact that Cleveland's Hungarian immigrants still accepted Jews as members of their community in the mid-1880s. Most Slovak-speaking people who came to Cleveland in these years, by contrast, would have thought of themselves as members of an oppressed minority ruled by Hungary, not as "Hungarians."[47] Grossman saw Cleveland's residents in ethnic terms, but in terms that derived from his own background.

Grossman arrived in a city that already had a significant Irish-immigrant population, some of whose members resented the discrimination that denied them access to jobs and resisted the arrival of newcomers. He belonged to the most advantaged group of immigrants, coming from a family that had been able to lease some land from the "waning nobility," and had been able to send him, with a coachman, to a Latin high school. The Latin he had learned "in Europe stood me in good stead in acquiring the English," he recalled. And Grossman did not arrive alone: not only was he part of a complete family unit, but his family came with friends.

The total population of the city when Grossman arrived was about 250,000. About 40,000 of these people had been born in Germany, and many more spoke German as their mother tongue. 14,000 or more had come from Ireland; perhaps 12,000 from the Czech lands. Grossman was among the first 3000 to come from areas ruled by Hungary; a similar number had also come from Polish-speaking regions ruled by Austria, Prussia, and Russia, and about 1500, mostly Jewish, from other parts of Russia. Six thousand were working in Cleveland's steel mills in 1889, and another 10,000 in foundries, forges, nut and bolt and wire factories, and in plants producing stoves, ironwork, hardware, tools, etc. Thirty-five hundred produced ships, rail cars, and carriages. Several thousand worked in warehouses and rail yards, moving goods from place to place. The ten steel plants averaged 600 wage earners each, but most Cleveland firms employed many fewer than 50 people, and employment was dispersed into a wide variety of industries.

Altogether, those who arrived in Cleveland in the 1880s and 1890s encountered a rapidly growing labor market that included many small and middle-sized manufacturing firms operating in distinct, and highly competitive, markets. Cleveland's dispersed manufacturers and rapidly growing residential neighborhoods also needed increasing numbers of shipping clerks, sales people, insurance agents, and lawyers. A number of the city's employers, professionals, and shopkeepers had migrated to Cleveland from the British Isles, from German-speaking areas, or from the Czech lands. Those who were literate, skilled, and entrepreneurial often found excellent opportunity. But with such a diverse population employed in such a wide variety of small, competitive firms, those who looked to promote worker solidarity found that Cleveland posed a very big challenge.

The Cleveland of the 1890s possessed many Protestant churches, but it also embraced a substantial and well-established Jewish community and an actively expanding Catholic Church. Wary of Protestant influence on the public schools, Catholic leaders responded by pressing the construction of parochial schools, and by the mid-1880s Catholics were supporting as many as 126 parochial schools in the Cleveland diocese, with an enrollment of 24,000.[48] Cleveland's Catholic Bishop Gilmour won national prominence as the author of parochial school texts. When Gilmour could not get legislation to provide public funds to Catholic schools in the 1880s, he worked to defeat state legislation designed to increase support for public schools.[49] Immigrants who arrived in Cleveland in the 1890s came to a city that was by no means dominated by Protestants.

Politically, Cleveland offered immigrants of the 1880s and 1890s a local scene that was very different from the politics of their homelands. From 1876 to 1932 Ohio voters divided quite evenly between Republicans and Democrats in national elections: the party whose candidate carried Ohio usually carried the presidency. Facing an electorate of men who were family farmers, keepers of small shops, and, increasingly, factory and transportation workers, Ohio's political leaders appealed to the property interests of the small producer. Republicans championed the tariff as a guarantee of the "American wage" for factory workers, as well as a strong government role in the banking and transportation systems. Workers of many backgrounds responded favorably to their arguments.[50]

In the 1860s, 1870s, and 1880s, Republicans had also looked for ways to support "moral reforms" advocated by evangelical Protestants, making it

easier for townships to restrict the sale of alcohol and strengthening the public schools. But by the 1890s Ohio Republicans were actively—if carefully—
seeking immigrant votes. Democrats generally sought the votes of farmers,
of men closely tied to the south, and of Catholics and Lutherans by opposing tariffs, "moral reforms," and most government action—except for subsidies to the transport systems and banks that served their constituents. In
1882, the Ohio Democratic Party platform characteristically called for limited
government that would guarantee "the largest liberty consistent with public welfare."[51]

In Ohio, political debate over the public role of religion inevitably engaged immigrants. Republican Rutherford B. Hayes, from the northern
Ohio town of Fremont about eighty miles west of Cleveland, won election
as governor in 1875 and then as President of the United States in 1876 in part
by courting the support of the American Alliance, an anti-Catholic group.
Hayes and his allies worked to pass compulsory school attendance laws
and to maintain the influence of Protestant clergymen in state institutions;
Democrats opposed these laws.[52] Leaders of both parties appealed to immigrant voters. Democrats emphasized their opposition to Republican interference with personal liberty, including the liberty to send children to
parochial schools. In his successful 1880 campaign, the Republican James A.
Garfield had endorsed public schools and opposed government subsidies to
"sectarian" schools, but he also listened to delegations of Germans and other
immigrants on the front porch of his home in Mentor, just east of Cleveland
along the lake shore.[53] William McKinley, a Republican who rejected anti-
Catholicism, moved further, appointing so many Catholics to public office
that the anti-Catholic American Protective Association opposed his bid for
the Republican presidential nomination in 1896.[54] McKinley worked closely
with Mark A. Hanna, leader of Ohio's Republicans, to broaden their party's
appeal. During his successful 1896 and 1900 campaigns for President of the
United States, McKinley listened to many delegations of immigrant voters
on the front porch of his home in Canton, forty miles south of Cleveland.[55]

Socialist appeals were very difficult in the U.S. context, with its very
strong emphasis on individual property rights and its strong Protestant and
Catholic communities. Appeals for the toleration if not the support of religious diversity and of national interests in Europe did win encouragement
from mainstream politicians. Despite rural opposition, Hanna and McKinley Republicans, including Samuel Mather in Cleveland, agreed to accept
the Catholic Church. When Woodrow Wilson endorsed the national aims
of many Central and Eastern European ethnic communities as the United
States entered World War I, nationalists in Cleveland's Czech, Slovak, Pol-

ish, and South Slav communities must have felt that their efforts of many years in America had at last borne fruit.

Immigrant women lacked the vote before 1920, just as they had in Europe, and just as did their native-born American sisters. A few responded by joining the campaign for woman suffrage as early as the 1890s, despite the heavy demands of housekeeping and work, the opposition of husbands and fathers, and the resistance of many of the traditionally-inclined immigrant women.[56] Some found new work opportunities in the United States. They also, often, found reasons to join unions and to strike for better wages and working conditions. When female workers sought the support of middle-class women, however, they were rebuffed, and reminded of the American virtue of individualism.[57] Many immigrant women did find ways to participate in American society, and to advance the national, religious, and workers' community causes that attracted them, by working through voluntary and religious organizations. The great expansion of Catholic schools and hospitals, in particular, would have been inconceivable without the work of the thousands of Catholic women who joined religious orders as teachers and nurses, and who also served as managers.[58]

By 1920, migrants to Cleveland from Hungary, Slovakia, Croatia and Slovenia had left territories recently emancipated from an Austria-Hungary that had been on the losing side in World War I. Reeling from the loss of 70% of its territory and 60% of its population, Hungary saw a communist revolution gain power for several months. Most of Croatia and Slovenia had become part of a new "South Slav" nation, Yugoslavia (some came from lands that had been granted to Italy). Despite Yugoslavia's democratic new constitution, many Slovenes and Croats objected to what they saw as the overbearing role of its largest constituent, Serbia. Poland, on the other hand, emerged from its long domination by Austria, Germany, and Russia. Some of those who came to the United States after World War I had identified too strongly with Austria-Hungary to be welcome in the new nations that succeeded it. Some had for a time thrown in their lot with left- or right-wing movements that had lost out in the struggles that immediately followed the war; many saw no economic future for themselves in the new Europe.

On arriving in Cleveland in the teens and twenties, new immigrants encountered one of the world's greatest industrial cities. 800,000 people lived within the expanded city limits in 1920; another half million or so in the adjacent suburbs of Cuyahoga County. More than a quarter of the city's people had been born in Europe—now more often in the former Austria-Hungary or Russia than in German lands, and almost as often in Italy. The Great Migration of African-Americans from the American South had begun during World War I, bringing Cleveland's African-American population to 35,000 and further increasing the diversity of the city's people.[59]

Cleveland now produced not only great quantities of steel: it was one of the nation's leading makers of sewing machines, auto parts, trucks, machine tools, batteries, electrical equipment, paints and chemicals, office machines, and clothing. The labor market—like the markets for financial, legal, engineering, and printing services—extended to several nearby cities: Euclid's products included heavy earth-moving equipment; Akron's rubber tires and conveyor belts made it the nation's "rubber capital;" Youngstown, Lorain, Canton, and Mansfield were major steel-producing centers. Other northern Ohio towns became major producers of refrigerators, washing machines, and vacuum cleaners—the great new "consumer durables" of the 1920s. Many of these industries grew at a rate of 10% *per year* between 1910 and 1929. Even as the production process became more routine, wages were generally good, and with the exception of occasional sharp recessions jobs were plentiful.

Working conditions were still very difficult in many industries, and it had become more difficult than ever to organize effective labor unions. American participation in World War I had the effect of reducing the legitimacy of immigrant and second-generation German, Czech, and Hungarian union leaders. Some of the more radical labor leaders were deported during the 1919 Red Scare—even as the communist government controlled Hungary. The increased diversity in the national origins of Cleveland's workers made it easier for large employers to complicate the lives of labor organizers by deliberately mixing their labor forces. When employees did succeed in organizing, some employers did not hesitate to use African-Americans, who had previously been excluded from the labor market, as strikebreakers.

People who arrived in Cleveland after 1910, and especially after 1920, found themselves in a community whose employers had successfully fought unions in manufacturing, but which had made extensive efforts to accommodate Catholic, Orthodox, and Jewish religious and social service organizations. The new Community Chest, created in response to Catholic complaints about the aggressive attitude of many Protestant agencies, raised funds for Catholic and Jewish organizations as well as for Protestants.[60] Within limits, Cleveland business leaders not only tolerated but encouraged and supported the mutual savings banks and other fraternal mutual benefit organizations created by Cleveland's immigrant communities.[61] The 1920s saw the greatest expansion yet of Catholic schools. And political leaders struggled to find ways to hold the ethic communities in the Republican party, or attract them to the Democratic side.

Slovene, Croatian, and German women pose at the drill presses of the Cleveland
Hardware Company, 1917. WRHS

What were the people who had moved from Europe to Cleveland becoming in the early decades of the twentieth century? We know that there were
several answers. Not a few were assimilating as rapidly as they could into
the society of white North America in general. Those who met certain broad
criteria of personal appearance, attitudes, and values, could be successful,
and they did have success in helping create a more inclusive definition of
American society. Some were most concerned with the fate of the nation
from which they had come. Numbers gladly returned after Versailles to live
in a Poland or a Yugoslavia or a Czechoslovakia that they had wished for,

as some of the essays that follow show. Others remained in the United States but made good use of American traditions of free speech and organization to advance the cause of those with whom they identified in Europe. Some joined the struggle to create and advance the labor movement in the United States. Perhaps as many devoted themselves to service through the Catholic Church.

As the studies in this volume emphasize, many worked from the 1890s through the 1920s to build new neighborhoods of mixed ethnic heritage in the United States. In the 1930s, Lisabeth Cohen has suggested in her study of Chicago, the Great Depression overwhelmed the church charities, mutual savings banks, and mutual benefit societies that the newcomers had created to sustain their lives in these neighborhoods. The New Deal, with its recognition of labor unions, bank insurance, home loan insurance, and aid to the old and disabled, helped shore up their neighborhoods—was in a real sense, she argues, "made" by these immigrant industrial workers.[62] But some of the Central European immigrants and their children opposed the New Deal with its stronger national government and higher taxes, and after World War II found themselves described as "Eisenhower Democrats," and later as "Reagan Republicans."[63] An influential recent group of historians has suggested that the most important story is the merging of many groups into an inclusive "white race," distinguished by its ability to monopolize access to economic and social opportunity. This perspective clearly applies to some extent to the Cleveland experience, though it is also true that the Catholic schools created by Central European migrants to Cleveland now serve large numbers of African-American children, and that the now-suburban Catholic descendants of the immigrants join some of Cleveland's Jewish leaders in subsidizing these schools. The question of identity has no easy answer: individuals have continued to go in many directions, and the story never ends. The essays included in this volume should provoke further exploration.

Notes

1. Kathleen Neils Conzen, et al., "The Invention of Ethnicity: A Perspective from the u.s.a.," *Journal of American Ethnic History* 12 (Fall, 1992), 6; Werner Sollors, *Beyond Ethnicity: Consent and Descent in American Culture* (New York: Oxford University Press, 1986).

2. David E. Green, *The City and Its People* (Cleveland: The Federated Churches of Cleveland, 1917).

3. For a clear and thoughtful discussion of some of these points, see Paul Krause, "Labor Republicanism and *'Za Chlebom'*: Anglo-Americans and Slavic Solidarity in Homestead," in Dirk Hoerder, ed., *"Struggle a Hard Battle": Essays on Working-Class Immigration* (DeKalb: Northern Illinois University Press, 1986), 143–169. As Krause notes, the key debate has to do with the nature and reality of a distinction between "private property for use and private property for accumulation," 165, and also, though he does not emphasize this point, with the relative role of government in controlling the uses of property.

4. This is one of the themes of the very useful book by John Bodnar, Roger Simon, and Michael P. Weber, *Lives of Their Own: Blacks, Italians, and Poles in Pittsburgh, 1900–1960* (Urbana: University of Illinois Press, 1982).

5. Eric Hobsbawm, "Mass-Producing Traditions: Europe, 1870–1914," in Hobsbawm and Terence Ranger, *The Invention of Tradition* (Cambridge: Cambridge University Press, 1983), 283–288.

6. Patrick Geary, *The Myth of Nations: The Medieval Origins of Europe* (Princeton: Princeton University Press, 2002).

7. For good accounts of the purposes and experiences of people who came to Cleveland from Italy, Romania, and Slovakia, see Josef J. Barton, *Peasants and Strangers: Italians, Rumanians, and Slovaks in and American City, 1890–1950* (Cambridge: Harvard University Press, 1975); John W. Briggs, *An Italian Passage: Immigrants to Three American cities, 1890–1930* (New Haven: Yale University Press, 1978); and several essays by M. Mark Stolarik, including "Immigration, Education, and the Social Mobility of Slovaks, 1870–1930," in Randall M. Miller and Thomas D. Marzik, eds., *Immigrants and Religion in Urban America* (Philadelphia: Temple University Press, 1977). John Bodnar, *Remaking America: Public Memory, Commemoration, and Patriotism in the Twentieth Century* (Princeton: Princeton University Press, 1992), provides an excellent analysis of the interaction of ethnic and patriotic impulses in Cleveland after World War II.

8. Thirteenth Census of the United States, *Census of Population*, Chapter IX, "Mother Tongue of the Foreign White Stock," Introduction, 959.

9. U.S. Census, 1910. "Instructions to the Enumerators," 30–31, nos. 139, 140, 142.

10. Ibid.

11. Jan Pankuch, *Dejiny Clevelandskch a Lakeswoodskvch Slovakov* (Cleveland, 1930), 42; translated and discussed by Gudrun Birnbaum in "Growth: Peoples and Industries of Cleveland," 8.

12. Wellington G. Fordyce, "Immigrant Colonies in Cleveland," *Ohio Archeological and Historical Quarterly* 45 (1936), 323.

13. Lászlo Katus with the collaboration of Gábor Gyáni, "Budapest 1850–1914," unpublished manuscript, 1990, 20.

14. Frank Thistlethwaite, "Migration from Europe Overseas in the Nineteenth and Twentieth Centuries," *Rapports, V: Histoire Contemporaine*, Xie Congrés International des Sciences Historiques, (Stockholm: Almquist & Wiksell, 1960), reprinted

in Stanley Katz and Stanley Kutler, editors, *New Perspectives on the American Past* (New York: Little, Brown and Company, Inc., 1972), 64–65. See also Walter Nugent, *Crossings: The Great Transatlantic Migration, 1870–1914* (Bloomington: Indiana University Press, 1992).

15. By the 1940s, there were seventeen railway stations in Budapest; Erdmann Doane Beynon, "Budapest: An Ecological Study," *Geographical Review* 33 (1943), 246.

16. Jerome Blum, *The End of the Old Order in Rural Europe* (Princeton: Princeton University Press, 1978), 438.

17. Blum, *The End of the Old Order in Rural Europe*, 426–429, 438. Blum details the many complexities of the emancipation of peasants from parts of western Europe in the late 1700s to Russia at the beginning of the twentieth century.

18. For a detailed account of the complicated system of voting rights in Budapest, for example, see Zsuzsa L. Nagy, "Transformations in The City Politics of Budapest, 1873–1941," in Thomas Bender and Carl E. Schorske, eds., *Budapest & New York: Studies in Metropolitan Transformation* (New York: Russell Sage Foundation, 1994), 41.

19. Károly Vörös, "From City to Metropolis (1849–1919)," in Ágnes Ságvári, ed., *Budapest: The History of a Capital* (Budapest: Corvina Press, 1975, 39; Katus, "Budapest 1850–1914," 35–36, citing Katus, "Magyarország gazdasági fejlödése," in *Magyarország története 1890–1918* [*History of Hungary, 1890–1918*], ed. Peter Hanák and Ferenc Mucsi (Budapest: Académiai Kiadó, 1978).

20. V. Sandor, "Die Entfalung der Grossmühlenindustrie in Budapest nach dem Ausgleich in Jahr 1867 (1867–1880)," *Acta Historica* X (1964), 233–271, cited in Katus, "Budapest 1850–1914," 40; Vörös, "From City to Metropolis (1849–1919)," 40.

21. Albert Shaw, *Municipal Government in Continental Europe* (New York: The Century Company, 1895), 439–441.

22. Lászlo Katus, "A gépipar fejlödésé" ("Development of the Machine Industry"), *Magyar Tudomány*, Uj folyam XXXIV (1989), 832–45, cited in Katus with the collaboration of Gábor Gyáni, "Budapest 1850–1914," 40.

23. Manó Somogyi, *Az óbudai hajógyár munkásainak helyzete* (Budapest, 1888), cited in Katus with the collaboration of Gábor Gyáni, "Budapest 1850–1914." 55–59.

24. Vörös, "From City to Metropolis (1849–1919)," 40; Rondo Cameron, *A Concise Economic History of the World From Paleolithic Times to the Present* second edition, (New York: Oxford University Press, 1993), 258–261.

25. Katus, "Budapest 1850–1914," 12.

26. I saw the interior of this apartment when it was featured in the former Hungarian Museum of the Worker's Movement in Buda; it is described in *A Magyar Munkásmozgalmi Múzeum Évkönyve 1989–1980* [*Yearbook of the Hungarian Museum of the Worker's Movement*] (Budapest, 1981), cited in Katus, "Budapest 1850–1914," 12.

27. Manó Somogyi, *Az óbudai hajógyár munkásainak helyzete* (Budapest, 1888), translated by Lászlo Katus in Katus, "Budapest 1850–1914," 55–58.

28. David S. Landes, *The Unbound Prometheus: Technological Change and Industrial Development in Western Europe from 1750 to the Present* (Cambridge: Cambridge University Press, 1969), 236.

29. Katus, "Budapest 1850–1914," 67.

30. David C. Hammack and Zsuzsa L. Nagy, "Urban Political and Social History in National Historical Perspective: The Development of Budapest and New York, 1870–1940," in *Papers of the 17th International Congress of Historical Sciences* (Madrid, 1992) pp 1075–1081.

31. Katus, "Budapest 1850–1914," 20–21.

32. Hammack and Nagy, "The Politics of Urban Development in New York and Budapest."

33. Robert A. Kann, *A History of the Habsburg Empire, 1526–1918* (Berkeley: The University of California Press, 1974), 290.

34. Kann, *A History of the Habsburg Empire,* 290–291. In all linguistic communities, many peasants simply considered themselves members of their own village. But they were also, and increasingly, exposed to both religious and nationalist claims on their identity and their loyalty. Historian Robert A. Kann, who assumed that the development of national consciousness was somehow an inevitable process, has argued that Austria-Hungary's nationalities had two different historical trajectories. Germans, Czechs, Hungarians, and Poles had for hundreds of years experienced "the mixed blessings of a nationally conscious nobility, gentry, and urban burgher class." Kann insisted that many aristocrats and intellectuals in these communities "possessed a strong national identity and consciousness.'" But there were many complexities. The Roman Empire and the Catholic Church had celebrated the universal identities of "Roman citizen" or "child of God." Latin remained the universal language of the Church; in the eighteenth century French was the language of diplomacy and culture across Europe. Aristocratic landlords often oppressed their tenants and were strongly tempted to identify and join forces with their Austrian or Hungarian counterparts in defense of aristocratic rather than national rights, especially after the French Revolution and the Terror of the early 1790s, and again after the revolutions of 1848. Other aristocrats resisted imperial Austria's efforts to protect the rights of peasants and townsmen by joining conservative but anti-Habsburg (and aristocrat-dominated) movements of Polish, Hungarian, or Czech nationalism. Robert A. Kann, *A History of the Habsburg Fmpire, 1526–1918* (Berkeley: The University of California Press, 1974), p. 290.

35. Kann, *A History of the Habsburg Empire,* 290–295.

36. Hammack and Nagy, "Urban Political and Social History."

37. Kann, *History of the Habsburg Empire,* 66.

38. Gudrun Birnbaum, "Growth: Peoples and Industries of Cleveland," incomplete, unpublished manuscript, 1990.

39. Krause, "Labor Republicanism and '*Za Chlebom*'; for a related discussion of Polish industrial immigrant workers, see Adam Walaszek, *Polscy Robotnicy, Praca*

I Zwiazki Zawodowe W Stanach Zhednoczonych Ameryki, 1880–1922 [*Polish Work-ers, Labor and Trade Unions in the United States, 1880–1922*] (Wroclaw: Zakład Nor-odowy im. Ossolińskich, 1988), 231–233.

40. For an excellent overview of related debates among intellectuals in the United States, see David A. Hollinger, *PostEthnic America: Beyond Multiculturalism* (New York: Basic Books, 1995).

41. David C. Hammack, "Economy," in *The Encyclopedia of Cleveland History,* edited by David D. Van Tassel and John Grabowski (Bloomington: Indiana Uni-versity Press, second edition, 1996), 371–376.

42. Emil H. Dunikowski, *Wsrod Polonii w Americye.* Druga seria 'Listow z Ameryke,' Lwow, Poland, 1893, 103, 53, translated by Adam Walaszek.

43. Frederic C. Howe, *The Confessions of a Reformer* (New York, 1925; reprint, Kent, Ohio: Kent State University Press, 1988), 80–81.

44. Charlotte Erickson, *Invisible Immigrants: The Adaptation of English and Scot-tish Immigrants in 19th-Century America* (Ithaca: Cornell University Press, 1972, 101–106; Bruce C. Levine, "In the Heat of Two Revolutions: The Forging of German-American Radicalism," in Dirk Hoerder, ed., *"Struggle a Hard Battle:" Essays on Working-Class Immigration* (DeKalb: Northern Illinois University Press, 1986), 31.

45. Michael J. McTighe, *A Measure of Success: Protestants and Public Culture in Antebellum Cleveland* (Albany: State University of New York Press, 1994), 16–21.

46. Joseph Grossman, "Some Reminiscences of the Fading 19th Century," and "Recollections of Businessmen of the 1880s," *Cleveland News,* Feb. 16 and Feb. 27, 1945. Cleveland Public Library Clipping files, "Cleveland History."

47. For a very good account, see M. Mark Stolarik, "Immigration, Ethnicity, and the Social Mobility of Slovaks, 1870–1930," in Randall M. Miller and Thomas D. Marzik, editors, *Immigrants and Religion in Urban America* (Philadelphia: Temple University Press, 1977), 103–116.

48. Jorgenson, *The State and the Non-Public School,* 123; Sally H. Wertheim, "Education," in Van Tassel and Grabowski, *Encyclopedia of Cleveland History,* 378; for an account of the close relation between Protestant leaders and Cleveland's pub-lic schools in the 1860s, see Michael McTighe, *A Measure of Success: Protestants and Public Culture in Antebellum Cleveland* (Albany: State University of New York Press, 1994), 147–48, 228.

49. Jorgenson, *The State and the Non-Public School,* 125.

50. H. Wayne Morgan, *From Hayes to McKinley: National Party Politics, 1877–1896* (Syracuse: Syracuse University Press, 1969), 116, 120–121, 165–170, 308–319, 518–519.

51. Quoted by Paul Kleppner, *The Third Party System, 1853–1892: Parties, Vot-ers, and Political Cultures* (Chapel Hill: The University of North Carolina Press, 1979), 236.

52. Lloyd P. Jorgenson, *The State and the Non-Public Schools, 1825–1925* (Co-lumbia: University of Missouri Press, 1987), 122–23.

53. Kleppner, *The Third Party System,* 233; Morgan, *From Hayes to McKinley,* 106.

54. Paul Kleppner, *The Cross of Culture: A Social Analysis of Midwestern Politics, 1850–1900* (New York: The Free Press, 1970), 347–352.

55. Morgan, *From Hayes to McKinley,* 484–485, 516–520.

56. Adam Walaszek, "The Polish Women's Alliance in America: Between Feminism and Patriotism—Immigrants and Their Children in the USA, 1898–1930," in Klemenčič, ed., *Ethnic Fraternalism in Immigrant Countries,* 199–200.

57. Lois Scharf, "A Woman's View of Cleveland's Labor Force: Two Case Studies," in Thomas F. Campbell and Edward M. Miggins, editors, *The Birth of Modern Cleveland, 1865–1930* (Cleveland: Western Reserve Historical Society, 1988), 172–194.

58. For the most comprehensive general account, see Mary J. Oates, *The Catholic Philanthropic Tradition in America* (Bloomington: Indiana University Press, 1995).

59. Kenneth L. Kusmer, *A Ghetto Takes Shape: Black Cleveland, 1870–1930* (Urbana: University of Illinois Press, 1976); Kimberley L. Phillips, *AlabamaNorth: African-American Migrants, Community, and Working-Class Activism, 1915–1945* (Urbana and Chicago: University of Illinois Press, 1999).

60. Brian Ross, "The New Philanthropy: The Reorganization of Charity in Turn of the Century Cleveland," unpublished Ph.D. dissertation, Case Western Reserve University Department of History, 1989.

61. For a general account of these organizations, see David T. Beito, *From Mutual Aid to the Welfare State: Fraternal Societies and Social Services, 1890–1967* (Chapel Hill: The University of North Carolina Press, 2000).

62. Lizabeth Cohen, *Making a New Deal: Industrial Workers in Chicago, 1919–1939* (Cambridge: Cambridge University Press, 1990).

63. Ruy Teixeira and Joel Rogers, *America's Forgotten Majority: Why the White Working Class Still Matters* (New York: Basic Books, 2000).

Conflict and Co-Operation:
Cleveland's Croatians, 1880s–1930s

IVAN ČIZMIĆ

Migration, Settlement, and Socioeconomic Status

Between 1880 and World War I, approximately four hundred thousand Croatians immigrated to the United States. Most of them arrived in New York and then continued on to America's industrial heartland—Pennsylvania, Ohio, Illinois, Michigan, and Indiana—seeking employment in centers of the steel, aluminum, and electrical machinery industries and the coal basins. In these areas there were many Croatian settlements, among which the largest were in Pittsburgh, Chicago and Detroit. Cleveland's Croatian settlement was somewhat smaller, but also significant.

The settlement had its beginning in 1888, when two brothers, Nikola and Elias Kekić, and Franjo Kovačić came to Cleveland. Elias Kekić brought his fiancee from the old country with him, got married in Cleveland, and opened the first Croatian saloon in the city on St. Clair Avenue and East 26th Street. This family-run establishment provided a welcoming haven for many of the Croatians who were starting to arrive in Cleveland in growing numbers. Franjo Kovačić, who had started by working in the Pennsylvania mines, also became a saloonkeeper and prominent Croatian businessman in Cleveland. Another pioneer in the formation of Cleveland's Croatian settlement was "Uncle" Janko Popović, whose boardinghouse also received many newly arrived Croatians.

By the beginning of the twentieth century, the settlement was taking shape. It was composed of immigrants from the Karlovac region, Gorski Kotar, Žumberak, and some other parts of Croatia. These regions bordered with areas of Slovenia from which Slovenes were already migrating to Cleveland. Informed by Slovene neighbors about the good opportunities life in Cleveland offered, Croatians increasingly joined them in migrating. In Cleveland, both groups together formed the main Croatian-Slovene settlement, which stretched along St. Clair Avenue from East 24th Street to East 79th Street, and south to Superior and Payne Avenues. Settlements also grew up in the Collinwood neighborhood, along Holmes Avenue, Waterloo Road, and adjacent streets; in the Nottingham area from East 185th to East 222nd Street; in Newburgh along Union Avenue from East 75th Street to East 110th Street; in Euclid along St. Clair Avenue from Bliss Road to Lloyd Road; and in Maple Heights along Broadway from Garfield Park to Dunham Road.

It is difficult to determine precisely how many Croatians lived in Cleveland between 1888 and 1930, particularly since their numbers fluctuated constantly, with migrants arriving from and returning to Europe, or moving to or from other Croatian settlements in the United States. According to the Immigration Commission, there were 3,846 Croatians in Cleveland in 1910. The 1920 census counted 3,498, while the 1930 census put the number at 3,607.[1] Although this may be a reasonably correct count of the first generation, it does not include the entire community. Croatian fraternal organizations had as many as 5,841 active members in 1930, and all Croatians did not belong to fraternals. One estimate gives a figure of ten thousand for the number of Croatians living in Cleveland on the eve of World War I.

The social and economic characteristics of the Croatian settlement in Cleveland did not differ greatly from those of Croatian settlements in many other parts of the United States.[2] Within Cleveland itself, the results of comparative research indicate that there was also no great difference between the social and economic status of Croatians and that of members of other ethnic groups such as Slovenes, Slovaks, and Magyars.

According to sample data on 264 Clevelanders of Croatian origin from the 1910 census, three-quarters of the population (76.9 per cent) was male and one quarter (23.1 per cent) female. Not surprisingly, most of the immigrants were young or middle aged: 70 per cent of the men were between 20 and 40 years of age, while 12.5 percent were between 10–19, and 9.5 percent from 40 to 50. Sixty percent were married, forty percent unmarried. Most did not reply as to whether or not they had children: 6.8 percent said that they had only one child, 2.8 percent two, 4.2 three, and 1.4 four or more.

Birth, marriage, and death records from Cleveland's two Croatian parishes, St. Paul's (Roman Catholic) and St. Nicholas (Greek Catholic), also shed light on the demographics of the Croatian community.[3] St. Paul's recorded 16 marriages in 1903, 87 in 1907, and 128 in each of the years from 1912 to 1914, after which the number of marriages declined, to 71 in 1917, and 30 in 1925, as first World War I and then restrictive laws reduced immigration to the United States. St. Nicholas parish recorded its maximum number of marriages, 18, in 1921. St. Paul's also had a temporary increase in that year, due perhaps to immigrants hastily bringing brides over before new immigration laws made it more difficult.

The marriage registers of the Roman Catholic church, in particular, show the close ties between Croatians and Slovenes, who had come from adjoining territories in Europe, and who lived side-by-side in Cleveland. From 1903 to 1914, 884 marriages were recorded at St. Paul's. Of the individuals married, approximately sixty percent came from Croatian, and thirty percent from Slovene provinces. Most of the others were second generation South Slav-Americans: girls born in Pennsylvania, Colorado, Indiana, and other states, who married newly-arrived immigrants. Among the immigrants, nearly half came from the Žumberak and Samobor hills, forty percent from the Croatian, eastern communes (Jastrebarsko, Samobor, Ozalj, and Duga Resa), and seven percent from the Slovene, western part (Novo Mesto, Breźice, Krśko, Metlika and Crnomelj). Other communes represented were Delnice, Karlovac, Brač, Daruvar, Pakrac, and Kutina (Croatian), and Cerknica and Ribnica (Slovene). Approximately sixty percent of the individuals married in St. Nicholas church during the same period came from the Croatian Žumberak communes. Nearly ten percent came from other European countries, and twenty percent were American-born, two-thirds of these being Cleveland natives. These second generation spouses included 26 men and 46 women. At St. Paul's church, not a single second generation groom was recorded.

While these figures illustrate the intermingling of the Croatian and Slovene communities in Cleveland, they do not indicate a substantial degree of intermarriage among members of the first generation. Like other immigrants, most first generation Croatian men married women of their own nationality. Some married in Europe; others established themselves in America and then sent money to cover the travel expenses of the bride-to-be. Occasionally young women came to the United States alone to join relatives, where they found numerous suitors among the lone young men. In the case of the marriages recorded in the Cleveland Croatian parishes, a sampling of individuals from representative communes indicates that sixty percent of Croatians, and two-thirds of Slovenes chose spouses from the same commune, with a substantial minority of marriages being between individuals from the same village. Ninety percent of first generation Croatians, and eight-five percent of first generation Slovenes married individuals of the same nationality. Records for second generation marriages give less conclusive results (for example, someone with a non-south Slavic name

Parish council members and clergy of St. Nicholas Greek Catholic Church pose for a 40th anniversary photograph. WRHS

might in fact have had a Croatian or Slovene mother), but indicate that children of Croatian and Slovene immigrants married members of other ethnic groups in up to three out of four cases.

Birth and death records say less about ties to the old world, but do give some idea about family life and living conditions in Cleveland's Croatian community. From 1903 to 1925, 5,102 children were christened at St. Paul's; 74 children were christened in St. Nicholas parish from 1902 to 1905, and 986 between 1913 and 1931. (Records from St. Nicholas do not cover the years 1906 to 1913.) In both churches, the number of children peaked in the mid- to late 1910s, following the upswing in marriages and concurrent with a period of economic prosperity. The number of christenings then decreased, as the first generation neared the end of its childbearing age, while most

St. Nicholas Greek Catholic Church. WRHS

members of the second generation had not yet reached it. In addition, Croatians were moving out of the old ethnic neighborhoods near the churches as they prospered and assimilated into American society.

To modern sensibilities, child mortality in the two parishes was high. Of the 2,115 St. Paul's parishioners who died in the 1903–1940 period, over forty percent were children under the age of five. Before 1917, sixty to seventy-five percent of the deaths in the parish were among those aged fifteen and under. Although poor living conditions and limited health care were contributing factors, it also must be remembered that this was a young immigrant community in the early part of the century. Many adults had barely reached middle, much less old age. Until the mid-1920s the most frequent cause of death among adults was tuberculosis, with pneumonia and then accidents following. In 1918 the influenza epidemic took a heavy toll. In subsequent years, the death rate of working-age and older immigrants increased as the population aged and, perhaps, succumbed to the years of hard work in often unhealthy surroundings. Death statistics for St. Nicholas parishioners were generally similar to those for St. Paul's.

Information on living conditions, as well as socio-economic status, can also be gleaned from data on home ownership. In 1910 only 10.2 percent of Cleveland Croatians were in possession of a house, either as owners or as principal tenants. Half of the total residents in a dwelling were members of the owner's family (wife, siblings, children), and half were boarders or lodgers, indicating cramped and potentially unhygienic living conditions.[4] The fact that only ten percent of Croatians possessed houses in 1910 shows that most of them either did not intend to stay permanently in the United States, or did not yet have enough money to afford a house.

Data on occupation and employment are particularly indicative of the migrants' socio-economic position in their new environment. They show that for the most part Croatians left behind the agricultural occupations that many of them had followed in Europe. According to the 1910 census sample, 66.3 percent were laborers, 22 percent were unemployed, and several were pensioners. The remaining 11.7 percent worked as merchants or clerks.[5] A number of these undoubtedly were the owners or employees of the Croatian businesses that grew up in the Croatian neighborhoods. Another source states that in the period before 1918 most Croatians worked in manufacturing concerns such as the American Steel and Wire Company, and others were employed by the railways, notably in the Collinwood shops of the Lake Shore and Michigan Southern Railroad. The National Screw and Tack Company employed many Croatian women. In the period after 1918 some Croatians did find work in the agricultural sector, on farms in the West Park area.[6]

The situation was similar in 1930, with most Croatian men still employed as workers in heavy industry. Although independent data for Croatians do not exist, census records for the areas where Croatians and Slovenes were most heavily concentrated indicate that over thirty percent of them worked in the iron and steel industry alone, with another ten to fifteen percent in automobile factories. Approximately ten percent were employed in wholesale and retail trade. The same records indicate the clothing industry, the electrical machine industry, and wholesale and retail trade and other service sectors as the largest employers of Croatian and Slovene women.

As for assimilation into the broader society, this did not occur significantly among Cleveland Croatians until well into the twentieth century. Before that, they had not attained one of the basic preconditions for assimilation (or even acculturation) to occur to any substantial degree: sufficient length of stay. Of the total number of Cleveland Croatians in 1910, only twenty-five percent had arrived prior to 1900, with the other seventy-five percent arriving within the previous decade. In 1910 only 7.2 percent of Croatian immigrants stated that they had been naturalized, with 28.4 percent intending to take out naturalization papers. In addition to length of stay and naturalization, general literacy and a knowledge of the English language also affect or are affected by the acculturation and assimilation process. According to their own statements (on which basis the figures must be taken with some reserve), 70.5 percent of the Croatian migrants in Cleveland in 1910 were literate, and 54.6 percent spoke English.

Cleveland Croatians in the American Fraternal Movement

Like other nationality groups, Croatian immigrants formed their own fraternal benefit societies to pay sickness and death benefits, thus providing a sense of security and stability in their new environment. Initially, however, most Cleveland Croatians showed little interest in American fraternalism. Only after they were convinced of the efficacy of insurance and fraternal organizations did greater numbers begin joining organizations such as the National Croatian Union (headquartered in Pittsburgh) and, later, the Croatian Union of Illinois (headquartered in Chicago).[7]

The Croatian fraternal movement in Cleveland had its beginnings in 1895, when a few individuals went from house to house trying to convince others that Croatians should form their own fraternal society. They managed to arrange a meeting for those interested in the plan, but although approximately three hundred people attended, only sixty promised to join the proposed society. In the end, thirty-seven people founded the first Croatian fraternal society in Cleveland, which after some vacillation among the members joined the National Croatian Union as Lodge No. 22, St. Nicholas. When one of the lodge's members died in 1896, his heirs received three hundred dollars in recompense. In the following year the heirs of another deceased member received five hundred dollars. As lodge membership increased, the amount rose to six and then to eight hundred dollars. The snowballing effect of greater membership leading to higher benefits, thereby attracting yet more members, resulted in Lodge No. 22, with a roster of 120, becoming the National Croatian Union's largest lodge in 1903.

Other Cleveland Croatians followed the successful example of the St. Nicholas Lodge. In 1899 the Croatian Roman Catholic St. Joseph Society, which became Lodge No. 99 of the National Croatian Union, was founded. Additional lodges of the National Croatian Union soon followed, and American fraternalism became firmly established in Cleveland's Croatian community.[8] Meanwhile, in 1897 Croatian women founded their own society, the Ladies' Association of Our Lady of Bistrica.

In 1906, the National Croatian Union held its third national convention in Cleveland, at Travikar's Hall on St. Clair Avenue. Thirty-five delegates from various American cities represented the Union's membership of 1,885. The event heightened interest among Cleveland Croatians and attracted more to the movement. The Union's twelfth convention in 1915 was also held in Cleveland, attended by 140 delegates representing a membership that had grown to 35,112. At that convention the decision to found Union youth lodges, in order to attract second-generation Croatians, was reached.[9] Another convention took place in Cleveland in 1925, during which delegates from nearly all of the Croatian fraternal organizations in the United States elected to unite into a single body, the Croatian Fraternal Union.

Individual Cleveland lodges also merged, since those with few members found it difficult to solve organizational problems and fulfill financial obligations, most importantly the benefits due to their members. Eventually English-speaking lodges were founded in the Cleveland area. These included the Pioneers, No. 663, in 1927, the Strivers, in 1928, the Crusaders, No. 840, and the George Washington, Nest 182.[10]

In 1918 the National Croatian Union had 42,746 members organized in 428 lodges, the largest number, 144, being in Pennsylvania, followed by Ohio's 30 lodges. By 1926 the number of Ohio lodges, most of which were in Cleveland, had grown to 49.[11] Before joining with the Croatian Fraternal Union in 1925, the Croatian Union of Illinois had four lodges in Cleveland,

Morning Star, No. 79, the Sons of Zagreb Concord, No. 102, Fraternal Concord, No. 108, and the Sons of Žumberak, No. 132. As of 1930 the united Croatian Fraternal Union had 11 lodges in the greater Cleveland area, with 3,069 full members and 205 spouse-members. There were also 6 junior nests, with 1,787 members, bringing the Union's total membership to over 5,000.[12]

In 1921 another fraternal organization, the Croatian Catholic Union, was founded in Gary, Indiana, by some Croatian priests, who did not agree with the progressive-leftist policy that increasingly prevailed in the National Croatian Union after World War I. Immediately after the new union's founding, its first lodge, St. Paul, was established in Cleveland "to fight against socialism and communism."[13] The newspaper of the Croatian Catholic Union, *Nasa Nada* (*Our Hope*) was published in Cleveland for several years. Its editor, Rev. Michael Domladovac of St. Paul's Church, described the paper's task as "promot[ing] the Catholic religion and morality among our people, who are pushed towards ultramodern ideas under strong influences."[14] His fierce polemics with Croatian leftists about the meaning of religion evidently did not always have the desired effect. A Slovene priest complained to the bishop that Rev. Domladovac's confrontational stance was pushing Croatians even deeper into religious indifference.[15] Nevertheless, the Croatian Catholic Union attracted its share of members, and as of 1930 had five lodges in Cleveland.

Cleveland's Croatian lodges held monthly meetings, usually in halls rented from Croatian or Slovene owners. Regular payment of membership dues was mandatory, since the provision of benefits depended upon this. Dues were collected at the end of the meeting so that members could not leave early. Members who went to saloons during sick leave were not supposed to receive financial aid, although some lodges were lenient in enforcing such rules. The most important post was that of the lodge accountant, who was therefore paid a small sum for his services. Records of one National Union lodge in Cleveland, No. 451, give the following expense report for 1921: $1,302.74 sent to the main office in Pittsburgh (from which death benefits were disbursed), $238 in payments made to sick members, and $100.18 in salary to lodge officials, for a total of $1,640.92.

During periods of economic difficulty, most notably the Great Depression, lodge budgets could come under strain. Lodges might tolerate late payment of dues, but could afford to do so only as long as there was money in the till to meet financial obligations. Units with more members, which had larger treasuries, could afford to wait longer for payment and thus lost fewer members. However, in 1930 Lodge 199 of the Croatian Fraternal Union lost 32 of 752 members during a ten-month period. "The effects of lay-offs can be seen [at] each of our meetings, when members come and ask the lodge to wait for them to pay their dues and not suspend them. They promise to pay, but when they will be able to do so they do not even know themselves."[16]

Even in normal times dues did not always cover expenses. Lodges therefore sponsored social events to raise additional funds. These cultural and recreational activities also added a dimension to the fraternal societies apart from their social insurance function, serving to promote group and ethnic solidarity among the members. Parties and dances were typically held two or three times a year, on religious holidays or at the New Year. Whenever possible, a lodge would have its own tamburitza orchestra, subventing the need to hire musicians. Attendance at some social functions was mandatory, and members absent without an excuse were fined.

"Lodge solidarity" also grew up among the various units. If the members of one lodge did not attend another lodge's social event, the latter might repay in kind, so that there was considerable pressure to accept such invitations. Interethnic solidarity, primarily with Slovene ethnic organizations, and later with Serbian and other Slavic groups, was also demonstrated. The Collinwood Croatian community, which was relatively small, readily cooperated with Slovenes, for instance participating in and financially supporting the construction of the Slovenian Workmen's Home in Collinwood.[17] National Croatian Union lodges also responded to the invitations of Serbian lodges to attend their celebrations.

Cleveland-area lodges of the National Croatian Union and the Croatian Union of Illinois identified with and supported the struggles for national liberation and democracy in the Croatian homeland. They usually did so as part of more general campaigns set in motion at the national level, but sometimes the decisions were made by the rank and file of specific lodges. Many times lodges decided for themselves whether actions the headquarters decided upon were appropriate or not. For example, during World War I they strongly supported assistance to Croatian war veterans and invalids, but boycotted campaigns to collect money for war orphans in Croatia, and for the Yugoslav Committee in London. In 1922 Cleveland lodges enthusiastically collected aid for their Slavic brothers in Russia. However, local lodge members found the goals of some welfare drives too abstract or geographically distant, and initiators of the campaigns not always plausible.

After the war, Cleveland lodge members generally preferred to help their compatriots within the city or the United States, especially the sick or injured. Sometimes they helped lodge members who had exhausted the fraternal benefits to which they were entitled under the organization's rules. During the Depression or other times of hardship some members were

assisted in making dues payments so that they would not be suspended. Fraternals also offered assistance in instances that were not specifically tied to
ethnicity. Lodges in Collinwood collected money for the victims of a tragic
school fire that took place there in 1908. Particularly after World War I,
Cleveland lodges demonstrated great solidarity with workers on strike. During a miners' strike in 1922 they established an aid fund for the strikers, and
in April 1925 Lodge No. 102 of the Croatian Union of Illinois decided to
donate twenty-five dollars from the treasury for "our brothers who are fighting against the mining baron." However, many lodge members did not like
the idea of touching their funds for purposes other than supporting their
own members and would not readily agree to give funds, whether for striking workers or other causes.[18] One lodge, for instance, refused donation
requests from both St. Paul's Church and a Croatian singing society.

Croatian Ethnic Parishes: St. Paul's and St. Nicholas

Before 1900 there were no Croatian parishes in the Diocese of Cleveland.
Until then Croatians attended a Slovene church, St. Vitus, a natural step in
view of the similarity of the languages and cultures. This was, however, only
a temporary solution. Croatians wanted their own parish, with religious services conducted in their own language. As early as 1895 the need for a Croatian parish had been discussed in the St. Nicholas Society, but it was not
until after the turn of the century that Cleveland Croatians took serious
steps to found a parish. The increase in the number of Croatians in the city
made this feasible, but it was a misunderstanding with the Slovene priest
of St. Vitus, who accused Croatians of not fulfilling their parochial duties
and reproached Greek Catholic Croatians for adhering to the eastern ritual
in church, that actually triggered decisive action. On the initiative of the
St. Joseph Society, Croatian Roman and Greek Catholics met in 1902 to discuss creation of a single Croatian parish and construction of a church, but
agreement was stymied by an impasse over the name of the church. The
Greek Catholics proposed the church be called the "Croatian Roman and
Greek Catholic Church," while the Roman Catholics favored the simpler
"Croatian Roman Catholic Church," arguing that no one in America even
knew what Greek Catholicism was.[19]

In the end, each group decided to build its own church. The Croatian
Roman Catholics had elected a church board on 31 January 1901 to "organize church matters and collect money." The board, which cooperated with
the bishop of Cleveland in its activities, raised funds in various ways. It
organized lotteries, performances, dances, and house-to-house collecting.

Initially, success was limited, with only eighty-four contributors coming forward during the first seven months. The board appealed to the St. Joseph Society membership for greater help, and also requested permission from the bishop to collect money not only among Croatians, but among members of other nationalities as well. Once the board had amassed enough money to make a down payment on a building site at East 40th Street and St. Clair, a letter was sent to Zagreb asking for a Croatian priest. The proposal, supported by the bishop of Cleveland, received a positive answer, with the archbishop allowing Milan Sutlić to go to Cleveland.[20]

When Rev. Sutlić arrived in November 1902, neither his residence nor the church were finished. He lived in rented rooms on St. Clair Avenue, and served mass in the St. Vitus school hall. Contributions increased after the arrival of the priest, who assisted with the door-to-door fund-raising. The St. Joseph Society gave four hundred dollars, the St. Nicholas Society three hundred. The first mass was held in the new church, St. Paul's, on Easter 1903. The dedication of the church in August was a landmark celebration for Cleveland Croatians and made the pages of Croatian newspapers throughout the United States. Financial problems remained, however, necessitating the collection of more money. In November 1904 Rev. Sutlić left the parish to return to the Zagreb Archdiocese, where, reportedly, "he spoke badly about Croatians here [in Cleveland] and said that he would rather beg in the old country than be [a] parson in America."[21]

The Croatian Greek Catholics had also organized a church board and applied to the old country for a priest. They wrote to the bishop of Križevci, emphasizing that they had already accumulated a good sum of money toward the founding of a church. "Since we are a people used to hard and tedious work, we found here permanent and plentiful earnings, which are not only sufficient for us and our dear ones to live comfortably, but thanks to the grace of God, we also have some savings." Informing the bishop that there were five hundred Croatian Greek Catholics in Cleveland, including forty-five families with children, they made their request: "and as we do not lag behind other nations in anything that is lovely, useful, wise and resourceful, it is the burning desire of our hearts for us . . . to beg Your Excellency, our good bishop, to send us a priest, preferably born in Žumberak, and then to begin the construction of . . . a Greek Catholic church and a parsonage." The priest would receive an annual salary of five hundred dollars plus pension rights, be furnished with rooms and firewood, and paid one dollar for a christening, six dollars for a wedding, and five dollars for a funeral. "We wish him to be of good health, to possess a pleasant ringing voice and to be unmarried."[22]

The bishop responded to the request, and Rev. Mile Golubić (from Žumberak but not unmarried) came to Cleveland in April 1902 as priest of the new parish, named St. Nicholas.[23] His parishioners, who had already put down a deposit on a small Lutheran church at East 41st Street and St. Clair, proceeded to purchase the building for $2,800 and prepare it for Greek Catholic religious ceremonies. But Rev. Golubić also did not remain long in Cleveland. Within a year he was writing back to the bishop, complaining about inadequate salary, separation from his family in Europe, poor health, the heavy burden of his work (which included fund-raising as well as religious duties), and even the air he breathed: "I cannot remain here under any circumstances. . . . Cleveland is always full of smoke gushing out of 2,500 factory chimneys in the city and forming a cloud. Since I have been here, the sky has not been clear over Cleveland for 24 hours at a time. Sometimes the atmosphere is so heavy that I can hardly breathe."[24]

In fact, Rev. Golubić's sudden decision to return home was the result of discord with the church board. In response to an inquiry from the bishop of Križevci, the board stated that many of Rev. Golubić's complaints were unfounded—his salary, for example, had been raised to seven hundred dollars a year—and charged the priest with tactlessness and an uncommunicative manner. He refused, they wrote, to teach Sunday School for children, and had threatened to leave for a Ruthenian parish, where the earnings were greater. The board also noted that the Russian government was providing moral and financial support to the Orthodox church in America, enabling Orthodox priests to convert Greek Catholics easily, "so we fear, God forbid, that if we were to remain without a priest of our own that some deserters would also be found among us." Warning that the Russian Orthodox Diocese in San Francisco had decided to build a church and school in Cleveland, the St. Nicholas parishioners asked the bishop to send them a younger and unmarried priest who would be ready to spend several years in Cleveland.[25]

The Bishop of Krizevci was prompt in finding another priest for the church, granting Rev. Makso Relić six years' leave to go to America. Rev. Relić came to Cleveland in 1903, where he faced the same tasks and problems as his predecessor. Disaffection with his salary and conflict with the parishioners again resulted in the departure of the priest from the parish, in 1905. The situation was further complicated by disagreement between the parishioners and the Roman Catholic diocese of Cleveland (under which jurisdiction St. Nicholas was at the time) over ownership of church property.[26]

The decisions of Croatian priests in Cleveland to leave their parishes and parishioners so suddenly were not isolated episodes, but part of a pattern of conflict that occurred within Croatian and many other ethnic churches in the United States, pitting church boards and allied parishioners against pastors and their supporting parishioners. The church boards of Cleveland's original Croatian parishes initiated and carried out many of the most important activities in the founding, financing, and development of their parishes. The board invited the priest, saw to his salary and housing, and included him in its work on the construction of the church. In all these activities the role of the church board was dominant. Most board members were pioneers of the Croatian colony in Cleveland, who had already attained relative prosperity and status: they owned boarding houses and saloons, managed Croatian ethnic banks, and served as correspondents of Croatian newspapers. They were also the founders of Croatian societies and organizations, and the leaders of the ethnic community, who had a stake in its successful development. Most were married men who had decided to remain in the United States permanently. Genuine religious beliefs and concern for the religious needs of their community certainly motivated such men to serve on the founding boards of churches. At the same time, the creation of Croatian parishes would further the consolidation of the Croatian ethnic community, thereby solidifying the position of its leaders.

This inevitably led to a conflict of cultures. In Europe, a Croatian priest had the role of a "good shepherd" who guided his parishioners. He, along with the doctor and the teacher, was one of the most important persons in the village. Consequently, many priests found it hard to accept a new, diminished position vis-à-vis their independent-minded American parishioners. A passage from Rev. Golubić's letter shows just how difficult this new situation was: "The people would be masters of their priest, they want him to dance as they play. And it is true that I have no say at all in the disposition of church funds. The people chose the president, treasurer and secretary from among themselves, and the priest must go around and collect alms and give everything he collects to the treasurer. I think that this makes the position the priest is in clear to everyone. . . . Anyone who thought of America in any better light must be as disappointed as I was on coming here."[27]

The three Croatian priests who came to Cleveland at the beginning of the century were from poor parishes in the old country, and probably would not have come at all were it not for the prospect of financial reward.[28] Their unrealized expectations heightened the tension between them and the church boards. Differing political views also played a part (although less so in Cleveland parishes than in some other cities), with young immigrants who had accepted more liberal ideas clashing with pastors from conservative parts of Austria-Hungary.[29]

Yet despite the significance of the conflict between priest and church board, it should not be seen as entirely excluding cooperation between clergy and laity. Institutionally, this cooperation was evidenced by the relationship between Croatian churches and fraternal organizations. The National Croatian Union's St. Joseph and St. Nicholas lodges, which gave much financial and moral support to the construction of St. Paul's Church, were referred to as church societies in the 1903 parish report. This organizational ambiguity stemmed in part from the fact that the Croatian community was still in the process of consolidating and building its institutions. Once churches were established, fraternal societies centered their activities more clearly within the framework of their own national and local organizations. On the other hand, two Cleveland Croatian priests, Rev. Relić and Niko Grśković, were active in the National Croatian Union, but as community leaders rather than as religious directors of the organization, which included members of various faiths and political views.

Rev. Grśković, formerly pastor of a Croatian parish in Chicago, came to Cleveland to replace Rev. Sutlić at St. Paul's in 1904. He became one of the most prominent Croatian leaders in the United States, propelling St. Paul's into a period of religious, educational, and political development perhaps unequaled in any other Croatian parish in the United States. In Chicago, Grśković had edited the newspaper *Hrvatska Sloboda* (*Croatian Liberty*), and in 1907 he started *Hrvatski Svijet* (*Croatian World*). Although *Hrvatski Svijet* was actually published in New York under someone else's editorship, Grśković gave direction to the paper's writing and edited the main columns. Along with *Nardoni List* (*National Gazette*) it was one of the two most influential and widely circulated Croatian newspaper in the country.

Within Grśković's own parish, thanks to his leadership and communication skills, not only Croatian Roman Catholics but also Croatian Greek Catholics and a large number of Slovene Catholics began to gather around St. Paul's Church. By 1912 the situation was such that Rev. Jernej Ponikvar, the Slovene priest of St. Vitus Church, complained to the bishop. "I cannot refuse these people because of the political or geographical differences they lived in Europe," was Grśković's response. (Less lofty was his observation that the Slovene priest had a reputation of laying claim to that which did not belong to him.)[30] Although many Slovenes did come to St. Paul's, it was also true that many Croatians belonged to St. Vitus. This crossing of ethnic lines occurred naturally among people who came from border regions in Europe, and lived side-by-side in Cleveland. Especially during the World War I years, political conflict in Cleveland's south Slavic community also played a part, since Rev. Ponikvar sympathized with pro-Austrian immigrants while Rev. Grśković led the pro-Yugoslav camp. In the end, Rev. Grśković's political work resulted in his departure from St. Paul's parish and Cleveland in 1917.

The next priest of St. Paul's was Rev. Michael Domladovac, who came to Cleveland from a Croatian parish in Youngstown, Ohio. Parishioners continued to expend energy and funds for parish development, and fundraising remained a constant preoccupation of the church board and the pastor. In 1918 and 1919 disaster struck St. Paul's, when fifty parishioners aged between twenty and forty-five died in the influenza epidemic, diminishing the parish's income in addition to causing shock and grief. According to Rev. Domladovac, the survivors rose to the occasion: "In that great tragedy our parishioners, both men and women, showed real Christian love. They helped the sick, cleaned their houses, dressed and washed children and took into their own homes children whose parents had been wrested from us by the disease." At the same time, Croatian clergy and laity were also contributing to causes further from home, as when Rev. Domladovac, together with the other Croatian priests and community leader Janko Popović, spearheaded a drive to raise money for victims of famine in Croatia following the end of World War I.[31]

Economic trends affected churches, as they did the fraternal organizations. St. Paul's church income fell by seven thousand dollars in 1921, a time of "great unemployment" among its parishioners, most of whom were factory workers. In 1923, employment circumstances had improved to the extent that the church was able to make a twenty-five dollars per family and twenty dollar per bachelor assessment to retire part of its debt. In 1926 the more typically American "Envelope System," with offerings of fifteen to thirty cents per couple or individual given in sealed envelopes every Sunday, was instituted to finance St. Paul's. The onset of the Great Depression again put the parish on shaky financial ground, raising fears that the parish school might have to be closed. By 1932 only thirty-five percent of the parishioners were employed, and Rev. Domladovac was asked to forego one-sixth of his monthly one hundred and fifty dollar salary.[32]

At the same time, the increasing dispersal of Croatians from the St. Clair neighborhood into other parts of the Cleveland area also affected St. Paul's. In 1928 Rev. Domladovac informed the bishop that he had no objection to the twenty Croatian families living beyond E. 185th Street becoming members of the Slovene parish of St. Christine's. He had always, he continued, considered that Croatian Roman Catholics who lived far from St. Paul's Church need not belong to it, although he would never turn away anyone who wanted to remain a parishioner for the sake of old ties and sentiment. By 1934 St. Paul's had only 250 families who attended church regularly, as Croatians moved to neighborhoods further away from the noise and dirt of the factories.[33]

A cultural, as well as a geographic dilution of the Croatian community was also taking place by this time, as assimilation did its work. Links with the old country persisted, but to a diminishing degree. In 1924, the visit of two Croatian Jesuit missionaries to St. Paul's drew hundreds of people: "Never were there so many men in St. Paul's Church as there were during these sermons. . . . Dalmatian music played in front of the church." But by 1934 Domladovac, asking the bishop for permission to have a mixed, rather than an exclusively male choir in his church, also requested to continue the practice of singing the Croatian National Anthem "because in the spreading Americanization that is all that remains for Croatians in their church."[34]

After Rev. Relić left Cleveland in 1905, St. Nicholas parish had remained without a priest for many years. Although some Croatian Greek Catholics attended the Rusyn Greek Catholic Church of St. John the Baptist during that time, most went to St. Paul's. In vain did the parishioners of St. Nicholas continue to petition the bishop in Križevci, in part because the American depressions of 1907 and 1908 decreased interest in immigration. Consequently, the board sold the church and the parsonage, deposited the money in a bank, and stored the church furnishings at St. Paul's. Cleveland remained without a Croatian Greek Catholic pastor until 1913. In that year Cleveland resident Vlado Hranilović, while in Croatia on a visit, persuaded his brother, Rev. Milan Hranilović, to come to Cleveland. By this time there was a separate Greek Catholic Diocese in America, seated in Philadelphia, from which Rev. Hranilović obtained permission to serve in St. Nicholas' parish.

As he had neither church nor residence, Rev. Hranilović at first lived in Janko Popović's saloon, holding mass there on Sundays. The parishioners soon purchased another Lutheran church at Superior Avenue and East 36th Street, as well as a parsonage. As at St. Paul's, financing of the parish proved a perennial problem. The parishioners were factory workers, not always willing or able to support the church with their modest earnings. In May 1914, for example, only half of the 146 married men, and only 45 of the 233 un-married parishioners had made the regular monthly contribution to the church. In 1925 the envelope system was also introduced as St. Nicholas, as a more efficient means of collecting money.[35]

Despite the difficulties, Rev. Hranilović used his organizational skills to renew St. Nicholas parish. He established a new church board and an altar society, and assisted in founding other supporting and fraternal societies in the parish. After he left the parish in 1928, the former parson of St. Nicholas, Rev. Relić, returned for a time, but due to bad health returned to Croatia and was replaced by Ilija Severović. In the thirties, the parish of St. Nicholas was financially and organizationally stable, with very active altar societies and a youth group which helped to keep Croatian national songs and music of the eastern rite alive in Cleveland.

During the tenure of Rev. Domladovac at St. Paul's and Rev. Hranilović at St. Nicholas, a high level of cooperation existed between the two Croa-tian parishes, despite the differences between Roman and Greek forms of Catholicism. This was due in part to personal ties between the two priests, who had been good friends in their seminary days in Zagreb. They agreed, and obtained the approval of the bishop, for both to perform rites for Croa-tians in either of the two Croatian churches. Only later, after Rev. Severović's arrival, did disagreement over performing Greek Catholic rites in the Roman church arise.[36]

The two Croatian parishes had long cooperated in fostering ethnic iden-tity by maintaining a Croatian school at St. Paul's. Land adjacent to St. Paul's had been purchased in 1907, and in 1910 the school started with three teach-ers and 154 students. It followed a curriculum similar to that of other Ameri-can Catholic schools, with the addition of classes in Croatian language and history. By 1918 the school had 320 students. The lay teachers were paid fifty-five dollars per month, and although Rev. Domladovac was pleased with their work, he also brought in nuns from Illinois in 1920, and a Croatian sister in 1921. "Our lay teachers were good in every way, but they came in the morning and left in the evening ... [while] the sisters ... are near the school-house or in it day and night. All Catholic schools realize this, especially as it is cheaper for the parish to engage nuns." The number of pupils kept growing right up to the first years of the Depression, when the trend re-versed. Croatian families moved away from the central city, could not afford transportation or schoolbooks (provided without cost in the public schools), and, Rev. Domladovac complained, increasingly practiced birth control, reducing the number of children.[37]

The fact that Croatian parishioners supported the school to the best of their abilities, despite the financial burden and the difficulty of finding Croatian schoolteachers, indicated its importance to them. They did so both for religious reasons and because they wanted to preserve their children's national consciousness. In Rev. Domladovac's view, Croatian schools in America in fact had a trifold duty: to rear children as good Catholics, to teach them about their Croatian heritage, and also to foster loyalty to the United States. "With just the Croatian language and a purely Croatian education all our children born here would remain—aliens. No one wants that, because it would serve no purpose."[38]

Cultural Life

In addition to national parishes and ethnic fraternal societies, in which communal identity was an adjunct, albeit an important one, to religious worship or the provision of social insurance, groups concerned primarily with preserving Croatian cultural life also grew up within the community from the beginning. Their activities promoted ethnic solidarity, and also represented a struggle for affirmation of the Croatian cultural heritage vis-à-vis other immigrants and native-born Americans. Work in mines and factories had greatly changed the rhythm and content of everyday life for Cleveland's Croatian immigrants, most of whom came from peasant stock. Nonetheless, ordinary women and men, mostly industrial workers rather than artists or intellectuals, continued to nurture their cultural traditions and values under new circumstances, according to their resources and abilities. The immigrants had brought with them their folk costumes, plays, poetry, songs, and dances, and their national folk instrument, the tamburitza, forming the basis for Croatian cultural life in Cleveland.

As early as 1905 Cleveland Croatians founded the "Prosvjeta" (Enlightenment) Singing and Dilettante Society, which from the beginning had a library of Croatian books. In 1913 Prosvjeta's eighty active members participated in a male choir, a mixed choir, and a drama group, which performed the play *Siget* before a large south Slavic audience. Prosvjeta later organized Croatian language classes, and until the end of World War I was the main proponent of cultural life among Cleveland Croatians, also attracting interest among other south Slavs.[39]

Croatians also founded the Ruzica Tamburitza Society, the Croatian Workers' Enlightenment Independent Society (both in 1914), and the singing society Hrvatski Sinovi (Sons of Croatia) in 1916. Members of the South Slavic Socialist Federation in Cleveland also developed their own social and cultural groups, such as the Red Banner (Crveni Barjak) Singing Society. Following the example of Slavic and fellow Croatian immigrants who founded Sokol (Falcon) organizations in almost all of their settlements, Cleveland Croatians established Hrvatski Sokol (Croatian Falcon) in 1911. In addition to its athletic program, the organization also emphasized ethnic traditions and pan-Slavic consciousness.[40]

In view of the difficulty cultural societies had in finding suitable premises for holding their events, Croatians decided in 1914 to build a Croatian National Home to house their activities. After its completion, the work of many Croatian organizations centered around the Home, which was located at 1402 East 40th Street.[41]

Almost all of the Croatian societies were founded by individuals or groups with some kind of political or class interests, who tried to gain the support of Cleveland Croatians for their goals through community and cultural work. Although this promoted social and cultural life among Croatians, the consequent political, religious, and class conflicts and power struggles hindered the long-term development of these societies. Not one of those founded before World War I survived after the war's end.

Their place was taken by the new cultural, educational, and athletic organizations that appeared in the interwar period. The South Slavic Workers' Music and Drama Society, "Abrašević," founded in 1921, was the most important of these. It aspired to high standards, with its drama group performing plays from Croatian and other literatures, while the music section staged operas from the standard repertoire. Meanwhile, in 1920, members of St. Paul's parish had organized the Columbus Croatian Catholic Society to promote church singing and to organize social events and cultural performances for the benefit of the parish. The society performed both dramas and comedies.[42]

In 1929 the "Lira" (Lyre) Croatian Singing Society was formed to "promot[e] cultural activities and singing among the Croatian people as a non-party organization." By 1930, Lira had about seventy singers, most of them American-born, making it the first society of any importance founded in Cleveland by second-generation Croatians. Lira performed for American as well as Croatian audiences. In 1930 it presented the Croatian play *Sokica* in English at Cleveland Public Hall, as part of the "Theater of Nations" Series of performances sponsored by the *Plain Dealer* newspaper, and also gave a concert in Gordon Park under the auspices of the city recreation department, which was attended by several thousand Clevelanders.[43]

The Theater of Nations was one of a number of multicultural programs organized in Cleveland in the late 1920s and early 1930s to draw upon the

talents and traditions of the city's numerous ethnic groups and to present
ethnic diversity as a civic asset. The city's Croatian community participated
in these events. In May 1928 the municipal administration had sponsored
the "Dance of Nations." Twenty-four groups, including the Croatians, presented their songs and dances. Croatian tamburitza players also performed
at the 1928 Labor Day Festival, celebrated in the city's Brookside Stadium
and attended by about one hundred thousand people. At one of the largest
events of this type, the All Nations Exposition, held in Public Hall in 1929,
Croatians exhibited handicrafts and folk costumes, and their tamburitza
orchestra and dancers gave a performance for twenty thousand people.
Encouraged by the success they had in presenting their cultures to the Cleveland public, representatives of the numerous ethnic groups that had participated in the Exposition founded the All Nations Council (with a member
of the Croatian community serving as its first head). In the 1930s, Croatians
participated in the city's Cultural Gardens program, in which various ethnic groups planned and constructed their own gardens along East and Liberty Boulevards. The planning group for the South Slav garden included one
Serbian, one Croatian, and one Slovene member. Work progressed slowly,
because not only were there three ethnic groups to be represented, but also
progressive and conservative factions, each of which wanted to place busts
of "their" national heroes in the garden. The Croatians finally decided upon
placing a statue of Bishop Joseph George Strossmayer, a progressive leader
and enlightener, in the garden to represent their nationality.[44]

Despite the Croatian community's efforts to preserve its cultural identity, the burden for the amateur societies was great, especially during the
Depression. The economic crisis compounded with demographic factors—
restrictions on immigration, aging of the first generation, and the dispersal of the older Croatian neighborhoods as many families moved into the
suburbs of Cleveland—resulted in the demise of many Croatian cultural
and social groups. The formation of larger and more permanent culture and
art societies had continued to be hindered by political and ideological differences within the Croatian community. Only two groups, both of which
drew their strength from one faction or the other, had any marked degree of
success: Abrašević, supported by leftists and the labor movement, and
Columbus, from St. Paul's parish.

Political and Labor Activism

Much of the political activity in Cleveland's Croatian community during
the period in question centered on two causes: socialism and the workers'

movement, championed by leftists, and the struggle for an independent south Slav state, which attracted support from across the political spectrum.

Adherents of the socialist cause, while fervent in their beliefs, were small in number. This was the case among Croatians in Cleveland, as it was in the south Slavic population in the United States in general. The first national south Slavic socialist organization was founded in New York in 1905, with a Cleveland branch forming at the end of 1907. Also in 1907, the national organization began publishing a newspaper, *Radnička Borba* (*The Workers' Struggle*).[45] There was, however, considerable dissent among the south Slavic socialists, particularly over the question of which of the two American socialist parties to support. Two factions developed, with the New York group inclining toward the Socialist Labor Party, while a rival Chicago-based group, which also published a newspaper, *Radnička Straza* (*Workingmen's Guard*), supported the Socialist Party.[46]

In the years 1908 to 1911 the two factions formally parted ways, organizing two separate South Slavic Socialist Federations (sssfs) allied with the respective socialist parties. The Chicago group had relatively more success overall, with supporters of the slp facing difficulties from the very beginning on account of their party's more radical and sectarian program. *Radnička Borba* suspended publication early in 1908, after its fifth issue. Cleveland adherents of the slp, however, refused to give up. The seat of the South Slavic Socialist Federation was moved to Cleveland from New York, and in 1909 *Radnička Borba* resumed publication there. The group received no assistance from the slp, presumably because the latter had no funds to spare, but managed to collect five hundred dollars to set up a press in Cleveland.[47]

This faction also held a number of its meetings in Cleveland. In 1911, in addition to sixteen delegates from the organization itself, two representatives of the Chicago organization attended and tried to convince their brethren to join them and adopt the principles of the Socialist Party, thus unifying the south Slavic socialist movement in the United States. Instead, the Cleveland-based Federation at this point decided to join the Socialist Labor Party as a foreign-language section. Membership remained small, however, totaling two hundred nationwide in 1915.[48]

During the first ten years or so the activities of the sssf-slp, especially in Cleveland, consisted primarily of maintaining and promoting the influence of *Radnička Borba*. Members kept the paper alive through donations, even though many of them were often unemployed. Editors came and went in rapid succession, partly because of low pay—the first editor in Cleveland, Blagoje Savić, received nine dollars per week—and partly

because of dissent with the editorial board. Many of them had few qualifications for the job. Savić's successor, Dragutin Kuharić, gained popularity
with workers through his abilities as a public speaker, but was only partly
literate and knew little about socialism. The next editor, Josip Kraja, was a
twenty-two-year-old student from Dubrovnik. Milan Jetvić, who took over
in July 1910, at last brought the skills of a professional journalist to the paper,
and with his thorough grounding in socialism, gave direction to *Radnička
Borba*. His autocratic and combative style, however, brought him into conflict with the editorial board, and he was released from his duties in 1912.
Finally, in 1913, Lazar Petrović was appointed and remained as editor for a
number of years. Although the question of editorship had been solved, the
paper continued to be plagued by financial and technical problems. Much
of the work on the newspaper was done on a voluntary basis by factory
employees during their off-shift hours. Despite the financial risk, the organization bought a costly typesetting machine in 1916, and hired Milan
Tomić, also their secretary and librarian, to handle administrative work on
the newspaper. In subsequent years, the Federation also published Marxist literature translated from English into Croatian, Serbian, and sometimes
Slovene, as well as works by Croatian and Serbian socialists, and an annual
almanac, *Deleonist*. These titles were sold in the *Radnička Knjižara* book-
shop at 2259 St. Clair Avenue, and helped to make this the most productive South Slavic immigrant publishing firm in the United States.[49]

In Cleveland, the rival SSSF-SP had few members and few subscribers to
its paper, *Radnička Straža*, among Cleveland Croatians, although it was
more successful among Slovenes. It initially had only one branch, No. 71,
in the city. By 1913, when the organization had 119 branches nationwide, the
number in the Cleveland area had grown to five, including two in Collinwood and one in Euclid. Cleveland branches No. 27 and 71 organized a rally
at the beginning of January 1914 to protest violence against striking workers
in Upper Michigan, printing one thousand leaflets on the subject. The rally
had no success, however, since neither the Croatian community at large nor
other south Slavic associations attended it. *Radnička Straža* reproached
ethnic leaders, and especially Rev. Grsković, with not understanding the
workers' struggle, and had equally harsh words for *Radnička Borba*, which
upheld the SLP's stand condemning strikes as a means of workers' struggle.[50]

One important reason for the lack of support for south Slavic socialists
within their own community was their attitude concerning national liberation in the south Slav homeland. As partisans of class liberation, they considered national liberation of secondary importance and during the war

opposed the cause supported by most south Slavic immigrants, the abolition of Austria-Hungary and the creation of a south Slavic state. This was especially true of SLP adherents. Such stands did not find ready sympathizers among south Slavs in Cleveland, who contributed to both the national cause and the American war effort enthusiastically.

American socialists' opposition to United States participation in World War I, and the successful Bolshevik revolution in Russia, had a profound effect on the American socialist movement, including its foreign-language sections. The SSSF-SP was dissolved, with Slovene and Serbian members remaining faithful to the Socialist Party, while Croatians increasingly accepted the radical ideas which were spreading throughout America at the end of the war following the events in Russia. When the Labor Party was formed the United States in 1921, Croatians immediately founded a Yugoslav section. The section worked through its branches, with active members in Croatian neighborhoods. An increasing number of Croatian immigrants read its paper *Radnik* (*The Worker*).[51]

As in other cities with a major south Slav presence, Cleveland had a district committee to coordinate the work of area branches, and the Labor Party's influence began to grow modestly within the community, partly through the agency of newspapers such as *Radnik, Delavska Slovenija, (Workers' Slovenia)* and *Daily Worker. Radnik* continued the socialists' internecine feud, conducting polemics with *Radnička Borba* and the SLP, and also verbally attacked south Slavic churches at every opportunity.[52]

During the 1920s Cleveland's south Slav socialist organizations tried to widen their influence in the south Slav ethnic communities, attempting to use culture as one weapon in the workers' struggle. The Abrašević singing society, for example, "by gathering workers around it, singing revolutionary songs, performs an important part of the elevated work for the liberty of its class." Croatian radicals concentrated hardest on gaining a foothold in Croatian fraternal lodges, believing that the National Croatian Union's decision to set up educational committees offered them a perfect opportunity. However, their efforts to promulgate their own cultural program through these committees generated conflict, which ultimately undermined the efforts of the committees and also demonstrated the weakness of the Yugoslav section and socialism in general in Cleveland's south Slav community.[53]

In the interwar period the Yugoslav section of the Communist Party of the United States was also active in Cleveland. In 1928, for example, communists held a large party in the Slovenian National Home featuring several tamburitza orchestras, with profits going to the aid of striking miners.

Nevertheless, none of the leftist factions ever managed to attract many Cleveland Croatians, having at most only several dozen active members. The local sssf-slp branch, for example, had twenty-four members in 1925. Although its parties and picnics attracted a reasonable number of paying guests in that year, with attendance reaching into the hundreds, its more serious public assemblies and classes drew an average of only thirty-one and fourteen attendees respectively. One Croatian observer later noted that slp members, popularly known as "Eselpists," were a sect unto themselves, completely separated from the masses, because they adhered rigidly to party ideology concerning the class struggle rather than helping workers attain their more immediate demands.[54]

As for the participation of Cleveland Croatians in more mainstream labor unions and particularly strikes, few records indicate any significant activity in this area before the late 1920s. The small interest they showed in labor unions can perhaps be explained by the fact that they relied on their fraternal organizations to give them at least rudimentary social protection and psychological support in case of need. Their disinclination to participate in strikes is also not surprising considering that on the left, *Radnička Borba* inveighed against strikes as a weapon of class struggle, while on the right, the priests of the two Croatian Catholic parishes disapproved of any kind of "radical activity." In this respect the situation in Cleveland diverged from that in some other Croatian settlements, because Croatians in Pennsylvania and Michigan in particular were active in strikes from the beginning of the twentieth century. The Yugoslav sections of the Labor Party and the Communist Party did call for worker solidarity with strikers, and in some instances, especially in the later 1920s, Cleveland Croatians responded with financial and other support.[55]

The enthusiasm of Cleveland Croatians for the cause of national independence was in marked contrast to their disinclination for leftist activities. From the first, Croatian immigrants tried to interest fellow Clevelanders in the plight of their compatriots living under the Austro-Hungarian Empire in Europe. Although they had some success on their own, they soon found that cooperating with other south Slavs, and with Slavic nationalities in general was more effective. Like other Slavic groups, Croatians upon occasion expressed their national sentiments in terms of opposition, particularly to Magyar activities, such as the erection of a Lajos Kossuth statue in 1902, and the visit of Count Albert Apponyi in 1911.[56] Although Cleveland was not as important a center of Croatian settlement as Pittsburgh or Chicago, its overall substantial Slavic population made it one of the prime foci for Slavic political activities in America.

Croatian immigrants founded their own nationwide political organization, the Croatian League, in 1912. Its purpose was to coordinate the political work of American Croatians to the end proclaimed in its slogan: "For the liberty of Croatia!" Although the Croatian League was founded in Kansas City, St. Paul's Church in Cleveland became its administrative center upon the selection of Rev. Niko Grśković as the organization's president. *Hrvatski Svijet* served as its press organ, and League lodges quickly formed in Cleveland. The first, the Liberty Lodge, had 158 members in 1912, and used the Croatian parochial school as a meeting place. The City of Zagreb Lodge was founded next, in Collinwood, and later, in 1918, the Flower of Žumberak was organized.[57]

Just as events in the Balkans served to ignite World War I, so did the outbreak of the war inflame nationalistic passions among south Slavs in America. It also drew the various south Slavic ethnic groups into close association, as they began working on the political front for the abolition of the Austro-Hungarian Empire and the creation of a south Slavic state. Cleveland became an important center of the campaign, and Rev. Grśković a primary spokesman for south Slavic political aspirations. Less than a month after war was declared in Europe, he addressed the Slavic Day rally at Grays Armory in August 1914. A second such rally in 1915 drew three thousand Croatian, Slovene, Serbian, Czech, and Slovak participants, as well as representatives of the broader community, including Cleveland mayor Newton D. Baker. In September 1915 the National Croatian Union held its convention in St. Paul's church hall. Since many of the delegates were active in Croatian Sokol and the Croatian League as well, those organizations held concurrent meetings and public events, including a Sokol athletic demonstration in which Slovenes and Serbs also took part.[58]

Also in 1915, south Slavic immigrants in Cleveland who supported the creation of a south Slavic state founded the Bratstvo (Brotherhood) South Slavic Enlightenment Club. In April 1916 representatives from a number of Cleveland's south Slavic societies gathered to found an umbrella organization, the Federation of South Slavic Associations in Cleveland, intended to promote Slavic solidarity and present a united front before the general public. All Croatian, Slovene, and Serbian societies were eligible to join the Federation, which organized meetings, rallies, and social gatherings. Later, in 1918, the Alliance of South Slavic Women was founded in Cleveland, also in the service of the pro-Yugoslav political program.[59]

During 1915 and 1916 members of the Yugoslav Committee in London, which led the international movement for a south Slav state, visited Cleveland as part of a campaign to organize support for their cause among

American south Slavs. In September 1916 the Committee opened an American branch office in Cleveland. The Yugoslav Office, as it was known, conducted fund-raising, distributed Committee publications, and served as an information center, working out of the Croatian Sokol Hall on East 40th Street. Although the Yugoslav Office was relocated to Washington, D.C., in February 1917, its five months of work in Cleveland served to strengthen dedication to the cause among the city's south Slavs.[60]

The city's south Slavic Sokol organizations had a higher profile during the war, as sports, too, mixed with politics. Speeches and resolutions supporting the national cause became a routine accompaniment to athletic exhibitions. This culminated in a multi-ethnic Sokol parade and performance in 1917, marking the fifth anniversary of Croatian Sokol in Cleveland and providing an opportunity for Rev. Grśković and others to praise the freedom enjoyed in America while calling for liberation of their homeland.[61]

South Slavic Sokol societies across the United States worked in cooperation with the Yugoslav Committee in London, the South Slavic National Council in Washington, and the Serbian government to organize volunteer units for service on the Salonika front with the Serbian army. On the whole, this effort was not especially successful, certainly not in Cleveland, which in 1917 fielded only forty volunteers as the Zrinski and Frankopan Company, named after two Croatian nobles who had been executed for defying the Habsburgs in the seventeenth century. However, the departure of the company for Europe amid great fanfare on the part of south Slav activists also marked the dissolution of Cleveland's Croatian Sokol society, with its members deciding to sell the organization's building and property and send the proceeds to the Yugoslav Committee. Members who did not volunteer as soldiers joined the Croatian Federation's Liberty Lodge. These actions were in line with the South Slavic National Council's policy, which advocated that Sokols dissolve and their members volunteer for the Salonika front. The call for volunteers continued after the company's departure from Cleveland, but most immigrants contented themselves with giving financial aid to the Yugoslav cause.[62]

Even before the war, Croatians living in America had annually commemorated the anniversary of the execution of the national heroes Zrinski and Frankopan. During World War I, the anniversary took on special meaning, giving historical perspective to the anti-Austrian feeling that was running high among Croatian and other Slavic immigrants. In 1917 the date followed close upon America's declaration of war. In Cleveland, a "Yugoslav Day" was held on May 6 and 7 to mark the anniversary. School children and the youth of the National Croatian Union marched through the city's streets, and south Slavic groups carried their national flags.[63]

The entry of the United States into the conflict, while officially aligning America on the same side as the Slavs opposing the Austro-Hungarian Empire, also brought pressure upon ethnic communities to redirect their energies in support of the American war effort. The campaign to Americanize immigrants was stepped up, and Liberty Bond drives called upon everyone to buy government bonds to finance the war. Like nationality groups everywhere, Cleveland Croatians seized upon this opportunity to demonstrate their loyalty to America while contributing to the defeat of the Central Powers by organizing a "Croatian Division" bond drive. Liberty Lodge called on all Cleveland Croatians to join the Croatian League because, it said, America recognized the work of the League. By 1918 the political activities of Cleveland Croatians were at a peak, subsuming organizational life in all areas, social, cultural, athletic, and even religious. Cooperation among Slavic groups flourished, and Croatians became better known to the general Cleveland public due to the publicity their efforts received and ultimately shared in the satisfaction of having contributed to the defeat of Austria-Hungary.[64]

Croatian immigrants did not, however, form a solid block of opinion. A pro-Austrian minority existed in Cleveland and nationwide. Events in Cleveland attracted the unfavorable attention of the New York newspaper *Narodni list,* which favored the pro-Austrian faction. The paper disparaged Cleveland's Slavic Day, calling it a "Slavic comedy," and charged that Cleveland Croatians were collecting money for the Serbian rather than the Croatian Red Cross.[65] But *Narodni list* saved its harshest words for Rev. Grśković, as the most prominent leader of Croatian nationalist sentiment. It printed letters attacking his practice of promoting the nationalist cause from the altar: "During the sermon I thought I was in a pub, not in a church ... and that this is not a church but a political rally." "He is not preaching Christianity in church, but Serbian politics." The paper also demanded that the St. Paul's church board ask for Rev. Grśković's resignation: "If the board ... does not do so, *Narodni list* will send an article in English to the Bishop of Cleveland and all the clergy to acquaint them with what an immoral man the Cleveland parish is protecting with its silence." At the instigation of the *Narodni list* faction, an anti-Grśković rally did take place in Cleveland, and a petition of complaint was sent to the bishop.[66] In December 1917 the controversial priest left Cleveland for Washington at the pressing invitation of the South Slavic National Council, which wanted him to devote all of his attention to politics. For days beforehand parishioners visited him to express their heartfelt thanks, regrets, and good wishes. Representatives from Cleveland's numerous Slavic associations attended his farewell party at Popović's tavern. Although the campaign to discredit him may have played a part in his decision, Rev. Grśković's main motivation, according to his successor Rev. Domladovac, was his awareness that he could not continue to divide his energies between his parish and the Croatian national cause.[67]

Elation over the victory of the Allied Powers and the imminent establishment of a Yugoslav state was short-lived. Objections to Italian claims on lands that Croatians and Slovenes regarded as their own, and fears that the Serbian government viewed the projected state as a "greater Serbia," as well as concern for the plight of war victims in the homeland, became the focus of Croatian activism following the war. Led by the priests of St. Paul's and St. Nicholas parishes, Cleveland Croatians, including some socialists and others who had been silent during the war, united to protest the imposition of an unsatisfactory settlement in Croatian lands, and called for self-determination through free elections. Throughout 1919 Cleveland remained a center of political activity for Croatians dissatisfied with the situation in their old homeland. The unity among south Slavic groups had dissolved.[68]

In April 1919 the "First Croatian Convention," organized by Croatian priests who had been skeptical of the pro-Yugoslav movement throughout the war, met in Cleveland. Although the convention's resolutions condemned Italian claims to the Adriatic coast, they did were not anti-Serbian as such, but merely called for a federal Yugoslav state. The convention's delegates also established a fund to assist war victims in Croatia.[69]

Political activity continued into the 1920s. In 1921 representatives from Croatian settlements nationwide gathered in Cleveland and founded the Croatian Republican League in America, with a political program mirroring that of the Croatian Republican Peasant Party in the homeland. The League's work was continued by the Croatian Peasant Party, founded in 1923 to support the struggle for the political rights of Croatians in the Yugoslav state, to acquaint the American public with the situation there, and to aid the Croatian Peasant Party in Croatia. The party attracted only fifty-three active members in Cleveland, however.[70]

By the end of the decade, involvement in nationalist politics had ebbed to a very low point among Cleveland Croatians, for several reasons. First, the enthusiasm stirred up by the events of World War I had died down, dampened in part by disillusionment with the reality of the Yugoslav state that so many had campaigned for so fervently. Secondly, the center of Croatian political life had moved away from Cleveland. Political organizations had only branches rather than headquarters there. Thirdly, the many years spent in America had by now had their effect. Cleveland Croatians were increasingly interested in the political life and problems of their new city. The foundation of the Croatian Political Club marked this transition. The club sought to bring together American citizens of Croatian origin or descent in order to increase their effectiveness at the ballot box and enlarge their role in Cleveland's politics and government. One of the club's founders, William Boyd (Milos Bojic), was elected an Ohio state senator from a Cleveland-area district in the 1930s.[71]

The World War I period had been a turning point for Cleveland's Croatians. Their endeavors to help their European compatriots achieve freedom had helped to coalesce their own community, and gave rise to extensive, if in some cases short-lived, cooperation with other south Slavic and Slavic ethnic groups. Perhaps more importantly, although their goal was in the old country, they worked toward it through the means available in their new homeland. Their activities, which attracted attention from Cleveland's politicians, journalists, and general population, served as an apprenticeship in American public life. Ultimately, the experience helped integrate them into the broader community in Cleveland and the United States.

Notes

1. *RIC,* vol. 26, Part VI, Cleveland, Statistics; U.S. Population Census, 1920; and Howard Whipple Green, *Population Characteristics by Census Tracts, Cleveland, 1930.* These sources are also the basis of the demographic statistics given in subsequent paragraphs unless otherwise noted. See also Howard Whipple Green, "Persons Born in Yugoslavia," *A Sheet-a-Week,* vol. 20, no. 10, 13 November 1952.

2. Ivan Čizmić, *Hrvati u životu Sjedinjenih Americkih Drzava* (Zagreb, 1982), 141.

3. Matrimoniorum Registrum, Registrum Baptizatorum, and Record of Interments for St. Paul Roman Catholic and St. Nicholas Greek Catholic Churches.

4. Ivan Čizmić, "The Role of Boarding Houses and Saloons in the Life of South Slav Immigrants in the U.S.A. (1880–1920)," *Lock Haven International Review* (Lock Haven, Pennsylvania): 6–13 (1987).

5. Croatian immigrants in Cleveland possessed their own ethnic businesses and institutions, making for a more or less self-sufficient community. Croatians could satisfy most of their needs by patronizing the businesses of their compatriots or their Slavic neighbors. Local businessmen assisted in the community's development by giving Croatians loans for opening stores and craftsmen's workshops, and building family homes. Cf. Andre Breton, "Institutional Completeness—," The advertisements that appeared in immigrant newspapers show that Croatians and Slovenes in Cleveland advertised their businesses together, and also that there were joint

Croatian-Slovene stores. Additionally, the presence of advertisements from non-Slav businesses indicates that the Croatian settlement was a market which attracted the interest from the general business community as well.

6. Eleanor Ledbetter, *The Yugoslavs of Cleveland* (Cleveland, 1918).

7. See Ivan Čizmić, "Yugoslav Immigrants in the U.S. Labor Movement 1880–1920s," *American Labor and Immigration History, 1877–1920s*, ed. Dirk Hoerder (Chicago, University of Illinois Press, 1983), 177–190.

8. *Souvenir Book, 35th Anniversary of the St. Nicholas Lodge, no. 22, CFU Cleveland,Ohio, 1895–1930* (Cleveland, 1930).

9. *Kratki pregled povijesti Hrvatske bratske zajednice 1894–1949* (Pittsburgh, 1949), 227.

10. *Zlatni jubilej (Golden Jubilee), Croatian Fraternal Union, 1894–1944* (Cleveland, 1944), 37.

11. *Zajedničar,* 6 October 1926, 2.

12. *Souvenir Book, 35th Anniversary,* 13.

13. Material from Status Animarum Reports, 1922, St. Paul Parish Papers, ADC.

14. *Ibid.*

15. St. Paul Parish Papers, ADC.

16. *Zajedničar,* 5 November 1930, 2.

17. Minutes from meetings of the Croatian Sons of the Town of Zagreb Association, Croatian Union of Illinois, Lodge 102, 13 August 1922.

18. Secretarial book of the Croatian Liberty Lodge, no. 235, National Croatian Union, 4 January 1925.

19. Josef Misich, *Fifty Years of St. Paul's Parish, Golden Jubilee, 1953,* (Cleveland, Ohio, 1953); *Seventy-fifth Anniversary St. Paul's Church* (Cleveland, Ohio 1978); M. Domladovac, "Hrvatska crkva Sv. Pavla, Cleveland, Ohio" *Naša Nada, Calender for American Catholic Croatians* (Cleveland, Ohio, 1930), 140. Also see chapter[s] by Kopanic [and Puskás], regarding Greek, or Byzantine Rite, Catholicism.

20. Secretarial records of the Croatian Roman Catholic Church, Cleveland, Ohio; Archives of the Archdiocese of Zagreb, Officium dioceseaneum, no. 100/1905.

21. M. Domladovac, "Hrvatska crkva Sv. Pavla, Cleveland, Ohio" *Naša nada,* Calendar for American Catholic Croatians, 1930, 153.

22. *Fifty-fifth Anniversary, St. Nicholas' Croatian Greek Catholic Church* (Cleveland, Ohio, 1957); Archives of the Križevci Diocese, Križevci, Croatia, no. 92/1902.

23. Archives of the Križevci Diocese, no. 100, 549/1902.

24. Mile Golubić to the Bishop of Križevci, 14 February 1903, Archives of the Križevci Diocese, Križevci, Croatia, no. 551/1903.

25. St. Nicholas Parish Church Board to the Bishop of Križevci, 24 February 1903, Archives of the Križevci Diocese, no. 831–1903.

26. Greek Catholic Parish in Cleveland, *Souvenir Calendar of the Greek Catholic Diocese of Križevci 1933* (Cleveland, 1933), 124–125.

27. Mile Golubić to the Bishop of Križevci, Archives of the Križevci Diocese, no. 551–1903

28. The register of the Diocese of Križevci records frequent demands made by Mile Golubić and Makso Relić, who had asked for the bishop's financial aid almost every year before leaving for America, because they could not meet the expenses of life in their parishes.

29. For instance, Franjo Glojnarić, Allegheny, Pa. to Bishop Strossmayer in Dakovo: "Unfortunately, it is true that there are semi-intelligent and faithless newcomers who spread the ideas of Freemasonry among our poor Croatian Catholics. These ideas are a source of evil and are very present in the Croatian press in America." 6 March 1900, JAZU Archives, Bp. Strossmayer Collection, XI A-Gloj. F.1.

30. Papers of St. Paul Parish, ADC. Also see chapter by Klemenčič, for the disagreement between the two priests.

31. Domladovac, "Hrvatska crkva," 159.

32. Papers of St. Paul Parish, ADC; Domladovac, "Hrvatska crkva," 166.

33. Domladovac to Bishop Schrembs, 9 June 1928, and Domladovac to the Bishop of Cleveland, June 1934, St. Paul Parish Papers (hereafter quoted SPPP), ADC.

34. *Medjelja* (published in Sarajevo), 8 June 1924, 4–5; Domladovac to the Bishop of Cleveland, 20 June 1934, SPPP, ADC.

35. *Souvenir Book printed for the 55th Anniversary of the St. Nicholas' Croatian Greek Catholic Parish, 1902–1957* (Cleveland, Ohio, 1957); St. Nicholas Parish Records, 5 May 1914 and 25 January 1925.

36. The bishop, citing church regulations, sided with Rev. Severović.

37. *Twenty-fifth Anniversary, St. Paul's School* (Cleveland, 28 November 1935); Status Animarum Reports, ADC.

38. Domladovac, "Hrvatska crkva," 127.

39. *Prosvjeta* (Zagreb), 15 March 1910, 198.

40. *Hrvatski svijet*, 23 December 1914, 2; 18 May 1916, 2; 25 February 1917, 2; 14 May 1917, 2; *Radnička straza*, 11 February 1914, 1.

41. *Narodni list*, 4 April 1914, 3; *Hrvatski svijet*, 14 Janaury 1917, 2.

42. *Znanje* (Chicago), 24 April 1922; *Souvenir Book, 35th Anniversary of St. Nicholas Lodge*, 43; *Nasa nada*, 1930 Calendar, 161.

43. *Souvenir Book, 35th Anniversary of St. Nicholas Lodge*, 39; *Cleveland Press*, 22 March, 15 August 1930.

44. *Souvenir Book, 35th Anniversary of St. Nicholas Lodge*, 41; *Zajedničar* (Pittsburgh), 29 March 1929; *Hrvat* (Zagreb), 17 April 1929; Vatroslav Grill, *Med dvema svetovima* (Ljubljana, 1979). Lucić often went to Croatia and collected folk instruments and folk costumes for use in the Cleveland Croatian community. *Jutarnji list* (Zagreb), 15 April 1931, 4.

45. For its tenth anniversary in February and March 1917, *Radnička borba* (by this time based in Cleveland) published a Series of articles about south Slavic socialists in the United States. The information in those articles is used in this section. Croatian, Slovene and Serbian socialists in the u.s. called their societies and associations South Slavic or Yugoslav, continuing the practice from the homeland, where socialists also used these terms.

46. I. Čizmić, "The Involvement of Yugoslav Socialists in the Socialist Party of America and the Socialist Labor Party of America 1903–1924," *The Press of Labor Migrants in Europe and North America 1880s to 1930s,* ed. Christine Harzig (Bremen: University of Bremen, 1985), 459.

47. *Ibid.; Radnička borba,* 15 February 1917, 3.

48. *Radnička borba,* 22 February; 1 March 1917, 3.

49. *Radnička borba,* 15, 22 February 1917, 1; 7 March 1917, 3. Lists of *Radnička knjižara* publications were sometimes advertised in *Radnička borba.*

50. *Radnička straža,* 1 April 1908, 1; 1 July 1908, 2; 29 September 1912, 3; 13 August 1913; 11 February 1914, 1.

51. Čizmić, *Hrvati u zivotu,* 211.

52. *Radnik,* 9 August, 22 November 1924, 3.

53. *Souvenir Book, 35th Anniversary of St. Nicholas Lodge,* 43; *Zajednicar,* 8 July, 28, 30 October 1925, 10 March 1926; Čizmić, *Hrvati u zivotu,* 211.

54. *Radnička borba,* 23 September 1926, 3; Stjepan Lojen, *Uspomeme jednog iseljenka* (Zagreb, 1963), 106.

55. For example, see above 30; *Radnik,* 9 May 1929.

56. See chapter by Kopanic and Ivan Čizmić, "The visit of the Hungarian Count Apponyi to the USA in 1911," *Zbornik Filozofickej Fakulty Univerzity Komenskoho,* vol. 22, Historica (Bratislava 1971), 170.

57. *Hrvatski svijet,* 3 January 1913, 2; 22 March 1913, 1; 12 May 1918, 3.

58. *Hrvatski svijet,* 12 August 1914, 2; 24 April 1915, 2; 22 September 1915, 1. Regarding the fraternals, see Čizmić, "Yugoslav Immigrants."

59. *Hrvatski svijet,* 10 October 1915, 2; 20 June 1916, 2; 5 March 1918, 3; Cleveland *Plain Dealer,* 20 June 1916. The *Plain Dealer* regularly covered South Slavic political activity.

60. *Plain Dealer,* 27 December 1915, 8 April 1916; *Jadran* (Buenos Aires), 1916, no. 51, 8.

61. *Hrvatski svijet,* 22 September 1915, 1; 27 May 1916, 2; 15 January 1917, 2; *Plain Dealer,* 11 March 1917.

62. *Hrvatski svijet,* 7 July 1917, 2; 4 October 1917, 2.

63. *Hrvatski svijet,* 10 May 1917, 2.

64. *Hrvatski svijet,* 31 July 1917, 2; 31 March 1918, 3; 2 May 1918, 3; 21 December 1917, 3.

65. Čizmić, *Hrvati u životu,* 94; *Narodni list,* 18 November 1915, 4; 20 May 1916, 2.

66. *Narodni list,* 6 January 1916, 2; 17 February 1916, 2; 14 July 1916; SPPP, ADC.

67. *Hrvatski svijet,* 12 December 1917,2; material from *Status Animarum Reports,* 1918, ADC.

68. *Narodni list,* 14 December 1918, 1.

69. *Narodni list,* 9 April 1919, 1.

70. Čizmić, *Hrvati u zivotu,* 285; *Souvenir Book, 35th Anniversary of St. Nicholas Lodge.*

71. *Souvenir Book, 35th Anniversary of St. Nicholas Lodge.*

Cleveland Czechs

WINSTON CHRISLOCK

Migration

Cleveland, Ohio, has over the past one hundred years competed with New York City for the distinction of being the second largest urban center of Czech settlement in the United States. Only Chicago has attracted more Czech settlers. Significant Czech settlement in the United States began in the wake of the revolutions of 1848.[1] Early centers of urban settlement were St. Louis, Missouri; Milwaukee, Wisconsin; New York City; and, Cleveland.

Following the arrival of a few individuals in the 1840s, a true Czech community began to develop in Cleveland in 1852. In that year, 16 families, apparently on route to Wisconsin, stopped in Cleveland and ended up settling there. These families, from Smetanova Lhota near Písek, had received letters from relatives and acquaintances in Milwaukee enticing them to migrate to the United States. By 1857, 95 Czech families had settled in Cleveland. From then until 1865, a further 137 families settled, 74 of them in 1864.[2]

The second half of the 1860s brought about several significant changes which stimulated Czech migration. On the push side, Austria underwent an economic crisis in the wake of its defeat by Prussia in the Seven Weeks' War of 1866. The defeat also led in 1867 to the adoption of a new constitution which eased emigration restrictions.[3] On the pull side, the conclusion of the American Civil War and dynamic economic growth in northeastern Ohio drew many Czechs to that area until the economic depression of 1873.[4] Ninety-three families arrived in 1865, and then 129 in 1866, 91 in 1867, and 97 in 1868. As of June 1869, a survey commissioned by a Czech fraternal lodge counted 696 Czech families in Cleveland. There were 1,749 males and 1,503 females, a total of 3,252 individuals.[5] By 1878, Václav Šnajdr, editor of *Dennice Novověku*, a Cleveland Czech newspaper, estimated that there were from fifteen to eighteen thousand Czechs residing in Cleveland, with the greatest number having arrived in the 1865–1873 period.[6]

Czechs continued to settle in Cleveland up to the beginning of World War I. The city government's annual reports recorded 301 Czech individuals arriving in 1874, 148 in 1878, and 868 in 1883. The number rose to 1,292 in 1891, but then dropped off to 508 in 1892, and in 1894 fell to only 69. The low influx of immigrants in 1894 was probably a consequence of the financial panic of 1893 and subsequent depression in the United States. By 1897, when the economy was recovering, arrivals had increased to 105, and then to 202 in 1899, 352 in 1900, and 336 in 1901.[7] By 1910 the Czech colony in Cleveland had grown to forty thousand first- and second-generation Czechs; as of 1920 it had increased to over forty-three thousand.[8]

The principal sources of Czech migration to Cleveland from the 1850s to 1873 were southern and western Bohemia, centered in the south around the districts of České Budějovice, Tábor, Milevsko, Vodňany, Rokycany, and Plzeň.[9] Prague and the Časlov and Chrudim areas to its immediate east were also important sources of early migration. Indeed, one source states that from 1866 through 1868 more than half of the emigration from Austria came from the Tábor, Budějovice, and Plzeň areas. These emigrants most likely migrated in family units, as statistics from the 1853 through 1862 period demonstrate. There were only slightly more men than women and nearly one quarter of the emigrants were children under seventeen years of age.[10]

Another characteristic of early Czech migration was its Jewish component. When the sixteen Czech families settled in Cleveland in 1852, Bohemian Jewish families were already there, including several from the Tábor and Písek regions who were very likely acquainted with some of the first gentile arrivals, who came from the same areas. Leopold Levy, from the Písek area, came to Cleveland in 1849 and opened a small dry goods store. In 1852 he allowed newly arrived Czech families to live on his property for about a week. Bernard Weidenthal emigrated from the Tábor area in 1849 and opened a clothing store, and Zigmund Stein, born in Vlaším, also arrived in 1849, by way of Prague, and opened a tavern and boarding house. These individuals were an integral part of the nascent Czech community, both by their own choice and by choice of at least some of the Czech gentiles.[11]

There is a general agreement that the causes of nineteenth century emigration from southern and western Bohemia were political, economic, and psychological. Tomáš Čapek, who wrote in the 1920s about Czech migration, noted that "there were two distinct kinds of emigration: the political one which had its origins in the revolutionary disturbances of 1848; the other emigration, due to economic causes."[12] Fifty years later, Bedřich Šindelář, a Marxist, wrote in nearly the same vein as Čapek. He emphasized two causes, first, political and national suppression of the Czechs by the governing German bourgeoisie following the 1848 revolution, and second, the factor of economic "pauperization" of the Czech countryside brought on by the onset of capitalism.[13]

Another study pointed to several contributing factors, beginning with the increased birthrate in the region. At the same time, the penetration of industrialism and capitalist relations into agriculture, which decreased demand for labor in rural areas, added to rural unemployment. However, the study noted, the southern and western districts of Bohemia were not its most impoverished regions. Some resources were required to make a move. Many individuals emigrated just as their standard of living was beginning to deteriorate. An additional factor in the motivation to migrate was the effect on the collective psyche of "exaggerated accounts of the life of the Czech immigrants in the United States." Nor did the study ignore the political factor, which impelled the revolutionary leaders of 1848, socialists and union activists of the 1870s and 1880s, and Czech nationalists to migrate.[14]

In the 1850s most Czech emigrants were from an artisan background, the skilled building crafts and the clothing sector in particular. Relatively few of them were shopkeepers or farmers.[15] By the 1860s industrialization in the Habsburg Empire was shifting increasingly to Bohemia. This encouraged migration from the countryside to industrial cities, particularly after the Seven Weeks' War. People whose families had lived for generations in a specific area or village were migrating to industrial cities such as Plzeň, Prague, Brno, Ostrava, or Vienna. It was only one step further to follow the dream of greater economic opportunity and personal freedom all the way to America. The findings of one study indicate that medium-size cities such as Liberec, Steyr, Linz, and others were only intermediate stages in a long Series of migrations from place to place.[16] The United States appeared a very attractive destination in the 1866 to 1873 period and again from about 1878 to 1893.

On the political side, dissatisfaction over the Austro-Hungarian compromise of 1867 led to ferment in the Czech lands, with mass rallies throughout the country during the spring and summer of 1868, and subsequent Austrian countermeasures. This forced a number of politically and culturally active Czechs into exile, including Václav Šnajdr, who in 1873 became editor of *Pokrok,* a free-thought Czech paper in Cleveland. Political developments also precipitated emigration in the 1880s when the Austrian government, fearing growth of socialism among the Czech working class, persecuted Czech social democrats, causing many of them to flee to America.[17]

These developments, combined with economic motivations and the favorable accounts coming from Czechs living in Cleveland, probably explain the increased Czech immigration to the city in the middle 1880s.

Czech migration had become systematic by the second half of the 1860s, and most migrants' journeys conformed to the following pattern. Prospective settlers traveled from their native communities in Bohemia and Moravia to either Bremen or Hamburg. They frequently journeyed in family groups, though by the 1880s an increased percentage traveled as individuals, with slightly more males than females making the journey.[18] In Bremen the firm of Kares and Stozky, and in Hamburg the Hamburg-American Line, for many through the agency of Josef Pastor, arranged passage for Czechs to Boston, New York, or Baltimore, and then from these ports of entry on to Cleveland. By the 1860s, Kares and Stozky had an agent in Cleveland—Martin Krejčí, from the Písek area—who assisted Cleveland Czechs in bringing over their friends, relatives, and acquaintances.[19] The story of Frank Vlchek, a prominent Cleveland industrialist and writer, illustrates some of the above generalizations.

Vlchek was born of peasant stock in Budyn, a village in the Písek district near the town of Vodňany, in 1871. He was the last of fourteen children. His upbringing provided him with literacy, Czech national consciousness, and deep Catholic piety. Because the family land could not support all fourteen children, most had to learn a trade, which for Vlchek was blacksmithing. When his older brother Josef acquired the family land from his father, young Frank, not wanting to be dependent on his brother, went out to make his way as an apprentice journeyman. As compensation for not inheriting land, he received 300 *zlatys,* and prepared himself for his *"vandr,"* or journey in quest of work. His travels took him through southern Bohemia to České Budějovice, where his exposure to town culture altered his outlook. For Vlchek, village life would never again suffice. While working with a blacksmith in České Budějovice, he learned about work in an armament factory in Steyr. The pay he received for his work as a machinist there caused him to conclude that village peasants underpaid village blacksmiths and expected too much of them. After Vlchek was injured at a tavern dance during an altercation possibly resulting from tensions between Czech and German workers, his employers fired him. Reluctant to return to the Czech countryside and settle into the meager existence of a village smith, he wandered about Austria picking up work here and there. Losing his employment with a blacksmith in a German-language area of Bohemia, he was finally forced to return to his home district and take on a job with a smith in a village near

Vodňany. The wretched living and working conditions caused him to leave that position and return to his own village. With his newly acquired urban outlook, he became very depressed about his prospects. There was nothing for him to do that winter except live with his brother, pick up odd jobs, and wait for spring when he would again go on his *vandr* seeking work. At that point the Vlchek family received a letter from the husband of Vlchek's older sister, who had immigrated to Cleveland. The description of life and opportunities there moved Vlchek to decide to follow his sister and brother-in-law, and another sister who had followed them, to Cleveland.

Vlchek acquired a suitcase and negotiated with a shipping agent in Písek for passage to the United States. He then tried and—being eligible for service in the Habsburg army—failed to get a pass from the Austrian district administrator that would enable him to leave Bohemia legally. In spite of this, Vlchek proceeded with his plans to emigrate, said his good-byes to friends and family, and agreed to take a friend and a cousin with him. Alone among the three, the cousin succeeded in gaining permission from Austrian authorities to travel legally to Germany. The young men left home, probably in 1889, and traveled by train to the German border. There an agent, who worked for the company with which Vlchek had booked his passage to America, met them and gave Vlchek and his friend instructions to wait in a conductor's booth in a railway car. He soon returned with train tickets for Bremen, and led them to another railway car, where the cousin was already sitting. The trio proceeded to Bremen by way of Berlin. Clearly the travel company had made some arrangement with Austrian officials to enable Vlchek and his friend to cross over into Germany, despite their lack of exit visas.

In Bremen they stayed one night in a not particularly clean immigrant hotel, and then took the short train ride to the port where Vlchek and his friend boarded their ship for New York. (The cousin had booked passage on another ship after meeting a Czech girl who was sailing on it.) The passage lasted eight days, and as long as they could be on deck and not inside, where the stench was unbearable, the voyage was tolerable. Once in New York, Vlchek had no trouble going through immigration. Heeding the advice he received in a letter from his sister, he ignored the blandishments of a Czech-speaking hotel hustler, unlike his friend, who went with the hustler. Vlchek instead found a telegraph office, where he inquired about train schedules to Cleveland and then wired his sister when to expect him. Upon his arrival, brother and sister recognized each other only with difficulty, not having seen each other in six years.[20]

The above account indicates that a sophisticated network of migration existed by the 1880s. Over seventy-five percent of the Czechs who settled in Cleveland in the 1850s and 1860s had been from the Písek and adjacent regions, and undoubtedly many of them sent back letters similar to the one sent by Vlchek's brother-in-law.[21] The travel company, probably Kares and Stozky of Bremen, had one agent in Písek, and another at the Bohemian-German border to obviate any problems there. Although the importance of the shipping agencies' role by this late date has been questioned, it seems clear that if they did not encourage emigration, they at least facilitated it by selling tickets and dealing with state officials.[22] Thanks to the shipping agency, Vlchek's trip went smoothly enough. He made a single overnight layover in Bremen and once in New York, wasted no time in finding his way to Cleveland.

Vlchek, a skilled worker who could have made some sort of a living in Bohemia, immigrated because he believed he could do better in Cleveland. If he did not have a job awaiting him, he at least had a specific destination and family to get him started. The existence of clusters of individuals and families from the above-mentioned Czech regions attests to the fact that many individuals, like Vlchek, immigrated to Cleveland to join family, friends, or acquaintances.

Formation of the Community

The first Czech settlement in Cleveland was on the east bank of the Cuya-hoga River in the vicinity of the intersection of present-day East 9th, Commercial, and Canal Streets.[23] By 1853 some Czechs had moved to the west bank of the river into an area known as Brooklyn.[24] This was the origin of the west-side Czech neighborhood, which by the late 1860s and 70s would shift south and west to an area bounded on the east by Fulton Road, on the west by West 65th Street, on the north by Clark Avenue, and on the south by Denison Avenue. On the east bank of the river the Czech colony gravitated south to open land owned by Harvey Rice, an early settler, land agent, and political figure. Rice, who employed some Czech gardeners and orchardists, sold part of his land to several of them on easy terms. Martin Krejčí, the shipping agent, who had emigrated from Netolice (a few kilometers south of Vodňany) in 1854, acquired some of this land, subdivided it into lots, and sold it to his incoming countrymen.[25] This became the Croton Street neighborhood, which was the center of Cleveland's Czech colony in the 1860s and 70s. Krejčí's activities were an important factor in the neighborhood's growth. His connection with European shipping agencies facilitated the immigration of hundreds, if not thousands, of Czechs to Cleveland, and his dealings in land led to the construction of scores of Czech-owned homes. Šnajdr noted in 1878 that Krejčí was one of the wealthiest Czechs in Cleveland. His home on the corner of Croton and Forest (later East 37th) Streets, where he also kept a general store, was among the finest owned by Cleveland Czechs. Many Czech immigrants reportedly spent their first night in Cleveland on its front steps.[26]

Czechs tended to settle in newly developing areas of the city rather than to displace previous groups. Initially, this was almost inevitable, since the settlers of the late 1850s and 1860s were part of an older immigrant stream. They arrived at a time when ample open land was still available, before Cleveland was transformed from a regional marketing and agricultural center to a major industrial city. Furthermore, they had sufficient skills and could obtain enough capital to build their own houses: usually a small wooden-frame, one-story structure standing on a lot with a vegetable garden. This semi-rural existence had some resemblance to the village life from which many Czechs had come.

From the Croton neighborhood, settlement initially fanned out in two directions in the 1870s and 1880s as more Czechs arrived in Cleveland. To the southeast, across Kingsbury Run, Czech settlement extended along Broadway as far, by the end of the 1890s, as Union Street, where Poles were establishing a neighborhood.[27] The other direction of settlement was to the east, along Central and Quincy Avenues in the area between 79th and 93rd Streets. By the beginning of the twentieth century Czechs had also settled portions of the Buckeye Road district and the Mt. Pleasant area around East 131 Street. Eventually, Czechs moved into suburbs bordering Cleveland on the south and east. Many Czech neighborhoods were known by names of towns in the homeland. Sections of the larger Croton and Broadway neighborhoods were designated as "Praha", "Žižkov," and "Karlín." Other names came from farther afield: "Videň" (Vienna), or even "Kuba" (Cuba).

Artisans from the villages of southern and western Bohemia who arrived in Cleveland during the 1850s and 1860s found that their trades filled a need there.[28] For example, when Andrews, Clark & Company, the embryonic Standard Oil, in 1865 opened its Excelsior refinery right on the fringe of the Croton neighborhood, many of the Czech coopers living nearby found employment with the company making barrels for the storage and shipping of oil.

Cleveland's transformation into a modern industrial city in the post-Civil War area affected the economic and social composition of the Czech community. Jobs created by the development of industries such as petroleum refining, iron and steel, machinery production, ship building, and textiles drew growing numbers of Czech artisans, craftsmen, and builders to Cleveland. Increasingly, the influx of Czechs in the late 1860s and throughout the 1870s, and indeed on up to 1914, was drawn to Cleveland by the growth of heavy industry.

At some point between 1869 and 1878 the number of Czechs employed as workers in industrial concerns came to exceed that of self-employed artisans. Šnajdr, writing in 1878, stated that ninety percent of the Czechs in Cleveland were workers, 2,500 of them employed either in the iron and steel mills or as coopers with the Standard Oil Company.[29] Crafts of some of artisans became obsolete, and they had to find another skill, go to work in a local industrial plant, or move on. However, not all of these immigrants or their children remained in the working class. Considerable socioeconomic variation developed within the Czech community, with some of its members themselves becoming owners of small or even large companies. Frank Vlchek, the Bohemian village smith, opened his own toolmaking business in Cleveland. By the 1920s the Vlchek Tool Company employed six hundred people, many of them Czechs.

In many ways the community was self-contained, though not isolated from Cleveland institutions. During the first years of Czech settlement, before a real Czech community had formed, immigrants had to rely to an extent on the assistance of non-Czechs, as evidenced by their association with Harvey Rice and with members of the German community, but this reliance was short-lived. Those Czech immigrants who arrived later, from the 1870s up through 1914, found a Czech infrastructure which provided them nearly everything necessary for existence in a modern urban environment. The settlers of the 1850s and 1860s had established not only churches, lodges, mutual benefit societies, and schools, but also newspapers, professional offices, taverns, and shops.

General stores, notary and shipping offices, taverns, and food retailers were the nucleus of the business community. Small general stores provided Czech Jews with their livelihood. Several Czechs went into partnership with Germans in the early years of settlement. Jindřich Hladík from Prague ran a produce, meat, poultry, and cheese store in partnership with a German (and became engaged to his partner's daughter).[30]

By 1869 Czechs owned at least sixteen shops and twenty-two taverns in Cleveland. During the course of the next ten years, as the Croton Street and west side neighborhoods reached maturity, and Broadway and Quincy-Central began to develop, the number of Czech-owned establishments grew to ninety grocery stores, eighty-six taverns, and fourteen butcher shops. The

professions did not advance quite as rapidly. As of 1878 the Czech community counted two editors, two doctors, two lawyers, one architect, three
priests, three schoolteachers, two subordinate city officials, and one former
city councilman.[31]

Surprisingly, establishing a viable brewery, a near-necessity for a self-
sufficient central European settlement, proved troublesome. Three attempts
to found breweries failed in the early 1870s. František Payer, who made a bid
in 1873, later attributed his failure to a warm winter which sent the price
of ice up to $25 per ton, as well as to high barley and hops prices. In 1894 the
Pilsner Brewery, which operated successfully into the twentieth century, was
established.[32]

In the 1860s and 1870s Croton Street was lined with Czech establishments.
By the 1880s some commercial activity had moved to locations along Broad-
way. Šnajdr, for example, published the newspaper *Pokrok* from a Croton
Street address, but later published *Dennice Novověku* from an office on
Broadway. *Američan*, a Czech-language Catholic paper, also had offices on
Broadway, as did *Svět* and *Svět Američan* at a later date. The office of *Amer-
ické Dělnické Listy*, the Czech socialist paper, was located at East 41st Street
and Broadway. The Pilsner Brewery's operations were on the west side at
West 65th Street and Clark Avenue. The Vlchek Tool Company was origi-
nally located on Central Avenue, but later moved to East 87th Street and
Quincy, and then to East 87th Street and Mt. Auburn. All these addresses
were in Czech-settled neighborhoods.

The growth of the city's Czech population in the 1880s and 1890s contributed to an increase in Czech-owned business and service concerns. By
1895 the number of Czech-owned shops had risen to include 167 grocery
stores, 187 taverns, 63 meat markets, and 18 dry goods stores. There were
eleven Czech doctors, nine lawyers, three architects, seven funeral directors,
and twelve music teachers.[33]

The first Czech-owned savings and loan organizations, founded in the
1890s, filled the community's need for its own financial institutions. When
immigrants first arrived, they generally did not know English. They frequently needed to borrow capital in order to build their homes or start
businesses, so settlers of longer standing who could speak English had to
accompany them to downtown banks as interpreters. In time the banks
hired Czech employees who could interpret, but leaders in the Czech community questioned why they should deal with foreign banks when they
could organize their own. Consequently, they established a savings association, "Včela" (The Bee), in the Broadway neighborhood in 1896. Včela
began on a very small scale with only about twelve members. Each member

initially contributed one dollar a week to the association and was obliged to find one new member each week. This led to the accumulation of a modest amount of capital, and after several months the association was able to make its first home loan. As Včela continued to grow, other Czech savings and loan associations also started up: "Mravenec" (The Ant) on the west side in 1897, and the East End Building and Loan Association in the Quincy-Central neighborhood in 1911. By 1919 the largest of the Czech-owned savings and loans was the Atlas, founded in the Broadway district in 1915. These organizations soon became subject to state regulation, and most were sound up to the Great Depression, partly because they were conservative in their lending practices. They did not issue second mortgages, and lent up to no more than sixty-five percent of the value of a mortgaged property.[34]

Czech newspapers began publication in Cleveland in February of 1871, when Karel Jonáš, owner of *Pokrok* (*Progress*), sold it to F. B. Zdrůbek, who then transferred it from Cedar Rapids, Iowa, to Cleveland.[35] *Pokrok* continued publication until 1876, when Šnajdr, its third and last editor, discontinued it. In the fall of 1877 he began publication of a new paper, *Dennice Nového věku* (*Dawning of a New Age*). Both papers were politically and religiously liberal.[36] Workers' or socialist opinion found representation in the mid-1870s with publication of *Dělnické Listy* (*Workers' News*) under editorship of Lev Palda, but he transferred the paper to New York in 1876. Also during the 1870s, Cleveland's Czech Catholics established the short-lived *Budíček* (*Alarm Clock*).

By 1900 the Czech neighborhoods had assumed their own characteristic appearance. Descriptions of them abound. When Vlchek first came upon the Broadway neighborhood in the spring of 1889 he saw "unpaved streets full of mud, no stone sidewalks, there was plenty of mud on them. Aside from that the homes were entirely new, several gaily painted, in front of the homes a piece of lawn and a garden with flowers . . . behind the houses were gardens in which they cultivated a variety of vegetables. By the sidewalk in front of each home was a wooden fence with an opening directly against the steps leading to the house. . . . Everywhere we heard the Czech language, and it struck me like Bohemia."[37]

Vlchek gave a further description: "The colony grew very quickly (i.e. Broadway). Our compatriots built small wooden houses. There were no sewers; only gas and water, but few of the compatriots had gas and water in their dwellings. Usually the workers constructed the houses from wood—living room and kitchen measuring 14 by 16. Behind the kitchen was a small "šanda" (Czech-American version of shanty), where there were supplies such as coal, firewood and other household necessities. Behind the homes there were usually small gardens, in which vegetables and flowers were cultivated. Some raised pigeons, others chickens or ducks and geese. In order that the wife helped to earn a little income she took in 'bordynkaře"—boarders—with whom the family was cramped into small rooms. . . . Because there was no central heating in such new homes, in the winter there was frost as severe as in an icebox in the bedrooms. To warm up the young and healthy body of the boarder a true Czech comforter and rye bread sufficed; to maintain the health and good humor of the boarder, he was given some beer, good beef soup and a piece of meat."[38]

Eventually, the growth of public transportation, especially during the early twentieth century, gave Czechs access to a greater variety of housing, and a greater choice of location, size, and price. In the spring of 1920 a typical house in the Broadway neighborhood, with six rooms and a toilet, would be advertised in a Czech newspaper at prices ranging from $2,700 for a house in the center of the district, to $6,300 for a place at the edge of the neighborhood in Newburgh Heights. Duplexes commanded from $4,000 for twelve rooms (without indoor toilet), to $8,650 for a ten-room structure (with indoor toilet) in the newer Corlett district, located south of the Mt. Pleasant neighborhood. A more expensive single house "on a boulevard in a Czech neighborhood" stood on a lot measuring 50 by 160 and had seven rooms, bath, and sunroom.[39]

Catholics and Freethinkers

Closely paralleling the growth of Czech neighborhoods was the growth of Czech religious and social-fraternal organizations, which contributed significantly to Czech community building. Indeed, a good indicator of the community's growth is the establishment of churches and lodges. As Czechs developed the Croton, west side, Broadway, Quincy-Central, and Mt. Pleasant neighborhoods, churches and lodges, the centers of communal and cultural activities, sprang into existence. A characteristic of Czech-Americans was their division along religious lines. The overwhelming majority of those who left Bohemia from the 1850s up to World War I were at least nominally Catholic, but once in the American environment many broke ranks with the Catholic Church. Most of these dissidents turned to a "free thought," or anticlerical religious rationalist ideology, although a small minority became Protestants.[40]

This was the case in Cleveland. Except for the few Jews who were included in the original Czech community, most of the original settlers were

Catholic, but a small free-thinking element grew up as well. (The relatively small number of Protestants joined churches established in Czech neighborhoods by Protestant denominations.) The establishment and growth of Roman Catholic Czech national parishes corresponded to Czech settlement across Cleveland, and a competing network of free-thought lodges shadowed the expansion of Catholic parishes, although there were far more Catholics than freethinkers until sometime in the 1880s.[41] From the beginning these two segments of the Czech community engaged in acrimonious disputes which only subsided when both cooperated in the struggle to gain American recognition and support for an independent Czechoslovakia during World War I. Divisions and conflicts also existed within each of the two groups.[42]

Members of the early Czech community attended mass at Cleveland's first Roman Catholic church, St. Mary on the Flats, worshipping with Irish and German Catholics. After the establishment of the German national parish of St. Joseph's in the city's Central district, Czechs, many of whom understood German, worshipped there. In 1857 a Czech priest, Antonín Krásný, recently arrived from the Habsburg Empire where he had been incarcerated for nine years following his involvement in the 1848 revolution, was assigned to St. Joseph's, where he ministered to both nationalities.[43]

With the development of the Czech community in the Croton neighborhood in the late 1860s, the diocese authorized creation of the parish of St. Wenceslas, and appointed Rev. Krásný its first priest. Construction of the church's original building began in 1867 at Arch (now East 35th Place) and Burwell in the heart of the Croton neighborhood. In 1892 St. Wenceslas moved to a new building nearby at Broadway and East 37th Street.[44] In 1874 west side Czechs received authorization to establish a parish, St. Procop, and built a church at the corner of West 41st Street and Trent.[45] With the growth of the Broadway neighborhood in the late 1870s and 1880s, Our Lady of Lourdes was established in 1882, on East 54th Street just off Broadway. The first priest there, Štefan Furdek, was a Slovak, and Slovaks, Slovenians, and Croatians, as well as Czechs, attended the church.[46] Also in 1882 Czechs living in the Quincy-Central neighborhood established the parish of St. Adalbert, building their church on East 83rd Street.[47] Further migration south and west in the Broadway area led to the formation of St. John Nepomucene parish with a church at Fleet Avenue and East 50th Street in 1902.[48] Eventually, as Czechs settled in the Corlett area south of Mt. Pleasant on the eastern fringe of Cleveland, Holy Family Church was established there in 1911.[49]

Membership in Czech Catholic Parishes, 1913–1923[50]

Church	Neighborhood	Membership		
		1913	1918	1923
St. Wenceslaus	Croton	1,451	1,160 (ca.)	1,200
St. Procop	West Side	2,000	n.d.	n.d.
Our Lady of Lourdes	Broadway	3,000	3,500 (ca.)	3,800
St. Adalbert	Quincy-Central	1,500	n.d.	1,000
St. John Nepomucene	Broadway-Fleet	2,885	3,282	3,227
Holy Family	Corlett	721	1,300	1,900

Protestant churches and missions were also established in Czech neighborhoods. These included: Broadway Methodist Episcopal Church (founded in 1872), Mizpah Congregational Church, and Bethlehem Congregational Church, all in the Broadway area; Cyril Congregational Church on the west side; and Emanuel Congregational Church in the Quincy-Central neighborhood.[51] In comparison to the Catholic parishes none of these churches had large memberships, but they all had "Bohemian Departments" and conducted portions of their services and activities in Czech.[52] Broadway Methodist had enough success in winning over Czech Catholics to alarm the priest of the newly established Church of the Holy Family. He wrote to the Bishop in 1917 that lack of facilities at his church was very damaging, because Catholic children were attending the Sunday school program at the Protestant church.[53] During the early 1890s Bethlehem Church had seven hundred children in its Sunday school.[54] The Czech Protestant churches probably reached their high-water mark around 1910, thereafter declining due to competition from other churches, changing demographics, and the supplanting of houses by factories.

Within the Catholic community there were tensions between the Diocese of Cleveland and Czech Catholics over establishment of these national parishes, and over the related issue of what priests would serve in them. The Catholic hierarchy in Cleveland was predominantly English-speaking and not always sensitive to the needs and wishes of Czech and other ethnic parishioners, while the parishioners had little understanding of the complexities involved in administering a multi-ethnic diocese.[55] The creation of national parishes led to the building of numerous churches in a single district, resulting in additional expense and breaking down the geographic logic of the city's parish structure.

Finding qualified priests fluent in the appropriate language was an additional headache for diocesan administrators. On several occasions Cleveland's bishop had to request the archbishops of Prague or Olomouc to send a priest to Cleveland from Bohemia or Moravia at the expense of the Cleveland diocese. However, it was difficult to find priests there who were eager to go to America. In many cases, when a priest of the appropriate nationality for a given national parish could not be recruited, a clergyman of a different nationality with at least a smattering of the language in question would be appointed. Rev. Krásný had originally served at St. Joseph's because he spoke German. Rev. Furdek, a Slovak, was able to minister to Czech congregations because he was fluent in the language. Oldřich Zlámal, a Moravian-born Czech, and Furdek's successor at Our Lady of Lourdes, was initially assigned to Slovak parishes.[56]

Parishioners, who had their own ideas about who should officiate in their churches, often expressed displeasure with the priests appointed by the bishop. Parishioners and diocesan hierarchy also disagreed over language, with the former seeing churches as a means of preserving and promoting their language and culture. The hierarchy, on the other hand, envisaged the acculturation of Czechs and other immigrants into the broader English-speaking American Catholic community, with use of the native language in churches only an interim measure. Another divisive issue had to do with church-sponsored societies and lodges, particularly the practice of holding meetings at the same time as church services. Many parishioners were workers whose only free time was on Sunday, and were inclined to attend lodge meetings rather than mass.

Instances of such conflicts occurred in many of the Czech parishes. At St. John Nepomucene, for example, the parish itself was established in the face of resistance from the bishop, as well as ridicule from freethinkers, by Czechs who desired not only a church but above all a Catholic school, so that their children did not lose either their faith or their mother tongue.[57]

In the parish of St. Procop's on the west side, problems were seemingly endemic, particularly after Josef Koudelka, the first priest, left the parish and moved to St. Louis to edit the Catholic newspaper *Hlas* in 1882. The diocese had difficulty finding a linguistically competent priest to satisfy the parishioners. In addition, they persisted in electing a parish board unacceptable to the bishop, Richard Gilmour, and in holding lodge meetings which conflicted with church services. In 1884, his patience tried, Bishop

Gilmour decided to threaten the parish with an interdict.[58] "For the last two weeks St. Prokop's church in this city has been a standing scandal before the public. For eleven months the church has been closed because of the disobedience and misconduct of a portion of this congregation." It had been difficult to find Czech-speaking priests at all and impossible, Bishop Gilmour declared, to find one able to cope with St. Procop's unruly parishioners. "There are three Bohemian priests in the diocese. Two, this congregation has crucified to death. The third refuses to be there, preferring to leave the diocese rather than deal with such people." Although the parish councilmen had been suspended, the dissident parishioners re-elected them, and then "broke into the pastoral residence, and ended in riot and bloodshed before the Church. . . . They demand the selection of their priest, then his management." The bishop laid down an ultimatum: "St. Prokop's is either Catholic or not. . . . If the refractory members of St. Prokop's wish to try their strength they can be gratified. Meanwhile the Bishop will maintain his own rights and the rights of St. Prokop's as a Catholic congregation . . . and see that St. Prokop's is governed as the other 217 congregations in the diocese are."[59] Stefan Furdek read the proposed interdict to the parishioners; their non-responsiveness caused Bishop Gilmour to interdict the parish the following week. The interdict remained in effect for eighteen months, until the church members agreed to the bishop's selection of a parish council, and a Czech priest able to pacify the congregation was found.[60] There were subsequent problems in the parish, but none as serious as those leading to the interdict.

Conflicts involving more than one parish also occurred. At the time Holy Family parish was created, many Czech families in the area already belonged to a Slovak parish, having been recruited by the parish's Czech-speaking priest. The bishop allowed them to continue attending the Slovak church, which irritated the priest and some church members at Holy Family.[61]

Some of the dissent within Cleveland's Czech Catholic community was blamed on the influence of freethinkers. A diocesan report noted that "of the upwards of fifteen thousand Bohemians [in the city], only about six hundred families lay any claim to Catholicity. . . . In Cleveland the Bohemian infidels and their followers have been the cause of much trouble to the several priests in charge of the Bohemian congregations, making use of every vile means to frustrate them in their work among those who wished to live up to the faith of their fathers."[62] One contemporary source referred to "a vicious fraternal struggle between church and non-church people" on the west side.[63] Wishing to stave off losses of membership to the growing freethought organizations, Czech Catholics tailored their religious practices to conform to Czech cultural ways, which often conflicted with American church practice and the bishop's authority. Parish reports complained that many families involved in free-thought societies attended mass only on holidays. Oldřich Zlámal wrote that freethinkers used the church to have their children baptized and thus obtain documentation to prove citizenship.[64] Church records tend to support this: in 1883, the children from free-thinking families baptized at St. Wenceslaus (174) outnumbered those from Catholic families (164).[65] Catholic-sponsored societies and lodges were looked upon by some priests and devout parishioners as a means of bringing free-thinkers back into the church.[66]

A later history of Holy Family parish lamented the freethinkers' "constant harassment" of church loyalists. "No other faithful body of Catholics in Cleveland endured a greater test of their loyalty to the Faith than did the Bohemian Catholics. Not only did they bear, as all Catholics of that early day did, the natural 'no Popery' scorn prevalent in a native New England community—that was understandable and forgivable—but alone among the Catholic pioneers in Cleveland, they were forced to witness the ungodly spectacle of mass apostasy and suffer the antireligious jeers and taunts of their own countrymen so corrupting had been the poisons of the German "Away from Rome" movement and French Rationalists . . . so disastrous to any level thinking had been the political repressions associated with a Catholic Emperor preserving a seventeenth century policy in a world of burgeoning democratic processes."[67] Such was the antagonism between the two sides that freethinkers, for their part, referred to the Catholic Church as "the claws of the Roman idol," something akin to a "werewolf."[68]

The network of Czech free-thought organizations began on a smaller scale than the Catholic, but by 1895 it had achieved if not surpassed its rival in influence and strength among Cleveland's Czechs. While several of the early settlers were freethinkers, this element was a decided minority until the 1880s.[69] The small cluster of original freethinkers was both well educated and determined to promote its ideas.

A major controversy between Czech Catholics and freethinkers erupted in early 1871 when the free-thought newspaper *Pokrok* printed a story that Father Řepíš of St. Wenceslaus church was having an affair with his housekeeper. Řepíš filed a lawsuit against F. B. Zdrůbek, the paper's editor. The latter was represented in the case by J. W. Sykora, co-owner of the paper and a leading freethinker. Zdrůbek faced the prospect of a $1,000 fine and a year in jail if he were to lose the suit. In the end his principal witness proved unreliable, and he had to print a retraction and apologize to the priest. Zdrůbek left Cleveland soon after.[70] His journalistic shoes were filled first by

J. V. Čapek and then, in 1873, by Václav Šnajdr, who served as the herald of religious rationalism in Czech Cleveland and, indeed, Czech America until his retirement in 1910.

Under Šnajdr's editorship *Pokrok* and then *Dennice Novověku* carried on the struggle against religion and more specifically against Catholicism. In a series of articles appearing in 1875 Šnajdr wrote that free thought was in the tradition of Czech history and that Catholicism was the Czechs' oppressor. He singled out Josef Koudelka, priest of St. Procop's, for many of his attacks. Alluding to a sermon in which the priest had assaulted Czech free-thought societies because they taught that humans were descended from apes, Šnajdr wrote that Rev. Koudelka fancied himself as a second St. Augustine.[71] After Rev. Koudelka's departure, and the eventual interdict at St. Prokop in 1884, Šnajdr observed that the closing of the church had no significant effect other than to give the parish's men more time to drink, talk, and play cards in the taverns. Noting that the interdict also closed St. Procop's school, he wrote that parents who cared about their children's education already sent them to the free-thought school on Wilson Avenue.[72] In retaliation for Šnajdr's attacks against things Catholic—specifically his ridicule of the revelation of the Virgin Mary to Bernadette of Lourdes—Bishop Gilmour decided in 1883 to name the newest Czech parish "Our Lady of Lourdes." Thus, "Our Lady of Lourdes" would receive satisfaction for attacks and insults made by anticlerical Czechs such as Šnajdr.[73] Šnajdr also criticized the role of Catholic and other clergy in the economic strife that plagued Cleveland in the 1880s, charging that they wanted a passive working class and were used by mill owners to break a strike.[74]

Czech free thought found its most effective organizational expression through fraternal lodges. The first free-thought lodge in Cleveland was a unit of "Slovanská Lípa" (Slavic Linden Tree), founded at Martin Krejčí's home in the Croton neighborhood in 1862. It functioned as a mutual benefit and educational society, and was the ancestor of many of the Czech free-thought societies in Cleveland. Its first hall was on Orange Avenue, but by 1871 it had dedicated a brick structure at Case Avenue and Croton. During this time a number of other lodges either broke off from Slovanská Lípa or were founded in the neighborhood. The dramatic society "Perun" was established in 1866 as a division of Slovanská Lípa, but as a consequence of disagreements among the members the two organizations went their separate ways. By 1877 both had disbanded.[75]

In the meantime, a lodge known as "Svornost" (Harmony) had been established. In 1870 it affiliated with the growing "Česko-Slovanská Podporující Společnost" (č.s.p.s., Czecho-Slavonic Support Association), founded in 1854 in St. Louis. Svornost became lodge No. 3 of the organization.[76] Membership was open to any healthy male between the age of 18 and 45 who could speak Czech. Dues were originally five dollars per year.[77] Svornost, which provided life insurance and support for spouses and children in the event of a member's death, also required its members to arrange and attend funerals of deceased members. Its original membership of 23 grew to 186 by early 1886, but by 1895 had declined to 163 because many of its members transferred to newly established lodges in other parts of the city. Indeed, Svornost itself changed its meeting place from Perun Hall in the Croton neighborhood to the Bohemian National Hall on Broadway in the 1890s.[78]

In addition to providing insurance, č.s.p.s. lodges acted to promote Czech national consciousness and religious liberalism, and to provide their members and sympathizers with recreational activities such as dances, dinners, plays, lectures, parades, and excursions. A "beseda" (festive dance) in March 1870 inaugurated a long Series of such activities underwritten by č.s.p.s. lodges in Cleveland. Because many of their members were skilled workers, the lodges often lent material support to striking Czech workers (for example, to Czech coopers in Cleveland in May 1877, and to New York cigar workers in November of that year).[79] Svornost contributed money toward the support and maintenance of living Czech-American leaders, as well as to the memory of deceased ones.[80]

In the 1870s free-thought lodges quickly multiplied throughout the growing Czech neighborhoods, many of them affiliated with the č.s.p.s. By 1875 the west side Czechs had a lodge, "Jan Žižka," and the establishment of lodge "Lídomil" in 1877 at the southern fringe of the Croton neighborhood reflected the latter's growth toward Broadway. Free-thinking Czechs on the east side founded lodge "Přemysl" in a private home in the Quincy-Central neighborhood and lodge "Bratři v Kruhu" (Brothers in Circle) in the new Broadway area. By 1878 there were at least seventeen different free-thought lodges spread throughout Cleveland's Czech neighborhoods.[81]

Free-thought women's lodges were also established, usually following men's lodges into the various neighborhoods. "Jednota Českých Dam" (JCD, Union of Czech Women), a national organization founded in Cleveland, was formed in the Croton neighborhood in 1870. The Quincy-Central women founded their lodge in 1878 and their sisters on the west side formed one in 1879. By 1880 JCD was established in the Broadway area and several more lodges followed in that vicinity and farther to the east.[82]

By the time of World War I the various free-thought societies had pooled their efforts to construct meeting halls in each of the neighborhoods. These buildings served their respective neighborhoods by providing space for celebrations, gymnastics, musical and dramatic performances, Czech-language schools, community meals, and general cultural and political events. For each hall, a board of directors or "patronat" consisting of representatives of the affiliated lodges was formed to administer the building. The most imposing of these halls, the Bohemian National Hall, was built on Broadway near East 49th Street and dedicated in 1897.[83] The Bohemian Sokol Hall, in a building purchased from the Hungarians, was located on Clark Avenue and served west side residents; the Bohemian American Hall was built in 1910 on Quincy Avenue; the Jan Amos Komensky Hall on East 131st Street provided a meeting place in the Corlett neighborhood; and the Bohemian Lodge Hall, built on Buckeye Road in 1916, provided a center for the sparser Czech population in that area.[84]

While not isolating themselves from events in their adopted county—Svornost, for instance, voted to have its full membership turn out for the burial in Cleveland of assassinated President James Garfield—local č.s.p.s. lodges took an interest in affairs that went well beyond the city's confines.[85] In a show of pan-Slavic support during the Russo-Turkish War of 1878, Svornost contributed a small sum for Montenegrin relief. Two years later, it made a donation toward the construction of the Czech National Theater in Prague.[86] The lodges also participated in and supported international free-thought organizations and activities. They established close relations with "Volná Myšlenka," a militant free-thought organization in Prague, and in 1910 sent delegates to a convention of the Union of Freethinkers in Brussels. They participated in planning a five-hundred year anniversary celebration of Jan Hus's martyrdom in 1915.[87] At nearly the same time as Svornost's members were discussing in 1914 whether or not č.s.p.s. members had to be American citizens to attend that organization's national conventions, they agreed to send contributions to the families of wounded and deceased Czech soldiers fighting in the Austro-Hungarian armies during the early stages of World War I.

č.s.p.s. members aimed to perpetuate free-thought precepts and Czech culture through education of their children. In 1880 the lodges Svornost and Budívoj agreed to cooperate in operating a Czech Sunday school. č.s.p.s.-sponsored Sunday schools were subsequently extended to all of Cleveland's Czech neighborhoods. Their curricula included Czech language, geography, history, literature, and folklore. Just as Catholic parochial schools stressed Catholic teachings, Č.S.P.S. Sunday schools emphasized the rationalist tradition in Czech culture.[88] Visits by educators from the old country were designed to generate local interest in these schools. Vojta Beneš, a

prominent Czech educator and later a leader in the Czechoslovak independence movement, came to Cleveland for this purpose in 1914. In a series
of lectures, he argued the necessity of Czech immigrants establishing their
own schools, without which, he warned, Cleveland's Czechs might lose their
identity. Beneš came under attack from *Američan* (a Catholic-leaning paper)
which construed his lectures as fostering divisions within the Czech community and working to halt assimilation of Czechs into American culture.[89]
Sunday schools were still in operation in the 1920s, but it is difficult to gauge
the enthusiasm of the children who attended them.

Education, Culture, and Sokol

In addition to such Czech-language Saturday and Sunday schools, Czech
children of course attended both public and parochial daily schools in large
numbers. In 1916, eighteen of Cleveland's forty-eight grade schools had
enrollments of over one hundred students from Czech-speaking homes.[90]
Each of the Czech Catholic parishes had grade schools attached to them, and
until the 1920s their enrollment consisted overwhelmingly of children from
Czech-speaking families. Indeed, the rationale for establishing several of
these parishes was to provide Czech-language schooling for children of
Catholic families. From 1880 to 1914 there were never fewer than two hundred children enrolled in any of these schools.[91] Children of free-thinking
parents were enrolled in public schools, and some attended the Czech Saturday and Sunday schools as well.[92] This emphasis on education did not
begin in America. The literacy rate of Czechs immigrating from the Austro-
Hungarian Empire during the second half of the nineteenth and the early
part of the twentieth century was the highest of any ethnic group in that
multi-national state. During the period of their mass migration, beginning
in the late 1850s, illiteracy among Czechs ranged from only 1.3% to 1.7% of
the population over fourteen years of age. The Cleveland Foundation's 1915
survey of immigrant school children found that fifty-five percent of Czech
pupils in high school and thirty-six percent of third- through eighth-graders
could read Czech.[93]

Intertwined with the high literacy rate was a high degree of cultural
development and national consciousness among Czechs. Cleveland Czechs
formed their lodges not only to provide insurance against times of crisis and
misfortune, but also to create an alternative to cultural isolation on foreign soil.[94] The lodges helped immigrants, the majority of whom were from
Bohemian villages and towns, ease into Cleveland's alien, urban, industrial

environment by seeking to emulate the culture of the old country. To this end they promoted language, literature, music, theater, recreation, and gymnastics, all of which were in a Czech national mold.

An important component of Czech national consciousness was language and literature. Nineteenth century Czech nationalism had grown out of the linguistic and literary revivals associated with the philological and literary works of Czech scholars. First-generation Czechs in America, determined that their children have access to this tradition through competence in the Czech language, sent them to Czech schools. National halls and church schools had Czech-language libraries. Slovanská Lípa bought books from Bohemia in the 1860s; in response to requests from the Czech community, the Cleveland Public Library established a Czech literature division in 1895.[95] The Czech language was so important that Václav Šnajdr, no friend of the Catholic clergy, praised the Czech readers and grammars authored by Rev. Josef Koudelka for use in Czech Catholic primary schools.[96]

Along with language, theater and music promoted national consciousness in Cleveland's Czech community from its inception. Slovanská Lípa began Cleveland's Czech theater tradition in 1863 with the performance of two Czech plays (the venue being a fire station). The Perun and "Budívoj" societies both originated as theatrical subdivisions of Slovankská Lípa. Budívoj continued to produce plays into the twentieth century. Many of the fraternal, religious, and recreational lodges supported or organized theater productions or musical ensembles, and accordingly equipped their halls with stages. People who worked in factories or offices participated in the production of Czech plays in their free time, among them community leaders like physician Jan Habenicht and lawyer Jan V. Sykora. By 1894 thirteen halls staged Czech plays in Cleveland. Music, too, was something of a national tradition. As early as 1865 Cleveland had a Czech string quartet, and by 1871 a brass band, which in time had many competitors.[97] No major Czech event in Cleveland could be without music, be it vocal, brass band, symphonic, or drum and bugle.

Another characteristic feature of Czech community culture was gymnastics. The most significant gymnastic organization was Sokol (Falcon), which had its inception in Prague in 1862. The Sokol movement fostered national consciousness and unity through physical training and education. Czech immigrants brought this concept with them to America, where the first Sokol lodge was established in St. Louis. This soon led to a national Sokol organization with affiliated units. Sokol came to Cleveland in August 1870 with an organizational meeting in Perun hall, resulting in the founding of Sokol Perun. A second group, Sokol Čech, was founded in 1879, and the two co-existed in uneasy harmony for nine years until Sokol Perun (re-named Sokol Cleveland) disbanded in 1888, bequeathing its property to Sokol Čech.[98]

The Sokol idea did not catch on immediately in Cleveland. Sokol Perun never had more than twenty-five members. Sokol Čech's members were ini-tially subject to ridicule when they trained in the open air along Kingsbury Run. In time, however, Sokol gained wider acceptance, and another unit, Sokol Tyrš (named after one of the Sokol movement's originators), was founded in the 1880s, holding its meetings in the Broadway district. Sokols Čech and Tyrš subsequently merged. The new unit, Sokol Čech-Tyrš, which became known as Sokol Čech, centered its activities in the Broadway neigh-borhood, and eventually built its own hall there in 1893. Sokol Čech also found representation in the patronat of the Bohemian National Hall, al-though its specifications for training facility space within the building were not accepted.[99] In the early twentieth century, costume, an important com-ponent of the Sokol idea, became a contentious issue within the unit. By 1908, many members were unhappy with the blue shirts worn by Sokol Čech. Some preferred red, as worn by Slovene Sokols, and so seceded, form-ing Sokol Havlíček. For many years the two units held merger discussions, finally combining in 1921 with the stipulation that former Čech members could wear blue while former Havlíček members could wear red.[100]

Sokols also sprang up in other Czech neighborhoods. Sokol Nová Vlast was founded on the west side in 1892. In 1907 it cooperated with several other Czech organizations to purchase the Hungarian Hall on Clark Avenue and West 43rd Street. The Quincy-Central neighborhood gained a Sokol, which was named Cleveland, in April 1895. Sokol Cleveland stagnated in the 1901–1909 period, reportedly due to bad financial conditions, an indifferent membership, and city ordinances that resulted in the prohibition of draft beer at their functions. In 1909, just as the unit's women had begun to revive the organization, Sokol Cleveland's host building, the Bohemian-American Hall, burned to the ground. In this case too, the patronat of the Bohemian-American Hall and the Sokol could not agree on plans for the new building, and Sokol Cleveland ended up acquiring its own facility on Quincy Avenue. In the Corlett area a new Sokol Tyrš, originally named Jan Amos Komenský as was the neighborhood's national hall, came into being in 1919. Again, fail-ure to come to agreement with the hall's patronat eventually resulted in Sokol Tyrš opening its own hall at East 131st Street and Melzer in 1927.[101]

Czech women gymnasts work on the uneven parallel bars at a Sokol meet in
Cleveland in the 1930s. WRHS

Cleveland's Sokol units were affiliated with the national organization headquartered in Chicago, and they enthusiastically participated in "slets" (Sokol festivals) held throughout the United States and after 1919 also in Czechoslovakia. The Sokol movement crossed ethnic lines. Indeed, the Sokol idea was not original to the Czechs. In Europe, the German Turnverein pre-dated Sokol by some forty years, and German immigrants established Turn-verein units in Cleveland. Sokol units sometimes borrowed or hired German Turnverein gymnastic instructors, and the two organizations competed in festivals on a fairly regular basis before World War I, one of the largest being a national festival held in Cleveland in 1894.[102]

Cleveland's Czech Sokols also cooperated with similar organizations among other Slavic groups, who had also adopted the Sokol concept. In 1904 Sokol Čech participated in the unveiling ceremony for the Kosciuszko statue in Wade Park, thereby demonstrating affinity with the Polish community. Sokol Čech assisted the Slovaks in establishing a Sokol in 1908. All Czech Sokol units in Cleveland maintained relations with South Slav groups. As mentioned, the Slovenes influenced shirt styles in the Sokol Čech organization. During World War I, Czech, Slovak, Slovene, and Croatian Sokols formed a "Cleveland Slavic Sokol Union."[103]

By the outbreak of World War I there were six Sokol units located throughout the city. While traditional Sokol appealed to free-thinking Czechs (Czech Catholics set up their own Sokol organization), it could not attract segments of the post-1890 immigration. Socialist ideas had spread among workers in Bohemia in the 1860–1890 period, and consequently some of the later immigrants sought organizations espousing socialist principles, which Cleveland Czechs' existing fraternal and gymnastic organizations lacked. In 1903 they organized a local Czech section of the American Socialist Party, Section Ferdinand Lassalle, which had representation in the patronat of the Bohemian-American National Hall by 1906. They also founded a Workers Physical Training Union in 1909, which then merged with Section Ferdinand Lassalle to form DTJ ("Dělnická Tělocvičná Jednota," Workers Gymnastic Union) Ferdinand Lassalle.[104] They believed that workers should belong to and train only with organizations dedicated to their class interests, thus ruling out Sokol, which anyone could join. Affiliation with the Bohemian National Hall, nonetheless, brought the group into contact with non-socialist Czechs, while its status as a section of the socialist Party brought it together with non-Czech Socialists, particularly Germans, who comprised a large percentage of the party's Cleveland membership. A similar organization, DTJ Karl Marx, served the Broadway Czech socialists from 1910 until it disbanded shortly after World War I.[105] During the war both units, faced with the choice of backing the socialists' anti-war stance or supporting the war as a means to the creation of a Czechoslovak state, ultimately opted to support the war.[106]

The Workplace

The economic and social status of Cleveland's Czechs varied over time, as affected by technological and demographic trends in society at large, and also by factors peculiar to the Czech community itself, such as a large nucleus of skilled artisans, a high literacy rate, and the existence of strong freethought and socialist sectors, not to mention the group's relatively early arrival in the city. During the later nineteenth century, the small shops where Czechs worked as skilled craftsmen gave way to large industrial plants employing hundreds or even thousands of semi- or unskilled workers, many of them immigrants, many of them Czechs. And from the beginning, and increasingly in the twentieth century, a few immigrant Czechs, and more often their children, entered the ranks of management and the professions in the city's maturing economy.

The transition from independent artisan to industrial worker could not find a more apt illustration than the changing fortunes of Cleveland's Czech coopers. Originally most were self-employed, or worked for small Czech-owned firms. With the growth of oil refining after 1865, many coopers found employment building barrels in that industry. By the early 1870s the largest employer of coopers in Cleveland was Standard Oil. Initially coopers were skilled craft workers, but technological change caused their status to degenerate quickly in the 1870s. By 1871 wood staves and steel bands for making barrels were machine-cut. Workers were paid by the piece to assemble the barrels, and as Standard Oil grew, workers' pay declined in stages from twenty cents for each barrel assembled in 1872 to ten cents per barrel by 1877. Whole families sometimes worked in the industry, with men assembling about ten to twelve barrels daily while boys made seven or eight. Women, girls, and boys brought the cut bands and wood to the men to assemble. Mass-produced barrel heads and staves were hauled to the assembly point in great quantities. Sometimes the work was dangerous and accidents occurred. One Czech employee in a Standard Oil cooperage, a man named James Bohaslav, had his hand severed when a wagon carrying staves overturned, and the falling staves caused him to lose his balance and catch his hand in the machine where he was cutting heads.[107]

As their wages and status declined, Czech coopers responded positively to efforts by František Skarda and Lev Palda to organize them in late 1874 and early 1875. Skarda and Palda were Czech socialists, leaders of a Czech labor club and editors of *Dělnické Listy,* a socialist-oriented newspaper which began publication in Cleveland in 1875.[108] When Standard announced a further pay cut to nine cents a barrel in April 1877, the coopers went on strike. There were perhaps as many as 1,500 coopers, of whom 1,000 were Czech. Most of the remainder were German or "English," and they, too, struck in April. The workers apparently were ready to return to work for ten cents a barrel, but Standard Oil was not receptive. A fifteen-member strike committee was formed. The strike leaders, in order to strengthen the coopers' position, attempted without success to persuade other trades to go out on strike, going so far as to attempt to foment a general strike in Cleveland. Standard decided to break the strike by resuming production, renovating discarded barrels, and bringing in barrels from other shops in the country. The cooperages, closed since April 19, were reopened on May 2. The coopers continued the strike, but their solidarity cracked when many of the Germans returned to work.[109] Czech free-thinking and Catholic societies both donated money and food to the strikers.[110] As the strike continued and the workers became more desperate, Standard more determined, and city officials more irritated, confrontations erupted between strikers and Cleveland police. At rallies held on Forest and Broadway on May 9 and 10, Skarda, speaking in German and English, and Palda, speaking in Czech, urged the workers to persevere and to persuade their non-striking comrades to join their ranks. Seventy-five more workers joined the strike. Standard then requested that police be sent to clear its entrance gates of pickets. At one gate, where there were both male and female pickets, the police used clubs. At a second gate, blocked mostly by women, the police, presumably reluctant to club women, called in the fire department to spray the women with fire hoses.[111] Samuel Andrews, Standard Oil's co-founder, met with the strike committee on May 12, and a settlement was worked out on Standard Oil's terms. The workers were to return to the shops at the nine cent rate, which the company would seek to raise when business improved. Only men were now allowed to work full time. On May 15 the workers returned, but two hundred of the former strikers were not reinstated because strikebreakers had taken over their jobs.[112] According to Frank Vlchek, the strike decreased the utility of Czech coopers in the mind of John D. Rockefeller, Standard's other co-founder, and he moved the cooperage operations to other areas.[113] Demand for barrels also declined because Standard increasingly used railroad tankers to move its oil. By 1880 there were very few Czech coopers left in Cleveland. Skarda and Palda left Cleveland for New York and Texas, respectively, shortly after the strike's conclusion, but the Czech working class's receptivity to collective action had been demonstrated.

Though not socialist, Václav Šnajdr's *Dennice Novověku* advocated worker militancy and organization among Czech laborers, eight hundred of whom worked for the Cleveland Rolling Mill Company.[114] In the late 1870s and early 1880s increasing numbers of Czechs took up employment in Cleveland's growing steel industry. The rolling and wire mills in Newburgh, an industrial district on the southeast bank of the Cuyahoga River in close proximity to the Broadway area, attracted Czechs to move from the Croton to the Broadway neighborhood. The Cleveland Rolling Mill Company, an iron and steel manufacturer with origins going back to the 1850s, employed five thousand workers by 1880. It had kept abreast of technological change in the industry, with the consequence that its skilled workforce was also giving way to an unskilled one that performed simple but arduous tasks. The skilled workers were primarily British and Irish, but there were also a few Czechs. Most of the unskilled workers were newly arriving Poles and Czechs. Many of the skilled workers joined the Amalgamated Association of Iron and Steel workers and a smaller number joined the Knights of Labor in late 1881 and early 1882. In May union workers made demands including payment on a scale set by their association, a closed shop for skilled workers, and reinstatement of fired union members.[115] The company refused to accept these demands, and the mills shut down on May 10. This gave the company the opportunity to remove skilled workers, whose services had become all but superfluous, and replace them with cheaper, unskilled labor suitable for the newer methods of steel production. On June 2 the company announced that it would be reopening its wire, rail, and blooming mills on a half-time basis, employing unskilled or semi-skilled non-union workers.[116] The strike was on, and Czech workers found themselves on both sides of the picket line.

Of the 800 Czechs working for the Cleveland Rolling Mills when the strike erupted, an indeterminate number went on strike. Certainly not all Czech workers did so, because *Dennice Novověku* reported that on May 25 "several Czechs, not participating in the strike were attacked and had their lunch pails broken by strikers," and Šnajdr editorialized that "Czechs who break solidarity with the workers are a disgrace to the nation." Strikebreakers hired to reopen the mills included 300 to 350 Czechs. Apparently they were challenged by Czech strikers, and 200 of them joined the latter's ranks.

The remaining 150 along with Poles and Hungarians "like a herd of Polish and Hungarian oxen [by] the shouts of the strikers were herded one by one into the factory," wrote Šnajdr.[117]

A major confrontation occurred on June 13 when strikers threw stones at strikebreakers and the police, who then charged the strikers with drawn clubs. Several were arrested, including two Czechs.[118] The strikers, however, were no match for changing technological and labor-supply conditions. As the mills expanded operations during mid-July, it was clear that the union had lost.

Czech participation on both sides in this conflict reflects their transitional role in the immigration process. By 1882 a substantial number had been in Cleveland for over a quarter of a century, and their economic interests put them in league with the British, Irish, and Germans. On the other hand, large numbers of Czechs were continuing to arrive, fleeing conditions in Europe, and along with the growing number of Polish and Hungarian immigrants, they were prepared to go to work in the mills even if it meant throwing their longer-established Czech co-nationals out of work.

The second strike against Chisholm's steel concerns came in the summer of 1885. As a consequence of a series of wage cuts, the unorganized workers, many of whom had been among the unskilled immigrants hired in the midst of the 1882 strike, walked off the job in July. The strike lasted into mid-September, and there were incidents of violence and property destruction.[119] Because of this, Czechs, along with Poles, were labeled by the English-language *Cleveland Press* as "foreign devils," "ignorant and degraded whelps," "the canaille of Europe," "vipers," and "Communistic scoundrels [who] have hoisted the red flag of Agrarianism, Nihilism and Socialism [and who] revel in robberies, bloodshed and arson."[120] The 1885 strikers won a partial victory because at the order of the mayor of Cleveland, the company rescinded the wage cuts in late September, and though it refused to rehire strike leaders, other strikers returned to work.[121]

Cleveland's Czechs, with varied success, attempted to organize their own Czech local unions in various trades. Local unions of Czech carpenters and cabinetmakers were established in the Broadway neighborhood (Local #39) and on the west side (Local #1615).[122] Czech foundry workers formed Local #303, though lack of success—perhaps because foundries operated on a piecework basis, making unionization more difficult—caused it to dissolve in 1914. It regrouped in 1917 as an educational club of Czech and Slovak foundry and core workers.[123]

Czech workers did succeed in organizing Czech-owned bakeries, where Czech employees had been working under medieval conditions reminiscent of those in Czech lands. Sixteen workers organized the "Česká pekařská a cukráská unie, č. 39" (Czech baking and confectioners' union, #39) in 1892. Its first victory, after a three-year struggle, was removal of the requirement that bakery workers needed to board at their employer's shop or home. The union, active only in Czech-owned bakeries, organized nearly one hundred Czech bakers, affiliated with the International Union of Bakery Workers, and by the late 1890s succeeded in reaching an agreement with the city's thirteen Czech-owned bakeries on wages and hours. From then on through World War I, except in 1900, the union signed a yearly agreement with bakery owners each May 1.[124]

When in 1900 the bakery workers failed to agree with the owners, they struck, demanding ten-hour shifts and a pay scale of twelve dollars a week for the two most experienced ranks of workers, and ten dollars a week for the lowest category. As the strike continued, the striking workers attempted to gain sympathy and support from the Czech public. On Saturday, May 12, they marched through the Broadway neighborhood. Leading the parade was a bakery wagon adorned with the slogan "Kupujte dělnický chleb!" (Buy workers' bread!) Parading strikers distributed leaflets publicizing the opening of three workers' cooperative bakeries.[125] These ventures soon collapsed, however, because of managerial inexperience. By 1909 the union had established its own sickness and disability fund.[126] Czech bakery workers were active in Czech cultural, social, and political affairs. They contributed funds toward construction of the Bohemian National Hall in the 1890s, and during World War I actively demonstrated support for the founding of a Czechoslovak state.[127]

The garment and textile industries employed numerous Cleveland Czechs, both as workers and as supervisory and management personnel. In January 1909 workers went on strike at the Joseph & Feiss company, which at that time employed 1,200 people, mostly Slovaks, Poles, Serbs, Magyars, Croatians, and Czechs. Joseph & Feiss was located on West 53rd Street in the west side Czech neighborhood. Its top workers earned twelve dollars a week, regular workers from two and a half to nine dollars a week.[128] Although Joseph & Feiss's management attempted to make the workplace pleasant— for example, by having music played—and thereby increase production, they likewise introduced detailed and, in the view of the workers, onerous regulations. The strike began when the company issued a twenty-one paragraph memorandum laying down a multitude of workplace rules.[129] It required workers to be at their jobs at two minutes before seven A.M., to wear an identification button while on the job, to inform the company of any change in their residence, and so forth. The strike started with the pressers, who walked out and then elected a three-person committee which went to management requesting a raise. Joseph & Feiss granted a wage increase but fired the committee. The pressers stayed out, and the company transferred workers in from other departments. More workers, possibly as many as nine hundred, went on strike. Their strike committee was headed by three people who could speak English, Czech, Magyar, and German.[130] The leaders demanded that the new work regulations be abolished, that wages be increased, and that the fired employees be reinstated. The strikers then voted to join the Union of Clothing Workers, and to hold charity bazaars to build up a strike fund. Joseph & Feiss kept production going, with its foreman and senior workers, many of them Czech, staying on the job.[131] Within a few weeks, a combination of wage increases, lack of worker solidarity, and the presence of hired private police contributed to break the strike.

A second, industry-wide strike of garment workers occurred when the International Ladies Garment Workers' Union attempted to unionize clothing factories in Cleveland.[132] It began in June 1911 when over five thousand workers from several companies walked off the job after owners refused to meet with union leaders and consider their demands. The strike lasted until late October.[133] Meanwhile, the owners maintained production by hiring strikebreakers, which was so successful that *Americké Dělnické Listy* resorted to printing names and addresses in an attempt to shame the strikebreakers, many of them Czech women from the west side. By October 27 the strike was lost, with *Americké Dělnické Listy* reporting that the owners had held together while workers had broken ranks, and decrying the lack of support from the Czech working-class community.[134] Indeed, by 1911 Cleveland Czechs had spread so far over the economic spectrum that maintaining both class and ethnic solidarity was all but impossible. If ethnic and class interests clashed, class interests usually prevailed, as the evolution of the Vlchek Tool Company illustrated.

Frank Vlchek's prolific writings provide a source to the interaction of ethnic and labor relations in Cleveland, specifically in the growing tool industry in the 1890–1920 period. After his arrival in Cleveland, Vlchek worked as a blacksmith for a German who employed only Czechs, and then for an Irish-American with whom he also lived and from whom he acquired fluency in English. Because of difficulties in collecting his pay from this employer, he went to work for a Czech freethinker. Uncertainties of employment and pay here, too, due in part to the depression of 1893, motivated Vlchek to go into business for himself in 1895. Equipped with the experience that he had gained while working for others and perceiving a market need, Vlchek set up business in a specialty that Cleveland's Czechs seemed to monopolize, the sharpening and manufacture of stonecutting tools. As an innovative toolmaker anxious to improve his financial standing, Vlchek made use of newer power-driven technology in his shop and concentrated on producing a few items such as cold chisels. He credited his American neighbor, a Dr. Snow, with helping him acquire technical expertise, and American merchants with encouraging him to produce better products and to improve his own lot in life. Vlchek had a low opinion of fellow Czech blacksmiths, regarding them as a backbiting group. As his firm grew, he hired more workers. While he thought little of his Czech competitors, he did not hesitate to hire Czech workers, whom he employed increasingly in the production of 15- to 20-foot drills for quarrying. His shop, located on Central Avenue in the heart of the Quincy-Central neighborhood, was destroyed by fire in 1909, but he transformed that misfortune into an opportunity by incorporating, issuing stock, and expanding his business. He received help in this from Dr. Snow, from a Jewish merchant, and from a fellow Czech.[135] Relocating a few blocks east on Central, he affected a change from "z kovárny do továrny" (shop to factory).[136] Increasingly, the Vlchek Tool Company, as it was now called, produced specialty tool kits for automobiles. Despite the firm's transformation into a corporation, Vlchek maintained a paternalistic style. He looked upon his Czech workers as his extended family, for instance giving preference to Czech foremen and master workers over employees of other ethnic backgrounds and Yankee bankers alike when he sold or issued stock.

On the other hand, when America's entrance into World War I provided him with expanding market opportunities as well as growing management and labor problems, Vlchek did not allow ethnic solidarity to interfere with economic interest. He traveled to Washington to assess the needs his company could fill, and succeeded in receiving major orders as a defense contractor. The benefit of a larger market for his products was partially offset by the possibility of increased government regulation or takeover of the firm if it was not able to maintain production. Work stoppages and strikes were the principal danger, and the heightened demand for labor provided the occasion. In June 1917 the company was struck. The Brotherhood of Drop Forge Trades was attempting to organize the factory, and when Vlchek discovered that two of his "trusted" workers had signed on with the union, he told them to renounce the union or be fired. When they chose the latter option, a number of other workers, predominantly Czech, walked off the job. The following day, the strikers held a meeting and formulated a list of demands. All fired workers had to be rehired, no one was to be harassed for union activities, and there would be a twenty percent wage increase, plus time and a half overtime and double time for Sunday and holiday work. Vlchek at first refused to negotiate, but his attitude softened slightly when a competing firm, Champion Forge and Machine Company, had to settle their own strike on terms favorable to the workers.[137] He sent a delegation of non-striking workers to the strikers, instructing it to inform them that he was prepared to take all of them back (except for a Latvian named Preedy), and that he would give pay raises to those workers he considered deserving of them.[138] Vlchek then proceeded to humor the strikers and the federal mediator they had been able to bring in, while at the same time taking measures to break the strike.[139] He gave his non-striking and returning workers raises and advertised for strikebreakers in *Szabadság*, Cleveland's Magyar-language newspaper.[140] This enabled production to continue, causing the strike and the union to be broken.[141] Having weathered this crisis, Vlchek ultimately relinquished control of the firm in November 1917 to a board of ten Cleveland financiers, presumably Yankee, but he continued as the company's president and principal policy maker.

The lessons seemed clear to Czech union and socialist adherents: workers needed to be better organized, especially in view of the influx "of Negroes and women into the workplace as shown by several factories here, e.g. Hardware, where there are many more women and Negro workers employed for lower wages than there are white male workers." Without their own union organization in the forge and metalwork industry, Czech workers could not hope to succeed.[142] To a certain extent, the steel workers' strike of 1919 demonstrated the point.

Czech workers in Cleveland played a prominent role in that strike, but they were not organized, as *Americké Dělnické Listy* advocated, into a specifically Czech branch of the steel workers' union. The strike, part of a national movement to organize the industry that had begun in Chicago the previous year, found a positive response among immigrant workers in Cleveland.[143] On September 20, 1919, *Svět* announced that nineteen thousand people would not go to work in the steel mills on Monday the 22nd, and that there would be a mass meeting at a park near the mills to inform workers about strike strategy. Approximately twenty thousand steel workers struck on September 22, and by the next day all production in the steel mills was shut down.[144]

Because the steel companies intended to break the strike by importing and hiring strikebreakers, confrontations were inevitable. Violence occurred on September 23 when picketing strikers confronted strikebreakers. Some incidents had racial overtones.[145] The Amalgamated Association of Iron and Steel Workers had recruited African American workers in Cleveland during World War I, and black workers backed the strike. Many of the strikebreakers, however, were also black, increasing the animosity of white strikers. Nationwide, the industry recruited thousands of African American strikebreakers, with the result that thirty thousand African Americans found employment in the country's steel industry during the three and a half month duration of the strike.[146]

Ethnic rivalries and alliances in fact played out in a number of ways. Striking workers were themselves targets of ethnic hatred in the form of nativist attacks, with opponents of the strike attempting to stir up further opposition by attributing it to immigrants and communists.[147] On the other hand, Czechs, although not organized in a Czech-language branch of the steelworkers' union, used their national origins in order to gain solidarity from workers in other industries. Peter Zeleny of the Carpenters' Council, a Czech local, appeared before a strike rally at Brookside Park to announce the support of his council and urge the strikers to hold out.[148] Eventually, as the importation of strikebreakers allowed production to resume, this strike, too, was broken. *Svět* reported on October 21 that some mills had reopened, including the McKinney mill in the Czech Broadway area. By mid-December the strike was dissipating with no negotiated settlement between industry and the National Organizing Committee of Iron and Steel Workers. Czech and other steel workers in Cleveland would finally gain union contracts in the 1930s.

Other Cleveland industries employing Czechs also experienced labor strife in the immediate post-war period. In the meatpacking industry, centered on the west side in close proximity to the Czech neighborhood, labor disputes found Czechs on both sides of the struggle, as workers or managers. The Amalgamated Meat Cutters and Butchers Workmen of North America, Local #577 of the A.F. of L., between 1919 and 1920 enlisted 1,500 Cleveland workers including many Czechs.[149] In the midst of the steel strike, 2,500 slaughterhouse workers, many of them Czech, struck two major meatpacking houses and a number of smaller ones, demanding union recognition and higher wages. When the companies met the wage demands halfway, the strikers, meeting in the Clark Avenue Czech Sokol Hall, voted on October 17 to call off the strike. In March 1920, a strike erupted again when workers charged that the companies had not kept their promises on wages. Nine hundred workers, many of them Czech, struck the Swift meatpacking operation, but in the end returned to work without achieving their demands.[150] Unionization of meatpacking would not occur until a decade and a half later, while Czechs would continue to enter the ranks of management in the industry in ever-increasing numbers.

The general failure of the unions to win favorable settlements in 1919 and early 1920 was one important factor in the weakening of labor's position relative to industry in the 1920s. Two other factors also played a role. There was a significant economic recession during the fall of 1920, with the resultant unemployment crippling labor in its attempt to pressure industry. Secondly, many Cleveland industries used the techniques of "welfare capitalism" during the 1920s. The Vlchek Tool Company, for example, created a social welfare department. It insured workers against job-related accidents and also provided them with life insurance. The factory worked on a system of bonuses. When sales were good, which was the case throughout most of the 1920s, workers received bonuses; when sales were bad, they did not. Vlchek hired a Czech-American by the name of Emil Bartunek to set up a school for the factory's workers, with courses in English, civics, and how to deal with the American bureaucracy. Bartunek encouraged immigrant workers to become American citizens; over one hundred Vlchek employees did so in the 1920s.[151]

While the preponderance of Cleveland's Czechs were workers, there were also many who were not, especially in the second and later generations. The Czechs' high level of education helped enable them to move out of the ranks of the working class. Even in the nineteenth century, many Czechs were self-employed shopkeepers, tavern keepers, contractors, or service personnel; others were foremen or managers in industries such as steel, garment-making, or meatpacking, and still others were city employees. After World War I, many workers' children moved out of their parents' socio-economic class into the professions, and often moved into the ethnically more amorphous suburbs, losing touch with the Czech community. If industrialist Frank Vlchek epitomized a "self-made man" of the immigrant generation, the life and career of lawyer and political figure Harry Payer served to illustrate the experience of the upwardly mobile second generation.

Born in the Broadway neighborhood in 1875, Harry was the son of František Payer, an immigrant from the Písek area. The elder Payer was active in Czech fraternal and free-thought circles and had involved himself in several entrepreneurial enterprises, such as the attempt to start a Czech brewery. Payer's mother was the daughter of Jan Kříž, who had immigrated to Cleveland in the first wave of Czechs and operated a small cooperage. The Payer family valued education. Harry and his two sisters received public schooling through high school, and the sisters then went on to higher education and became educators in the Cleveland school system, with one also active in the Y.M.C.A.'s Americanization program. Harry attended Adelbert College in Cleveland, receiving his B.A. in 1897, and then the local Baldwin University Law School, where he earned a law degree in 1899.[152] In 1902 he married a non-Czech schoolteacher named Florence Graves. The young Payer also became active in Cleveland politics as a Democrat. From 1901 to 1907 he was assistant solicitor for the city of Cleveland, and he played a prominent role in the mayoral campaigns of the reformist Democrat Tom Johnson.[153] In 1907 he embarked on his private law career, becoming senior partner in the firm of Payer, Winch, Minshall & Karch.

As he scaled the professional ladder, his ties to the Czech community apparently weakened. He lived in suburban Cleveland Heights, and was not active in Czech fraternal life. But in another way, he identified with his Czech roots. He played a prominent role in supporting the Czechoslovak movement for independence during World War I, and developed a close association with Tomáš and Jan Masaryk.[154] He was president of the Czechoslovak Club of Cleveland during the war, and after its conclusion became chairman of the Czechoslovak Chamber of Commerce in Cleveland. In 1920 the Czechoslovaks feted him and his family in Prague for his role in the Czechoslovak liberation movement. After the election of Franklin D. Roosevelt in 1932, he held several positions in the United States government, including assistant secretary of state, and special counsel on foreign trade matters for the Reconstruction Finance Corporation. After the collapse of the Czechoslovak Republic in 1938 and 1939 he again worked for Czechoslovak independence, and hosted Czechoslovak cultural and political leaders including Jan Werich and Jiří Voskovec.[155] Although few could match the level of his success, a number of other Cleveland Czechs who moved up in the professional or business world conformed to the Payer model in that they moved out of the local Czech community but still identified with their Czech culture and heritage.

Politics

Cleveland's Czechs were politically engaged at all levels from the time that they formed an identifiable community in the city. They sought and eventually gained representation on the city council and the school and library boards, and by the 1870s had sufficient political leverage to obtain neighborhood improvements and city jobs. The first gentile Czech United States congressman, John Babka, was elected from Cleveland in 1918.[156] Several factors enabled the Czechs to exert political influence. The group's relatively large size as early as the 1870s, and concentration of their numbers in defined areas of the city provided them with a geographic power base. Also, their early arrival in Cleveland gave them a head start with respect to other east central European ethnic groups in nailing down claims on municipal offices and services. Czechs generally affiliated with the Democratic party irrespective of the Catholic-freethought division, although some adherents of both factions voted Republican, and a small portion of freethinkers voted Socialist.

The rapid growth of Cleveland's Czech community in the early 1870s led in April 1871 to Czechs petitioning city council to publish its proceedings in Czech.[157] The fifth signature on the petition was that of Ferdinand Svoboda, who in 1875, as a Democrat, became the first Czech elected to Cleveland's City Council. During Svoboda's two years in office, he proposed that city councilmen be paid per session or year for their services (apparently a revolutionary proposal at that time), worked to expand Cleveland's public bathing facilities, and had some success in getting the city to upgrade streets, sidewalks, and public services in his Ward 14.[158] The city's largest newspaper, the *Cleveland Leader,* which supported the Republican party, was uncomplimentary: "Mr. Svoboda is called the Henry Clay of the Council. There is more clay than Henry in his eloquence, however."[159] After Svoboda's departure from the council no Czechs served there until Frank Karda was elected, also from Ward 14, in 1882. The record shows that thirteen Czechs served on the council between 1875 and 1929. With the exception of Anton Sprosty, a Republican, all were Democrats.[160]

In elections where ethnic and party loyalty conflicted, results were unpredictable. In a city council race in 1903 in Ward 16, which incorporated the Croton neighborhood, many Czech voters and *Dennice Novéhŏku* supported the non-Czech Democrat Erdman against the Czech Republican Dolezal, even though the Czech Democratic paper, *Volnost,* supported the latter.[161] Another test of ethnic loyalty occurred when Czechs ran against non-Czech Socialist party candidates. *Americké Dĕlnické Listy* usually endorsed the straight Socialist ticket for city offices, generally consisting mostly of candidates with German, Jewish, or English backgrounds, but deviated from this in the heavily Czech Ward 16 on several occasions. In the 1909 elections, when both the Democrat incumbent Zinner and the Republican challenger Sprosty were Czech, it refrained from endorsing a Socialist candidate.[162] In 1917, Charles Kadlecek, a popular Czech-speaking Democrat, carried Ward 13 (the Broadway area) where Czech Socialists, in the midst of interethnic harmony promoted by the effort on behalf of a Czechoslovak state, again did not endorse the opposing Socialist.[163] Czech Socialists later attempted to win election to the city council when Josef Martinek, editor of *Americké Dělnické Listy*, ran in the 1920s, but with the diminution of nationalistic fervor following the war, Czech Democrats would not return the favor and abandon their party to vote for him. Not surprisingly, Martinek did not win.

The Czechs' political influence helped them find employment in municipal departments. The police and fire departments hired them in significant numbers. In 1869 there were already Czechs on the police force; by the 1890s Czechs held nine positions there and twelve in the fire department.[164] Cleveland's growth during the early twentieth century witnessed corresponding expansion of the police force and fire department, and increasing numbers of Czechs found employment there. By June 1918 there were 45 firemen and 105 (of 800) policemen with Czech names.[165] Czechs also held administrative positions in public safety. As early as 1891, John Vanek was Director of Police Security, and in the immediate pre-World War I years Anton Sprosty became Director of Public Security. By April 1918 twelve Czechs had positions of rank on the police force.[166]

Czechs attained other offices and positions as well. When the Cleveland school board was elected from districts in the late nineteenth century, Czechs placed two of their number on it, but after electoral reform mandated elections at large no Czech succeeded in winning a seat.[167] In the early 1890s the city's accreditation commission for teachers had a Czech member, and Václav Šnajdr's election to the library board directly influenced the Cleveland Public Library's decision to create a Bohemian literature division in 1895.[168] During Tom Johnson's mayoralty (1901–1909), John Prucha became chief of the Department of Public Welfare's Immigration Bureau.[169] Czechs also found employment in the city engineer's office, the health department, water works, division of parks, division of streets, and as teachers in the public schools.[170]

John Babka's election to the United States Congress in 1918, although not strictly speaking a manifestation of city politics, demonstrated the Czechs' ability to work together across confessional lines within their ethnic community in Cleveland and to coalesce with other groups within the Democratic party. Babka was a second-generation Czech Catholic from the Broadway neighborhood. He began as a foundry worker, but put himself through evening law school, passed the bar, became a lawyer, and entered politics. He served as an assistant prosecuting attorney for Cuyahoga

County, and in 1918 ran successfully for Congress from the 21st District, which included several of Cleveland's Czech neighborhoods. Babka ran on a pro-Wilson, anti-German, win-the-war platform, and did not hesitate to emphasize his Czech origins. Speaking in Czech, he addressed meetings in Czech halls, and advertisements, editorials, and endorsements appeared in *Svět* and *Američan.* He served only one term, however. Along with numerous other congressional Democrats, he was defeated in the Republican sweep of 1920 and returned to the practice of law.[171]

Conflicts and Causes

Various issues and causes brought Czechs into conflict and cooperation with other groups. Generally, Czechs sought to cooperate with other Slavic nationalities on issues of ethnic import, and came into conflict primarily with Magyars and, especially during World War I, Germans. Many Czech organizations labeled themselves as "Čechoslovanský", that is, Czecho*slav,* to emphasize their Slavic identity and align themselves with other Slavic nationalities in order to strengthen their status vis-à-vis the Irish, Germans, Magyars, Yankees, and, in the twentieth century, African Americans.[172]

Conflict with other groups at its basest level consisted of brawls, riots, and occasionally murders. Early Czech settlers suffered ridicule and even beatings at the hands of English-speaking Americans. According to *Česká osada,* "Americans weren't accustomed to seeing these type of people . . . barefoot women with scarves. . . . American youth threw stones at Czech children when they went to town. . . . Czechs were regarded like an Indian tribe."[173] Ethnic gatherings, especially out-of-doors, sometimes generated antagonism from other nationalities. A Czech lodge picnic on the outskirts of Cleveland in 1899 attracted some Irish curiosity seekers, leading to an altercation. By the time it was over, a Czech man, the marshal of the picnic, had been shot dead.[174] Sometimes interethnic battles took place in a sanctioned forum: the boxing ring. Advertisements appeared in April 1918 announcing a boxing match between James Freyhouf, "Czech Champion," and "Hungarian Champion" Charles Oackly.[175] (In addition to ethnic pride, a two hundred dollar side bet between the participants was at stake.)

On another level, even seemingly minor local issues had the potential to serve as arenas in which the conflicts of Europe were fought, with words if not with fists or guns. In Cleveland, one of the best-known examples of this was the 1902 battle over the Kossuth statue, which pitted Slavic nationalities against a Magyar proposal to erect a monument to Lajos Kossuth in the center of Cleveland.[176] Although Czechs, whose homeland was not in the Hungarian part of the Habsburg Empire, did not feel the same intensity of bitterness toward Hungarians and Kossuth as did the Slovaks and Croatians, they joined in the opposition in a show of Slavic solidarity. Twelve years later, with the onset of World War I, the fight for freedom was taken up in earnest. If the Kossuth statue affair brought old-world issues home to Cleveland's ethnic communities, the possibility that Slavic lands could break away from Austria-Hungary during the course of the war drew these communities, including the Czechs, into the conflicts of the old world not only symbolically, but in very real ways.

For Czechs, the struggle to form a Czechoslovak state overcame intra-community rivalries. It contributed to a rapprochement between free-thinkers and Catholics that carried over into the post-war years.[177] Besides bringing Czechs of different political and religious views together, the common desire for liberation from Austria-Hungary led to cooperation with Slovaks, Serbs, Croatians, and Slovenes. (Since Poland was partitioned among countries fighting on both sides in the war, Poles were in a somewhat different situation and did not align themselves as closely with those seeking to dissolve Austria-Hungary.)

In 1915, free-thinking Czechs formed a national umbrella organization to coordinate the activities of the numerous smaller Czech organizations in promoting the cause first, of Czech relief, and then, of independence. This was the Bohemian National Alliance (České Národní Sdružení). A key meeting of free-thinking leaders from the United States' major Czech settlements took place in Cleveland in March 1915. At this meeting, goals and procedures for the Alliance were agreed to, and the organization's name formally adopted.[178] Although the organization located its headquarters in Chicago, a Cleveland Alliance bureau was set up, which soon expanded to include representatives from thirty-four free-thought organizations and lodges.[179]

Cleveland Alliance organizers were anxious to recruit Czech socialists into their movement. Initially, several obstacles stood in the way. In the Czech homeland, the Czech Social Democratic Party, with which Cleveland's socialists maintained close links, had gone on record at its Eleventh Party Congress in 1913 as favoring the Czechs' continuing association in a democratized and federalized Austria-Hungary. It followed an Austrophile policy until September 1917.[180] Closer to home, Cleveland's socialist and free-thought newspapers had recently engaged in a series of polemics. Also, the tendency of socialists to form separate fraternal, cultural, and gymnastic organizations did not promote understanding between the two groups. The

American Socialist Party opposed the war, and Cleveland's Czech socialists initially did not disagree with that position. Josef Martinek, as editor
of *Americké Dělnické Listy* and *Právo*, criticized Austria for its repressive
actions against Czechs and other Slavs, but also voiced opposition to Tsarist
Russia and its oppression of Ukrainians and Poles.[181] This placed him and
his comrades apart from the many Czech-Americans who looked upon
Tsarist Russia as the Czechs' Slavic savior.

Czech-American socialists' statements and actions regarding support for
any Czech national effort were mixed until the spring of 1915. By stages,
Cleveland's Czech socialists drifted into cooperation with their free-thinking, bourgeois co-nationals. They called on Austrian subjects living in Cleveland to ignore the Austrian consul's call to Austro-Hungarians to register
for conscription. Resisting the blandishments of the local Austrian consulate, Martinek in April 1915 printed an editorial in support of Czech independence and alignment with the Bohemian National Alliance, though he
soon made it clear that for socialists, political independence alone would not
suffice: "In a free country, we want free people." Cleveland socialists were
soon publicly cooperating with the Alliance and were officially represented
there after the latter's reorganization in September. This cooperation lasted
until well after the conclusion of the war.[182]

As the Bohemian National Alliance gained support from Czech free-
thought and socialist groups, it also sought to cooperate with other Slavic
nationalities. The Cleveland Slavic Sokol Union, uniting Czechs, Slovaks,
Slovenes, and Croatians, had been formed in 1914 to provide relief to Slavic
peoples in Austria-Hungary who were suffering due to the war, but by 1915
it was calling for destruction of the Habsburg Empire and the establishment
of independent Czecho-Slovak and Yugo-Slav states.[183] To this end the
Union organized "Slavic Days," which served as propaganda and fund-
raising events, in part designed to demonstrate antipathy towards Austria-
Hungary and sway the American public. Two of these gatherings took place
at Grays Armory, the first in April 1915. The mayor of Cleveland, Newton D.
Baker, was invited to greet the leaders and musical groups from the Czech,
Slovak, Slovenian, and Croatian communities appearing at the event. The
Slavic Day celebration in May 1916 drew an even larger range of participants: the Slavonic Sokol Union, the Bohemian National Alliance, the Slovak League, Slovene and Croatian organizations, and also Serbs and even
Poles. Though the event was intended as a show of Slavic solidarity, according to a Czech account one Polish speaker proved somewhat of a loose can-
non, informing the audience that the Poles needed help from no one and
intended to fight for freedom in their own manner.[184]

By July 1915 the Bohemian National Alliance was working in conjunction with the movement being established in Europe by Tomáš Masaryk for the creation of an independent state. Because Masaryk's movement envisioned a state of Czechs and Slovaks, the Alliance sought cooperation and contact with Slovak organizations. In October the Alliance and the Slovaks' umbrella organization, the Slovak League, held a joint meeting in Cleveland.[185] This was the beginning of a series of cooperative efforts between these two nationalities, and their relationship remained good until 1919.[186]

Among the last of Cleveland's Czech organizations to fall into line on behalf of a Czech state were the Catholic churches and lodges. Statements by Czech-American prelates, such as the one made by Josef Koudelka (by 1914 serving as a bishop in Wisconsin) to the newspaper *Staatszeitung* in support of Austria-Hungary shortly after the outbreak of the war, seemed to indicate Catholic satisfaction with the status quo.[187] The Alliance, nonetheless, sought Catholic support both nationally and locally, having concluded that Catholic participation was vital to their movement. Alliance leaders worried that Austrian publicists would seek to attribute the Czechoslovak independence movement solely to "unbelievers, rebels, and dissatisfied people whereas the Catholics are satisfied and do not demand severance from Austria."[188] Cleveland Alliance leaders were heartened when they heard in July 1916 that Hynek Dostal, a Czech Catholic editor, had declared that Czechs would be better off under Russia than Austria. This statement came during a meeting at Our Lady of Lourdes. Consequently, the Alliance sent three representatives to visit Oldřich Zlámal, the recently installed priest of Our Lady of Lourdes parish, to invite him and his parishioners to participate in the work of the Alliance. Although Rev. Zlámal was sympathetic, he refused to commit himself before consulting with Cleveland's other Czech priests. He found that Rev. Hynek of St. Wenceslaus was pro-Habsburg, Rev. Červený of St. Procop was for a high degree of Czech autonomy under the Habsburgs, and that second-generation Czechs Rev. Hroch of St. John Nepomucene and Rev. Becek of St. Adalbert were politically naive about the situation in Europe.[189]

Despite the lukewarm attitude of the Czech clergy, Rev. Zlámal and likeminded Catholics moved to organize on behalf of Czech liberation. In November 1916, Rev. Zlámel published an article in the Lourdes parish paper stating his reasons for wishing to cooperate with the Bohemian National Alliance, and subsequently, at a meeting at Rev. Hynek's parish residence, the Catholic leadership decided to support the independence movement. In December representatives of Catholic lodges and societies agreed to transform the Cyril-Methodius Society, which Czech Catholics had established as a relief organization for the homeland, into an organization with political goals. In January 1917 they decided to affiliate with a Catholic organization headquartered in Chicago, the National Union of Czech Catholics (Národní Svaz Českých Katolikú). The National Union remained organizationally apart from the Bohemian National Alliance, partly, it was said, because Catholics did not want freethinkers to obtain all the credit in the event that their cause prevailed. In any case, the two organizations worked well together.[190]

In Cleveland, the cooperation of freethinkers and Catholics reaped substantial success. Their activities included fund raising, political agitation and lobbying for the recognition of Czechoslovakia by the United States, and mobilizing Czech Americans to work and contribute to their cause.[191] In 1917 the Alliance staged a bazaar in order to raise money in Cleveland. While the National Union of Czech Catholics did not officially participate in the bazaar, it encouraged Catholics to attend, and several Catholic societies donated money to it. The event, in which the Slovak League also participated, raised $30,000.[192] During the summer of that year the Alliance and the National Union both organized picnics and national celebrations in the public parks, taking care to cooperate and coordinate their efforts.

The Alliance and the National Union jointly levied a "National Tax" (Národní daň) in late 1917 and again in late 1918. In Cleveland, the two groups compiled a list of every Czech household and organization and sent teams out across the city to collect money. Each team consisted of one Catholic and one freethinker, the theory being that prospective donors could not then turn the collectors away because they were of the wrong persuasion. These efforts raised $18,000 in 1917, and over $41,000 in 1918 when as many as 8,000 individuals and organizations contributed. Even on the west side, where Father Cerveny of St. Procop's parish refused to support the National Union in this endeavor, Czech Catholics worked independently to collect money, which they sent to National Union headquarters in Chicago.[193]

Czech-Slovak cooperation continued. In September 1917, and again early in 1918, the Alliance, the National Union, and the Slovak League met together in Cleveland. The agenda included recruitment of Czechs and Slovaks into the Czechoslovak Legion, and formation of the Czechoslovak National Council. Cleveland Czechs and Slovaks also staged joint public events during 1918, notably a mass meeting at Engineers Hall where national leaders spoke about the Czechoslovak movement world-wide.[194]

The Alliance and the National Union also strove to demonstrate their support of the United States. *Svĕt, Ameriĉan,* and *Americké Dĕlnické Listy* all carried advertisements and articles urging their readers to buy Liberty Bonds. Czech civic leader D. J. Zinner spoke publicly before both Czech and English-speaking audiences to promote the bonds. In 1918 the Alliance and the National Union planned a Czech fair to be held from July 4 through July 7, but when Cleveland's War and Americanization Committee "requested" ethnic groups' participation in an Independence Day celebration, the Czech organizations surrendered the first day of their fair at considerable financial loss.[195]

The socialists' participation in the Bohemian National Alliance, and then their support for the American war effort, caused some dissension within their ranks. Nonetheless, although the American Socialist Party had passed a resolution opposing the war, Martinek and a majority of Cleveland Czech socialists backed American participation.[196] At the same time, they did not lose sight of the struggle for workers' rights, as demonstrated by their support of a strike against the Vlchek Tool Company. While comrades-in-arms on the national issue, Vlchek and Martinek were antagonists on economic matters.

By the time of the First World War, Czechs had gained sufficient political influence in Cleveland to ensure passage of Councilman Charles Kadlecek's resolution urging President Wilson to support independence for the Czechs and Slovaks. This was in 1918 after the President had made his "Fourteen Points" speech, which called only for autonomy for the nationalities of Austria-Hungary.[197]

Also in 1918, Tomáš Masaryk visited Cleveland. By this time Masaryk's independence movement, which commanded a significant number of fighting troops, had gained conditional recognition from the Allies. After arriving in the United States in May, Masaryk traveled on to a number of cities. Cleveland Czech leaders made elaborate preparations for his visit. When his train arrived on the morning of June 15 delegations of Americans, Czechs, Slovaks, Slovenes, and Serbs met him. He spoke on "America and Small Nations" at the Cleveland City Club and was honored by a reception and, on the following day, a parade down Euclid Avenue to Wade Park which drew fifty thousand people as either participants or spectators, making it one of the largest Slavic events in Cleveland's history. Cleveland's Czech organizations turned out in force to march in the parade, and were joined by organizations representing numerous eastern European ethnic groups. At the front of the parade, a mounted guard of Sokol members and American soldiers of Czech and Slovak descent escorted Masaryk and other dignitaries. During the program at Wade Park, the mayor of Cleveland, Bohemian National Alliance and National Union of Czech Catholic leaders,

Czech and Slovak clergy, and several American army officers joined Masaryk on the tribune. In the evening there was a large assembly with speeches in Czech and English.Masaryk himself addressed the audience in both languages.[198] In terms of visibility this event was the high-water mark for Cleveland's Czech community.

The 1920s

Though the activity and visibility of Cleveland's Czech community was at its peak during the World War I period, by the war's end there were indications of an incipient decline. Geographic concentration in several neighborhoods was beginning to dissolve; members of the second, third, and fourth generation could not speak Czech; some Czech organizations began conducting their business in English; attendance at lodge functions decreased; United States immigration restrictions effectively cut off the infusion of new immigrants; and the Americanization process, which had been intensified during the war, reinforced an already extant trend. This is not to say that the 1920s witnessed a sharp decline in Czech national consciousness. Czech organizations continued to function. National parishes did not close their doors. Czech music and theatrical societies gave performances, fraternal lodges met, Czech-language Saturday and Sunday schools held classes, Czech-language newspapers published, Czech festivals and outings took place. But the nationalistic euphoria which accompanied Masaryk's visit and the creation of the Czechoslovak state would never again be duplicated.

Two Czech neighborhoods were starting to disappear in the 1920s. Croton fell victim to industrialization, railroads, and general blight; a large influx of African Americans was rapidly changing the ethnic character of the Quincy-Central area. Although Broadway preserved its Czech identity, this was increasingly mixed with Polish and other elements. The west side, too, retained a Czech presence, but Czechs were moving from both these neighborhoods to the southern and eastern suburbs.

By 1940 Croton was practically a neighborhood of the past. A decision in 1919 to route most passenger trains to the Cleveland Union Terminal, which increased rail traffic through Croton, hastened the replacement of residential areas by industry and railroad yards, a trend which had already started before World War I.[199] Indicative of the neighborhood's decline was the consecration in 1923 of a new Czech national parish, St. Wenceslaus Catholic Church, in the suburb of Maple Heights. Its parent church, St. Wenceslaus on Broadway and East 37th Street, was rapidly losing members as they moved to the outlying districts. By 1940, though some of the old Czech public buildings remained, there were no more than three or four people of Czech extraction in the Croton neighborhood.[200]

During World War I, as industrial production increased and immigration from Europe was cut off, large numbers of African Americans migrated from the south to take jobs in northern industrial cities like Cleveland, where they tended to settle in the older, central parts of the city. As African Americans moved into the Quincy-Central neighborhood, whites moved away. By 1930 the neighborhood was more than seventy percent black.[201] Frank Vlchek wrote that he left a very comfortable eight-room house on Central Avenue for suburban Shaker Heights in 1918, and that many other Czechs moved out as well.[202] Writing in 1929, authors of a history of Sokol Čech noted that it was only a matter of time until Sokol Cleveland's hall at East 89th and Quincy would close, since the neighborhood was becoming black rather than Czech.[203] African American settlement was also changing the ethnic make-up of the adjacent Corlett/Mt. Pleasant area, although there was a Czech presence until after World War II.

The conclusion of World War I was itself also a factor contributing to dissipation of the Czech community. While cooperation between freethinkers and Catholics during the war led to a more or less permanent reconciliation, their organizations had done their jobs so well that it was difficult to return to normal activities. Indeed, both the National Union of Czech Catholics and the Bohemian National Alliance questioned whether they should continue to exist. They decided to do so, but increasingly confined themselves to relief and fund raising for the benefit of the old country. At the same time, the good relations that they had established with the Slovak League crumbled amid disputes between Czechs and Slovaks over Slovak status within Czechoslovakia.

Like their bourgeois co-nationals, Cleveland Czech socialists also experienced a difficult time of transition. They had to both heal the rift with the American Socialist Party caused by their pro-war stance, and deal with the communist-socialist split of 1919–1920. They had reasonable success, forming a Czech Socialist Organization of Men dedicated to "the platform of the American Socialist Party as had been formulated at its last Congress in May 1920."[204] Nonetheless, their organizational life reflected a struggle for survival during the 1920s, difficult years for the socialist movement in general in the United States.

Czech cultural leaders recognized the serious problems they faced. B. E. Ptak, writing in 1929, analyzed Cleveland's Czech cultural institutions.[205]

To begin with, two or three hours a week of attendance in Czech-language schools was insufficient for children raised in America to learn Czech. He urged parents to support preservation of the tongue by speaking it in the home. As for the program of the Sokols, Ptak suggested that instructors remember that according to the original Czech Sokol philosophy, physical training was not meant merely to produce accomplished gymnasts, but aimed ultimately to educate youth toward Czech national consciousness. He viewed Czech music as an important element in preserving Czech national identity because it drew on themes from the Czech past and kept the language alive. He thought Czech theater significant because it represented life in Czech villages and towns, and hoped that Sundays would continue to find audiences attending Czech theatrical performances. Finally, he pointed to the impressive literary resources built up by or at the behest of Cleveland's Czech community, notably the Czech literature division in the Cleveland Public Library and the large number of Czech book collections in societies and lodges.

Yet despite these many cultural and educational resources, Ptak concluded pessimistically. In his analysis, Cleveland's Czech immigrants were so busy developing institutions to promote ethnic consciousness that they concentrated on organizational infrastructure while neglecting to train their own descendants to carry on the lodges' and societies' work and traditions. As an example, he pointed to Czech theater, which the older generation actively and attentively patronized, while the youth, though they attended performances, were noisy and inattentive. Ptak attributed this in part to the fact that they came mainly to attend the dances that followed the theater productions, and also, more significantly, to the fact that they did not know Czech and therefore could not follow the plays' dialogues. He blamed his own generation for failing to pass on the language.

Many Czech institutions were becoming Americanized. While Catholic churches continued to have Czech-speaking priests, the use of English increased because younger people did not understand Czech. Lack of interest made it difficult for Catholic schools to keep the Czech language as part of their curricula. Parish publications included a greater percentage of English language articles and advertisements; individual advertisements sometimes used both languages.[206] Many lodges, Catholic and free-thinking alike, either switched to English or established "junior" branches in which the official language was English.

A subtle change in attitude had been evolving, as was reflected in some of the societies founded after 1900. The Organization of Czech Settlers was established in November of 1909, in part to help its members deal with American conditions and increase their self-reliance, and in part to bring together the "old" Czech settlers scattered throughout Cleveland.[207] Its first major task, in 1910, was the production of a flyer instructing its members how to respond to the upcoming U.S. census. The authors recommended that people simply state their nationality as Czech, since the census officer would certainly not "break his head" trying to understand the finer points of central European geopolitics, but likely would lump Moravians and Silesians together with German Austrians and thus undercount the Czech nationality.[208] While social activities made up a large part of its program, the Czech Settlers group also acted as an advocate for its membership vis-à-vis the broader American community.

Another organization, which had a similar purpose but appealed to a slightly different clientele, was the Bohemian-American Club, founded in 1912. It also sought to bring people scattered across Cleveland into a single recreational, educational, and mildly political organization, but unlike the Czech Settlers, the club kept its minutes in English, and its membership combined "Americans of Bohemian parentage" and "Bohemian born Americans." It existed to "encourage and foster among its members the use of the Bohemian language and to assist in the advancement of Bohemian art, music and literature and in the general uplift of the Bohemian race."[209]

The ability to use the English language in daily life—which Czech leaders, Catholic, free-thinking, and socialist alike, recognized as a necessary skill for members of their community if they were to prosper in America—also contributed to the gradual disintegration of Czech national consciousness. Cleveland's government and schools sponsored evening English-language schools in Czech neighborhoods, and many employers, like the Vlchek Tool Company, offered instruction in English to their employees. Czech leaders and publicists urged people to take advantage of such opportunities. In September 1917 *Americké Dělnické Listy* printed an article entitled "Utčte se anglicky!" ("Learn English!")[210] In 1918 *Svět* suggested that Czech immigrants dissatisfied with conditions in Cleveland were partly to blame for their own problems if they had neglected to learn English. The paper promised that knowledge of English would gain the immigrant more respect, make life more satisfactory, and indeed change his whole outlook.[211] But the notion that English was a necessity also carried the implication that Czech was a luxury in America.

Ironically, the Czech organizations' efforts to expand or at least maintain membership by switching to English or establishing English-speaking units

to attract second and later generation Czechs and thereby keep Czech culture alive in America was in the end self-defeating, since the foundation of
Czech national feeling was language. Cleveland's Czech-language DTJ units,
for example, established English-language branches and youth organizations in the early 1920s. By the end of the decade, *Americké Dělnické Listy*
had an English-language section, and the DTJ was publishing its constitution
in two languages and conducting classes where students could learn "how
to talk, write and read" the now-forgotten "language of their fathers."[212]

To stave off the decline of Czech, freethinkers still attempted to maintain
Saturday and Sunday schools, and even founded new lodges. As late as 1935
free-thinking lodges in Cleveland still supported Czech free-thought schools
in the Broadway, Mt. Pleasant, and west side neighborhoods, which reportedly had six hundred students. In April 1930 twenty-eight Czechs established
a new branch of the Association of Czech Freethinkers in Mt. Pleasant and
named it Václav Šnajdr.[213] This branch helped to promote the free-thought
school in its district.

Another vector of change in the Czech community was the upward mobility of its members, which tended to go hand-in-hand with acculturation.
Although Cleveland's Czech settlement had always had its doctors, lawyers,
and journalists, their numbers had increased so that by the 1920s even a
mainstream newspaper was noting that over the course of the past fifty years
Czechs had produced more than their share of these and other professionals.[214] The Bohemian Lawyers' Club, founded in 1932, had its headquarters
in a downtown office building rather than in a neighborhood national hall,
and one of its goals was to enrich America with Bohemian culture rather
than simply to perpetuate the latter.[215] The Independent Business Men's
Association, founded in 1933 with 350 members "to better conditions for the
independent Czech dealer," did not even have the words "Czech" or "Bohemian" in its name.[216]

The decade of the 1920s thus witnessed a trend whereby Cleveland's
Czechs continued to maintain their identity, but the "American" in the term
Czech- or Bohemian-American was acquiring more relative weight. Loss of
language, pressure of Americanization through schools and official culture,
intermarriage with other groups, dying-off of the immigrant generation,
severing of the immigration flow, upward mobility, and movement to the
suburbs, contributed to a gradual melting of the settlement.[217] Although
Cleveland's Czechs could claim in 1930 that there were over 100,000 "Czecho-
slovaks" in the city, many of these were Slovaks, or members of the third,
fourth, or even fifth generations among whom Czech national feeling was

often weak at best. Increasingly, Czech ethnic consciousness was focused on food, music, gymnastic meets, and lodge and church anniversaries and not on political or economic issues. The growth of African American settlement on the borders of Czech neighborhoods tended to increase a sense of commonalty with other European-American ethnic groups, such as the Poles, Croatians, Serbs, Slovenes, Slovaks, and even the Magyars, with whom they were in close proximity. This ultimately led to fusion into a white ethnic identity, as east European ethnic groups in Cleveland continued to retreat before the advance and growth of African American population and eventually political power. Conflict and cooperation among white East European nationality groups in the 1890–1930 period gave way after World War II to conflict and cooperation between European- and African Americans.

Notes

1. See Tomáš Čapek, *Naše Amerika* (Prague, 1926), 152, 153, 625, 626; Josef Polišenskí, ed., Začiatky českej a slovenskej emigracie do USA: Česká a slovenská robotnicka emigracia v USA v období I. internacionaly (Bratislava, 1970), 142.

2. *Česká osada* a její spolkový život v Cleveland, O. (Cleveland, 1895), 26.

3. Polišenský, Začiatky, 23.

4. Václav Šnajdr, "Cleveland a jeho Čehové," Amerikán: Národní Kalendář, I (1878), 94.

5. *Česká osada*, 26.

6. Šnajdr, "Cleveland," 94.

7. The Annual Reports of the Department of Government of the City of Cleveland (Cleveland, 1874), 422; (1878), 348; (1883), 868; (1891), 559; (1892), 710; (1894), 684; (1897), 721; (1899), 721; (1900), 708; (1901), 760.

8. Čapek, *Naše Amerika*, 625.

9. Polišenský, Začiatky, 32; *Česká osada*, 26; Jan Habenicht, *Dějiny Čechův Amerických* (St. Louis, 1910), 690.

10. Čapek, *Naše Amerika*, 160–162.

11. Theodore Andrica, "Czechs Came in Force to City 100 Years Ago," Cleveland *Plain Dealer*, 17 December 1951; Čapek, *Naše Amerika*, 189; *Dennice Novověku*, 18 May 1902; *Česká osada*, 14.

12. Thomáš Čapek, *The Čechs (Bohemians) in America* (Boston and New York, 1920), 28; Čapek, *Naše Amerika*, 28.

13. Polišenský, Začiatky, 16.

14. Jiří Kořalka, Květa Kořalková, "Basic Features of Mass Migration from the Czech Lands during the Capitalist Era," *Les migrations internationales de la fin de XVIIIe siecle a nos jours* (Paris, 1980), 505–507.

15. Polišenský, Začiatky, 16.

16. Heinz Fassman, "Patterns and Structures of Migration in Austria," in Dirk Hoerder ed., *Labor Migration in the Atlantic Economies: The European and North American Working Classes during the Period of Industrialization* (Westport and London, 1985), 75.

17. Kořalka, *Basic Features,* 507.

18. Ibid.

19. Jan Habenicht, *Dějiny Čechův,* 691.

20. František J. Vlček, *Povídka meho života: Historie Amerického Čecha* (St. Louis, 1928), 6–104.

21. Habenicht, *Dějiny Čechův,* 690, 691, gives the names and origins of many of the early settlers from the 1850s and 1860s. 75% of them are from a fifty-mile radius of Písek.

22. Kořalka, *Basic Features,*506; Emily Greene Balch, *Our Slavic Fellow Citizens* (New York, 1910), 80.

23. *St. Adalbert: Cleveland, Ohio: 1883–1958* (Cleveland, 1958), ADC, 22.

24. Eleanor E. Ledbetter, *The Czechs of Cleveland* (Cleveland: Americanization Committee, 1919), 8.

25. *St. Adalbert Parish,* 22; Habenicht, Dějiny Čechův , 691.

26. Šnajdr, "Cleveland a jeho Čechové," 94; Ledbetter, *The Czechs of Cleveland,* 9.

27. Ledbetter, *The Czechs of Cleveland,* 9.

28. *Česká osada,* 26, provides a list of occupations as of 1869.

29. Šnajdr, "Cleveland a jeho Čechové," 94. According to Šnajdr, of 1,500 coopers at Standard Oil, 1,000 were Czechs.

30. Habenicht, Dějiny Čechův, 690; *Česká osada,* 14.

31. *Česká osada,* 26; Šnajdr, "Cleveland a jeho Čechové," 96.

32. *Česká osada,* 20, 24, 186.

33. *Ibid.,* 185, 186.

34. F. J. Vlček, *Náš Lid v Americe (Sebrané články a Verše)* (Týn nad Vltavou: Czechoslovakia, 1935), 37, 39; Ledbetter, *The Czechs of Cleveland,* 11.

35. F. B. Zdrůbek to Bedřich Jonáš, 10 November 1870, Charles Jonas Papers, Wisconsin State Historical Society, Madison, Wisconsin (hereafter cited as CJP).

36. See the inventory to the Václav Šnajdr papers in the WRHS.

37. Vlček, Povídka mého života, 109.

38. Vlček, *Náš Lid v Americe (Sebrané články a Verše)* (Tyn nad Vltavou, 1935), 41–42.

39. *Americké Dělnické Listy,* 30 April 1920.

40. See Karel Bicha, "Settling Accounts With an Old Adversary: The Decatholicization of Czech Immigrants in America," *Histoire Social. Social History* (no. 8, 1971), 45–60; also Čapek, Naše Amerika, 362–405.

41. *Česká osada,* 23.

42. *Holy Family Parish Cleveland: Golden Jubilee, 1911–1961,* (Cleveland, 1961).

43. *St. Adalbert's Parish: Cleveland, Ohio: 1883–1958* (Archives of Diocese of Cleveland, 1958 [?]), 23.

44. *Diamond Jubilee: St. Wenceslaus Parish: Cleveland, Ohio: 1867–1942* (Archives of Diocese of Cleveland, Cleveland, 1942).

45. *Centennial: 1874–1974: St. Procop Church, Cleveland, Ohio* (Archives of Diocese of Cleveland, Cleveland, Ohio 1974).

46. *Historical Report of the Parish of Our Lady of Lourdes: Cleveland, Ohio: From the Time of its Erection to December, 1945* (Archives of Diocese of Cleveland); Oldřich Zlámal, *Povídka mého Života* (Chicago: Tiskárna Českých Benediktinů, 1954), 73.

47. *St. Adalbert Parish* 21.

48. *Památník 25 letého Střibrného Jubilea Osady sv. Jana Nepomuckého* (Cleveland, 1927, found in Archives of Diocese of Cleveland), 1.

49. *Holy Family Parish: Cleveland: Golden Jubilee: 1911–1961* (Archives of Diocese of Cleveland, 1961[?]),

50. Church Reports, Diocese of Cleveland, 1879–1923 (Archives of Diocese of Cleveland).

51. Ledbetter, *The Czechs of Cleveland,* 24; Esther Yukl, "Bethlehem Church in its Social Setting: A Study of the Neighborhood Comprising the Parish of Bethlehem Church and the Group Work Program Carried Out by that Church," (Masters thesis, Western Reserve University, 1931, found in the Western Reserve Historical Society), 33, 79–83.

52. Yukl, "Bethlehem Church," 94–98.

53. Fr. Faflík to Bishop Farrelly, 21 April 1917 (Holy Family Church, Archives of Diocese of Cleveland).

54. Yukl, "Bethlehem Church," 103.

55. There was also an Irish-German division within the hierarchy with the Czechs usually supporting and identifying with the German faction. Father Josef Koudelka was closely linked to the German faction. See Henry Leonard, "Ethnic Tensions, Episcopal Leadeship, and the Emergence of the Twentieth-Century American Catholic Church: The Cleveland Experience," *Catholic Historical Review* 71 (1985), 394–512.

56. Zlámal, *Povídka mého Života,* 37–8.

57. *Památník 25. Letého Střibrného Jubilea Osady sv. Jan Nepomuckého,* n.p.

58. *Diamond Jubilee, November 13, 1949: St. Procop's Church: Cleveland* (Cleveland, 1949, in the Archives of the Diocese of Cleveland); typescript of the interdict message read to the congregation on 3 February 1884.

59. Undated document in Archives of the Diocese of Cleveland.

60. *Ibid.*

61. John Svozil to the Bishop, 9 June 1913, Holy Family File (Archives of the Diocese of Cleveland).

62. *St. Procop's Congregation, Cleveland, Ohio, 1874–1880* (found in the Archives of the Diocese of Cleveland).

63. *Česká osada,* 52.

64. Zlámal, Povídka mého Života, 115.

65. Church Reports, St. Wenceslaus, 31 December 1883 (Archives of the Diocese of Cleveland).

66. Fr. Panuška of St. Procop to Bishop Horstmann, November 30, 1898 (Archives of Diocese of Cleveland).

67. *Holy Family Parish: Golden Jubilee.*

68. *Česká osada,* 24.

69. *Ibid.*

70. Zdrůbek to Bedřich Jonáš, 10 and 18 November 1870; 27 January, 2 February, 16 April, 4 June 1871; J. V. Sykora to Bedřich Jonáš, 28 November 1870; Bedřich Jonáš to J. V. Sykora, 31 November 1870 (Charles Jonas Papers, Wisconsin State Historical Society, Madison, Wisconsin). The correspondence deals with the lawsuit, the sale of the paper from Charles Jonas to Zdrůbek, and the transfer of Pokrok from Cedar Falls, Iowa, to Cleveland. Cf. also Zdrůbek in Amerikán: Národní Kalendář, I (1878), 125; Habenicht, *Dějiny Amerických Čechův,* 727.

71. Pokrok, 8, 22, 24 April 1875.

72. *Dennice Novověku,* 21 February, 21 October 1884.

73. Zlámal, *Povídka mého Života,* 72.

74. *Dennice Novověku,* 27 July 1882.

75. *Česká osada,* 97–98; Šnajdr, "Cleveland a jeho Čechové," 95.

76. Cf. Josef Martínek, Století Jednoty č.s.a. Dějiny Jednoty Československých Spolků v Americe (Cicero, Illinois, 1955).

77. Proceedings of "Svornost" 26 January 1870, see the minutes of the meetings in Czechoslovak Society of America Records, 26 January 1870, wrhs (hereafter cited as csa).

78. *Česká osada,* 30–95.

79. May and November 1877 minutes of Lodge "Svornost", csa, vol. 1–4.

80. *Česká osada,* 43; Minutes of Lodge "Svornost", July 1882, č.s.a.; cf. also Minutes from August 1902 and June 1910, csa.

81. *Česká osada,* 57, 61; Šnajdr, "Cleveland a jeho Čechové," 94.

82. *Česká osada,* 115.

83. *Památník Zlatého Jubilea České Nár. Síně na Broadway* (Cleveland, 1947), title page.

84. Ledbetter, *The Czechs,* 26.

85. *Česká osada,* 44.

86. *Česká osada,* 43–45.

87. Cf. "Počátky české volnomyslenkárské a bezvěřecké organizace," *Československý Časopis Historický,* 33 (1984), no.2, 218–249; minutes of Lodge "Svornost", July and September 1910, May 1915, csa.

88. Minutes of Lodge "Svornost" May 1910, csa; *Česká osada,* 44.

89. *Americké Dělnické Listy,* 30 January 1914; American, for the week of 10 February 1914. *Americké Dělnické Listy* over the same period defends Beneš.

90. Cf. Herbert Adolphus Miller, *The School and the Immigrant* (Cleveland, 1916), 78, 80.

91. Cf. the parish reports from St. Wenceslaus, St. Procop, Our Lady of Lourdes, St. Adalbert, St. John Nepomucene, and Holy Family in the Archives of the Diocese of Cleveland.

92. *Česká osada*, 138–140; on number of children attending these schools see Czech Freethinker School Association of Cleveland Records, WRHS.

93. Josef Chmelář, "The Austrian Emigration, 1900–1914," *Perspectives in American History, VII. Dislocation and Emigration* (Cambridge, Mass., 1974), 345; Čapek, *Naše Amerika*, 29; Miller, *The School and the Immigrant*, 29, 30.

94. *Památník Padesatiletého Trvání Sokolské Jednoty Čech-Havlíček* (Cleveland, 1929), 172.

95. *Česká osada*, 10, 98; Ledbetter, *The Czechs*, 33.

96. Cf. Šnajdr, "Cleveland a jeho Čechové," 97 writes that Koudelka speaks and writes correct Czech.

97. *Česká osada*, 101, 104; Habenicht, *Dějiny Čechův Amerických*, 721.

98. Památník Padesatiletého Trvání Sokolské Jednoty Čech-Havlíčcek, 13–14.

99. *Ibid.*, 13–14, 21; *Památník Zlatého Jubilea České Nár. Síně na Broadway: 1897–1947* (Cleveland, 1947).

100. *Pamatník Padesatiletého Trvání*, 39.

101. *Ibid.*, 150, 155, 158, 162.

102. *Ibid.*, 25.

103. *Ibid.*, 30–31, 56.

104. *Památník k Desetiletému Trvání I.D.T. Jednoty Ferdinand Lassalle* (Cleveland, 1912),

105. Frank Bardoun Papers (Western Reserve Historical Society).

106. *Ibid.*

107. *Amerikán: Národní Kalendář*, XLIII (1920), 285; *Cleveland Leader*, 20 April 1877; *Annals of Cleveland: Court Cases*, Abstract 7, "Accidents & Disasters, Industrial, James Bohaslav vs. The Standard Oil Company," 7–8.

108. *Amerikán*, XXXIV, 270.

109. *Cleveland Leader*, April 20, 24, 25, 26, May 2, 3, 10, 1877; Šnajdr, "Cleveland a jeho Čechové," 94.

110. Vlček, *Povídka mého Života*, 122.

111. *Ibid.*; *Cleveland Leader*, 10 May 1877.

112. *Cleveland Leader*, May 14, 16, 1877.

113. Vlček, *Povídka mého Života*, 133.

114. *Dennice Novověku*, May 11, 1882, This title began publication on October 10, 1877, about six months after Pokrok's demise.

115. Henry Leonard, "Ethnic Cleavage and Industrial Conflict in Late 19th Century America: The Cleveland Rolling Mill Company Strikes of 1882 and 1885," *Labor History*, 20 (Fall 1979), 526–528.

116. *Ibid.*, 528. See also chapter by Walaszek, on this and subsequent iron and steel workers' strikes in Cleveland.

117. *Dennice Novověku*, 11, 25 May, 8 June 1882.

118. Leonard, "Ethnic Cleavage," 531.

119. *Ibid.*, 536–543.

120. As quoted in *Ibid.*, 539.

121. For an account of both the 1882 and 1885 strikes see Leslie Hough, "The Turbulent Spirit: Violence and Coaction among Cleveland Workers, 1877–1899" (Ph.D. dissertation, University of Virginia, 1977).

122. *Svět*, June 15, 1918.

123. *Americké Dělnické Listy*, 2 March 1917.

124. *Ibid.*, 13, 27 April 1917; *Dennice Novověku*, 3 May 1900.

125. *Dennice Novověku*, 3, 10, 17 May 1900.

126. *Americké Dělnické Listy*, 27 April 1917.

127. *Ibid.*; *Svět*, 16 June 1918.

128. *Americké Dělnické Listy*, 8 January 1909.

129. *Dennice Novověku*, 14 January 1909.

130. *Americké Dělnické Listy*, 8 January 1909.

131. *Ibid.*; *Dennice Novověku*, 21 January 1909.

132. *Americké Dělnické Listy*, 9 June 1911. For an account of the strike see Lois Scharf, "A Woman's View of Cleveland's Labor Force: Two Case Studies," in Thomas F. Campbell and Edward M. Miggins (eds.), *The Birth of Modern Cleveland* (Cleveland: Western Reserve Historical Society, 1988), especially 175–183. Scharf suggests that Czech subcontractors defected from the strike after two weeks of united action, but she does not elaborate on their position or role in the industry or the strike.

133. *Americké Dělnické Listy*, 9 June 1911; every issue from 19 June through 27 October contains a report on the progress of the strike.

134. *Ibid.*, 27 October 1911. This breaking of solidarity may have referred to the Czech subcontractors' defection mentioned by Scharf.

135. Vlček, *Povídka mého Života*, 133–144, 154, 173, 192, 209–211.

136. *Ibid.*, 211–212; *The Encyclopedia of Cleveland History*, David D. Van Tassel and John J. Grabowski, eds. (Bloomington, Indiana: Case Western Reserve University and Indiana University Press, 1987), 1014.

137. *Americké Dělnické Listy*, 8, 15 June 1917; Vlček, *Povídka mého Života*, 245.

138. *Ibid.* In his memoirs Vlček mentions that a Lithuanian threw an object at him in the plant, and was then carted off to jail. It is possible that this man and the "Latvian" Preedy may be the same individual.

139. Faulkner wrote a preliminary report on 14 June 1917, stating that 75 employees were directly affected and 275 were indirectly affected. He also stated that the plant was crippled but "in part operation." "Preliminary Report of Commissioner of Conciliation" to Department of Labor, Cleveland, Ohio, 14 June 1917, in National Archives.

140. *Americké Dělnické Listy*, 22 June 1917. Szabadsag, 19 June 1917, may carry the advertisements for workers. Vlček employed a number of Magyars and stated that he had their interest at heart. See Vlček, *Povídka mého Života*, 340.

141. Vlček, *Povídka mého Života,* 249; *Americké Dělnické Listy,*

142. *Americké Dělnické Listy,* 29 June 1917.

143. David Brody, *Labor in Crisis: The Steel Strike of 1919* (Philadelphia and New York: J. B. Lippincott Company, 1965), 62, 65, 73.

144. *Svět,* 23 September 1919; *Američan,* 23, 24 September 1919.

145. *Američan,* 24 September 1919.

146. Brody, *Labor in Crisis,* 162; Kenneth L. Kusmer, *A Ghetto Takes Shape: Black Cleveland, 1870–1930* (Urbana, Chicago, London: University of Illinois Press, 1976), 197.

147. Brody, *Labor in Crisis,* 134–136; *Američan,* 7 October 1919.

148. *Američan,* 26 September 1919.

149. *Americké Dělnické Listy,* March 5, 1920; *Encyclopedia of Cleveland History,* 992.

150. *Svět,* October 11, 18, 1919; *Americké Dělnické Listy,* March 5, 1920.

151. Vlček, *Povídka mého Života,* 308, 340.

152. Harry Franklin Payer Papers, Western Reserve Historical Society, Cleveland, Ohio.

153. Newton D. Baker, later to be Cleveland's mayor and then Woodrow Wilson's secretary of war, was city solicitor at the time. Payer's political career would benefit from Baker's political fortunes.

154. When Tomáš Masaryk was in Cleveland in June 1918, Payer entertained him in his home. See Payer Papers.

155. Werich and Voskovec were progressive actors and writers in Prague's Osvobozené Divadlo (Liberated Theater). They were and are still regarded as a Czech cultural institution. Werich wrote of Payer that he had a large law firm and was one of the Cleveland Czechs who lived among cream of Cleveland society. He also notes that Payer spoke Czech with a hard American accent. See Jan Werich, Vzpomíná vlastně Potlach (Prague: Melantrich, 1982), 128.

156. Congressman Sabath from Illinois, who preceded Babka into the House of Representatives, was Jewish; Babka was a Catholic.

157. The petition reads as follows: "To the Honorable Council of the City of Cleveland. We, the undersigned citizens of Cleveland respectfully represent to your Honorable Body, that more than seven thousand of the population of our city are of Bohemian birth, who by reason of their want of knowledge of the English language are deprived of the means of a ready acquaintance with the laws and ordinances by which they are governed, and as it is their desire to be placed in this respect—on an equal footing with those of their fellow citizens, as are able to read the Laws and Ordinances in the newspapers, they pray your Hon. Body to cause the ordinances and other advertisements of this City to be published in the Bohemian language. And your petitioners will ever pray." In the Cleveland City Council Archives.

158. City of Cleveland "Council Proceedings," 18, 25 April, 20 June, 1 July 1876. In Cleveland Public Library.

159. *Cleveland Leader,* 6 December 1876, in *Cleveland Newspaper Digest:* 1 January to 31 December 1876, 903.

160. City Council Reports, in Western Reserve Historical Society. These councilmen were:

1875–1877	Ferdinand Svoboda	Ward 14
1881–1882	Frank Karda	Ward 14
1883–1884	Joseph Pták	Ward 12
1891–1892	" "	District 10
1885	Emanuel Payer	Ward 14
1888–1889	J. M. Novák	Ward 14
1888–1890	Frank Turek	Ward 40
1890	John Havlíček	Ward 24
1891	" "	District 8
1901–1902	Joseph Štibr	District 7
1906–1910	D. J. Zinner	Ward 16
1910–1911	A. B. Sprostý	Ward 16
1926	" "	Ward 13
1926–1929	" "	District 2
1914–1915	J. E. Votava	Ward 13
1916–1923	Charles Kadleček	Ward 13
1922–1923	Edward Sklenička	Ward 30

161. *Dennice Novověku,* 9 April 1903.

162. *Americké Dělnické Listy,* 29 October 1909.

163. *Ibid.,* 26 October 1914.

164. *Annual Reports of the City of Cleveland: 1901,* 721; *Česká osada,* 187. As a basis of comparison, in 1901 246 police officers were native born, and 46 were Irish born.

165. *Svět,* June 14, 29, 1918.

166. *Annual Reports of the City of Cleveland: 1891,* 671; *Svět,* April 26, 1918.

167. *Česká osada,* 187.

168. Ledbetter, *Czechs of Cleveland,* 33.

169. *Annual Reports, 1915,* 1435.

170. *Česká osada,* 187. The number of workers was not large, ranging from one to four in each department, but the point is that they worked their way into city jobs.

171. *Svět,* June 21, August 8, November 6, 1918; obituary in "Czechoslovak" Clipping File, Cleveland Public Library.

172. Česko-Slovanská Podporující Společnost (C.S.P.S.) is one example. Many English translations of this name erroneously render it as "Czechoslovak."

173. *Česká osada,* 16.

174. Coroner's report on Frank Heyduk, June 18, 1899, in Cuyahoga County Archives, Cleveland, Ohio. The report does not say who actually committed the murder.

175. *Svět,* April 2, 1918. This also demonstrates cooperation on the part of the Magyars, who apparently agreed to have their "champion" fight in a Czech venue.

176. See chapters by Puskás and Kopanic.

177. Zlámal, *Povídka mého Života*, 116; Josef Mašek, *Památník Českého Národního Sdružení v Clevelandu, O.: 1915–1920* (Cleveland: České Národní Sdružení, n.d.), 3.

178. Vojta Beneš, *Československá Amerika v Odboji: 1. Od června 1914 do srpna 1915* (Prague: Nakladatelství Pokrok, 1931), 273–276.

179. Mašek, *Památník Českého Narodního Sdružení*, 12.

180. C. Winston Chrislock, "Reluctant Radicals: Czech Social Democracy and the Nationality Question, 1914–1918" (Ph.D. dissertation, Indiana University, Bloomington, Indiana, 1971), 35–38.

181. *Právo*, August 4, 1914.

182. *Ibid.*; Beneš, *Československá Amerika*, 217, 230–231; *Americké Dělnické Listy*, April 16, and 30, 1915. Martínek was on the executive board of the Bohemian National Alliance in Cleveland, see Mašek, Památnik Českého Narodního Sdrueí, 12, 13.

183. *Památník padesátiletého Trvání Sokolské*, 56, 88.

184. *Ibid.*, 92; Mašek, *Pamatník Ceského Národního Sdružení*, 23.

185. Mašek, *Památník Českého Národního Sdružení*, 16.

186. See below, 61, and chapter by Kopanic.

187. Zlámal, Povídka mého Života, 39.

188. Mašek, Památník Českého Národního Sdružení, 24;

189. Mašek, *Památník Českého Národního Sdružení*, 24–6; Zlámal, Povídka mého Života, 52–53, 56–59.

190. Zlámal, *Povídka mého Života*, 56–59; Mašek, *Památnik Českého Národního Sdruženi*, 24; František Šindlář, *Z boji za Svobodu Otciny* (Chicago: Národní Svaz Českých Katolíků, 1924), 226. Šindelář, Mašek and Zlámal all write very positively about one another in their accounts of these activities.

191. By the fall of 1915 Czech opinion was not yet entirely behind this effort. On some problems related to fund rising campaigns (of Vojta Beneš). *Američan*, the main opponent of V. Beneš' actions finally moved to the independence camp in 1917. Cf. Mašek, *Památník Českého Národního*, 16.

192. Mašek, *Památník Českého Národního Sdružení*, 24, 27, 30, 32; Šindelář, Z Odboji, 18.

193. Mašek, *Památník Českého Národního Sdružení*, 43, 63; Šindelář, Z Odboji, 237.

194. Mašek, *Památník Českého Národního Sdružení*, 40, 49; and see chapter by Kopanic.

195. *Svět*, May 10, 1918; Mašek, *Památník Českého Národního Sdružení*, 61; Šindelář, *Z Boji za Svobodu*, 235.

196. *Americké Dělnické Listy*, May 4, 1917.

197. *Svět*, February 5, 1918.

198. *Svět*, June 15, 16, and 17, 1918.

199. John Mihal, "March of City's Business, Industry Chokes Out All but a Few of Croton Area's Czechs," [1940?], "Czechoslovak" Clipping File, Cleveland Public Library.

200. *Diamond Jubilee: St. Wenceslaus Parish, Cleveland* (1942).

201. Cf. Kenneth L. Kusmer, *A Ghetto Takes Shape: Black Cleveland, 1870–1930* (Urbana: University of Illinois Press, 1976), map between 146–147.

202. Vlček, *Povídka mého Života*, 306.

203. *Památník Padesátiletého Trvání*, 158–159.

204. "Protokol z ustavijící schůze české socialistické organisace mužů v Cleve-landu," Sunday, n.d., December 1920, in "Protokoly schůzí české socialistické organ-isace mužů," in Czech Socialist Organizations, Records, WRHS.

205. *Památník Padesátiletého Trvání*, 164–174.

206. *Památník 25. létéhostříbného Jubilea Osady Sv. Jana Nepomuckého;* Farnik, 1933, Archives of Diocese of Cleveland.

207. "K Zlatému Jubileu Spolku Starých Českých Osadníkú" and "Zápisky první schůze Starých Českých Osadníkú," November 7, 1909, in Czech Old Settlers Orga-nization Records, WRHS (hereafter cited as COSO).

208. Attachment to minutes, March 20, 1910, COSO.

209. Constitution of the Bohemian-American Club Inc., revised in 1928 ([Cleve-land, 1928]), found in Bohemian American Club Records, WRHS.

210. *Americké Dělnické Listy*, September 28, 1917.

211. *Svět*, October 8, 1918.

212. "English Section," *Americké Dělnické Listy*, December 29, 1929.

213. "Around the World in Cleveland—No. 117," "Czechoslovak" Clipping File, May 24, 1935, Cleveland Public Library; "První Protokol ze zakladající Schuze a Slavnosti Odbočky Svazu Svobodomyslných v Mt. Pleasant," April 19, 1930, Free-thinkers Association, Václav Šnajdr Branch, Records, 1930–1957, WRHS.

214. "Czechoslovak" Clipping File, Cleveland Public Library.

215. "Around the World in Cleveland—No. 119," "Czechoslovak" Clipping File, Cleveland Public Library.

216. *Ibid.*

217. Precise data on intermarriage is difficult to find because Czechs marrying outside of the Czech community frequently did so in the churches of the group into which they were marrying or they had civil ceremonies. Church marriage records in Czech parishes may give an idea of "mixed marriages" performed within those parishes, but that does not help to determine what percentage of Czechs married outside of their ethnic group.

The Magyars in Cleveland, 1880–1930

JULIANNA PUSKÁS

Immigration and Settlement

During the period between the 1880s and the 1920s, a large number of ethnically mixed immigrants from the Hungarian part of the Habsburg Empire, among them a considerable number who spoke Magyar as their mother tongue, arrived in Cleveland, eventually creating the largest concentrated settlement of Hungarians in the United States. Because these migrants had come from something of a "melting pot" society, the development of their communities in America was more complex than that of other ethnic groups that left the Austro-Hungarian Empire.[1]

Significant immigration of Hungarians to Cleveland, as to other parts of the United States, began in the 1870s. Earlier, in the 1850s, some of the thousands of people who left Hungary for America following the 1848–9 revolution had settled in Cleveland. Although not all were political refugees as such, the immigrants of this period, mostly from the bourgeois and educated classes, tended to identify with the "freedom fighters" of 1848.[2] Their social background and motivation differed from that of the immigrants who arrived in Cleveland from the 1870s on within the framework of the great labor migration of the late nineteenth and early twentieth century. The small numbers of craftsmen, small merchants, and miners who came during the 1870s pioneered what became a mass movement of peasants-turned-laborers by the turn of the century.

These immigrants were not an ethnically homogenous group, although most of them spoke the Magyar tongue. Overseas migration had in fact begun from the northeastern part of Hungary, where the population was mixed, with the first to undertake the journey being Jews, Germans, and a large number of Slovaks. The ethnic Hungarians, the Magyars, joined them, following the route they had traveled, and soon migrants were departing from other regions of the country as well. They came to work in America's mines and factories, attracted by wages much higher than those in Hungary. Before World War I most Magyars, like members of other ethnic groups, did not leave Hungary with the intention of settling permanently in the United States. They planned to stay only until they had earned enough money to improve their financial position back home. With this goal in mind, young men, many of them single or newly wed, bid good-bye to their families for what they believed would likely be a few years' separation. They did not seriously consider the possibility that they might never again see the land of their birth.[3]

Migrants from the northeastern county Abauj, from the villages of Buzita, Csécs, and Göncz, came to Cleveland in the years 1879 and 1880, and were the real founders of the city's Hungarian community, although migrants from the western part of the country (e.g., the county of Sopron) were also present.[4] As migration continued over the following decades, Cleveland's Hungarian settlement developed into one of the largest in the United States. Before 1900, Slovaks were the most numerous group among immigrants to Cleveland from Hungary, but the city's Magyar population grew rapidly after the turn of the century.

Between 1874 and 1901, 12,265 immigrants from Hungary arrived in Cleveland. Following the turn of the century, the rate of arrival increased considerably, with 13,107 newcomers recorded between 1902 and 1907.[5] It is likely that the numbers were actually higher. For example, migrants coming to Cleveland from other parts of the United States, like the mineworkers of Pennsylvania and West Virginia, had sometimes jumped trains or arrived on foot, and were not necessarily included in such figures. Although individuals coming from every region of the homeland could be found among Cleveland's Hungarian immigrants, those from the northeast, from Abauj and Zemplén Counties, continued to predominate.[6]

Quite early on, Hungarian Jews settled in the area between East 55th and East 65th Streets near Woodland Avenue. In the 1880s large numbers of non-Jewish Hungarians followed, and Cleveland's Hungarian community began to crystallize around certain workplaces and nearby neighborhoods, in part due to the activities of some of the early immigrants. János Makranszky and András Kuzma, who were among the first to serve as ombudsmen for their countrymen, finding work and lodging for acquaintances and relations, sent almost everyone to industrial plants on Cleveland's east side: the National Malleable Casting Co., known as the "old" factory, or else to the "new" factory," the Eberhardt Manufacturing Co. ironworks, both of which employed over one thousand workers by the turn of the century. These factories produced metal parts for various kinds of manufactured goods, from carts and coaches to stoves and kitchen-ranges. A large Hungarian settlement developed east along Woodland Avenue and East 79th Street. Irish and German residents withdrew from the area as Hungarians came (in the words of the newspaper *Szabadság*) "in swarms."[7] The factories concentrated near East 79th Street provided employment, and were within walking distance. Living conditions were not necessarily pleasant; in the 1880s, the streets were not yet paved or lit. Moreover, native-born Americans and members of longer-established groups evinced hostility toward the newcomers, disparaging the Magyar-speaking "Tatars" and sometimes even stoning them. As more and more migrants arrived, the settlement extended southeast along Buckeye Road.[8]

On the city's west side, Tivadar Kundtz (1853–1937), a German-Hungarian cabinetmaker from Metzensef in Abauj County, who had arrived in Cleveland in 1873, set up his own workshop in 1878. He soon contracted with the White Sewing Machine Company to produce sewing machine cabinets, and by 1900 the Theodor Kundtz Co. was one of Cleveland's largest employers, with 2,500 employees, the overwhelming majority of them Hungarian.[9] Most Hungarian migrants on the west side (many of them from Kundtz's home village) lived fairly close to the Kundtz Co., located in the Cuyahoga valley Flats district, and to other factories where they worked. They did not, however, bunch together like the east side Hungarians, but instead lived in mixed neighborhoods with Germans, Czechs, and Slovaks. As their numbers increased, a certain degree of Hungarian ethnic concentration developed on Franklin Street and Lorain Avenue between West 22nd and 47th Streets, but the west side Hungarian neighborhood always remained an ethnically mixed district.[10]

Establishing Fraternal Organizations

According to extant records, about twenty Hungarian organizations were founded in Cleveland before 1900. They fall into two general categories: secular mutual aid and cultural organizations; and religious mutual aid and "church-building" societies.

The impetus to form a Hungarian mutual aid society came in 1886, when a Hungarian man, who had no relatives in the city, died and was taken away in the middle of the night without arrangements for burial. Horrified by the news, some Hungarian craftsmen, at the urging of a doctor of Polish origin, joined to form the "Count Lajos Batthány Social and Relief Society."[11]

Additional secular, non-confessional benefit societies followed, also named after Hungarian historical figures revered as freedom-fighters. Many members were not of Magyar origin. The German-Hungarian Tivadar Kundtz and the Hungarian-Jewish József Black and Martin Deutsch took leading roles in giving both moral and financial support to such organizations. Upon the occasion of the Batthány Society's second anniversary, Black's mother donated a Hungarian flag.[12]

In the community's early years, before 1900, Cleveland's Hungarian migrants were slow to commit themselves to fraternal and other ethnic institutions. In 1894 an article in *Szabadság* criticized Hungarian immigrants' lack of enthusiasm for the fraternal movement, and urged them to organize themselves.[13] Individuals who arrived later (mostly craftsmen) did join fraternal organizations, but in general membership grew slowly until the 1920s. Interest in the fraternal movement was evidenced more by the founding of additional societies than by growth in membership of those organizations already active.

Secular patriotic and cultural societies worked to promote national pride, enshrining the ideals of the 1848 bourgeois revolution and promulgating the cult of Lajos Kossuth.[14] They led the way in organizing the celebration of various national holidays commemorating the events of 1848–49. This patriotic national ideology had been established by the post-1848 immigrants, and by Hungarian Jewish merchants, craftsmen, and intellectuals, whose status in the Cleveland community was already high in the 1880s. Through newspapers and fraternal organizations they made efforts to transmit this ideology to the growing population of peasant-worker immigrants. In using Kossuth as a symbol for Hungarian nationalism, they chose a name that had been honored by the American people and government as well; Kossuth had been cheered by crowds in many American cities during his visit in 1851, and, a particular point of pride for Hungarians in America, had been the second European politician (after Lafayette) to address the United States Senate.

From the 1890s on, not only representatives of the patriotic ideology, but Magyar-speaking socialists also appeared and started to organize in Cleveland. Their numbers were small; most were craftsmen and skilled workers who belonged to trade unions or the Social Democratic Party in Hungary. There, craftsmen used German as their trades' language. This multi-lingualism helped Hungarian craftsmen in general to accommodate themselves to their new surroundings, and was especially useful for socialists, since organizations like the Socialist Labor Party had many German members.

Hungarian socialists in Cleveland founded the "Petőfi Sándor Szocialista Munkás Egylet" (Petőfi Sándor Socialist Workers' Association) in 1894, and

Cleveland's Hungarian community dedicates the Kossuth Monument at University Circle in 1902. WRHS.

began publishing a newspaper, *Amerikai Népszava* (named after the Hungarian Social Democratic Party's paper) in 1895. It promulgated socialist ideas in general, and supported the program of the Socialist Labor Party in particular. The socialists distinguished their stand from the nationalistic line taken by other Hungarian newspapers, stating: "In the *'Amerikai Népszava'* it is not the Hungarian language that comes first, but what we say in Hungarian. We do not call you to read this paper, because it is written in Hungarian but, first and foremost, because what we write is in the interest of the workers."[15] Financial and other problems forced the staff to take *Népszava* to New York in 1896.

As for the religious mutual aid and church-building societies, Hungarian immigrants began establishing them in Cleveland in the late 1880s. Again, the first activists in this area were craftsmen, mostly from the villages, although peasant-worker migrants played a more important role in these denominational societies than they did in secular ones. In 1888, a Roman Catholic fraternal benefit society named after the medieval Hungarian king

Szent László (St. Ladislas) was founded, with a multiethnic membership, mostly Slovak and Magyar. The society's main goal was to build a Roman Catholic church where both Slovaks and Magyars could worship in their mother tongues. In later years, Hungarian migrants looked back with nostalgia to this period, when nationalism had not yet disrupted fellow-feeling based on geographic origin, and cooperation in building churches, fraternal organizations, and social institution seemed a natural thing.[16]

Building Religious Institutions

Hungarian migrants varied denominationally as well as ethnically. Most (approximately sixty to sixty-five percent) were Roman Catholic, and the rest were Calvinist, Lutheran, Greek Catholic, or Jewish. The Jews were the first among the immigrants from Hungary to establish a religious community in Cleveland. In 1866 Herman Sampliner gathered sixteen people as founding members of a congregation, which they named B'nai Jeshurun. It was not a congregation of typical '48ers. It reflected the early arrival of a different kind of Hungarian Jew in Cleveland. They were the forerunners of the mass migration of the 1880s.[17]

Slovak and Magyar immigrants worked together to build their first Roman Catholic church, St. Ladislas (named after a Hungarian King) in Cleveland at the corner of East 92nd Street and Holton Avenue in 1889. Cooperation between Magyars and Slovaks was short-lived. A major quarrel erupted in 1891 over the consecration of the Magyar St. Imre fraternal organization's banner during a Sunday mass, necessitating police intervention. Magyars claimed that the "Slovaks threatened to kill the priest [who was a Slovak] if he held a Hungarian speech"; Slovaks made similar accusations against the Magyars.[18]

In the end, the church had to be divided along ethnic lines, with Slovaks retaining St. Ladislas, and Magyars compelled to found a new parish. The bishop of Cleveland requested the primate of Hungary to "send me a zealous and meritful priest for the Huns, i.e. Hungarians, abandoned in the Cleveland diocese." Károly Bőhm, from upper northern Hungary, who spoke Magyar, German, and Slovak, came to Cleveland as the city's first Hungarian priest at the end of 1892, and almost immediately posted the following advertisement in *Szabadság:* "The next church service will be held in the Szent László Church [which we still share] with the Slovaks, but after that there will not be any room there for the Hungarians anymore.... We have to procure a church by our own effort, so that it can be called Hungarian."[19]

In 1893 first Hungarian Roman Catholic church in the United States, named after St. Elizabeth of Hungary, was built in Cleveland, on the corner of Buckeye Road and East 98th Street, and consecrated in the same year.[20] Károly Bőhm started the first Hungarian Catholic church newspaper in America, *Szent Erzsébet Hirnöke* (*St. Elizabeth's Herald*), in the late 1890s. During the decade, St. Elizabeth's parish grew steadily. In 1892 church membership totaled 1,287, including 220 families and 340 single adults. By 1901, 300 families, or thousands of individual Catholics attended the church.

Marriages, Baptisms and Burials held in St. Elizabeth's Chuch, 1891–1899[21]

Year	Marriages	Baptisms	Burials
1891	15	95	33
1895	31	98	32
1896	21	108	26
1897	24	100	34
1898	24	115	46
1899	43	116	52

In the year 1893 a parish school was built beside St. Elizabeth's church. It had 67 pupils enrolled in 1894, and 317 in 1899. Ursuline nuns taught most subjects, with the priest giving Magyar language lessons. Magyar children, however, attended Cleveland's public schools in larger numbers than children from other central and southeastern European ethnic groups.[22]

Greek Catholic Hungarians also founded their own church in Cleveland. In 1891 eighteen Greek Catholic families founded the Szent Mihály Sick Benefit Society to provide fraternal benefits and to build a church. The society merged with the St. Anne Society for Women to form the St. John Society. Following the request of the society's leaders for a priest, Rev. János Csurgovich came to Cleveland, and led the effort to organize a parish. St. John's parish was founded in 1893, and within a year the parish church opened its doors on Rawlings Avenue as the first Greek Catholic church in the United States. Its members came from various ethnic groups, but were in some degree assimilated to the Magyars.[23] Although the Greek, or Byzantine, Catholics owed allegiance to the Roman Catholic pope, their rites and traditions (particularly the acceptability of married clergy), which grew out of a combined Roman Catholic and Eastern Orthodox heritage, caused controversy within the American Catholic church.[24]

The first Hungarian Protestant church in Cleveland was founded in 1890. In that year, the Reformed Church of the United States, a Calvinist denomination of German origin, called a Hungarian clergyman, Gustav Jurányi, to serve the needs of Cleveland's Hungarian Protestants.[25] Rev. Jurányi met with great difficulties, primarily financial, in establishing a church. When asked to join the congregation, many potential members "answered that they came to the u.s. only for a short time, they will return home soon and are paying the church fees at home in the mean time." Out of the 100 to 150 individuals who attended Rev. Jurányi's first service, only 50 to 60 were willing to become paying members of the church.[26]

The minister delivered his first Magyar-language sermon in Cleveland in a German church on the west side. Calvinists from both the west and east sides of the city attended. In 1891 the Hungarian Evangelical Reformed Church of Cleveland, more generally known as the First Hungarian Reformed Church, was officially organized, initially housed in a rented German church, and after 1894 in its own building at East 79th Street and Rawlings Avenue.[27] Three ministers came and went during the first eight years of the church's existence. At that time, the clergyman in Cleveland was the only minister for the Hungarian Calvinists of the entire state of Ohio and of Michigan. He visited eighteen to twenty settlements, traveling "in the heat, in rain, or cold, on the rails or a coach or by foot," as one pastor recalled. "Carrying my cloak, my bible and my hymn-book in my bag, I set out to the huge plains," going from one *tanya* (farm) to another, "where I preached to the members of the congregation, who gathered together to the appointed place on foot, on horseback or in coaches from near or far."[28]

According to the First Hungarian Reformed Church's registers, the congregation grew from 50 or 60 founding members in 1891 to 800 adult congregants by 1901, although more than half of these were only nominal members. During this first decade 313 children were born, of whom more than one-third died in infancy. From October 1890 to the end of December 1899, 114 couples were married in the church. Both spouses hailed from the same village in only 11 cases, but 68 couples had both partners coming from the same county (Abauj, in most cases), while 35 individuals married someone from a different county. In fifty of these marriages, the spouses did not belong to the same denomination, a relatively high proportion. The church was too small and ill-funded to be able to run a full-time day school, but the clergyman was commissioned to teach the congregation's children the Magyar language on Saturdays and during the summer holidays.[29]

The organization of the Hungarian Calvinist churches took place in coordination with the home missions of the American Protestant churches. In these early years, most Hungarian immigrants were young laborers who did not plan to put down roots in America. It would thus have been very difficult for Hungarian Protestants, who were in any case outnumbered by their Catholic compatriots, to organize and maintain churches without any assistance from American Protestants. The relationship between the two was not easy, however, due to cultural differences. From the beginning, these differences led to doubts among the Hungarian clergymen and church members as to "whether the constitution and the teachings of the mother-church and the assisting church did not contradict each other?"[30] The Hungarian clergymen affirmed, after some discussion, that the Hungarian and American churches were nearly identical in their essentials, that is, their articles of faith, even though church practices and organization might differ somewhat. At the same time, in 1896, they asked for permission to found a Hungarian Reformed Diocese in America, in the hope that this would help stop the missionary efforts of other denominations among Hungarian immigrants. The American Reformed Church authorities, who considered maintaining an ethnic branch within their denomination as inimical to Americanization, refused this request. The Evangelic Reformed Church establishment in Hungary also did not give the support and acknowledgment that their Hungarian brethren in the United States requested. Nonetheless, the Reformed Church was more successful than other Hungarian Protestant denominations in America, which before the turn of the century had so few members that they could not think of setting up their own churches. Many Lutherans and other Protestants joined the Hungarian Reformed Church, which tended to dilute the homogeneity of the denominations.

Yet even with the support they received from the American church establishment, whether Catholic or Protestant, the immigrants' churches were by and large the product of their own work. It was they who started the process by deciding to found a parish or congregation. They then proceeded to organize a church-building society, raise funds, and find a clergyman. Together with the clergyman, they conducted the affairs of the church (not always in harmony since the Hungarian clergy were not accustomed to this degree of lay participation) and through their voluntary contributions made possible its continued existence. Considering the itinerant nature of the migrant population, the building of churches with more or less permanent memberships was a substantial achievement by those small groups forming the active core of the community.

It did not take long after the churches' founding for the bickering among the denominations common in the old country to reach the new.

In Cleveland, for example, the Roman Catholic priest Károly Bőhm and the Calvinist minister Sándor Harsányi soon became embroiled in religious polemics. In 1901, *Szabadság* lamented the effect of "the ever present denominational quarrels" on Hungarian unity.[31]

Expansion of the Settlement

Following the turn of the century, Cleveland's Hungarian community grew rapidly, with Magyars outnumbering Slovaks and Germans from Hungary. Many of the Magyars who initially worked in mines in the United States moved on to factory jobs in Cleveland and other cities as soon as possible. They were more likely to have lived on the plains of the old country, tilling the soil, and found life in mining areas much more alien than did Slovaks, who came from a more mountainous landscape. The influx of Hungarians to Cleveland was so large that in 1914 the Austro-Hungarian consul met with the area's Hungarian clergymen to discuss ways of reducing this massive migration. The clergymen without exception attributed it to problems in the Hungarian homeland: lack of land, of money, and opportunity, combined with the oppressive actions of civil servants and the military, and the disdainful attitude of the upper classes. But these were problems too large to solve during the few years left to the Empire, and meanwhile the Cleveland settlement continued to grow.[32]

As the east side neighborhood continued to grow east and south, Buckeye Road became its major east-west artery. This was an outlying district of the city. Before World War I there were open fields nearby, and a little wood with springs on Woodland Hill that was a popular site for Sunday excursions and picnics. The less-concentrated west side neighborhood, which was growing in a southwest direction, had its "Main Street" on Lorain Avenue.[33]

Palpable differences existed in the social backgrounds of people on the east and west sides. On the east side large numbers of industrial day-laborers— the peasants from back home—had settled. Among the Hungarians who lived on the west side there were relatively more skilled workers, who had been factory workers or craftsmen in Hungary. This latter group did not cling so much to their traditional culture and folkways. They had more in common with immigrants from northwestern Europe, and their contacts with these peoples, particularly the Germans, were enhanced through some of them being in fact assimilated Germans, and also through the ability of the skilled craftsmen to speak German.[34]

According to the 1910 census, New York had more Hungarian residents than any other American city. Although Cleveland's settlement was somewhat smaller, it was much more concentrated, and especially on the east side, national customs were more in evidence. Thus, Hungarians viewed Cleveland as the "American Debrecen," that is, the second largest Hungarian city after Budapest. A contemporary observer described the Buckeye Road neighborhood in 1910: "The extensive Hungarian quarter on the East Side is truly and clearly Hungarian. One can hardly hear another language spoken; can hardly see another shop. The Hungarian institutions, churches, schools, halls of the fraternals are all together. They keep the Hungarian customs more than anywhere else. The women are not ashamed to go out with a scarf on their head, even barefooted in the summer; the men stay 'greenhorns' in their appearance. The houses are in the hands of Hungarians, Hungarian song can be heard in the streets, and newsvendors are shouting out the titles of Hungarian papers."[35]

Strong ties to the homeland helped maintain the "Hungarianness" of the community. People came and went, with some returning to Hungary, and others newly arriving from there. Some went home for summer harvests and returned to America in the fall.[36] Others moved about within Ohio and the neighboring states, to the industrial plants of nearby Lorain and Akron, or away from the mines of West Virginia, Pennsylvania, and Ohio, drawn by the lure of factory jobs in Cleveland. The demographic characteristics of the Cleveland settlement in the first decade of the twentieth century illustrated first, the newness of the community relative to some other ethnic groups, and second, the fact that many Magyar immigrants did not plan to make the United States their permanent home. These characteristics were that the population was nearly two-thirds male, with a high ratio of young adults and relatively few young children.[37] Only about a third of Cleveland's Magyars could speak English, only eight percent were United States citizens, and only nineteen percent hoped to become so.[38]

Labor

More than two-thirds of the male heads of the household were laborers. The rest worked at skilled trades, either as factory employees or as independent tradesmen, or in the services, and a few owned small businesses such as grocery shops or taverns.[39]

For the laborers, wages were low, generally less than four hundred dollars a year, and hours long, with a working week of sixty hours and more.

"My father always used to join the family circle with tired body and soul, and the first thing he did was to put his aching feet into warm water." The factories in which they worked produced standardized products, be it iron and steel parts or clothing, at a rapid pace and often on a piecework basis.[40]

Some Cleveland Hungarians, both men and women, did participate in strikes during the pre-World War I years, first at the Standard Iron Foundry in 1893, for better wages; at the Joseph & Feiss clothing factory in 1909, over work rules and conditions; in the garment workers' strike of 1911 organized by the i.l.g.w.u., with demands for a shorter work week and the prohibition of subcontracting; and in a 1913 strike at the Mechanical Rubber Company organized by the i.w.w.[41] However, since many Hungarians viewed themselves as temporary sojourners, they had short-term goals that lessened their enthusiasm for strikes and organized labor. They wanted to work and make money at any cost, so that they could return to their homeland and their families as soon as possible. They reacted to wage cuts or strikes by moving on to look for other work and better wages, or they returned to Europe. Their itinerant condition thus both affected and was affected by their attitude toward the workers' struggle.

Housing

As in the case of other immigrant groups, Hungarians' fanatical desire to save money resulted in a standard of living lower than that of American-born workers, which helped to create the negative feelings and prejudices so prevalent among "Yankees" and longer-established groups. Even other Hungarians commented unfavorably upon the way some scrimped on food and housing to amass money. "We have to shudder to think of the miserable food our compatriots consume. They buy the cheapest, the lowest quality of everything. Living this way it is only natural that after a few years they save up a nice capital."[42]

Like other immigrants, most Hungarians lived in one- or two-story frame houses, with small yards and front gardens. Conditions were actually better in the 1890s, when the east side neighborhood was still more or less of an outlying district, with woods and meadows nearby. Residents could pursue some of the traditional activities of a peasant household, growing vegetables and keeping small livestock—chickens, pigs, and sometimes even a cow or two which could produce dairy products for the market.[43] As the population of the city grew, largely due to the flood of new immigrants, the municipal government began restricting such activities. Residential density increased markedly, so that by the 1910s the average number of households per lot was 2.28. In the Franklin Avenue area on the west side, where more than forty percent of the households were Magyar and nearly twenty percent Slovak, residential structures included everything from two-story frame houses to brick tenements. Most of them were not in good condition, and were set flush with the street, with little yard space at the side or back. Magyars tended to live in the better houses, with Slovaks and Irish in the poorer ones. About one-third of households fell into each of the following categories: one to three persons; four or five persons; six or more. On the east side, houses accommodated one to four families. The houses on lower Buckeye Road were smaller, and on some side streets shanties were not uncommon.[44]

Prior to 1914 Hungarians did not place any special value on owning a house. They moved frequently, and interspersed rental and ownership one with the other. Along Buckeye Road, houses were typically multiple-family, or attached to a shop, both of these patterns providing extra income for the owner-occupant. Many households took in boarders, "*burdosok*," another source of income.[45] In fact, according to the Immigration Commission, among immigrant groups Magyars had the highest proportion of families taking in boarders or lodgers, 53.4 percent (Poles were next with 42.7 percent, and then south Italians with 40.5). Over seventy percent of the wives in Magyar families either earned wages or took in boarders, compared to less than sixty percent in Polish families and under fifty percent in Italian and Slovak families.[46] The "*burdos* family" helped immigrants adjust to life in the new world, as well as to save money by providing an inexpensive form of lodging. This type of communal living was familiar to peasants who had worked as migrant agricultural laborers in Hungary, and provided a pseudo-family for both unmarried and married men who had left their own families behind.[47]

Institution-building, 1900–1914

Despite the fact that individuals came and went, during the fourteen years prior to World War I the overall number of Hungarian immigrants in Cleveland increased considerably. The Hungarian settlement became more firmly established as an identifiable ethnic community with its own neighborhoods and institutions, both religious and secular. By 1911 approximately one hundred Hungarian associations functioned in Cleveland.

During this period, Hungarians living on the west side left the east side churches to establish their own parishes and congregations. In 1904 Roman Catholics founded St. Emericus Hungarian Church (Szent Imre Magyar

Hitközség), with 162 families and 432 single people joining. The church building was consecrated in 1905, and a parish school opened next to it, with two teachers and 115 pupils.[48]

The west side's first Hungarian Reformed congregation started off with 122 members in 1906 and grew very slowly, to 203 members five years later, and to 350 families in 1919. The congregation rented, then purchased a German church on West 32nd Street, and held frequent services despite the relatively small membership. From 1907 to mid-1916, 650 Hungarian children were baptized there and 135 had their confirmation; 257 couples were married; and 165 persons died. To hold a summer school, the minister did the best he could with little money by renting an old building, which provided four walls and nothing more. He solved the problem of seating by having every child bring a chair from home.[49]

On the east side, congregations felt sufficiently strong and solvent after the turn of the century to build new houses of worship, bigger and more ornate than their first structures, more like what they had known in Hungary. Cleveland's original Hungarian Jewish congregation inaugurated its second synagogue building in 1906, on the corner of East 55th Street and Scovill Avenue. As the formerly orthodox congregation became ever more liberal over the years, dissident groups separated from it.[50]

When in 1904 the east side Reformed church consecrated a new building on East 79th Street, the city's entire Hungarian community, together with people from nearby communities, gathered to celebrate. Ministers from a number of cities including Chicago and Pittsburgh participated in the service, saying prayers, giving the sermon, and serving communion. One clergyman baptized four children, another confirmed twelve girls and four boys, and yet another married two couples. The church's own minister, Elek Csutoros, closed the service, and in the evening a dinner was held in the Hungarian Hall.[51] The east side Roman Catholic Church, St. Elizabeth's, built a hall in 1917, which it used as a church until a new stone building with neo-baroque style decoration was completed in 1922.

Not only new church buildings, but new denominational congregations grew up as well. The Hungarian Lutherans separated from the Calvinists in 1905, with the leadership and assistance of the Lutheran Church of America. The First Hungarian Lutheran Church of Cleveland was chartered in 1906. Its first minister, István Ruzsa, arrived from Hungary in 1907, and the congregation soon purchased a church building on Rawlings Avenue. The church founded the first Hungarian orphanage in the United States in 1913. Like other early Hungarian churches, First Lutheran was multi-ethnic, with Wends being the most numerous group apart from the Magyars.[52]

Hungarian Baptist congregations were also formed in Cleveland after the turn of the century, on the east side in 1903 and in 1907 on the west side. A Baptist Magyar-language monthly journal was published in Cleveland. Relations between American and Hungarian Baptists were slow to develop, however, due to the language barrier. The Baptist Church concerned itself more with spiritual matters than involvement in "worldly" politics, so that conflict among the multi-ethnic Hungarian Baptists (including Slovaks, Rumanians, and Croatians) did not occur to a significant degree until during World War I. Groups outside the mainline Protestant denominations, such as Seventh-Day Adventists, Sabbatarians, and Pentecostals, also began to organize small Hungarian churches in the early twentieth century, with the assistance of German and American congregations.[53]

The situation among the Protestants was further complicated by competition among the home missions of the mainline American churches, particularly between the Reformed and the Presbyterian, to proselytize the Hungarians (who, unlike most eastern or southern European immigrants, already had a relatively strong Protestant tradition and thus seemed especially likely candidates for conversion) and absorb their churches into the American denominational structure. "So that we shall be able to Americanize them, they need to get Christianized first. If we are to do our duty by 'these strangers within our gates' and by their American-born children, we must give them the Gospel," declared a Presbyterian synod.[54]

At the same time, the Reformed Synod back in Hungary was calling on Hungarian churches in the United States to recognize its authority, to "'affiliate' in the best interest of their national and ethnico-religious life, for the fostering of the feeling of national fellowship and of the Hungarian Calvinist creed." The government in Hungary was present in the background of the "Hungarian Action" program directed toward the immigrants, which had the goal of "keeping alive the people's feelings of a relationship to their homeland" by strengthening organizational links with the immigrant churches and giving financial backing to their presses.[55]

The first United States diocese of the Reformed Church in Hungary was formed by the affiliation of six churches in October 1904. It acted under the authority of the church in Hungary, its bishop resided in Hungary.[56] This action helped to increase conflicts and animosity among the Hungarian Reformed membership in the United States, drawing sharper lines between the "affiliated" (with the church in Hungary), "non-affiliated" and the "Presbyterians," sometimes tearing communities apart and inevitably drawing clergymen into the controversy. Opponents of the "affiliated" accused them of ingratitude for the financial and other support they had received from the American home mission, and even of being "political agents," while the affiliated "branded the 'non affiliated' ones as traitors of Hungarianhood, who would sell the Hungarian characteristics of their churches for an American charity dole."[57] In general, members of non-affiliated churches exhibited greater similarity in their ideas, customs, and behavior to the broader American society than affiliated church members. They had less interest in nationalistic causes and more in social problems.[58]

Despite opposition from the American Reformed Church, to which many of the Hungarian churches in the United States had belonged prior to the formation of the overseas diocese of the church in Hungary, the number of affiliated churches grew to become the biggest group of Hungarian Protestant churches in the United States by the 1910s.[59] Cleveland's Reformed congregations joined their ranks. "It took a fight of the year and a half until the Reformed Church in the u.s. let the East Side Church go." A loan from the homeland helped enable the west side church to affiliate.[60] The Presbyterians entered the fray, but convinced only a handful of members to leave the east side Reformed church in 1914 for Presbyterian authority, and participate in activities, like English language classes and a nursery school, that hastened assimilation.[61]

During the first two decades of the twentieth century, ethnic consciousness strengthened within the Hungarian immigrant community, and this affected religious life. By appealing to national sentiments, Hungarian churches attracted adherents. "It is undeniable that our people can be only saved for the church, for the sacred community of Catholic belief by showing an explicit Hungarian feeling and nursing it. . . . As a Hungarian [the immigrant] can be quickly moved to enthusiasm, to build a church. Everything he performed until today, he did as a Hungarian," wrote Rev. Bőhm in 1913.[62] Rev. Béla Perényi observed that since there were already plenty of Catholic churches in America: "We . . . require a Catholic church only in the second place. We need a Hungarian church in the first place."[63] As in the Protestant denominations, issues related to national feeling sometimes led to tensions within the Roman Catholic church. An Episcopal council stated the matter frankly: "We American bishops do not sympathize with the Hungarian priesthood, moreover, the Panslavic priests purposely agitate their bishop against the Hungarians, as against a people who suppress the Slavs in [their] own country."[64]

Many immigrants to the United States, however, were unmoved by religious and nationalistic blandishments alike and were not linked to any church. Although definitive figures are difficult to come by, it seems that just after the turn of the century a third or more of Magyars, and in the 1910s forty to fifty percent at most belonged to one or the other of the churches.[65]

In addition to churches, many cultural, civic, and community service associations were founded in Cleveland's Hungarian community during the 1900–1914 period, some of them affiliated to church organizations, others secular. While the two were not necessarily inimical—the secular societies sometimes put on benefits to raise funds for the churches—some competition arose when the churches tried to become social as well as religious centers. Their social organizations included women's and men's circles, singing societies, and amateur theater groups. The pastor of St. Elizabeth's church, for example, mentioned eight such confraternities in 1911.[66]

Among the secular associations, one of the most active was the Hungarian Self-Educating Circle (Magyar Önképzö kör), founded in August 1902 on the west side by fourteen young craftsmen. The Circle organized various kinds of cultural events and educational activities, including English language courses for migrants. The group bought a building on Lorain Avenue to house its activities, featuring a library, reading rooms, a large hall with a stage, and kitchen facilities. The Circle regularly performed Magyar-language dramas and operettas, the first group in Cleveland to do so. Churches followed this example and organized their own amateur troupes; in 1904 the King St. Stephen Catholic Hungarian Society at St. Elizabeth's formed its Dramatic Club. The Hungarian community, like other ethnic groups, also had its own athletic organizations. In 1908, eleven young men started the Hungarian Athletic Club, at first holding their meetings in rented halls, and then purchasing their own building on Vestry Avenue (on the west side) in 1911.[67]

As well as religious and mainstream secular groups, cultural societies with a socialist orientation existed. One of the most successful was the Hungarian Workingmen's Singing Club (Cleveland Általános Magyar Munkás Dalkör), organized in August 1908 "by workers of liberal views to furnish a healthy outlet for the cultural efforts of the Hungarian neighborhood and to support the working people in its struggles for social advancement." The Club built a hall and clubhouse on Lorain Avenue in 1911.[68]

In general, the workers' movement in Cleveland was fragmented in the years after the turn of the century, in large part because of differences in culture and experience between American and European socialists. Hungarian socialists tried to keep aloof from the divisions in the American socialist movement between the adherents of the more typically "American" Socialist Party with its politically oriented program (less relevant to non-citizen immigrants, who could not vote), and loyalists of the Socialist Labor Party (SLP), which had a more "European" program based on class struggle. Inevitably, however, they were drawn in. The small group of Cleveland Hungarian socialists reorganized itself as part of the national Workers Sick Benefit and Self-Education Federation (Munkás Betegsegélyzö és Önképzö Kör). As Hungarian socialists began to align themselves with one or the other of the American socialist parties, this organization went the way of the Socialist Party (despite the fact that at this time most Hungarians were more inclined to support the SLP), and also started a new publication, *Előre (Forword) (1905)*, since its former newspaper *Népakarat* (People's bill) remained in the hands of SLP adherents. The Federation's Cleveland branch, No. 15, was housed in the Hungarian Workers' Home on West 25th Street, and had its own cultural group, the Progress Singing Circle (Haladás Dalárda). SLP adherents started a new mutual aid society, the Hungarian Workers' Sick Benefit Federation (1906), Branch No. 2 of which was established in Cleveland's east side Hungarian neighborhood.[69] Beyond the internecine quarrels, Cleveland's Hungarian socialists naturally came into conflict with the churches, both Catholic and Reformed ones, since in the course of propagating atheism and anticlericalism they often verbally attacked church followers and priests.

In subsequent years a group of Hungarian carpenters and cabinetmakers started a Hungarian branch, No. 1180, of the American Federation of Labor. They set up headquarters in the Hungarian Workers' Home and chose *Előre* as their official newspaper. The I.W.W. also had a presence among Cleveland's Hungarian migrants, with small but active groups on both the east and west sides.

Ethnic Leaders: The Rise of the Hungarian Middle Class

Hungarian immigrants were to be found in every branch of industry employing unskilled workers, doing the hardest, dirtiest, and most physically demanding jobs, known as "foreign jobs" and shunned by native-born Americans. Immigrants themselves had a different view, considering American working conditions better than those of Hungary. Moreover, life in the American cities' immigrant neighborhoods offered at least a limited chance for social mobility, in contrast to the more rigid social structure of the old world. A contemporary described a typical formula for success: "The simple Hungarian who gets to America breaks himself with body killing work and his biggest wish is to become a 'boss' of boarders and then a 'salooner' as soon as possible."[70] By taking in a few lodgers, a migrant and his family could begin to amass a small amount of capital, which was then used to open a business such as a tavern or a small grocer's or butcher's shop. The petit-bourgeois shopkeeper who emerged in this way from his peasant-worker origins seldom looked much like a modern entrepreneur. He did business within the confines of the immigrant neighborhood, relying on a network of kinship, friendship, and ethnicity. Most of these businesses were family-run affairs, often operating out of the home, and making the most of the family's own human capital. Even children had their chores assisting in the boardinghouse or shop, leaving them little time for play. Girls, especially, were important to the boarder economy. One second generation woman remembered washing by hand and ironing the clothes of boarders at an age when she was hardly big enough to reach the wash tub, as well as cleaning the rooms and helping her mother with the cooking.[71]

In the earlier years of the Cleveland settlement, the migrants who set up as small entrepreneurs tended to be those who had worked as tradesmen or craftsmen in their native villages, with peasants rising to this status only after the turn of the century. In the 1890s lower Buckeye Road was still ethnically mixed, with a variety of stores owned by English, German, Scottish, French, Dutch, and Hungarian families. Hungarian businesses flourished by catering to the particular needs of their co-nationals, providing goods imported from Hungary or prepared according to Hungarian custom, like home-distilled brandies, wines, and "sligovica," or pork to be processed into white and black puddings and sausages. A Hungarian business or store was not merely a purveyor of goods, but also functioned as a social center where immigrants met with their fellows and discussed politics or gave and received advice in their own language, none so more than the Hungarian-owned "korcsma" (saloon). The neighborhood had numerous examples of these; in 1897 there were at least seven of them on Holton Street alone. The owners of the saloons and other businesses tried to attract customers by placing short, inviting slogans in local papers: "The Hungarian House's owner is Hungarian, his friendliness is also Hungarian," or "The Buzitai Csárda is on Holton Street, Ferenc Lukács is its good innkeeper." József Pipi, who for a time leased the Hungarian House, advertised his tavern with a three-verse rhyme:

A Tavern (dedicated) to Hungarian Freedom

The old Hussar is restless because there is no war
For who can stand this peace time, it just becomes a bore
The enemy is nowhere, neither near nor far

The old Hussar gets angry, and opens up a bar.
Hungarian Freedom is the name of the saloon
Open all the time, be it morning, night or noon.
Needless is to say, there is lots and lots to drink,
Food is also plentiful and served in just a wink.
So friend, if you live within, or have to come to town
Come to see the old Hussar, he'll never let you down.
Magyar is the food he serves, and if you taste the wine
You'll feel like a young Hussar, fiery all the time.

Another tavernkeeper, János Juhász, also used verse to advertise his business:

The "Magyar Ház" became Hungarian again,
Only now did the real life surely begin.
Boss Juhász is here the owner of land.
The wine that he offers is fiery brand.
In the "Magyar Ház" here,
We shall sing old songs,
As we did not for years,
Up till now, not once.

Another road to middle-class success was the career of the immigrant banker. These men, who played a key role in the migrant communities, also built up their careers from the bottom.[73] "Nearly everybody among the pen-holders had also pursued heavy work. . . [or] he was a travelling 'peddler' and then became a 'banker.'"[74] Joseph L. Szepessy opened the Buckeye neighborhood's first Hungarian bank, exchange, and notary public in the early 1890s. Szepessy, from Abauj County, arrived in the United States in 1880, at the age of eighteen. After an astonishingly peripatetic ten years, which he spent in locales as different as Brooklyn, Albuquerque, Denver and Wilkes-Barre, at jobs including factory worker, court interpreter, cowboy, bartender, and tea merchant, he settled in Cleveland and soon set up his bank. He also sold groceries and real estate. He took part in the founding of *Szabadság*, was a leader in Hungarian fraternal organizations, and himself owned a considerable amount of real estate.[75] The early banks often combined multiple functions, and the bankers themselves served as intermediaries between the immigrants and both the American and Hungarian authorities. "Owing to my position at home and due to my connections, I can settle legal deals

quickly on favorable terms," advertised Károly Dobay. "I send money, attend
to law-deals, sell boat tickets, [handle] house and building lot sales and various insurance transactions."[76]

Other small entrepreneurs also found that they could expand their success by diversifying. János Weizer, who arrived in Cleveland as a sixteen-year
old youth with his father in 1882, began by working in the "old" and then the
"new" factory, after which he opened a grocery in the east side neighborhood in 1891. A few years later he added a clothing shop, where, he informed
his "honored compatriots," they could also "get a ticket for any shipping line"
or "send money through me to Hungary cheaply and safely." By becoming
a notary public and dealing in real estate, he eventually became one of the
east side's wealthiest Hungarian businessmen. He was a founder of the St.
Ladislaus Sick-Relief Organization and a founder and chairman of St. Elizabeth's church council.[77]

The relatively homogenous society of manual laborers thus soon became
differentiated, as some individuals gained social and occupational mobility
by serving the daily needs of their fellow immigrants. Not all members of
the Hungarian immigrant middle class came from the laboring classes, however. This middle class was formed by people with strikingly diverse social
and ethnic roots.

In the case of those who arrived in the United States before the mass
migration started, many were people who had belonged to the middle or
even upper classes in Europe, but had gotten themselves into financial or
legal difficulties and found it expedient to start new lives in America. In
many cases, this meant entering at the bottom of society and performing
manual work for a shorter or longer period of time. Some of them stayed
there for good, although most, after the first "dog years" following their
arrival, managed to escape from the despised manual labor and latch on to
an occupation having greater social prestige, even if it was not more remu-
nerative. A number did in fact establish successful careers, with journalism being a popular choice of occupation. Most of the Hungarian journalists
and publishers in America at this time came from the *déclassé* gentry or
the Hungarian Jewish community, and were not trained journalists. Their
higher level of education (some had been to university) allowed them to
escape the rigors of physical labor.[78]

The developing Hungarian middle class was ethnically as well as socially
mixed, including many assimilated Hungarian-Germans and -Slovaks as
well as Hungarian Jews. "Hungarian" shops could often serve their customers
in one of the three languages, Hungarian, German, or Slovak. Hungarian
Jews were well represented among the small cadre of professionals, including

physicians and lawyers, and were also active in Hungarian associations, particularly those with a cultural emphasis. Not only the lay leadership, but the clergy also was socially and ethnically mixed. A number of Roman Catholic priests were of national minority origin, assimilated into Magyar culture to a greater or lesser degree. Along with the journalists, the church leaders, particularly the Calvinist ministers but also the Catholic priests, had an ever-increasing role in mediating the ideology of nationalism to the peasant migrants after the turn of the century. For this multi-cultural middle class of varied social origins, identification with the traditions and culture of Hungary was a matter of choice as much as of birth.[79]

The settlement's Hungarian businessmen did their share in organizing the Hungarian community and developing its national consciousness. Almost without exception they held leadership positions in church and fraternal organizations. They promoted the cause of Hungarian identity based on their convictions, but it is also true that like the clergy and the journalists, they served their own material interests by doing so. It was good business for them to serve the needs of their co-nationals, just as Hungarian newspapers would have readers and Hungarian churches' congregants to the degree that people were conscious of themselves as Hungarians. By the 1910s, the Buckeye neighborhood had formed itself into a structured micro-society, with its own internal status hierarchy. By emphasizing ethnic solidarity, middle-class leaders endeavored to downplay conflicts arising between those of differing class and ethnic origins within the Hungarian community, and to gain the adherence of the itinerant workers and peasant migrants to their own ideology. Yet, inevitably, the followers also shaped the institutions that "led" them.[80]

Szabadság: The Role of the Ethnic Newspaper

Attempts to start Magyar-language newspapers in Cleveland before the turn of the century were abortive, lasting a few months or (in the case of the socialist *Amerikai Népszava*) a few years at most.[81] Only *Szabadság* (*Liberty*), which was founded in 1891 and became the city's most important Magyar-language newspaper, had long-term success, although its early years were not promising.[82] Its publisher and founder, Tihamér Kohányi, had been born into the gentry in County Sáros.[83] As a young man, he migrated to the United States to escape his gambling debts, and worked in the mines, and then as a cleaner, a peddler, and a newspaper agent before starting his own publication. Kohányi did not find a ready-made reading public for his newspaper, and had to depend on the goodwill of a few well-to-do Hungarians for funding. When they abandoned him, he fell back on other business ventures, like selling books published in Hungary, and contracting to do printing work for others. He persisted, however. Realizing that his readership would have to come from the large numbers of peasant-workers, he tried to address his newspaper to their concerns. *Szabadság* regularly printed information on where work could be found, which factories were trying to use strikebreakers, and which ones were raising and which ones cutting wages. As migrants developed the habit of newspaper-reading, they grew to expect their papers to write about the main events of their family and community life, and successful publications like *Szabadság* responded to this demand. In 1906 *Szabadság* became a daily, the most important Magyar-language newspaper in the United States outside of New York City. By 1911, when Kohányi celebrated *Szabadság's* twentieth anniversary with a gala banquet, the paper's subscription level stood at forty thousand. The influence wielded by the newspaper and its publisher can be gauged by the fact that Cleveland city leaders and even President William Howard Taft saw fit to attend the event.[84]

Kohányi envisaged his paper's true task as awakening the national consciousness of Hungarian migrants, and building cohesion among them. To achieve this he drew attention to Hungary's glorious past and cultural and political supremacy in the Danube basin. In 1896, on the occasion of the millennium of the Hungarian state, he invoked "the world-historical calling of the Hungarian race," declaring: "The misjudged, misunderstood, often despised 'Hunky' holds his dignified head as if he would tell every American that he is the son of a people, of a land, which can look back on a thousand-year-old culture."[85] As leaders of the nationalities, particularly the Slovaks, took advantage of America's free political environment and began to voice their grievances, Kohányi, like others in middle-class and intellectual circles, found the growing ethnic rift troubling, and, tried to attribute it to pan-Slavic machinations. Ethnic Hungarians needed their own press to "counteract the Pan-Slavic agitation, the goal of which is to discredit the Hungarians of the old country and the immigrant Hungarians in the eyes of the Americans."[86] From the turn of the century on, this attitude of defensive nationalism colored the editorial outlook of *Szabadság*.

In later years commentators criticized it and other Hungarian newspapers of the day, stating that they did not live up to their potential of becoming truly progressive agents for educating the migrants and shaping public opinion.[87] Instead, the newspaper writers, most of whom had entered

journalism merely to escape manual labor, promulgated the nationalist ideology of the Hungarian ruling classes, and on the one hand gave pride of
place to events in Hungary and on the other pandered to the lowest common denominator by chronicling trivialities within the confines of the local
Hungarian community. While this view has a good deal of truth to it, it
must be said in favor of *Szabadság* and similar publications in the first place
that, if nothing else, they inculcated the habit of reading among the migrant
population. They could not realistically be expected to advance literary and
intellectual standards to the point of divorcing themselves from their reading public. As for their emphasis on news of Hungary, the links of the emi-
grating masses to their new surroundings were still weak. Many factors
served to keep alive the ties with the homeland, not least the fact that many
migrants expected to return there. Moreover, *Szabadság,* despite or because
of its nationalistic stance, also criticized political and social conditions in the
old country. While ethnic minorities within Hungary's borders were seeking autonomy, a Hungarian democratic opposition was struggling to break
free of the Austro-Hungarian Empire. This opposition viewed the migrants
in the United States as a potential base of moral and financial support.
Austro-Hungarian government authorities considered all significant Hungarian papers in America as excessively nationalistic or radical, and for a
time *Szabadság* was in fact banned from circulating in Hungary.[88]

Ties to American and Hungarian Political Parties

Like all ethnic communities, Cleveland's Hungarian settlement was linked
to the homeland by ties both sentimental and practical, but was at the same
time, whether by expedience or by desire, developing a relationship with the
host country that would inevitably end in the assimilation of at least some of
its members.[89] The large size of the settlement gave it greater significance
for the political leaders of both Cleveland and Hungary, and its relative concentration made it easier for those leaders to reach and exert influence upon
it. Members of the Hungarian immigrant middle class in Cleveland posi-
tioned themselves to mediate between the migrant masses and the power
structures of both the sending and the receiving societies.

The Hungarian Jews, who rapidly rose to prominence in Cleveland's
business life, paved the way in establishing relations with the representatives
of political power. By inviting the mayor and other government officials to
attend Hungarian fraternal organization festivities, for instance, they and
other middle class leaders were able to use such occasions to inform local
politicians about matters concerning the Hungarian immigrants and to con-

vince them of the importance of Hungarian votes. Along with their devotion to Hungarian nationalism, the middle-class members of the fraternal
organizations and clubs held the opinion (at least until World War I) that
they should be the major link between migrant Hungarians and the broader
American society.

In the 1890s, middle-class and would-be middle-class Hungarians joined
Democrat and Republican clubs; approximately seven hundred people gathered at the first meeting of the Hungarian Democratic organization. During this period, *Szabadság* did not develop a clear preference for one party
or the other, but recommended candidates on the basis of what they had
done for the city and its Hungarian residents: "At city elections political
views must be put aside. The question is not whether the candidate is a good
Democrat or a good Republican but whether he is a good mayor."[90] Significant Hungarian involvement in the city's political life, however, had to
wait, with the first steps taken in the 1930s and more notable participation
occurring in the 1940s. Up through World War I and its aftermath, the situation in Hungary remained the chief concern of most politically active Hungarian migrants.

As a result of transatlantic communication, the continuing arrival of
migrants and visitors from the homeland, and group activities that helped
to maintain political contacts, events in Hungary seemed part of daily life
in the Cleveland settlement. Ethnic leaders put forth the notion that the
migrants had a historical vocation to forward Hungarian nationalism. In
point of fact, at the time when Hungarian communities began to form in
the United States, nationalism was confined to those who were members
of the upper and educated classes. The peasant-worker migrants identified
with the sending society on a personal level only, that is, with their own
village or region. Initially, they had little notion of a national culture and felt
little solidarity with people from other regions or other classes. In the years
preceding World War I, as nationalist political movements gained strength
among Hungary's various ethnic groups, leaders of those movements tried
to gain financial and political support from the migrants. This, combined
with the natural tendency of migrants to band together with their own in
a new and alien environment, and the continued efforts of fraternal and
cultural societies, journalists, and other ethnic leaders, raised ethnic consciousness among migrants from Hungary in the 1900–1914 period.

The relative concentration of the settlement of Hungarians and their
organizations made it easier for the political leaders of Cleveland and those
of Hungary to reach the Magyar inhabitants of Cleveland and exert influence on them. In 1902, the leaders of Cleveland's Hungarian community,

with the encouragement of some American contacts, proposed to the city
government that a monument be erected to commemorate the fiftieth anniversary of Lajos Kossuth's visit to Cleveland during his tour of the United
States in 1851–2. Although funds would be raised privately, the project required, and received, permission from the municipal government to place
a statue of Kossuth on Public Square in the heart of the city's downtown.
The Slovak community, joined by Czech and other Slavic groups, vehemently and publicly opposed this honor to the memory of a man they saw
as an oppressor.[91] Hungarians then organized a rally to protest the protests
of their "pan-Slavic" opponents. The Kossuth statue controversy brought
the politics of European nationalism to the city's migrant communities and
also its general public in a highly visible, if symbolic, fashion. In the end city
council approved a compromise, approving the erection of a Kossuth monument in University Circle, a growing cultural-educational hub on the city's
east side.

When the statue (a reproduction of a similar memorial in Hungary) was
unveiled in September 1902, the ceremony, attended by up to 60,000 people,
included speeches by Cleveland Mayor Tom L. Johnson, U.S. Senator Mar-
cus L. Hanna, and the governor of Ohio. A 16,500-member procession, in
which members of Hungarian fraternal and other organizations from across
the country joined their Cleveland compatriots, preceded the ceremony.
Leaders of the city's Hungarian community, some garbed in elaborate
hussar attire, featured prominently among the marchers, as did mounted
horsemen, Hungarian orchestras, and girls in folk dress. Roman and Greek
Catholic, Protestant, Jewish, and secular organizations turned out en masse
for the occasion; community members unaffiliated with any organization
also took part in the procession, as did a large number of Cleveland-area
Italians. The parade was a milestone in the Cleveland Hungarians' development of ethnic identity.[92]

The Kossuth statue affair set a pattern for similar events during subsequent years. It raised national self-consciousness, provided an impetus for
organization-building within the Hungarian community, and strengthened
the migrant settlement's identification with political currents in the homeland, while also serving as a focus for the opposition of the non-Magyar
nationalities, who were no longer willing to accept their subordinate rank.

In 1904, Count Albert Apponyi, chairman of the Independence party of
Hungary, visited the United States, making a stop in Cleveland where he met
with Hungarians at St. Elizabeth's church and at Hungarian halls on the east
and west sides. Upon this occasion, as well as at the time of Apponyi's return
visit in 1911, the non-Magyar nationalities in Cleveland and across the United

States voiced their opposition in no uncertain terms.[93] Transatlantic political ties were also maintained through the visits of immigrant leaders to Hungary. Kohányi, whose American activities had served to reestablish his prestige in certain circles of the gentry, made a return trip during which he spoke on "the position of Hungarians in America" and the "Pan-Slavic danger."[94]

A governmental crisis in Hungary in 1905–06 attracted considerable attention in the immigrant communities. In Cleveland, more than one thousand people attended a meeting at the Hungarian House on Holton Street. Nationwide, the representatives of two hundred Hungarian settlements in America formed the American Hungarian Federation in 1906.[95] "We, the one million [sic] Hungarians in America do not only demand, but will also [ensure] that the peoples of Hungary will have the same freedom, the same justice, the same well-being, which . . . exists in that America, of which we are citizens."[96]

With the resolution of the crisis, patriotic fervor abated and the Hungarian Federation's 1907 program emphasized the interests of Hungarian immigrants in America. The Federation's leaders, however, were out of touch with the average worker's concerns, and by the time of World War I the organization existed only on paper.[97] The Hungarian elections of 1910 revived political interest somewhat, with *Szabadság* among the supporters of the opposition Independence Party.[98] Although the governing party gained a majority, the election of Independence candidates in the "emigration region" counties caused people in Hungary to recognize that Hungarians in the United States were a political factor to be reckoned with. Apponyi's 1911 visit, during which he addressed a large gathering from the steps of St. Elizabeth's, was meant to attract the support of immigrant leaders and bring their influence to bear upon public opinion in Hungary in favor of the Independence party.[99]

Leaders tried to mobilize the masses through the Hungarian-American press for political movements of interest to the homeland. By the 1910s, using slogans such as people's rights, personal freedom, and democracy, the middle class and the radicals had strengthened the politcal consciousness of the immigrant. When in 1913 Hungarian socialists in America, following the lead of the Social Democratic Party in Hungary, allied with middle-class elements in support of universal suffrage in the homeland, a new factor entered the political scene. Up until that time socialists, who objected on principle to nationalism, had kept themselves aloof from the Hungarian movement in the United States and all its manifestations (in Cleveland, for example, they did not donate any money toward the Kossuth statue), and most migrants had in turn kept aloof from the socialists. The magic words "universal suffrage" opened doors for the latter, who used the opportunity to attempt to disrupt the national unity promoted by the mainstream associations and rally the more radically inclined migrants to the red banner.[100] The differences among various groups notwithstanding, the Hungarian migrants' views overall did become more democratic and radical by the 1910s.

In 1914 one of the leaders of the Hungarian opposition, Count Mihály Károlyi, visited all of the larger Hungarian communities in the United States. Accompanied by representatives of the Hungarian Social Democratic Party, he asked for moral and financial support for the "Independence and 1848 Party." Hungarian politicians had taken note of the way in which Irish immigrants were at that time involving themselves, to great effect, in the political struggles of their homeland, and sought to create a similar movement among Hungarian immigrants. In Cleveland, a rally held at Gray's Armory welcomed the Hungarian visitors. In response to the zeal of the Károlyi Committee and the press, ten thousand people, including the mayor and other prominent citizens, also attended.[101] Patriotic enthusiasm was rekindled in the city's Hungarian community, but the outbreak of World War I changed the course of events both abroad and at home.

Ethnic Identity and Class Consciousness before 1914

In the new environment, migrants' social and leisure-time activities were guided by the traditions and customs they brought with them. Just as young men would have socialized in the village pub or visited each others' homes, they now frequented one of the numerous neighborhood saloons or boardinghouses. The meeting halls, the "Hungarian House" on the east side's Holton Street, and the "Hungarian Hall" on Grand Avenue on the west side, also served as social gathering places.[102] In the saloons and the halls, friends met, talked, drank, made music, and danced, as they used to do at home, to relieve the drudgery and homesickness of immigrant life. The alcohol consumed on such occasions heightened bravado, leading to quarrels, sometimes even knifings. Native-born Americans, in condemning such "barbaric behavior" as typical of the "Hunkies," did not stop to consider that this was a natural outgrowth of the uncertain lives led by itinerant workers, most of them young men far away from their families. Since they did not plan to stay in the United States, they initially showed little interest in American society, and instead organized their own social activities. Beginning in the 1890s Saturday night dances became a mainstay of leisure-time activity in Cleveland's Hungarian community.[103] Hungarian traditions lived on in such social gatherings, whether those of the peasant-workers on the east side, or the craftsmen and middle-class people on the west side. Poor village youth had originally made their own music, while the gentry hired gypsy musicians. After gypsy bands started to appear in Cleveland in the 1890s, they became an indispensable feature at any formal dance.[104]

Religious and family festivities in particular manifested the continuity of traditions and village customs. At Christmas time Reformed church members went caroling, while Catholics took their "Bethlehem plays" to the streets. Rural people transplanted to the city continued to gather for harvest feasts, vintage balls and pigkillings, even though they had, in most cases, grown neither grapes nor pig themselves. Weddings and christenings gave cause for traditional celebrations the whole year round.[105] The Eastertime "sprinkling," in particular, when young men tried to douse with water "the girls who were skipping about to escape," was a carryover of village folk ritual to the American city.[106]

Communal celebrations like these helped to develop group consciousness in a natural way, without any intention on the part of the participants. Fraternal organizations did the same through a planned program, defining norms, giving praise, or inflicting punishments (for instance, levying fines on members who did not attend meetings). By organizing social gatherings to benefit a church or a fraternal benefit fund, they linked entertainment with community-building.[107] Although not altering the behavior patterns of the migrants overnight, such internal influences had greater effect than regulations imposed from outside. The intimate atmosphere of small groups encouraged the unfolding of individual aptitudes. Some migrants learned to read and write through their church or fraternal organization. Others, who had not picked up a book since leaving elementary school, resumed the habit of reading in their new surroundings. Shopkeepers, tradesmen, and workers went on stage as members of drama groups, or learned how to conduct meetings and speak in public through their fraternal organizations.[108]

Most scholars agree that a sense of national and ethnic identity evolved considerably faster in immigrants in America than it did among the rural population in their country of origin.[109] This may be explained by the combined effect of many factors. Encounters with people of other backgrounds overseas gave migrants cause to define their own identity, which they had been able to take for granted in their native environment. Moreover, the small communities of immigrants that formed in the strange new environment of a sometimes unfriendly host society became a welcoming "us" as opposed to a hostile "them" outside, and served as a natural framework for

a burgeoning ethnic consciousness. National identification came to supersede regional identification at least to a degree, as immigrants (many of
rural background) who came from diverse regions with different traditions,
who were socially and culturally stratified, here mixed together and were
bonded by language. The very settlement patterns, wherein migrants of a
given nationality would concentrate within a small geographic area, reinforced these tendencies.

Among the Hungarians, the feeling of "us" versus "them" had special
meaning, and was a key characteristic of their developing ethnic consciousness. "They slander us at every step, they belittle the Hungarians," wrote one
journalist. The view that "the Hungarian people have no relatives among the
people of the world," that the Magyars were a "solitary people," a "kinless"
nation, was often expressed.[110] The Hungarian-American press was quick
to point out that this ethnic isolation had political implications. "A permanent peril is threatening Hungarians both in Hungary and in the United
States. Over there they want to make 'Gross Österreich' (Greater Austria),
annexing Hungary to Austria. Here the pan-Slavs blacken us with verbal
and written slanders. They attack us in public meetings and in books with
the aim that the people, who at one time bowed to the greatness of Kossuth will hate the Hungarians."[111]

The growing ethnic awareness was not without its price. Some individuals among the assimilated minorities experienced a deep identity crisis. "I
am Slovak for the Hungarians and Hungarian for the Slovaks," wrote one
immigrant in a letter sent home.[112] Others chose to make a clean break with
the Hungarian elements in their past and focussed on their ethnic roots. To
some Hungarians, the new attitudes of formerly compliant subjects seemed
to smack of treason, or at least ingratitude: "When he left he was still a faithful Hungarian but later became a belligerent nationality agitator. Who can
look into the soul?"[113] Attitudes in general had to be adjusted more and
more to the ideological requirements of ethnic identity, as in some contexts
individuals were increasingly judged on the basis of whether or not they
were a "good Hungarian" (or Slovak, or Croatian, or Slovene, depending on
the group in question).[114] Social organizations used outward appurtenances
like flags, medals, and uniforms to demonstrate communal solidarity. Members of Cleveland's Hungarian Greek Catholic fraternal society, for example,
attended cornerstone layings, church and school openings, organizational
anniversaries, and other such events as a group, wearing their uniforms.[115]

The founders of the first Hungarian fraternal organizations in Cleveland
were mostly members of the middle-class, who aspired to lead within their

community. Eventually, however, leadership of the fraternal societies passed over into the hands of self-made men and workers. Generally speaking, the Hungarian immigrant community in Cleveland fell into three social classes—the peasant-workers, the craftsmen and skilled workers, and the middle stratum. Although mixing of the classes frequently occurred in the immigrant communities, each group maintained its own cultural characteristics as evidenced by, for example, the way in which they organized their social activities. The middle class, which included the upwardly mobile, took the entertainments of the Hungarian gentry as a model for their social gatherings, balls and banquets. For the peasant-workers, social life generally meant congregating with their friends on an informal basis. They tended to hold themselves aloof from the "well-dressed" people, taught by experience both in Hungary and in the new setting to be distrustful. The skilled workers were the most likely to belong to socialist and similar organizations that offered self-education as well as entertainment in their singing circles, theatrical groups, libraries, and lectures.[116] Like other Hungarian groups in Cleveland, the socialists honored Hungarian national anniversaries like March 15 and October 6, but their speeches stressed social progress rather than national independence, and criticized the remnants of feudalism that still existed in Hungary.

The role of migrants in the development of the political-national movements of their home countries should not be underestimated, nor should it be romantically overestimated. In the immigrant settlements, development of ethnic consciousness was intertwined with community development and lifestyle, with social and cultural activities becoming a vehicle for political ideologies. They conveyed social and political views imbued with ideological content to the ordinary immigrant, even when politicization was not necessarily intentional. The "patriotism" embraced by so many of the Hungarian migrants easily shaded over into the demand for Hungary's independence from the Austrians (or for the autonomy of the Slovaks and other groups from the Magyars).[117] At the same time, most of these migrants accepted their socioeconomic status in the United States.

Politicization on the part of the socialists was more intentional, aiming to integrate immigrants into the working class movement. Although the organizers' goals were international, they depended on the Magyar language and their common culture to gain acceptance among Hungarian migrants. Thus, ethnic considerations colored even the socialists' activities.[118] The fact that both the patriotic and the socialist organizers dispersed their views through the channels of cultural programs indicates that national culture had more relevance than political ideology for the migrant community. Such cultural activities fulfilled a need within the community, and thereby helped to promote group consciousness which was sometimes used for political ends.

Up to 1920s the movement for national independence and democracy in the homeland was the foremost political concern among Hungarian migrants. Assessing the intensity of group consciousness within the rank and file, however, is very difficult. Hungarian sources suggest that only a core group of more educated migrants within the Cleveland community involved themselves to any great degree in political activity and, by promoting their ideas to other immigrants, influenced the development of group consciousness. Nonetheless, it is clear that ethnic awareness was accelerated among Hungarians in the United States.

The effect of migration on the development of class consciousness is less clear. Observations of some contemporaries seem to indicate that it had a retarding rather than an accelerating effect. Zsigmond Kunfi, one of the leaders of the Social Democratic Party in Hungary who accompanied Mihály Károlyi on his trip to America in 1914, argued that: "Emigration weakens the social and political struggles of the working class at home. . . . Hungarians in the u.s. are in large part judged as being more retarded in the political and social sense than the Hungarians in Hungary. It is certain, that the patriotic and church ideology, the leadership of the church are not as strong in Hungary as they are among the Hungarians in the u.s." Kunfi based his conclusions mainly on observations made during his stay in Cleveland.[119] According to another contemporary, Géza Hoffmann, "The bulk of the Hungarians does not even want to hear about the socialists. It is characteristic what an agitator reports: 'I started my speech naturally like this: "Dear Workmates!" Now I got in for a hot time! The compatriots, who were all workingmen, started to yell: "We are not workmates. We are gentlemen. We are members of the association!"' Thus the complaints often voiced by the [conservative] circles in Hungary that the people who return from the u.s. bring socialism with them are based on error . . . fewer socialists leave the shores of the u.s., than leave Hungary. But if the reemigrant from the u.s. does not find such conditions in Hungary, like he got used to here, he either joins that party which speaks up against the existing conditions or reemigrates."[120] When remigrants returned to the streets of their native villages demonstrating a new dignity and self-assurance, the estate owners and bureaucrats, used to demanding servile compliance from villagers, labeled every change in their behavior as "socialist," whether or not this accurately described their political views.[121]

World War I: Divided Loyalty

The outbreak of war made events in Europe an immediate concern for the entire Hungarian community, not only the politically active core. Personal contact ceased as emigration stopped, and those who were preparing to return could not do so. The news that family members were in danger, that fathers or brothers were fighting on the front line, reinforced the weakening attachment to and fading memories of the homeland. Migrants prayed in the Hungarian churches for the victory of the motherland, for the lives of Hungarian soldiers, for the well-being of family members. They organized charitable events, held sales, and collected funds to purchase medicine, bandages, and clothing to send to the Hungarian soldiers through the Red Cross. They responded to requests from Hungary for subscription to war bonds.[122]

With Hungary, as part of the Habsburg Empire, fighting on the side of the Central Powers, the leaders of "patriotic" Hungarian organizations hoped that the United States would maintain its neutrality rather than enter the war in alliance with the Triple Entente. They repeatedly asserted that the United States did not have any interest in the war and so should remain neutral, and openly criticized the war contracts concluded with the powers of the Triple Entente.[123] Meanwhile, within the ethnic communities of non-Magyar migrants from Hungary, the campaign against the Austro-Hungarian Monarchy intensified. Ethnic leaders and particularly journalists realized that the war could open up a free road to their national aspirations, and now called for complete independence instead of mere cultural autonomy. From the beginning of the war, they sympathized with the Entente powers.

The degree to which immigrants identified with their homelands dismayed many "indigenous" Americans, and seemed to belie the image of the United States as a melting pot. As the country prepared for war, American nationalism also strengthened, as did suspicion and hostility toward those of recent foreign extraction, especially Germans but also Hungarians. The "Dumba affair" of 1915, which resulted in the president of the United States calling upon Austria-Hungary's ambassador to resign after the discovery of an apparent sabotage plot, seemed to bear out these suspicions.[124] It was charged that the ambassador, Mr. Dumba, together with Márton Dienes, a former editor of *Szabadság* and Hungarian parliament member, had planned strikes and sabotage actions in order to hamper the production of military material in American factories. The Dumba affair brought about a huge press scandal, which the leaders of the nationalities attempted to use to their own advantage, since it focussed negative public attention upon the Hungarians.[125]

After the United States's entry into the war on the side of the Entente in 1917, hostility toward immigrants from Central Powers countries increased. Leaders of the Hungarian communities tried to assuage this and convince Americans of their good intentions by drafting various "declarations of loyalty." *Szabadság*, which had up to this time taken a pro-Hungary line, now supported the United States, praising the "rightfulness" of its cause with the same enthusiasm it had previously devoted to Hungary's war effort. The fast turnabout disturbed many readers and did not improve the paper's prestige. Similarly, community leaders who had promoted the sale of Hungarian war bonds now urged their fellow migrants to buy Liberty Bonds and take out naturalization papers "so that their loyalty should not fall under suspicion in their adopted country."[126]

Along with the city's other ethnic groups, all of which felt compelled to demonstrate their loyalty to the United States, Cleveland's Hungarians took part in a huge Fourth of July parade and celebration organized by Cleveland officials and other mainstream leaders in 1918.[127] Only the socialists were absent upon such occasions. American socialists considered the conflict an internal one among imperialist powers and did not support the participation of the United States in the war.[128] The i.w.w., with its vociferous anti-war stand, became a particular target of government suspicions. In May 1916 government agents had come to Cleveland to investigate i.w.w. agitation among factory workers. It was charged that the i.w.w. had sent four hundred agitators, most of them Hungarians, to foment a workers' revolt in the city. Members of the organization were threatened with the loss of their jobs; those who were immigrants were barred from American citizenship.[129]

Strikes and other union activity did take place during the war years, not as acts of sabotage, but because workers were in a better position to press their demands. In 1915, workers struck in the Kundtz factory in Cleveland. With Hungarians involved on both the labor and management sides, it was the west side's Hungarian Reformed clergyman who served as president of a committee which eventually worked out a compromise settlement to end the long-protracted strike.[130] Most of Cleveland's Hungarian immigrants were employed in the iron and steel industry. War contracts and, later on, war preparations enhanced the importance of these industries. This brought prosperity, increased demand for workers, and higher wages. To keep production going, the government intervened in labor disputes when necessary, thereby restricting the power of the employers, and sometimes supporting the workers' demands for higher wages, better working conditions, and even shorter hours.[131] Trade unions were able to take advantage of the situation, particularly in the steel industry where long working hours and low wages had been the norm prior to the war.[132] During the war years, especially in 1917, Hungarian workers finally joined unions in large numbers.

From late 1918 to 1920 the situation in Hungary changed rapidly. As war ended, and the Central Powers went down to defeat, the Austro-Hungarian Monarchy dissolved, and Hungary became a separate state. Within Hungary a bourgeois democratic revolution occurred in the autumn of 1918, followed by Béla Kun's Bolshevist dictatorship from March to August 1919. After a period of chaos, a new elected government had no choice but to accept the peace treaty of Trianon, which reduced the historical Hungarian territory by approximately two-thirds.

Just what effect these events would have on Hungarian immigrant communities in the United States was not immediately clear. During the spring of 1919, word that the working class had taken over power in Hungary (together with the general ferment in socialist circles following the success of the Bolshevik Revolution in Russia) heartened the small groups of Hungarian socialists in America, and also Hungarian immigrant workers in general. According to *Szabadság*, "Bolshevik agitation" caused a large number of Hungarians in the United States to believe "that Hungary changed into a workers' Paradise without problems."[133]

Hungarians participated in a general May Day demonstration in downtown Cleveland in 1919, which devolved into a riot in which two people died. A crowd also gathered in the east side Hungarian neighborhood "and refused to disperse even at the order of the police. Somebody shouted: 'Long live the Industrial Republic!'" The man was arrested, precipitating a clash between the crowd and the police. During the day many arrests took place, including the mass arrest of two hundred people at Szabó Hall, a Hungarian saloon that served as a meeting place for east side radicals. American nativists used the participation of immigrants in the May Day events to propagandize against foreigners.[134]

With the end of the war, government control of industry ended, and conflict between management and labor flared up again. The wave of strikes in 1919, particularly the nationwide strike against U.S. Steel, which had great impact in Cleveland, was also attributed to "foreign" and "red" agitation in order to sway public opinion. "For every radical movement, for every strike, the immigrant workers are made responsible," complained *Szabadság*.[135] At the end of 1919 and the beginning of 1920, Hungarian adherents of the I.W.W. were arrested in Chicago, Detroit, and Cleveland. In November, seven Hungarians alleged to be radicals were arrested in a small restaurant on Lorain Avenue; in December, police raided Cleveland's Hungarian socialist club, and arrested its secretary, József Gács, in his home.[136]

While some in the United States advocated an aggressive nationalism, and ultimately succeeded in restricting the flow of "undesirable" peoples from southern and eastern Europe through discriminatory immigration laws in the 1920s, others believed that education and Americanization was the best response to the perceived threat posed by unassimilated foreigners. Americanization programs, some begun during the war, were continued and strengthened in the post-war years. In Cleveland, the work of the Americanization Committee of the Mayor's War Advisory Committee, which included organizing naturalization classes for immigrants, was carried on by the non-profit Citizens Bureau. Three members of the organization's board and committees were of Hungarian origin: Louis Petrash, Helen Zöldi, and Joseph Andrássy. Petrash, a second-generation American raised in the Buckeye neighborhood, was a lawyer who later became a councilman and municipal judge.[137] Americanization programs aimed at "educating the Hungarian people, furthering their culture and entertaining them" included educational centers in schools on Rawlings and Woodland Avenues on east side. Petrash taught a citizenship course at the Woodland Avenue center. Hungarians participated in Americanization efforts in other ways as well: for example, in October 1919 *Szabadság* reported that two municipal employees, a Hungarian, Piroska Hornyák, and an American, Alice Flint, drove through the immigrant neighborhoods and, stopping at street corners where people were gathered, extolled the advantages of American citizenship.[138] Two local Hungarian publications, the Magyar-language *Amerika,* produced by Láaszló Pólya, and *Speak English,* edited by Arthur Winter and Joseph Reményi, also promoted Americanization.[139]

Permanent Settlement and Changes in Ethnic Ideology

Following the end of the war, some middle-class members of the Hungarian community tried to renew the American Hungarian Federation. They hoped to influence American public opinion in the interest of Hungary in order to preserve the territorial integrity of the country at the upcoming Paris peace conference. By then, however, the Federation commanded little attention, even in Cleveland, where it was based. Its loyalists managed to produce some English-language publications, and to have their case presented at a U.S. Senate hearing, but, further weakened by growing divisions within the Hungarian community, the organization's attempts to affect the outcome of events in Europe came to nothing, as evidenced by the conditions of the peace treaty signed at Trianon in 1920.[140]

Much of the territory lost by Hungary was in the areas with large non-Magyar populations. However, many ethnic Magyars had also emigrated from those regions, and were living in the United States when the war broke out. Up to this time many were still planning on returning to Hungary, as a publication of the west side Reformed Church had stated: "When the terrible War abates and along comes the long-awaited and hoped-for peace, then we will return home to support our sweet Hungarian motherland, and to help to make it happy. We could take this church apart and everybody could take away a brick as this church is ours."[141] In the 1920s, however, increasing numbers of Magyar immigrants began to consider the option of remaining in America permanently.

The new national boundaries influenced many to stay, including some who during the war were still planning to return to Hungary.[142] This factor did not, however, play as decisive a role as some Hungarians claimed. Their links to their homeland were still strong, and at least in these early years they did not want to confess that it was, in most cases, the economic prospects offered by an industrialized society that kept them in America. Only later on did people speak more openly about these real reasons.

The situation in America compared favorably with that in Hungary, especially during the prosperous years of the 1920s. Workers experienced significant real growth in their wages. As they came to think of themselves as permanent residents in the United States, rather than itinerant workers bent on taking their savings back to Hungary, their behavior, lifestyle, and shared ideology altered considerably. They gave up, for instance, the practice of amassing money at any price and the self-enforced privations this entailed. They were also much less inclined to purchase land in Hungary, and more inclined to accept "American values" unequivocally. Their lifestyle differed much less significantly from that of Americans of a comparable social class than it had in former years.[143]

In Cleveland, economic prosperity in combination with this new outlook motivated Hungarian immigrants to use their savings or take out loans to build houses. More than at any time before or after, the 1920s were a period of expansion for the Buckeye neighborhood. During those years, with the building of new houses, churches, and commercial buildings, it took on the outlines and appearance that would characterize it over the following decades. The upper Buckeye Road area was built up to 140th Street. By the 1930s Hungarian businesses predominated in the entire Buckeye area, from the vicinity of East 79th Street and Woodhill Road to East Boulevard and East 130th Street.[144] As the Hungarian neighborhood expanded, it reached Cleveland's boundary with the suburb of Shaker

Heights, where wealthy Americans were building large homes. The implications of this juxtaposition of two utterly different worlds were not lost upon the maturing youth of the second generation: "being Hungarian we are poor, they are rich because they are real Americans."[145]

Between 1920 and 1924 family reunification shaped Hungarian migration and remigration. Although some of the married men who had had to stay in the United States during the war now returned home, many others brought their families to America, so that most of the newcomers during that period were women and children.[146] Within the United States, many Hungarians moved from mining areas to industrial cities like Cleveland during this period. Others, mostly young, left Cleveland for Detroit, attracted by the automobile industry. Some Hungarians bought agricultural land in the Cleveland area, rather than in Hungary, with the money they had saved. This strengthened the family's economic position, since in most cases the head continued to work in industry, while the wife and children worked the farm.[147]

As immigrants gradually put down deeper roots in the United States, attitudes toward political activity that focussed on Hungary inevitably changed as well. The unpleasant experience of World War I had already given pause to those who had promoted the political interests of the homeland within Cleveland's Hungarian community. The trend toward Americanization now worked against their efforts, and internal rivalries further reduced their effectiveness. At any rate, most peasant-worker immigrants still had an aversion to politics, considering it "the roguery of the gentlemen." Eventually even the activists, mostly intellectuals or would-be intellectuals, became discouraged and grew tired of making collections or organizing, particularly since arguments seemed an inseparable part of such activities. News about the "white terror" and the anti-Jewish and undemocratic steps of the Hungarian government during this period also created a negative image of the country among the capitalist class and well-known intellectuals, many of whom were Jews. Along with leftist groups, they opposed the Horthy regime, notably through the World Federation of Hungarian Jews.[148] Any contributions from radical and labor organizations went to support victims of the white terror and communist and social democrat émigrés, rather than the Hungarian government. The unceasing requests for aid to Hungary from factions representing the entire political spectrum met increasingly with suspicion and indifference.[149] As interest in the governing of the old country diminished, interest and involvement in local politics grew, evidenced by the election in 1921 of Louis Petrash as Cleveland's first city councilman of Hungarian descent.[150]

Attitudes toward non-political issues relating to their lives in America also reflected Hungarian immigrants' greater integration into the new society. Even though Cleveland's Hungarian community entered its most flourishing stage culturally and socially during these years of expansion and prosperity, Americanization had also made significant inroads, and inevitably affected this cultural and social development. In the 1920s, the phrase "Let us become Americans, let us stay Hungarians!" expressed the change in ethnic ideology. Nearly all fraternal and other communal organizations had in their statutes a passage stating their intent "to help and further the permanent cultivation of the Hungarian language and culture."[151] Handing down the Hungarian language to the second generation remained important in theory, but the actions taken to accomplish this were often ineffective.

By the 1920s the second generation's desire to flee the ethnic communities, or at least to view themselves as Americans first even while recognizing their Hungarian descent, was unambiguous, and proponents of ethnic ideology had to revise their thinking. Realizing that parents had to accept Americanization in order to maintain some influence over their children, and hoping in the same way to keep the second generation within the community, they retreated from their earlier position and now claimed that identity lay not so much in language as in sentiment. In the Hungarian religious schools, religious education began to overshadow teaching of the Magyar language and inculcation of ethnic awareness. A newly opened school adjoining St. Margit Church initially had no facilities for teaching Magyar. At this time, in the 1920s, more than one thousand pupils attended the St. Elizabeth's church school. Even though it was the second largest church school in Cleveland, and even though public schools were criticized as tools of Americanization which disparaged eastern European immigrants while indoctrinating pupils with the superiority of the American way, many Cleveland Hungarians nonetheless sent their children to public schools. It was not by chance that the Americanization programs designed for Hungarian immigrants were organized at the public schools in the Hungarian neighborhood.[152]

Other community institutions and activities were also affected by the trend toward Americanization. News about American events gained greater prominence in the pages of *Szabadság* and other newspapers, which devoted less space than before to matters concerning the Hungarian community alone. At the same time, the former coalition of newspapers, churches, and fraternal organizations in community leadership weakened, as breaks in their ranks appeared, and as the immigrants' Americanized children drifted away from their influence. These institutions themselves were to a greater or lesser degree integrated into American society at large. The Hungarian Calvinists in fact split over this issue, particularly after the "Tiffini Convention" of 1921, when Hungarian Calvinist clergymen reached an agreement with the Reformed Church of the United States. Although many Hungarian Reformed churches, including Cleveland's east and west side congregations, returned to the jurisdiction of the American Reformed Church, others opposed this move and remained independent. "There is no other goal of our continuance than the safeguarding and tending to our heritage we received from God, and that is the Hungarian Calvinisim."[153]

Although the Hungarian Roman Catholic community always was less fragmented than its Protestant counterpart, the forced assimilation of the 1920s also brought conflict. Joseph Hartel, pastor of St. Elisabeth Parish respectfully alerted Joseph Schrembs to the problems caused by replacing Hungarian hymns with Latin chant. "My people are immigrants from Hungary where from their earliest years the Mother Church permitted them to sing the praises of God in Hungarian, while the priest at the altar sang his proper part in Latin. They think it was good there, why does the church forbid [it] here." As for the Hungarian Jews, who had played such an important leadership role in earlier years, many began to identify more with the American Jewish community than with Hungarian gentiles, partly in reaction to the anti-Jewish actions of the government in Hungary.[154]

During the 1920s, the small radical faction of the labor movement divided along ideological lines. Some of the Hungarian i.w.w. members became communists, while others remained loyal to i.w.w. ideology, which they propagated in their newspaper *Bérmunkás, (Wageworker)* edited in Cleveland.[155] The national Workers Sick Benefit and Self-Education Federation was taken over by the recently arrived communist emigrants, who had been active in the events in the 1919 Hungarian Soviet Republic. The activities of the Cleveland branch, which was headquartered in the Buckeye neighborhood, came to be imbued with communist ideology.[156] Therefore, in the 1920s the other radical fraternal organization, the Workers Sick Relief Federation, was able to attract those who supported the left wing of the workers' movement but preferred to remain separate from the communists. The second-largest branch of this Pittsburgh-based group operated in Cleveland.

Cleveland's Hungarian radicals, carrying on the progressive traditions of the i.w.w., would play a role in the organizing of the cio in the 1930s.[157] By this time Hungarian workers in general had become more integrated into the American working class, as the second generation of adults distanced themselves from their ethnic roots. Like other Americans, they were affected by the Great Depression. According to estimates, during the peak of the Depression about half of Hungarian workers were unemployed. This was caused not only by discrimination against them, but also because the impact of the Depression was felt mainly in industries such as the steel works and coal mining, where most of them were employed. Many lost their homes as well, evicted when they could not pay the installments on their mortgage loans. Hungarian and Slovak owners of the modest houses in the Buckeye neighborhood united to protest this, using even violent means to stop the evictions.[158] Even before the full impact of the Depression, however, a lot of Cleveland's Hungarians still had not purchased homes and lived in rented dwellings.[159]

As of 1930, the east and west side neighborhoods remained stable, but Hungarians were by this time also dispersed throughout the city. The community had matured, and so had the first generation of immigrants. In the 1910s, most of the migrants had been young men, under thirty. In 1930, the most populous age groups of first generation immigrants were those over forty-five, and women now apparently outnumbered men. Most Hungarians still worked in the iron and steel works and related industries, but a considerable number were active in other occupations, such as small business ownership.[160]

During the fifty years prior to 1930, Cleveland's Hungarian settlement had grown to become one of the largest in the United States. With the coming of age of the second generation, whose members knew no country other than the United States, the migrants' community entered a new phase. Its sheer size, combined with the substantial institutional framework of churches, fraternal and cultural organizations, and neighborhood homes and businesses that had been built up over the years, ensured an enduring Hungarian ethnic presence, one that would continue as a significant element in Cleveland's cultural mosaic during the decades to follow.

Notes

1. Although, as indicated in the title, it is primarily the Magyars that are the subject of this chapter, in the United States their communities were known by the broader term "Hungarian," which the author therefore uses throughout the essay. "Magyar" is used here only in reference to the language, or to specify Magyar ethnicity as opposed to Hungarian national culture.

2. Susan Papp, *Hungarian Americans and their Communities of Cleveland* (hereinafter: S. Papp, "*Hungarian Americans.*") (Cleveland: Cleveland State University, 1981), 155. Among these early immigrants, the Jewish Black family, reputed to be the

first Hungarians to settle in Cleveland, were particularly prominent, with sons Lajos and Jozsef Black becoming active in business and politics. For more on the pioneers of the Hungarian Jews in Cleveland see Robert Perlman, *Bridging Three Worlds, Hungarian Jewish Americans, 1848–1914* (Amherst: University of Massachusetts Press, 1992), 101–104.

3. Cf. Julianna Puskás, *From Hungary to the United States (1880–1914)* (hereinafter Puskás, *From Hungary*) (Budapest: Akadémiai Kiadó, 1982), 5–45, and, for more on centers of emigration in Hungary, 56–63.

4. *Szabadság 10. jubileumi sz.,* (Szabadság 10th Anniversary) (hereinafter *Szabadság 10*) ed. Tihamér Kohányi (Cleveland, 1901), 18–19.

5. David D. Van Tassel and John J. Grabowski. *The Encyclopedia of Cleveland History* (Bloomington: Indiana University Press, 1987), 542–543 (hereafter cited as ECH).

6. Cf. marriage registers of the Hungarian churches in Cleveland, and biographical data in the *Szabadság 50. jubileumi száma* (Szabadság 50th Anniversary) (hereinafter *Szabadság 50*), 1941, 32–86.

7. *Szabadság. 10*, 18–9, 47–8; J. Palasics 1976, History of Cleveland's Hungarian Community, manuscript, 43.

8. *Szabadság 10*, 18. See also Karl Bonutti and George Prpic, *Selected Ethnic Communities of Cleveland, A Socioeconomic Study for Cleveland* (Cleveland: Cleveland State University, 1977).

9. "The Life of Tivadar Kundzt"; ECH, 601–2; see also Theodor Kundzt, *Cleveland und sein Deutschtum,* German-American Biographical Publishing Co., Cleveland, 1897–1899; *Napsugár,* (Sunbeam). 1910, for advertisements of small entrepreneurs from Metzensef.

10. Geza Hoffmann, *Csonka munkásosztály az Amerikai Magyarság* (1911), 37.

11. Kende Géza, *Magyarok Amerikában, az Amerikai Magyaok tötténete.* (Hungarians in America). Cleveland: Szabadság Publishers, 1927, vol. II, 67–8.

12. *Szabadság 10*, 18–19. They aim at organizing artisans or higher educated persons.

13. *Szabadság,* November 1894.

14. As homage to Kossuth, to commemorate his name-day, in a Hungarian Hall a fete was organized in 1891; *Szabadság,* 21 October 1892. At the time of Kossuth's funeral in 1894 Hungarian fraternal organizations gathered to mourn his death. Cleveland Poles, referring to the brotherly relations that had bound the two nations together for centuries, offered to join Hungarians at the memorial service, *Szabadszág,* 4 April 1894.

15. *Amerikai Nepszava,* (American People's Voice) 15 January 1897.

16. Puskás, *From Hungary,* 253–4; *Dongó,* (Wasp) a Hungarian-language humor periodical was started in 1903 by György Kemény, who for twenty years was a leading figure in Cleveland's Hungarian public life. *Dongó* became a successful paper bringing gaiety and humor to the Hungarian immigrants, 18 April 1908.

17. J. Palasics, History of Cleveland's Hungarian Community. 1976; Perlman, 1992.

18. *Szabadszaág*, 1892. See St. Elizabeth Church Papers, ADC (hereafter cited as SEC), Bishop Hartman's letter to the Archbishop of Hungary, 1890, Hungarian Archbishop's Archive, Esztergom CD. 181.

19. Archive of the Primate of Hungary, Esztergom (hereafter cited as APHE), 181–1890; *Szabadság*, 25 December 1892.

20. *Elizabeth's Hungarian Catholic Church, Cleveland, Golden Jubilee, Cleveland, Ohio, 1892–1942* (Cleveland, 1942).

21. SEC, 1891–1914, ADC.

22. Church and School Reports, 1894–1899, SEC.

23. *St. John the Baptist Byzantine Catholic Church. Jubilee Album* (Cleveland, 1984), ; *Szabadság 10*, 25.

24. See, concerning this, the reports of the ambassadors and consuls of the Austro-Hungarian Monarchy in Washington, for example, the papers relating to the Hungarian Greek-Catholic churches. Cf. Országos, Levéltár, A Miniszterelnökség Központilag Iktatott és Irattározott Iratai. [The Centrally Registered and Filed Documents of the Prime Minister's Office, National Archives, Budapest], 1867–1944, (hereafter cited as OL ME) K26, XXXI. 650. See also "Die Ortodoxe Propaganda unter Unsere Griechisch Katholische Immigranten", Nr. 16. A–B 1896 Nov. 28 SA PA W XXXIII USA.

25. Louis Kalassay, "Educational and Religious History of the Hungarian Reformed Church in the United States" (Ph.D. dissertation, University of Pittsburgh, 1939), 30–33.

26. *Jubileumi Emlékkönyv*, (Jubilee Memorial Book) ed. Sándor Tóth (Pittsburgh, 1940), 54.

27. Papers and Minutes of the First Hungarian Reformed Church, Cleveland, Hungarian Collection, Immigration History Research Center, St. Paul.

28. Elek Csutoros, *Az Árpádházi településről* (The Árpád Home Colony) *Tizév a clevelandi west side-i magyar Református Egyház történetéből*. (Ten years of the history of the Hungarian Reformed Church Life, 1906–1916), Cleveland, 1917. (hereinafter: Csutoros, 1917.) 122.

29. Records of the First Hungarian Reformed Church, November 1890 to 31 December 1899, First Hungarian Reformed Church, Cleveland, Ohio.

30. Aladár Komjéthy, "The Hungarian Reformed Church of America. The Effort to Preserve a Denominational Heritage" (Ph.D. dissertation, Princeton Theological Seminary, 1962), passim, describes in detail the endeavors of the U.S. Protestant churches to assimilate the immigrants. He emphasizes the prejudices of the leaders of these churches in the U.S., and the enforcement of assimilation.

31. *Szabadság 10*, 26.

32. Kivándorlási Tanács Iratai, (Minutes, Papers of the Emigration Council) vol. I–VI. Budapest, 1924–1930.

33. Daniel E. Weinberg, "Ethnic Identity in Industrial Cleveland. The Hungarians 1900–1920," *Ohio History*, 86 (1977, no. 3), 179; J. Puskás' interview with Ilona Palasics, Cleveland, 1988.

34. Weinberg, "Ethnic Identity," 179.

35. *Szabadság*, 21 March 1893.

36. See for example *Kivándorlási Értesitö*, (Emigration Gazette) 22 November 1903; Cf. reminiscences of elderly people, Imre Sári Gál, *Amerikai Debrecen*. (The American Debrecen) (hereinafter I. Sári Gál) (Toronto, 1966), 15.

37. *Reports of the Immigration Commission: Immigrants in the Cities*, 1910, vol. 26, Tables II and III (hereafter cited as RIC). The Immigration Commission survey distinguished Magyars as a specific ethnic group, rather than combining them with other ethnic groups from Hungary.

38. RIC, vol. 26, 596, 598.

39. Senate, Documents, 61; Congress 2nd session 1901–1910 vol. 66, 497–502, vol. 67, 190–2, in Weinberg, "Ethnic Identity," 177.

40. Seventy percent of the Hungarians earned less than $400. RIC, vol. 26, 575; interview with Mrs. Farkas, Cleveland, June 1988.

41. *Szabadság*, 21 March 1893; 7, 8 January 1909; Van Tassel and Grabowski, eds., ECH, 43.

42. *Amerikai Magyar Népsvava*, Julieumi Diszalbuma, 1899–1909 (Deluxe Anniversary Album of the American Hungarian People's Voice) Ed. by Géza Berkó. (hereinafter AMN 10. 1910) (New York 1910), 41.

43. Interviews with members of the women's circle of the First Hungarian Reformed Church and St. Elisabeth Church, May and June 1988. Most of the women belonged to the second generation being children of the immigrants.

44. RIC, vol. 26, 511; Table 33; I. Sári Nagy, 166, 16.

45. Weinberg, "Ethnic Identity," 180; interview with J. Palasics, Mr. Sabo and others who belonged to the second generation, June 1988.

46. RIC, vol. 26, 579.

47. AMN 10., 1910, 41; Sárkozi Zoltán, A summások (The seasonal workers) in Istvan Szabó, ed. *A parasztság Magyarországon a kapitalizmus korában, 1848–1914* (The peasantry in Hungary during the time of capitalism, 1848–1914) 2 vols. (Budapest: Akadémiai Kiadó, 1965); (hereinafter: Szabó, 1965).

48. Kapri Ferenc, *The Story of St. Emeric Church* (Cleveland, 1979); Ferenc Kapra, *Bőhm Károly pápai porelátus élete és korrajz. 1885–1907* (The life story of Kátoly Bőhm, papal prelate and a portrait of the period) (Cleveland: Classic Printing, 1994), 11–21.

49. Csutoros, (1917).

50. S. Papp, "Hungarian Americans," 120–1.

51. *Kivándorlási Értesitö*, (Emigration Gazette) 26 June 1904; SEC records, ACD.

52. Mrs. I. Ruzsa, "Ruzsa István első Magyar ág.h.e. Amerikai Magyar Lelkész Életrajza és működése." (Biography and work of István Ruzsa, first Hungarian minister of the Augustan Confession) Unpublished, 1967.

53. E. L. Kautz, "The History of the Hungarian Baptist Work in America." (Dissertation, 1957). The History of American Baptists (1958),19; *Evangéliumi Hirnöke* (Gospel Messenger) (the official paper of the Hungarian Baptist Association in the

u.s., published in Cleveland beginning of 1909); Mihaly Almási, *A Clevelandi Magyar baptista misszio 85 éves története Jubileumi Emlékkönyv*, (The eighty-five year history of the Cleveland Hungarian Baptist Mission) Cleveland, 1984.

54. "Mission Among Our Foreign-Speaking Population," in Minutes of the Synod of Pennsylvania, 1900, 10.

55. "Guidelines for the American Hungarian Action," 27 March 1903, typescript, OL ME 126.

56. "American Hungarian Action" files, Committee for Foreign Affairs of the Convent, Archives of the Reformed Church Synod of Hungary.

57. Zoltán. *Kuthy*, 1917, 42–3; *Emlékkönyv az Amerikai Magyar Reformáttus Egyházmegye 25 éves évfordulójára az Egyesült Államokbeli Reformáétus Egyház Keleti Magyar Egyházmegyéje, 1904–1929* (Memorial Album for the 25th Anniversary of the Hungarian American Reformed Diocese. The Hungarian Diocese of the Reformed Church of the United States in the East, *1904–1929*). Compiled by Géza Takaró, Ernő Komjáthy, and István M. Böszörményi (Bridgeport, Conn., 1929), (album, 1929), 19, 403.

58. Hoffmann, *Csonka Munkasosztaly*, 200.

59. Sándor Harsányi, *Az Amerikai ref. Egyház Története*. (The history of the American Reformed Church.) Homestead, 1911.

60. Csutoros, 1917. OL ME K 26, 1910, XXI, Batch 8760.

61. Their first church was built on the corner of Buckeye Road and East 103rd Street in 1915. The second church was completed in 1918.

62. Bőhm, Memorandum, 1913, APHE [Primate's Archives, Esztergom].

63. *Bevándorló*, (Immigrant) 7 May 1907.

64. Minutes of the Board of Bishops, 22 January 1913, APHE.

65. Cf. Paula Kaye Benkhart, "Hungarians," *Harvard Encyclopedia of American Ethnic Groups*, ed. Stephen Thernstrom (Cambridge: Harvard University Press, 1980), 462–471.

66. Church Report, 20 December 1911, SEC.

67. Newspaper clippings, Cleveland Public Library.

68. John Körösföy, *Hungarians in America. Az Amerikai Magyarság aranykönyve* (Cleveland, 1941), 48.

69. Organizational news column, *Népakarat*, (People's Will) 1909.

70. György Kemény, "Az Amerikai Magyar életböl," (From the Hungarian life in America) in AMN 10. 1910. 221.

71. J. Palasics, manuscript, 1976, 63; interviews with two elderly women, both members of the second generation, in the Buckeye neighborhood at the time of my first visit in Cleveland, 1977.

72. J. Palasics, 61; *Dongó*, 1904, no 19; *Cleveland Magyar Recorder*, 1897.

73. Cf. their biographies in Körösföy, *Hungarians in America*. 1961.

74. AMN 10. 1910.

75. *Szabadság*, 20th anniversary issue, 21 December 1911; i.e. September 1918.

76. *Szabadság Naptár*, 1915, 190.

77. *Szabadság*, 1897; 20th anniversary issue, 21 December 1911.

78. *Bevándorló*, 1907; Gy. Kémeny, 1909, 216.

79. *Szabadság*, 10 50; on the rise of the immigrant middle class see György Kemény, "Az Amerikai Magyar életből," (From Hungarian life in America) in AMN 10. 1910, 80, 221; see *Napsugár; Szabadság*, including 20th anniversary issue.

80. See *Napsugár; Szabadság*, including 20th anniversary issue.

81. There was also a comic newspaper, *Dongó*, founded by György Kemény in 1902, which lasted for some decades; and a literary paper, *Napsugár*, produced by Gyula Rudnyánszky. Both of these editor-publishers were poets. Cleveland's first Hungarian daily, the *Hungarian Daily Paper*, began publication in 1902 but was taken over by *Szabadság* after a six-year campaign on the part of the latter.

82. At its founding, J. Black and T. Kundtz contributed 600 dollars each. T. Kohányi was paper's editor, J. Szepessy assistant editor. The owner of the newpaper was Szabadság Ltd. The paper appeared twice a week, on Monday and Thursday.

83. For Kohányi's life, see Márton Dienes, *Kohányi Tihamér élete és küzdelmei* (The life and struggles of Tihamér Kohányi) (Cleveland, 1913).

84. *Szabadság*, 20th anniversary issue, 21 December 1911; Dienes, *Kohányi Tihamér;* Cf. the history of *Szabadság* in Otto Táborszky, "The Hungarian Press in America," (M.A. thesis, Catholic University of America: Washington, 1955).

85. *Szabadság*, 1896.

86. Márton Dienes, *Kohányi Tihamér*, 48.

87. R. E. Park, 1921, 115–141.

88. Haus-, Hof- und Staatsarchiv, Wien, Aufstellungsverzeichnis des Politischen Archivs des Ministerium des Aussers, 1848–1918, XXXIII, usa, Washington [herereafter cited sa pa w], Report 1903, no 31.

89. Regarding the ethnic community vis-a-vis the countries of origin and settlement see Helena Znaniecki Lopata, *Polish Americans* (Prentice-Hall, Englewood Cliffs, New Jersey), 1976, 21.

90. *Szabadság*, 25 February 1897.

91. See chapter by Kopanic.

92. *Szabadság*, 30 September 1902; Géza Kende (Cleveland, 1927), 208–227.

93. Monika Gletter, 245; ol me K 26 1904–XV. 5089; [see chapter[s] by Kopanic and Čizmić].

94. *Szabadság 10*, 9–42.

95. Tihamér Kohányi was chairman of the Federation. Other officers were: vice-chairmen, Imre Fecső, Rev. Elek Csutoros, Rev. Biró; chief treasurer, János Németh; banker/treasurer, V. Gusztáv Hámory; banker/secretary, György Kemény; assistant secretary, Henrik Baracs.

96. *Szabadság*, February, March 1906.

97. Jenó Pivány, *Egy Amerikai kiküldetés története* (1943), 42; Puskás, *Hungarian Migrants*, 249. "The Federation—being established in stormy weather—remained a dead letter . . . there were so few attending the meeting that they could not even carry a resolution." *Bevándorló*, 1907.

98. *Szabadság*, April 28, 1910.

99. For a first-hand account of Apponyi's visit to the United States, see Ernő Kovács, *Utazásom Amerikában Apponyi Alberttá* (My trip to the U.S. with Albert Apponyi) (hereinafter: Kovács, Budapest, 1911) (Budapest, 1911).

100. See articles in *Előre, Amerikai Népsvava*, and *Szabadsag*, March 1913; Béla Vasady, "The 'Homeland Cause' as Stimulant to Ethnic Unity: The Hungarian American Response to Károlyi's 1914 Tour," *Journal of American Ethnic History*, 2 (1982, Fall), 39–64.

101. Vasady, *ibid; Szabadság Naptár*, 1915, 82–94. See also Mihály Károlyi, *Hit illuzio nélkül* (1977).

"Under the influence of the Szabadság's articles, Cleveland's Hungarians rallied into one unified camp. There was not one dissident voice. All of them., from the wealthiest Hungarian, Tivadar Kuntz, to the most simple Hungarian worker ten thousand rallied as one at the thought of taking an active part in the continual struggle for an independent Hungary" *Szabadság Naptár* (1915), 92.

102. Both opened in 1891. The east side facility had a saloon, grocery, and butchery, as well as a meeting hall, stage, ballroom, and summer recreation room. *Szabadság*, 18.

103. The Magyar-language press repeatedly complained of the way Hungarians were "scolded . . . without reason" by the mainstream society and its newspapers. See for example *Szabadság*, 13 May 1897. However, self-criticism also occurred. In 1899 *Szabadság*, in an article entitled "Eternal Carnival," fulminated against the Hungarians' many revelries, which, it complained, drained the community's pockets, with only the breweries growing wealthier; see also K. Bőhm's article, "Suggestions for our carousing Hungarians," in *Magyarországi Szent Erzsébet Amerikai Hirnöke* (Cleveland), 14 July 1899.

104. *Szabadság*, 1892; advertisement for Andrós Miká's uniformed band, 6 June 1894.

105. *Szabadság*, 21 January 1897; *Szabadság* 10 (American Messenger of St. Elizabeth of Hungary) *Dongó*, various issues; interviews with second generation members, June 1988, at the First Hungarian Reformed Church and St. Elizabeth Church; S. Papp, "Hungarian Americans," 235–237.

106. An interesting report can be read for example of the Easter spraying, how the traditional forms change in the altered surroundings. *Szabadság*, 19 April 1900.

107. In the forefront of organizing balls and theatrical performances were the Self-Educating Circle, the various amateur theatrical societies formed at the turn of the century, and the Youth Organization, founded in 1891.

108. *Bevándorló*, 1907; April 6, 1911.

109. Greene, 1975; Znaniecki, 1976; Puskás, 1982.

110. *Napsugár*, 16 January, 27 May 1910.

111. *Napsugár*, 10 May 1910. Cf. also *Bevándorló*, 18 March, 19 May 1911.

112. Bishop of Munkács to the Archbishop, "The Care of the Soul of the Catholics in the United States," 1910, Office of the Archbishop, APHE

113. Letter, 27 October 1905, OL ME, K 126.

114. Kovács, Budapest 1911. Béla Vasady, "Mixed Ethnic Identities among Immigrant Clergy from Multiethnic Hungary: The Slovak-Magyar Case, 1885–1903," in Peter Kivisto, ed., *Ethnic Enigma* (Philadelphia, 1989), 47–66.

115. *Szabadság*, 26 April 1900.

116. G. Hoffmann, *Csonka munkásosztály*, 1911, 130–6.

117. See Monika Glettler, *Pittsburgh-Wien-Budapest. Programm und Praxíes der Nationalitätenpolitik bei der Auswanderung der ungarischen Slowaken nach Amerika um 1900* (Wien, 1980), 391–401.

118. See the socialist newspapers founded in the years as follows: *Amerikai Népszava* (1895), *Nepakarat* (1903), *Előre* (Socialist Party, 1905), *Munkás* (Socialist Labor Party, 1910), *Bérmunkás* (I.W.W., 1912).

119. *Előre*, 25 January 1915.

120. Hoffmann, *Csonka*, munkásosztály, 1911. 136.

121. Puskás, *From Hungary*, 1982, 84–91; Kemény G. Gábor.Iratok a nemzetiségi kérdés történetéből Magyarországon a Dualizmus Korában. (Documents concerning the question of non-Magyar ethnic groups at the age of dualism) Budapest, vol. 1, 1952; vol. 2, 1956; vol. 3, 1964; vol. 4, 1966; vol. 5, 1971. Budapest: Akadémiai Kiadó.

122. For instance, Karoly Winker, the Hungarian Royal Chief Consul, spoke at the September 1914 board meeting of the Rákóczi Sick Benefit Association (one of the four nationwide fraternal organizations) and asked for support for war orphans and widows. The national mutual aid societies (except for the socialist organizations) used part of their assets to buy Hungarian war bonds. Cf. Puskás, *From Hungary*, 304–305.

123. Cf. *Református Hiradó*, 7 January 1915, quoted in Puskás, *From Hungary*, 305.

124. Mark Stolarik. *Slovak Migration from Europe to North America, 1870–1918* (Cleveland: Slovak Institute, 1980), 116–22.

125. Papers relating to the Dumba affair, 1915, National Archives. Cf. "Resolution of the Slovak League of America," sent to Joseph P. Tumulty, 14 September 1915: "We citizens and intended citizens of the U.S.A. of Slovak descent are aroused by the impertinent actions of the said Dumba and his co-conspirators, and further be it resolved that we rejoice in the patriotic and prompt actions of our esteemed and beloved President, his Excellency Dr. Woodrow Wilson and his Excellency Robert Lansing, Secretary of State of the United States of America, in removing said Dumba from our country, and proving to all our enemies that even [a] peace loving country will not suffer interference beyond a certain limit." However, reports about explosives being planted in some factories could not be confirmed by this author's research in the archive (National Archive).

126. In 1918, *Szabadság*, which had been pro-Hungary became pro-American. Dr. Cserna: *Szabadság*, 1918.

127. *Szabadság*, 5 July 1918.

128. *Előre*, 1916; Milton Cantor, *The Divided Left, American Radicalism 1900–1975* (New York: Hill and Wang, 1978), 56.

129. National Archives; F. Thomson, *The IWW. Its First Fifty Years, 1905–1955* (Chicago, 1955), 109–10; M. Dubofsky, *We Shall Be All: A History of the Industrial Workers of the World* (Chicago: Quadrangle Books, 1969), 376–93, on the I.w.w. and World War I.

130. *Szabadság*, October 1915; Csutoros, lo 1917; *Előre*, 1915.

131. David Montgomery, *Workers Control in America* (Cambridge: Cambridge University Press, 1979), 98.

132. D. Brody, *Labor in Crisis: The Steel Strikes of 1919* (Philadelphia: Lippincott, 1965), 73–75.

133. *Szabadság*, 7 September 1919.

134. Van Tassel and Grabowski, eds., ECH, 667; *Szabadság*, 2, 3 May 1919.

135. *Szabadság*, 1 November 1919.

136. *Szabadság*, 13 November and 2 December 1919. The I.w.w.'s paper *A Szabadság* (Chicago) reports on it; in its issue of the 19th July 1919: "their strongest groups in this city (Cleveland) are amongst the Hungarian workers. 11 of our members were sentenced to deportation. More than 200 members were arrested. On the first of May, one of our members was murdered, they shot him through and smashed his head to pieces."

137. Executive Committee, Citizens Bureau; also see Americanization Committee, Mayor's War Board. Andrássy was manager of the "Foreign Department" of the Buckeye branch of the Garfield Savings Bank, and spoke Hungarian and German.

138. *Szabadság*, 7, 18 October 1919.

139. S. Papp, "Hungarian Americans," 533.

140. The Federation's secretary, Jenő Pivány was an American citizen but had returned to Hungary before World War I. He came back to the United States in 1919 to get support from Americans before the peace conference, serving as a representative of the "League Defending the Territorial Integrity of Hungary," and publishing a pamphlet, *Some Facts about the Proposed Dismemberment of Hungary* (Cleveland, 1919). He later wrote about his mission in *Egy kuldetes tortenete* (The history of a mission) (Budapest, 1943).

141. Csutoros, 1917.

142. *Szabadság*, December 1919.

143. Van Tassel and Grabowski, eds., ECH, 606; J. Palasics, 72–5, Puskás, Kivándorló Magyarok, 1982..

144. Káldor, 1937, 18–19; Sari Gal, *Amerikai Debrecen;* interviews of second generation members of the Hungarian community at the St. Elizabeth Church and First Hungarian Reformed Church, May–June 1988.

145. Van Tassel and Grabowski, ECH, 884. Geographicaly there was not a distance between the Shaker Heights and the Hungarian neighborhood (on East Side) on the other hand, socially it was so much larger ; interview with J. Palasics, who recalled how he used to compare the two worlds while picking up the tennis balls of the rich. As he told, the Hungarian immigrants "the inhabitants of Shaker Heights were only referred to, as, the masters, or the Englishmen."

146. I. Ferenczi, Willcox, *International Migrations,* vol. 1, (New York, 1929) 431.

147. That happened with the Szabó Family and some others around Cleveland. Interview with Mr. Szabo, a son of a Hungarian immigrant family on his farm near Cleveland, June 1988.

148. J. Puskás, "Hungarian Immigration and Socialism," In Marianne Debousy *In the Shadow of the Statue of Liberty: Immigrants, Workers and Citisens in the American Republi,c 1880–1920.* St. Denis, 1988, 138–151.

149. For requests for support and aid, see for example Károly Huszár's New Year's greetings and request to the Hungarian people in the United States, published in *Szabadság,* 19 December 1919; Béla Kun's letter to the Hungarians in America, *Előre,* 17 May, 23 June 1920. For a reaction, see József Reményi, 1934, 423–426, including the ironic remark, "It seems as if the role of the savior of our Fatherland would await the Hungarians in America."

150. Kőrösfőy, *Hungarians in America,* 1942, 62. Petrash served on the council for ten years.

151. Cf. statutes of the Verhovay Association.

152. J. Palasics, manuscript, 1976; Church and School Reports for the Year ending December 31, 1922, ADC; Herbert A. Miller, *The School and the Immigrant,* Table 5.

153. For text of the Tiffin Agreement see Kalassay, "Educational," 1939, 139–144." Tiffin is Our Trianon," wrote a minister of the Independents, György Borsy-Kerekes in his book, *Az Egyetlen Út* (The only road) (Duquesne: Magyar Egyház Társaság, 1930), 24.

154. By the 1930s Hungarian Jewish organizations, whether religious or secular, had all but disappeared. Perlman, 1991, 155, 234–237. *Bérmunkás Naptar,* (Wageworker's Calendar). 1923.

155. *Bérmunkás Naptar,* 1923.

156. *Előre Naptár,* 1927. Roy Wortman, *From Syndicalism to Trade Unionism: The I.W.W. in Ohio, 1905–1950* (New York: Garland, 1985), 139–140.

157. Cf. R. T. Wortman, 1985, 123.

158. J. Palasics interview, June 1989.

159. Howard Whipple Green, "Population Characteristics by Census Tracts, Cleveland, Ohio, 1930," (Cleveland, 1930). Although the data is given according to country of origin rather than by ethnic group, correlating it with the known location of the Hungarian/Magyar neighborhoods gives at least a general grasp of the demographic and social characteristics of the Magyar ethnic group.

160. *Ibid; RIC.*

Polish Americans

ADAM WALASZEK

The Decision to Migrate

After 1795, Polish territories were partitioned among Russia, Austria, and Prussia. Complex motivations impelled many inhabitants of these territories to migrate. First and foremost was the desire to better one's material situation. Rapid population growth, overpopulation, and lack of land characterized Polish villages following the emancipation of the peasantry from their remaining feudal bonds in the mid-nineteenth century (as late as 1864 in the case of Russian Poland).

Plagues and economic crises of the late nineteenth century combined with other push factors to impel migration. Migration, as sociologist Florian Znaniecki has noted, "like any other social phenomenon with an economic background, is conditioned by a rise of new needs among the people, and by a knowledge that these needs can be fulfilled and how." In the emancipated villages, surplus income was scarce, but people still had to pay debts, buy more land and cattle, and take precautions against possible crop failures and other misfortunes. The indebtedness of rich and poor peasants alike increased twelvefold between 1885 and 1905. Money was an important new reality in the Polish peasant's life. Banks and savings and loan associations eventually appeared. But acquiring money was difficult in the countryside. Thus, people started seeking it abroad.[1]

Peasants' horizons were also broadening. During fairs and in the market places people heard about migrants' adventures and the marvels of the outside world. In 1861 Feliks Boroń from Czernichów, a village not far from Cracow, set out on foot to Rome, Paris, and Jerusalem. Travels like this had been almost unheard of among the peasantry, but now trains and steamships were beckoning. In village taverns, conversations frequently revolved around migrants' tales. In the 1880s Wojciech Łagowski was the first person from Krzywa, a Galician village in Ropczyce County, to cross the Atlantic. "There was so much talk in the village, so much fear. A year later a second, then a third person left, and after these sent back a few dollars to their families a real hysteria started. Everybody borrowed money, wherever he could, and left for the golden land."[2]

Emigration was an act of revolt against fate, an attempt to escape: from oppression, from the authorities, and from military service; from families, elders, and the traditional way of life. "Finally I revolted against my fate and my parents," declared one migrant. "I escaped from the house." In 1907, during a conference of religious authorities in Poland, priests discussed the reasons for emigration, noting that among them was "a wish for freedom, a desire to escape from parents' supervision."[3]

Beyond financial hardship, and the simple desire to escape, the motivations for some migrants lay more in the realm of the imagination: curiosity about the outside world, a longing for adventure, and the dream of becoming a grander, richer, enviable person. An old woman living in Chicago, who had left Poland before World War I, remembered how it had been: "I wanted to go to America, I wanted to know." There had been no economic necessity for her to emigrate; her parents were fairly wealthy peasants who employed some agricultural workers, and the girl herself owned "six coral strings." Another girl was inspired by a photograph, sent back by an acquaintance who had left their village for America six months before. "What a lady, a hat, feathers, beautifully dressed. . . . Her mother came to mine to show [the photograph of] Filomencia. And my mother calls: 'Józia, come, you'll see Filomencia, look what a lady.' I looked: 'Filomencia, so, here you were such a beggar and your father worked for my parents just for food, and now you're such a lady!' I said nothing, but later to my mother—'Mother I go to America. . . . I don't want to work on a farm, I go to America.' I wanted to be a lady, like this colleague of mine. . . . I wanted to be here, [and] send a photograph, see."[4]

In the case of America, as Ewa Morawska notes, "a positive motivation" always existed. People were not only pushed out of the old world by the need to survive but were also drawn to the new by a wish for social betterment. Advancement, a better future, prestige: these were of course understood in the contexts of people's own culture.

For those of peasant stock, socioeconomic status was based on "the possibility of having an independent life without a necessity of work in dependency," rather than on the extent or value of landholdings as such. However, it was also true that "Property secured that [independence] in the best way." Work in the fields provided a living often basic at best. Cash received from outside the village made economic stability and social mobility possible. Returning migrants could build a house, achieve higher status, and buy more land.

People went to America "to make their pile of krutzers," or "to buy a farm to run" in Poland. Emigration created an opportunity to direct the course of one's own life. The expanding economy of the United States in the late nineteenth century offered peasants a chance to fulfill "their aspiration for social advancement as defined by their own hierarchy of values." Two weeks of work there could bring in as much as a whole season's labor in German or Hungarian agriculture. At this time, most migrants considered their stay abroad as temporary. Before World War I re-immigration to the homeland and circulation back and forth across the ocean were common. These "birds of passage" could in fact be considered the migrant workers of the transatlantic economy. Available data indicate that the return rate was about thirty percent of the emigration rate.[5]

Chain Migration

Emigration was typically organized through networks of families and friends. There were close ties between those who left for America and those who remained in the European villages. This was true for Cleveland as elsewhere. Letters between husbands and wives, parents and children, and friends and relatives were constantly crossing the Atlantic. This everyday dialogue was conducted at very great distances with the help of agents (*pisennicy*) who were able to write letters. However trivial or dull the subjects of some of these communications might seem to the outsider, they were important to the correspondents. The migrants sent advice as well as money to the old country. "And if you are going to lease the land then let the lessees have it but for 6 years, and let him pay for the lease to you in advance if he can. . . . And if you have straw to sell, leave it on the land and the dung as well. Tear down the fence and chop it up for firewood unless he wants to pay you for it," one man wrote to his wife. They also persuaded friends and relations that they, too, should leave, setting in motion a chain of migration. "As regards Władek, I'd like to ask you to help him to come overseas, as you are his uncle, and I will try to get a steamship ticket for him if he sends the money. For one must have at least 40 rubles for this journey, and to come to Cleveland one may need over 47." One of the most common statements of all in migrants' letters was, "I will send you a steamship ticket if you wish it."[6]

The agents bringing families to America and making trip arrangements also gave information about all details of the journey. "When you are in Prussia and when they ask you where you come from, you should tell them you come from some little town or village in Prussia; thanks to that, you will have an easier journey." "Only ask God that the Lord Jesus will allow you to cross the border safely so that they will not catch you [emigration from Russian Poland was illegal]." Migrants were advised that after arriving in America, "When they ask you where you are going, you should say you are going to Cleveland and if they ask you whether you have a job there, you should answer in the negative and say that you will take up any job they give you." One husband instructed his wife regarding the journey: "You should take with you on the trip thick bread and smoked dried fatback, sugar and vinegar"; and also on the disposal of household items: "... the pictures, those which are nicer take them out of the frames and bring them with you, and sell the frames and the glass. . . . The iron take with you and the large one too, but do not waste the bedding."[7]

Mutual help continued in America, with relatives and friends seeking out accommodation and often jobs for new arrivals. Train tickets were sent to poorer relatives.[8] At the end of the long journey from Europe, Polish migrants were comforted by the sight of familiar faces, and sometimes even surprised by the strong ties between the new communities and the old country. One man recollected that when he arrived at the railway station in Cleveland, "Of course my sister-in-law and an uncle that we had here . . . all came for us. It was like salvation, coming to put sad immigrants into a strange country. So we went home with them . . . they were my brother and uncle, and . . . my brothers' wives, and we lived there."[9] On the evening that immigrant John Gallka arrived in Cleveland's Kantowo neighborhood, everyone who had once lived in or near his village came to ask for local gossip. "This is not America! It's Tarnów, Stanislawów!" exclaimed Emil Dunikowski, a Polish journalist who visited the United States in the 1890s.[10]

Building Neighborhoods: 1873–1900

The City

Cleveland was one of the main American destinations for Polish immigrants by the turn of the century. Based on the impressions of Polish visitors and immigrants to Cleveland in earlier years, this might have seemed unlikely. A Polish journalist described his first view of the city in 1892: "I never thought that such a big and almost 60-year-old city could have such a strange appearance. One has the impression of the Far West, where house after house is being built, where everything is only just being delineated and remains unfinished. For it is here that the wild forest or the virgin prairie push in between the streets and houses, and the beautiful buildings filled with modern objects exist side by side with unbridled jungle." A visitor to Cleveland might find a broad street suddenly giving way to a steep wall overgrown with weeds. Similarly, "going from one part of the city to another, we have to wade through a knee-deep gorge cutting across the eastern part of the city, while further north there are numerous steel plants." Detroit, also a destination for Polish migrants, with "broad streets covered with asphalt or paved with timber cubes, clean houses" was "a beautiful city!"; Cleveland, a backwater.[11]

Through the nineteenth and into the beginning of the twentieth century, Cleveland was still expanding. This had a great impact on immigrants' experiences. Polish neighborhoods, until the 1920s located principally along the city's fringes, were relatively isolated. This did not mean, however, that they had no contact with other similar neighborhoods, or with the outside world. As these settlements developed, their character also changed. The city's first Polish neighborhoods, Warszawa, Poznań, Kantowo, Kraków, and Jackowo, were well-established by the end of the nineteenth century. After 1900, three smaller settlements, Corlett, Barbarowo, and Josephatowo, took shape. Areas of Polish concentration also developed in the suburbs of Lakewood, Newburgh Heights, and Garfield Heights.

Warszawa

The number of Polish immigrants coming to Cleveland started to grow in the 1870s. The few Poles already in the city were living in or near Czech-settled areas, on Willson (later East 55th) Street and in the Broadway neighborhood about a mile from the Cleveland Rolling Mill Company, a major steel plant and a prime factor in attracting immigrants to Newburgh, at the southeast edge of the city. By 1873, there were enough Poles in Cleveland to organize a mutual aid association, St. Vincent de Paulo, which laid the foundation for the community's first Roman Catholic parish, St. Stanislaus.[12]

The parish's first church building, a wooden structure, was not built until 1881. By this time Poles had begun creating their own community near the intersection of Tod (later East 65th) Street and Fleet Avenue, separated from Broadway by streams and ravines. The church was built on a site at the corner of Tod and Forman Avenue, on a property bought from landholder

Ashbel Morgan. To everyone who purchased a lot for the church, Morgan offered a separate lot free of charge. Thirteen lots were bought that way. The neighborhood that developed became known as Warszawa. In the year 1883 200 Polish families reportedly lived there; between 1879 and 1883 455 children were baptized and 84 weddings conducted. Parish registers recorded the following numbers of families living within the St. Stanislaus/Warszawa area: in 1878, 70; 1883, 425; 1893, 825; 1897, 875; 1901, 905; 1903, 850. The 1890 census counted 2,848 Poles. Police registers stated that 20,488 Poles arrived in the city between 1885 and 1905.[13]

Birthplaces of Newlyweds in the Parish of St. Stanislaus[14]

Year	Prussian Poland	Russian Poland	Others (incl. unknown)
1875	13	2	1
1876	8	2	
1877	5	1	
1879	2	14	

Initially, the inhabitants of the parish were primarily migrants from Prussian Poland; gradually, during the 1880s and 1890s, migrants from Russian Poland began to dominate. Extant copies of money transfers sent in the latter half of 1892 through the agency of Michael P. Kniola, a Polish entrepreneur and travel agent in the Warszawa neighborhood, confirm this. Out of 278 transfers, 260 were sent to Russian sector of Poland, with 227 of those in turn destined for the Plock guberniya (including 88 to the county of Mława, and 81 to Rypin). An analogous register for the second half of 1903 recorded 179 money transfers sent to Russian Poland (including 119 to the Płock and 43 to the Łomża guberniya), 14 to Prussian Poland, and 27 to Galicia.[16]

In the nineteenth century Polish migration to Cleveland was predominantly male. A considerable number the migrants from Russian and Austrian Poland, in particular, planned to return to the old country. By the beginning of the twentieth century, however, married couples predominated among Poles settling in Warszawa. Out of ninety-nine couples whose marriages had taken place during the preceding eleven years, only eight had taken their vows after arriving in the United States. This pattern, along with the large number of children born in Warszawa, would seem to indicate a stable immigrant community.[17]

In 1890 the neighborhood stretched from Morgana Ravine and Heisley Street in the north, east to Broadway Avenue and the Czech settlement, west to Willson Avenue, and south to Gertrude and Fullerton Avenues and Harvard Cemetery. Scots, Irish, and Welsh lived nearby. Streets were being laid out and homes built on land that had belonged to Morgan, or to other individuals surnamed Hickox, Hosmer, Bates, Smith, and Reed. Land in the area north of Harvard Avenue was owned by the pastor of St. Stanislaus, Antoni Kolaszewski.

Poznań

During the 1880s, immigrants from Prussian Poland also settled in an outlying area, in the vicinity of industrial plants then being constructed along Lake Erie near East 79th Street and Superior Avenue. The presence of German immigrants in the area was also a factor in attracting Poles there. Initially, the streets were few and far between, and building lots were only just being staked out.[18]

Rev. Kolaszewski promoted the idea of creating Cleveland's second Polish parish in this area. He wrote to Bishop Richard Gilmour of the Cleveland diocese: "There is a large number of Polish families residing near the Lake Shore Railroad. . . . There are a number of men of the Polish tongue whose families reside at present in Newburg or around the church located there who have to travel a distance of 6 or 8 miles for work in the shops situated along the shore of the Lake Erie."[19] These men could move their families nearer their workplaces, were there a church in the lakeshore area.

In 1892, a Polish church committee persuaded a German landowner, Joseph Hoffman, to donate a lot on Sowinski Avenue for the building of a church, noting that he would "sell many lots for homes to Polish people if the parish were once organized."[20] The Poznań neighborhood grew around this nucleus. Jan Urbanowicz, chairman of the parish committee and organizer of the lot sales, advertised: "Soon a Polish church is going to be erected in the Poznań quarter, thus the area will become a very good place for those who wish to buy lots, for the land in this part of town is valuable. . . . Here there are many plants, and if you don't have jobs, you may go there and jobs will be found. The building lots in Poznań are flat, dry, and shaded by beautiful trees."[21] The parish, named St. Casimir, was established in 1893.

"It is funny how fast everything moves here in America. This Polish colony has only existed for two years and already . . . the houses go up like mushrooms after the rain, and the Polonia numbers grow almost daily. Things still look pretty primitive; the streets have only just been laid out, and one wades ankle-deep in the alluvial sand or in the mud of the prairie, but no doubt things will soon improve." For a long time Poznań was a small neighborhood, surrounded by various other ethnic groups. So diverse was the area that in 1912 Germans, Irishmen, Slovaks, Slovenes, and Lithuanians lived side by side with Poles in a single building. By the time of World War I Poles from Galicia (Austrian Poland) had begun to predominate in Poznań.[22]

West Side Settlement: Kantowo and Lakewood

The third concentration of Polish settlement was in the vicinity of Columbus and Fairfield Streets, on the west bank of the Cuyahoga River. This part of the city, known as Tremont, was ethnically very mixed. In the mid-nineteenth century, it was inhabited by Germans, Irish, and English. During the 1870s and 1880s, Russians, Slovaks, Slovenes, Greeks, Syrians, Rusyns, Ukrainians, and Poles began to settle there in increasing numbers, attracted by the steel plants located at the foot of the hill on which Tremont was situated.

The number of Poles in the area increased to the extent that in 1897, at the initiative of a lay committee, a Polish parish was founded. Services were first conducted in the nearby church of St. Augustine, and then transferred to a barn building until the new parish's own church could be completed on land located between Professor, Fairfield, and College Streets. Tremont's Polish community would come to be known as Kantowo, after the name of the church and parish, St. John Cantius. Initially, migrants from Galicia outnumbered other Poles there, with most of them coming from Samokloski parish in southern Poland. As of 1899, three hundred Polish families were reported to be living in Kantowo. "Very close to the big plants in the northwestern part of the city there is also a Polonia, but it is somewhat poor, as its people live in tiny wooden houses belonging to the plants. Seemingly, these people don't think about settling there for good," wrote Dunikowski.[23]

Another area of Polish settlement on the west side was located in Lakewood, an inner-ring suburb immediately west of the city. Poles moved to the area after the opening of the National Carbon Company plant at Madison Avenue and W. 117th Street in 1892. (National Carbon, a manufacturer of electric-lighting carbons and batteries, became part of Union Carbide in 1917.) Poles and Rusyns initially attended the neighborhood's Slovak church, Sts. Cyril and Methodius. A Polish parish, St. Hedwig, was founded in 1906. At first a mission parish, it became a separate parish in 1914.[24]

Kraków and Jackowo

Warszawa remained the core of Polish settlement in the city. It was from here that new settlement plans, or at least support for them, came.

Its religious leader, Rev. Kolaszewski, helped to form additional Polish neighborhoods in Cleveland, including not only Poznań, but also Kraków and
Jackowo.

Kraków, located across the ravine from Warszawa at Harvard and Ottawa
Roads on the southeastern fringe of the city, was first settled in the late 1870s.
Its inhabitants practiced small-scale agriculture or worked in industrial
plants in Warszawa or the Cuyahoga River valley. Initially they attended St.
Stanislaus church, more than a mile distant. In 1888 Rev. Kolaszewski orga-
nized a mission in Kraków, and after the creation of the neighborhood's own
Sacred Heart of Jesus parish in 1889, consecrated its first church building
in 1890.[25]

He also helped to form the parish of St. Hyacinth (*Jacek* in Polish), in
an area northeast of Warszawa near Tod Street and Francis Avenue. Poles
began settling there in the 1880s, attracted by the availability of jobs nearby
at the Empire Plow Company or in plants along Kingsbury Run. There were
two hundred Polish families in the area by the early part of the twentieth
century. Like the residents of Kraków, they at first belonged to St. Stanislaus
parish. The new Polish parish was not created until 1906; its church was completed in 1908. The neighborhood became known as Jackowo, after the name
of the parish.[26]

Developing communities: 1900–1920s

The Growth of Settlement

At the beginning of the century Warszawa remained Cleveland's largest
Polish community. With Fleet Avenue as its main thoroughfare, it extended
to Broadway in the east, East 55th Street in the west, and Lansing Avenue
in the south. Southward growth continued until Warszawa and Kraków,
which was growing northward, met near Harvard Avenue in about 1914; the
communities retained their separate identities, however. Although existing Irish and Welsh communities seemed to block Warszawa's expansion to
the southeast, Polish settlement ultimately continued on beyond and surrounded them by the mid-1910s. This development was made easier by the
introduction of new streetcar lines, which enabled workers to live farther
away from their jobs. In 1904 the population of Warszawa was 15,000. The
diocesan census of 1913 recorded 1,532 families (7,584 individuals); that of
1915, 2,077 families (11,015 individuals), but noted that "the quoted number of families is imprecise, as one may suppose that not everybody permitted his name to be recorded."[27]

Additional Polish communities continued to be founded in Cleveland during the years 1900–1920. The proximity of a streetcar line and, possibly, the existence of a Czech settlement along E. 131st Street in the Corlett neighborhood helped create a Polish settlement in the Harvard Avenue-East 131st Street area. In 1914, sixty families were reported to be living there, prompting the creation of another Polish parish, Our Lady of Czestochowa, at East 142nd Street and Harvard. It had 80 families in 1915, 194 in 1920, and 175 in 1923.[28]

Two other Polish communities, Barbarowo and Josaphatowo, developed prior to World War I. In the 1890s, Poles began settling in the western edge of the Cuyahoga valley near Denison Avenue. They were employed by the Grasselli Chemical plant or nearby steel mills. In 1905, the 750 Poles living in the area founded a parish, St. Barbara; its first church was constructed the following year.[29]

The parish of St. Josaphat was created in 1908 to serve the needs of the one hundred Polish families living near the intersection of East 33rd Street and St. Clair Avenue, not far from the central city. This was also an area of south Slavic, primarily Slovene, settlement. Poles, mainly from Russian and Austrian Poland, began settling there a little before 1900. St. Josaphat church was erected in 1917.[30]

Between 1920 and 1940 Poles and people of Polish origin constituted Cleveland's most numerous ethnic group. Warszawa filled the entire area available for its growth, extending south to Harvard Avenue and west to East 49th Street. Suburban communities also developed southeast of the city limits, in Newburgh Heights and Garfield Heights.[31]

Polish Born Population in Cleveland, 1870–1970[32]

Year	Polish Born	% of Total Population
1870	77	0.08
1880	532	0.33
1890	2,848	1.09
1900	8,592	2.25
1910	19,483*	—
1920	35,024	4.39
1930	36,668	4.07
1940	24,771	2.82
1950	23,054	2.52
1960	19,437	2.18
1970	6,234	0.83

*—J. B. Galford, "The Foreign Born," p. 127

Neighborhood Appearance and Living Conditions

Teodor Dłużynski, one of the 'pioneer' immigrants from Prussian Poland and later a community leader and editor of the weekly newspaper *Polonia w Ameryce* (*Polonia in America*), recalled that around 1890, "[I] bought a lot in Fleet Ave., after I got additional money through working. I kept on investing in lots. A man named Hickox had died and his son had come into a lot of property. The son would come to me from time to time saying, 'Buy another lot. I'll sell cheap!' I kept on buying off him until I had ten lots, all on Fleet Ave. The street at the time was a quagmire. For fifteen years I was unable to sell even one of these lots. But after that I sold all of them within the space of one year."[33]

Civic improvements were noticeably lacking in Cleveland's Polish neighborhoods during the first few decades of their existence. Most of Warszawa's side streets were not paved, nor did sidewalks exist. One man later recalled that during his youth in the neighborhood, he "would run out and put the ashes from the coal stoves that were used then, onto the walks after rain to hold the earth together and prevent muddy surfaces."[34] Although East 65th Street was paved between Lansing and Fleet Avenues, sidewalks were not installed until 1918. Morgan Avenue, near East 75th Street, received sidewalks in 1922. Poznań, having obtained paved streets and sidewalks at the beginning of the twentieth century, presented a better appearance. In Kraków, however, around the turn of the century, inhabitants "could hardly walk for the mud" after spring and fall rains. By 1912 sellers of building lots there were able to reassure potential buyers that the streets "had been leveled and stone sidewalks had been built."[35]

The first street lamp at the corner of Lansing Avenue and East 64th Streets was not lit until 1921; the eastern side of Broadway received electric lights in 1922. The darkness perhaps contributed to the numerous street accidents, in many of which carts, trams, and automobiles knocked down pedestrians. Other accidents involved workers who took shortcuts on their way home from the plants by walking along railway tracks, a dangerous venture after nightfall.[36]

The stench from the sewers and canals flowing into Kingsbury Run was so obnoxious that, it was asserted at a meeting of Cleveland City Council in 1921, "Conditions [are] detrimental to the health and comfort of those residing in the vicinity of said streams." Finally, in 1923, Councilman Frank Orlikowski introduced resolutions for a modern sewage system.[37]

For a generation or even longer, Polish neighborhoods had the appearance more of villages than of towns, having been established on previously uninhabited land. (The more centrally located Josaphatowo neighborhood was an exception to this; its Polish residents moved into already existing homes.) "I found nothing when I came out to this parish [Warszawa] but fields," Rev. Kolaszewski wrote. Vegetable gardens and fruit trees surrounded the houses of the new settlements; residents kept ducks, hens, chickens, and geese. It was not by coincidence that Kraków was also called Goosetown. As in Polish villages, the lots were separated from the streets by wooden fences, here allegedly "propped up" by bored and idle youth.[38]

One-story wooden dwellings were the most common sort of residence, although there were exceptions. "Polish houses, which are mostly made of wood, are spacious and clean, and testify to the well-being of their inhabitants. However, one also finds brick houses and real palaces such as for instance the villa of Mr. Orlikowski," Dunikowski had reported in 1893. In Warszawa in the early 1900s, 3.5 percent of residential structures were built of brick; 10 percent of residential structures were apartments.[39]

Unlike Dunikowski, inhabitants of other parts of the city who visited these neighborhoods, as well as contemporary native-born social workers and scholars, expressed mostly unfavorable impressions. They claimed that "Foreign landlords' . . . low standards and [lack of] responsibility baffle every effort for improvement," and that the houses in worker neighborhoods were "[not able] to meet any of the city requirements regarding property, such as the installation of sanitary plumbing with sewer connection."[40]

In 1909, 31.2 percent of Kantowo's houses were categorized as decisively substandard or barely satisfactory. Warszawa received higher marks, with only 7 percent of its houses being regarded as dirty and neglected. Eight percent of apartments and houses in Warszawa and 37 percent of those in Kantowo relied exclusively on outdoor wells for water. In 1914 52 percent of the families in Warszawa had no toilets in their dwellings; 21 percent had to share facilities with other families. In Kantowo, only 7 percent had their own toilets. Nevertheless, contemporary observers stated that sanitary conditions in the homes inhabited by Polish immigrants were by no means the worst in the city.[41]

Although intended as objective studies, buttressed by endless figures and statistics, the reports of social workers in various American cities who visited "Hunkie" neighborhoods reflected either horror or disgust. Immigrants' letters and diaries, on the other hand, do not express comparably significant critical comments. Living conditions and dwellings in American cities were in many cases more comfortable than those in the old country. Suffice it to say that in 1921, 85 percent of the houses in Poland were built of wood and typically consisted of one room and a corridor. Outdoor toilets were still a common phenomenon.[42]

Boarders and Families

Nothing provoked a greater outcry from native-born social workers and surveyors than overcrowded housing conditions. In 1914 in Warszawa an average of nine persons lived in a single house; in 1909 in Kantowo, there were between two and three persons to a room. It was primarily the practice of taking in boarders and lodgers that increased the density of habitation. With little regard as to the size of their apartments, tenants often sublet a part of them. The immigrants had quickly adopted the boarding system, already long established in America, together with the name "boarder," or *bortnik* in Polish. A similar system was also customary in some Polish territories, for instance among agricultural workers in Russian Poland. Thus, although the average family in Warszawa numbered seven persons in 1914, the number of persons living in one apartment was nine. Boarders and lodgers constituted 14 percent of all inhabitants, and they lived in 36 percent of Polish households. The 622 boarders living in St. Stanislaus parish in 1913 made up 8 percent of its inhabitants. Cases existed of families taking on as many as twenty-five boarders.[43]

Immediately after arrival in America, a person who had come alone usually stayed with a family, often relatives, but sometimes total strangers. There, the lodger took meals and slept. Sleeping arrangements were less than luxurious, sometimes just a mattress on the floor. Individuals who worked different shifts at their jobs might occupy a single bed space in shifts. Little room was left over for other purposes in these cramped quarters: "There [were] beds everywhere, like in a hospital." Laundry dried on lines strung across the room, overcoats hung on hooks driven into the wall, personal items and linen were kept in cupboards assembled from wooden boxes. Although sharing a bed with someone else, a common practice, was not the most comfortable arrangement, it was cheaper. And, after all, it was not so different from life in the cottages in the old country.[44]

In a new and alien land, Polish migrants developed a sense of kinship with their co-nationals, even those from other parts of the Polish homeland. The new arrivals slowly came to feel that living in a Polish neighborhood in America was "like being in their own home." "We felt like one big family." The boarding system, by providing greenhorns with a makeshift "family," eased their transition to new urban world. For landlords it was equally if not more advantageous, providing income. It was also the quintessential family business. It gave women an opportunity to add to the household's budget, and at the same time kept them at home. Even children could and did help in various ways.[45]

Like those of other immigrants, Poles' wages were low. In many cases, the money brought home from the factory by the chief breadwinner did not meet family expenses. Thus, it became necessary to augment the income from additional sources. Quite often, other members of the household contributed to the family budget.[46]

Women's work was mostly connected with the home. The Immigration Commission found that in the Kantowo neighborhood, 69 percent of Polish women remained at home, 14 percent were employed in domestic and personal services, and 17 percent in manufacturing and mechanical work. It was above all young, single women who worked outside the home, often in the same companies where relatives also worked, generally in the clothing industry, in laundries, or as maidservants.[47]

Children's work, long required and accepted in the old country, also supplemented family budgets in America or at least contributed to the running of the household. Even the youngest children had to help with household duties; their older siblings were expected to bring in wages. Teodor Dłużynski gave up school in order to go to a plant where "we had to wind wire on spools.... After a while I was put on a night shift." Józef Sawicki took up his first job, on the piecework system, when he was fourteen. In order to get the job, he had to put on long pants and lie about his age.[48]

Not all children and youth were forced to work. Neither did those who worked always do so under threat of punishment. Helping one's parents was regarded as a duty; contributing to the family budget was a matter of pride, and the first step on the way to independence. Quite often, the children themselves decided to give up school to start earning money.[49]

Work

Teen-aged boys, like their fathers, generally walked to their jobs. As has been noted, Cleveland's first Polish neighborhoods formed in locations near large factories, as did other ethnic neighborhoods. To help sell lots in Warsawa, Michael Kniola advertised them as being "just 12 minutes walk" from the Newburgh plants. Neighborhood children could "run up and take the lunch to the father, you know, just like in Europe."[50]

Most Polish immigrants worked as unskilled laborers in the iron and steel and related industries. Just as a network of relatives and friends had helped bring them to Cleveland, so that same network assisted them in finding employment after their arrival. Sometimes, a factory worker might put in a word (perhaps accompanied by a few dollars or a box of cigars) with his foreman to get a newly arrived compatriot a job. In other cases, community leaders like Kniola and Rev. Kolaszewski used their wide circle of contacts and acquaintances to find jobs for Polish immigrants. "If a man has no work, he comes to me and I write him a letter to the boss of the mill to get him a job. I write thousands of letters every year," noted Rev. Kolaszewski. Kniola, who made job referrals for a fee, received requests from employers as well as would-be employees. The ethnic press also ran help-wanted ads from employers looking for immigrant workers. The sentiment that "Hunkies . . . are crazy to work" was common among industrial plant managers.[51]

At the same time as Poles were arriving in Cleveland, technological changes were creating a greater demand for unskilled laborers, while reducing the need for skilled craftsmen, in the city's growing factories. An observer found the Cuyahoga Valley's industrial landscape "at night . . . picturesque in the extreme. The whole valley shows a black background, lit up with a thousand points of light from factories, foundries, and steamboats, which are multiplied into two thousand, as they are reflected in the Cuyahoga, which looks like a silver ribbon flowing through the blackness." Inside, however, the reality was hellish: "the roaring thunder, the flowing sea of flames, the choking smoke. . . . From up above there come rain, soot, and ashes. . . . The air is poisonous in the plants, and it is incredibly hot near the furnaces. In the vicinity of some of them, the temperature is so high that the human organism can stand it for only a few minutes." A Polish worker described the scene of his twelve-hour day: "Great red-hot furnaces were standing in a row and next to each of them, there was a big hammer. Altogether there were 14 of them. When everybody started hammering, the noise was tremendous all day long. . . . The red-hot bars of steel were pulled out of the furnaces toward the hammers by means of iron pincers."[52]

In such workplaces, injuries were common. In the wire plants, for example, where workers drew out wires of red-hot steel and wound them onto huge reels, it was easy to lose a finger, and possible to be fatally entangled in the wire. One Polish worker, who fell asleep in a Cleveland factory, was burned to death when another worker, equally tired, threw hot ashes onto him. One of Cleveland's Polish-language newspapers later wrote that, after years of hard work in America, immigrants gathered "the fruit of Polish American culture, in the shape of т.в., general exhaustion, mental break-down, various types of permanent injuries, and many other similar gifts."[53]

Nonetheless, Poles, like most immigrants, rated their jobs as good or bad depending on how much they paid, and on their permanence. Working conditions were a secondary consideration. According to the Immigration Commission's survey, the average yearly earnings of foreign-born males in Cleveland was $350, compared to $447 for native-born men. For women, the comparable figures were $178 and $256. Poles living in Tremont earned $339 on the average; a quarter of them earned less than $200. City-wide, the average Polish family income was $391, compared to $486 for all foreign-born and $577 for native-born Americans. These Polish families paid an average rent of $5.31 per month. It was possible, under these circumstances, to save much more money than in the homeland—that is, so long as the job lasted. "In America [life] proceeds as if someone were playing cards, for America is the worst country of all the others. If there is work in America it is good, but if there is no work, then there is no greater misery, than there is here."[54]

Strikes and Unions

Immigrants changed jobs often, either voluntarily, in search of better pay, or involuntarily, when let go by their employer. Things were particularly difficult in years of economic downturn, such as 1893, 1896–1897, and 1907, and ratios of return migration were always highest during such periods. Although they had no job security and little power, they did not turn out to be the submissive and docile strikebreakers that some employers had hoped. Even in the Polish territories, there had been a tradition of passive resistance and occasional active revolt among agricultural laborers, and in the years immediately before and after 1900, proletarized villagers (who had worked as industrial or construction laborers) helped set off waves of strikes in rural areas. Immigrant Poles, who came from a similar background, soon began to participate in strikes against their American employers. The Cleveland Rolling Mill strikes of 1882 and 1885 illustrated how quickly the role of the immigrant could change from strikebreaker to striker.[55]

The Rolling Mill's skilled workers—mostly of British and Irish origin but including some Czechs—who had joined the Amalgamated Association of Iron, Steel, and Tin Workers (AAISTW), went on strike in 1882. To break the strike, William Chisholm, president of the company, used agents to hire unskilled and semiskilled workers, mostly Poles and Czechs, from outside the city. In New York City, agent Charley Franklin, who spoke five languages, offered newly arrived immigrants "steady work" at wages of $1.50 to $2.00 per day. Despite the initial resolve of the union to use peaceful means, the strike soon turned violent, with strikers stoning strikebreakers and police, and was eventually broken. The incident left a residue of ill will between Poles and Irish living in the neighborhoods near the mill.[56]

In 1885, economic conditions led to three successive wage cuts. This time the unskilled Polish and Czech workers led a spontaneous strike against the Rolling Mill. An empty lot in the Warszawa neighborhood known as the "Peach Orchard," became a gathering place, where speakers exhorted workers in English, Polish, Czech, and German. Groups of over a thousand workers marched to Chisholm's office, and to the H. P. Nail and Union Steel Screw companies (in which Chisholm also held stock) to stop work there as well. These actions were reminiscent of rural uprisings in the Polish homeland, when agricultural laborers and villagers would march upon the manor houses. Also similar to village unrest was the participation of entire families in demonstrations and even violence. Women, "arriving on the scene with their aprons full of bricks and other missiles," stoned policemen in front of the Rolling Mill. Strikebreakers as well as policemen were attacked by the strikers during the course of the strike, resulting in numerous arrests, and injuries on both sides. A strike committee including both English-speaking and Polish and Czech workers was later formed, but misunderstandings persisted between the groups, and the skilled workers blamed the greater violence of this strike on the unskilled "radical" immigrants. The strike was ultimately successful, in that the mayor of Cleveland, desiring an end to the unrest, ordered Chisholm to restore higher wages, but success came at the cost of the jobs of many of the Poles and Czechs, whom the company refused to rehire.[57]

Another strike involving Poles, this one against the American Steel and Wire Co. in 1898, was described in the press as particularly peaceful. *Polonia w Ameryce* called for workers' solidarity, warning Poles against "various superintendents and wire mill bosses who visit Polish houses and recruit people, replacing strikers. People should remember that those who enlist not only do harm to themselves but also bring shame on the Polish name." Cleveland's Poles did, in fact, by this time, show support not only for fellow Poles, Slavs, or steelworkers, but also, in the case of the Cleveland streetcar drivers' strike of 1899, for a group with whom they had no particular ethnic or occupational affiliation. Poles were among those arrested for setting up obstacles on the tracks; Polish shop- and tavernkeepers joined in pitching stones at passing trams, which, being subject to a boycott, ran mostly empty. Even the elderly were expected to join in boycotting the streetcars. As in the village, non-conformist behavior met with little tolerance in ethnic neighborhoods. A letter published in a Polish weekly illustrates the sort of community pressure that operated: "Mr. Edmund Szczygliński publicly admits the mistake which he made with relation to Mrs. Sawicka, the owner of a clothing shop in Fleet [Avenue], about whom he had spread rumors that she had ridden on a streetcar driven by scabs. The foregoing turned out to be untrue."[58]

The 1885 Rolling Mill strike was defensive in nature, with Poles and fellow workers reacting to a wage cut. Other early labor actions by immigrants also most often had a simple primary goal: higher wages. Initially, relations of unskilled immigrants, including Poles, with American labor unions were characterized by mutual distrust. The AAISTW (which federated into the AF of L) accepted only skilled workers and their assistants as members in Cleveland in 1882, which meant that except for some Czechs, few of the newer immigrants were eligible. In 1884 the AAISTW supported restrictive immigration legislation at the Congressional level. The Knights of Labor was one of the few labor organizations that did not discriminate against unskilled workers, and thus attracted some recent immigrants, including some Cleveland Poles, into its ranks during the 1880s. As the number of Poles in the city grew, calls were made for the organization of specifically Polish unions, but met with little response. A few skilled workers tried to organize ethnic craft unions in Cleveland, for instance a Polish Carpenters Union in 1902, but ultimately did not succeed. Polish skilled workers sometimes joined with other nationalities in American unions, as in the German-organized Building Laborers Union Local 8430, which also included Irish and African American Clevelanders. The positions of secretary and business agent in this local were both filled by Poles; Poles also served as officers of various other craft union locals around the turn of the century.[59]

During the period after 1900 the relations between unskilled and skilled workers and between them and the unions changed. Recognition of unions and the introduction of the closed-shop rule became demands as important as wage increases. Many employers now depended on their immigrant work force of "machine tenders" as much as they had formerly relied on skilled workers. In times of economic prosperity, many companies were plagued by high turnover, as unskilled workers in particular changed jobs frequently in search of better wages. Especially during World War I, production in the heavy industries where many Poles and other immigrants worked increased, and so did wages. Beginning before the war, and continuing on after it, employers introduced various "welfare capitalism" programs to attract employees and enhance their productivity, including profit-sharing plans, safety measures, accident insurance, and educational benefits, including English-language and other Americanization-related classes.[60]

Unions also became more interested in organizing unskilled immigrant laborers, and in 1918, in part to accommodate the desire of these workers for a greater voice for the rank and file within the union, the AF of L agreed to the creation of shop committees. Workers in the Cleveland Furnace Company formed a multiethnic shop committee with ties to the AAISTW-AFL. The number of Polish union activists in Cleveland grew during this period. Poles held office in several construction industry locals, as well as in locals representing other occupations, including bakers, typographers, and chemical workers. Constantine Urbanowicz was president of Fireman's Union Local 93 in Cleveland, and in the 1920s served as a trustee of the Cleveland Federation of Labor.[61]

Strikes occurred at a number of Cleveland companies during the World War I years, a period when large numbers of workers joined unions.[62] These were only a prelude, however, to the great steel strike of 1919, which followed upon the AF of L's effort to organize the steel industry nationwide. The union's Cleveland organizers included twenty-five individuals fluent in the various languages spoken by immigrant steelworkers. A Cleveland resident, Antoni Piławski, played a particularly important role in organizing Polish workers. Born in Russian Poland in 1882, Piławski came to the United States in 1901, and eventually settled in Warszawa. He worked as a machinist at the Belle Vernon Mill Co. and the Cleveland Steel Casting Co., and also sold insurance and wrote for the local radical weekly *Jutrzenka* (*Dawn*). Piławski had joined the International Machinists Union in 1906, and was for a time a member of the Socialist Party, running unsuccessfully for a city council seat on the Socialist ticket. Although conservative members of the Polish community regarded him as a dangerous radical, Piławski, though an activist, in fact chose to work within the system. He was a member and officer of Polish National Alliance lodge No. 6, sold Polish Liberty Bonds, and in 1920, helped organize anti-Bolshevik meetings among immigrants. In 1919, Piławski served as president of Steelworkers Local 114 and led the effort to rally Poles to the union, frequently addressing meetings of Polish and other Slavic workers.[63]

Across Cleveland, the union gained nearly 18,000 members. The Polish-language *Wiadomości Codzienne* (*Daily News*) supported the organizing effort, for instance publishing a notice that "Polish workers . . . should come tomorrow afternoon to an organizational meeting of the American Federation of Labor." Every Sunday meetings were held in Tremont, and editor and activist Stanisław Dangel addressed audiences on "how to search for justice and truth, in a legal way," turning "passive people into unionists who understand what they want and where they are going." Tremont's Local No. 140 quickly attained a membership of 1,860, many of them Poles. There was also a local in the Poznań neighborhood.[64]

When union leaders called for a nationwide strike against U.S. Steel in September 1919, all locals voted in favor of the action, and in Cleveland 18,000 workers walked off their jobs. Nearly all elements of the Polish community, including the press, the PNA, and the clergy, while calling for moderation and non-violence, supported the union and the strike. The pastor of St. Stanislaus defended the worker's "right to organize for his own defense," maintaining that "such organization is in accord with Christian principles." Józef Sawicki was the only community leader who openly opposed the strike, having copies of a Detroit-based Polish publication which defamed strikers distributed in Cleveland. Indignant residents burned it on the streets, shouting, "Rag!"[65]

Ultimately, the strike collapsed, in part because nativist propaganda revived the old antipathy between English-speaking and other workers. In November the AAISTW ordered its members back to work; the strike ended in January 1920. Piławski and others still continued to agitate; each Friday meetings were held in the Polish National Hall to organize workers under the auspices of the AF of L. In advertising his merchandise a Polish grocer found it effective to state: "For your special use this store has brought in cigarettes from unionized factories, produced by union men. Their taste far surpasses other cigarettes." Overall, unions were on the defensive during the 1920s, initially due to reasons including economic recession and unemployment, a hostile attitude on the part of federal and state authorities, and the fear of radical movements and foreigners as manifested by the Red Scare and the Palmer raids. Later, prosperity muted workers' dissatisfaction. However, pro-union sentiment remained strong in Cleveland's Polish community throughout this decade, which bridged the ferment of the war years with the American labor movement's revival in the 1930s.[66]

Coexistence with Other Groups

At first, the Polish neighborhoods being built up in Cleveland had to make use of the existing networks of shops, businesses, and services created by their nearby neighbors, mainly Czechs. For example, the Cleveland funeral home patronized by Poles in the 1870s was owned by a Czech named Wolf. Czech merchants, shop and saloon keepers, and other dealers advertised their services in the Polish press. "In my place you can speak Polish," advertised a Dr. Prochaska. This contrasted with the situation in some shops owned by native-born Clevelanders, about which complaints were made that they "did not want to employ Polish clerks" and had only German and Czech salesmen, despite the fact that there were so many Polish customers.[67]

Neighborhoods were not ethnically homogeneous; on the same floor, in the same house, Poles might live side by side with people of four or five different nationalities. Children speaking different languages played together in gardens and yards and on the streets. Czechs, English, Germans, Irish, and even an Asian Indian lived in the Broadway area. Different ethnic mixtures existed in different districts. "This was a German neighborhood," Jackowo residents later recalled. "Some German and some Irish." "The Germans were good people."[68]

The lifestyle in ethnic neighborhoods in the late nineteenth and early twentieth centuries promoted interaction among residents, especially within their own ethnic group, but also with neighbors of other nationalities. One-story wooden houses often had porches and verandas jutting out into the street, and also little gardens where people met, talked, gossiped, and drank beer on Sundays. Empty lots afforded space for social meetings, particularly in times of tension or crisis. Public wells and water taps were popular meeting and discussion places for women and the young. The saloon was the magnet for men, serving as a neighborhood rendezvous, a political center, a plebeian "club." There one could confide in others, ask for advice, and form opinions about current affairs, while drinking a glass of vodka or beer. There, the parish committee might meet to plan the founding of a church. There, union members and strikers sometimes congregated, as in Warszawa during the 1885 Rolling Mill strike: Poles and Czechs ". . . were observed in front of saloons and on the street corners, holding animated conversations."[69]

Contacts between Poles and members of other ethnic groups were not limited to conversation and gossip. They often involved assistance, in matters both small and large. The paternal role of the saloonkeeper transcended nationality. Shortly after his arrival, John Gallka, who lived in Kantowo, had walked a friend to the gates of the factory where he worked. Making his way home alone, Gallka walked in the wrong direction. "I finally ended up a dozen streets from home," he remembered. "Realizing that I had gotten lost,

I went into an inn whose owner was a Slovak with whom I could communicate and tell him what my problem was. The Slovak sent along a friend to see the lost stranger home."[70] In 1903 a woman arrived in Cleveland from Poland only to learn that her husband had been imprisoned for forging a check. She was rescued from her extremely difficult situation by the sympathy and help of a German woman.[71]

At the institutional level, contacts between ethnic groups took place, first of all, within the parish framework. In many instances Cleveland Poles borrowed other churches, some of which belonged to ethnic parishes, prior to building their own. Before St. Stanislaus church was built, services were held in the church of St. Mary on the Flats (Irish); in 1879 they were transferred to St. Joseph's church (German). In St. Casimir parish, services were first held in a nearby Irish church; in St. John Cantius they were conducted at St. Augustine church; in St. Hyacinth's, in the churches of St. Edward (Czech) and St. Lawrence (Slovene); and in Lakewood, Poles first joined a Slovak parish, Sts. Cyril and Methodius. Later, as the Polish community grew and developed its own religious infrastructure, Polish priests delivered sermons and took part in missionary work among Slovaks and Croatians, sometimes serving as substitute vicars.[72]

Intergroup contacts were most frequent in ethnically mixed Tremont. In Warszawa, Poles came into contact mainly with Czechs. Czech newspapers usually recorded events in the Polish colony. A Czech musical group played during the first mass in the Polish church of the Immaculate Heart of Mary. Until World War I the meetings of some Polish organizations took place in Czech or German meeting halls. As late as 1924 a Polish amateur performing arts group used a Czech hall. Some economic undertakings also involved intergroup cooperation. For instance, in 1903 Poles and Czechs created a joint company for the purpose of building a brewery.[73]

In April 1894, Polish societies participated in Magyar-organized memorial events following the death of Lajos Kossuth. Interaction with fellow Slavs, however, was more common. In 1897 or 1898 a Slavic aid union was created, followed in 1903 by the founding of the Slavic Alliance of Cleveland. The Alliance's first president was a Czech, V. Svarc; Michael Kniola succeeded to the post in 1904. The organization was made up of "Polish, Czech, Slovak, Croatian, and Slovenian people." Its activities ranged from recreational outings and neighborhood beautification to, in 1905, sponsorship of the Slavic Handicraft and Industrial Exhibition "in order to acquaint the general public with the life of Slavs, [including] Poles." The exhibition was intended to help the wider community recognize the cultural heritage of the

Slavic immigrants, and to showcase characteristic elements of this culture. Doing so, according to Svarc, would also "surely in time enrich our art and literature and in their broader and more immediate influence develop a higher standard among the great masses of our people."[74]

In this phase of the immigrant communities' development, contacts with other groups were mostly friendly, the most notable exceptions being the clashes with Irish, Welsh, and others of British ethnicity during the Rolling Mill strike of 1882. Misunderstandings between the Polish and Irish communities, in particular, continued to occur, in large part due to church-related matters: the differences between Polish and Irish Catholicism, and Poles' perceptions of an oppressive "Irish" church hierarchy in Cleveland.

Democratization via Churches and Parishes

People coming to Cleveland from Polish territories were overwhelmingly Roman Catholic. The creation of their own parish was one of the first communal decisions that Polish immigrants, as represented by their lay committees, made. The newcomers wanted to reconstruct the familiar religious institutions that had shaped their lives in the old country. In Europe the aristocrats and gentry had built churches. In America the immigrants, many of them former peasants, took on this task, and they were proud of what they achieved.

Apart from purely religious functions, ethnic parishes also served their communities in many other important ways. Adjacent to the churches, associated buildings such as parochial schools, meeting halls, and even orphanages were often constructed. Each parish founded dozens of religious, semi-religious, social, charitable, national, cultural, and recreational organizations and societies. The ethnic parish and all the institutions clustered about it provided an organized social and cultural network in which immigrants could live and function more easily. Although this served to support and preserve ethnic solidarity, the parish, on the other hand, also played an assimilationist role. Its institutions prepared immigrants for participation in American society, while teaching them about their own culture, and educating their children.

Parish life was not, however, without tensions and conflicts—within parishes, between parishes, and with the American church hierarchy. Such conflicts suggest that the integration of migrants into the "democratic" political system initially took place via self-determination within the parish structure, rather than through secular political institutions. Only after such self-determination had been practiced within the familiar setting of the parish, could participation in the American political system follow. To a considerable extent parish conflicts were due to the democratization of parochial communities. The peasant founders of parishes used their positions on lay committees to exert an influence on parish activities, an influence that clerical authorities sometimes found excessive.

Most commonly, conflicts stemmed from disagreements over financial and related matters, such as ownership of church buildings, or collection and allocation of parish funds. Parishioners felt that they were justified in their demands for more say in the governance of their parishes, since they provided the money, in the form of donations, collections, pew rents, and other fees, that made possible the existence of parishes and construction of churches. In many churches, pew rents from parishioners constituted the most regular source of income. The annual pew rent in the Sacred Heart of Jesus parish, for example, was six dollars. St. Stanislaus parishioners were warned that "Who[ever] has not paid for his pew for the past year, has already lost his right to it. . . . So let nobody be angry, if on the following Sunday he or she will find somebody else in his/her place."[75]

Parishioners' voluntary donations were also vital. However, the generosity of church members did not always meet the wishes of the priest. According to a sermon delivered by St. Stanislaus's vicar in 1915, his parishioners "did not spare money for the church, neither in the good old days, nor in the hard times of today . . . There were a lot of complaints this year of some people against the others that they never put money in the collection box. Sometimes, the basket passes 3 pews and there are merely 7 cents in it! Especially in the chapel! One must have no shame at all if one takes the basket into one's hand and then passes it on to another putting nothing in it." It was similar later: "the collectors in the church complain all the time that there are so many people who never put anything in the basket . . . that sometimes the basket passes the entire pew and only one person puts [in] money."[76]

Besides financial issues, the appointment of parish priests and their subsequent leadership style and activities was also a prime cause of conflict in ethnic parishes. Polish Catholic parishioners quickly perceived the benefits of the Protestant practice of a congregation "calling" a clergyman of its own choice. The arbitrariness of the church hierarchy, frequent transfers of priests, and disregard for public opinion were met with resistance.[77]

Cleveland's Polish parishes had their share of conflicts involving priests, parishioners, and middle-class community leaders. Among these, the most colorful were without doubt those involving Rev. Antoni Kolaszewski. In 1883 Bishop Gilmour appointed Rev. Kolaszewski as rector of St. Stanislaus parish. For the next ten years, and beyond, Rev. Kolaszewski was indisputably a leader in Warszawa. He gave advice, encouraged education, and helped get people out of trouble with the law. His influence reached into matters both public and private: "I work for the good of the poor. . . . If husband and wife argue they come to me in order that justice and peace might be preserved. If children disobey or parents are cruel the issue comes to me and I resolve it."[78]

A seemingly laudable project, the building of a grand new church for the parish, caused Rev. Kolaszewski to end up at the center of a conflict. Despite warnings from the bishop—"Before I can further discuss the erection of your new church you will please make formal application for its erection as required by diocesan statute"—and a regulation requiring the bishop's permission before a congregation's funds could be spent, Rev. Kolaszewski began to build his church in 1886. Completed in 1891, the immense St. Stanislaus was "the biggest" and "the most beautiful church," according to proud parishioners. A passing traveler had similar, although qualified, praise: "the church in the Gothic style is quite impressive though its interior decoration is exaggerated." It was for a time the second biggest Gothic-style church in the United States, after St. Patrick's Cathedral in New York.[79]

This glory was not without cost, however. By June 1892 parish debts amounted to the huge sum of $100,453. Various methods were used to cover the costs of construction. Parochial societies "sponsored" window frames and doors for the church, as well as banners and pictures. Rev. Kolaszewski reportedly required parishioners to contribute twenty-five dollars each, and also set fees for some services; for instance, "confession tickets" were introduced. (It should be noted that similar practices were not uncommon in other churches at the time.) Concern and resentment grew among the St. Stanislaus parishioners, leading to protests. As was often the case in such circumstances, some of them accused the priest of debauchery.[80] However, money was at the core of the problem. Diocesan authorities were also concerned about the size of the debt. Finally, the bishop forced Rev. Kolaszewski to leave the parish, asking: "Why is it that only amongst the Poles throughout the u.s. do we find these scandals?" In 1892 the controversial priest officially resigned his office and was sent to a Syracuse, New York, parish.[81]

The conflict did not end there. Some St. Stanislaus parishioners opposed the priest appointed to succeed Rev. Kolaszewski. This group, supported by *Jutrzenka*, enthusiastically welcomed the latter back to the city in 1894. He made a speech addressing the complaints and grievances against the "Irish-German" bishops of United States. He demanded the right of equal participation in American Catholicism for Poles and other immigrants, the right of the parish to control its own property, and the right of parishioners to have a priest and religious services appropriate to their ethnic background. "The despotism and tyranny of the American bishops is unbearable. The Poles are treated by them like cattle," he charged. "We want the priest to be approved and dismissed not by the bishop, but by the parish itself. . . . We shall recognize the bishop's power, but not in lay matters or in matters of this life."[82]

The final result of the impasse was a schism within the parish. In 1894 Rev. Kolaszewski and his supporters established the independent Immaculate Heart of Mary parish. "Now, Bishop, please read this, that you may know that we are no longer your cattle, your dirty swine, your mad dogs. We declare to you that we are men, American citizens and you . . . will have to treat us like men," declared the dissidents. "Our main objective is to maintain Polish churches in Polish hands and at the same time, protect you, beloved priests against the injustice and frequent willfulness of the bishop," stated an Immaculate Heart of Mary Church committee. The consecration of the new church was accompanied by public disorder. A crowd of Irishmen loyal to the diocese attacked the Polish procession and threw mud and other objects at its members. In the ensuing fight between Polish "cavalrymen" and the attackers, several people were injured.[83]

The fundamental conflict, however, was between the parishioners of the new parish and those of St. Stanislaus. People from Immaculate Heart were called "Barabbases," or traitors, and those from St. Stanislaus "Romans." The suspicion that someone belonged to the new parish might lead to his removal from a fraternal organization or other society.[84] The parish never did join the independent Polish National Catholic Church (PNCC) headquartered in Scranton, Pennsylvania, however. Although Rev. Kolaszewski had been excommunicated during the course of the schism, he always maintained that his quarrel was not with the Roman Catholic Church but rather with the American hierarchy, and hoped to come to terms with Rome. An agreement was reached in 1908. Rev. Kolaszewski resigned as pastor of Immaculate Heart, whereupon the parish was admitted to the diocese and he was readmitted to the church.[85]

Another major conflict occurred in the parish of St. John Cantius. In this case, opposition did not coalesce around the activities of a charismatic clergyman. Rather, it grew out of the parishioners' own desire for self-determination, with the emerging ethnic middle class rebelling against what they viewed as the priest's domination of the neighborhood, high-handed treatment of the laity by the clergy, and lack of democracy in church affairs.

"Frequently these advocates of lay trusteeism and parishioner democracy were themselves devout yet ambitious members of the rising immigrant middle class," observed historian John J. Bukowczyk. "More serious still, secular Polish nationalists, without disavowing the faith, often objected to clerical domination over immigrant politics. In fact the Polish National Alliance, the immigrants' most important fraternal benevolent organization, typified this position, to the consternation of the immigrant clergy."[86]

Tensions between the church hierarchy and the democratic inclinations of St. John Cantius's immigrant laity had appeared as early as 1898, the first year of the parish's existence. In December 1898, Bishop Ignatius Horstmann told the vicar, Rev. Hipolit Orłowski, to ensure the election of "reliable councilors" from among the parishioners, who would be amenable to the guidance of the pastor—"a distinct contrast to the more independent role laymen had played in the planning and establishment of the parish," as one commentator remarked. However, Rev. Orłowski allowed the parishioners to choose their own representatives, thus smoothing over the differences between his flock and the bishop.[87]

Tensions resurfaced after the appointment of Rev. F. F. Doppke as St. John Cantius's rector in 1909. He turned out to be very strict about pew rents and refused all religious services to those parishioners who did not pay their rent installments. Complaints were made that "Rev. Dobke [sic] treated people as if they were cattle; he shouted, said stupid things in the church, called his parishioners calves from the pulpit." The parishioners' committee rebelled and demanded that the priest be replaced: "If we do not get a satisfactory answer from your Lordship several days from now we will be forced to seek justice somewhere else."[88]

What gave the conflict between clergy and laity in the Kantowo neighborhood a particular edge was the fact that the secularist Polish National Alliance (PNA) fraternal organization was exceptionally strong in Kantowo and, contrary to the situation in the more religiously oriented Warszawa, tended to dominate communal life. Five PNA lodges were active in Kantowo. In 1905, at the initiative of Paweł Kurdziel, these lodges formed District Council 88 (DC 88). Leaders of DC 88 operated from a secularist point of view and sometimes forged links with socialists.[89]

These leaders were people representing a new generation of immigrants. Kurdziel, for many years president of DC 88, kept a saloon, owned a butcher shop, and also published a weekly newspaper, Narodowiec [Nationalist], beginning in 1909. Stanisław Dangel, who headed DC 88 in the years 1911–1913, had come to the United States in the 1890s, and worked in Chicago and in

Scranton, Pennsylvania, before coming to Cleveland. He edited *Narodowiec* and, with Kurdziel, founded *Wiadomości Codzienne* as an outgrowth of *Narodowiec*. Dangel also edited the PNCC weekly *Straż* (*The Guard*), and clearly sympathized with socialism. As community leaders in Kantowo, these activists from the lower middle class aided and encouraged parishioners in their struggle for democratization and control over the parish.[90]

This struggle lasted for a long time. Although the Doppke episode was eventually smoothed over on the surface, the underlying tensions between laity and clergy remained. Bishop John Farrelly wrote to parish's pastor in 1916: "Your people must learn to recognize that the statutes of the diocese must be observed by them just the same as they are by every other congregation in the diocese. In voting for [parish] councilmen it is the exclusive right of the pastor to present the names of those who can be voted for. If the voters disobey that law, the Bishop then appoints the councilmen." And even in 1925, Rev. Farrelly's successor, Joseph Schrembs, still had cause to refer to the parish's tradition of conflict. "St. John Cantius Parish has borne a reputation of being a rebellious parish," he wrote. "They have been in constant trouble with their pastors. Right within the heart of this parish there is the only existing Independent Polish Parish in the city of Cleveland today, and this—no doubt—has a disturbing influence upon otherwise troublesome members of the parish."[91]

The independent parish in question was that of the Sacred Heart of Jesus, formed in Kantowo in 1914 by individuals, including some of the dissidents from St. John Cantius, who favored lay ownership of church property, and the right to nominate pastors and administer the parish. Sacred Heart parish affiliated with the Polish National Catholic Church, which had broken with the American "Irish" church hierarchy over these and similar issues. Those instrumental in the creation of the new parish had backgrounds similar to those of other Kantowo leaders. Jakub Galiński, for example, was a contractor and a PNA member. Sacred Heart was not the first breakaway church with which he was involved; he had been vice-president of the independent Immaculate Heart of Mary parish in Warszawa before moving to Kantowo. Sacred Heart parish and its pastor maintained close contacts with leftist, democratic, and secularist groups in Kantowo.[92]

In the Poznań neighborhood, too, members of St. Casimir church had wanted control over the parish's activities as early as the end of the nineteenth century. The first two pastors there asked to be dismissed from their duties, citing an "unruly element." Yet, the parish committee, despite their disagreements with St. Casimir's clergymen, rejected the advice of *Jutrzenka* to join the independents; in fact they went so far as to forbid people to buy and read the publication. St. Casimir's fourth pastor, Rev. Konstanty Łaziński, finally won the approval of the parishioners. But his successor, Rev. Ignacy Piotrowski, again became the target of complaints in the years 1910–1912. The parishioners accused him of various abuses, including refusing religious services to those who had not paid their parish dues, and stated that they could "no longer . . . bear up with such treatment." The priest reacted to the revolt by saying: "It is a piece of work of a skunk, whom I would like to know," incurring a reprimand from the chancellor of the diocese.[93]

The controversy divided the parish community. Two-thirds of the parishioners demanded the dismissal of the priest and the parish committee, which supported him. At the end of February 1911 riots broke out near St. Casimir's vicarage; two people were killed. Subsequently, the introduction of new regulations relating to charges for religious services reinflamed the dispute. Influential parishioners like Stanisław Lewandowski, one of the lay leaders of Poznań, vehemently opposed these regulations, which included the stipulation that: "No adult will be admitted to church unless he produces [an] admission ticket and pays 10 cents admission at the door." Rev. Piotrowski was finally replaced, but conflict over governance of the parish continued.[94]

These and similar conflicts were the rule rather than the exception. Most, if not all, of Cleveland's Polish Catholic parishes at one time or another went through battles that pitted diocese against parish, clergy against layman, or one parish faction against another. After the First World War, the conflicts intensified rather than otherwise as social conditions changed. All along, many of the religious arguments had been stimulated by social tensions, and the growth of a new and confident middle class in the community.

The Ethnic Middle Class and Ethnic Leadership

As Polish neighborhoods grew, the ethnic middle class gradually developed a network of small businesses, many of which catered to the needs of the immigrant community. Early on, Polish-owned businesses included drugstores, grocery stores, saloons, and even a carriage factory and a printer. In 1905 there was one such business per every fifty inhabitants. Ethnic middle-class entrepreneurs were gaining prominence. They tried to ensure their customers' loyalty and maintain their own positions by appealing to ethnic pride: "Support your own, not foreign people, support Polish industry, so

Michael Kniola's store and travel bureau on Tod (East 65th) Street in Cleveland's Warszawa Polish neighborhood, ca. 1890. WRHS.

that you may deserve the name of an honest man."[95] These and similar appeals were buttressed by a proposal that a Polish business center be founded in the heart of Warszawa. It was to be similar to the Czechs' "beautiful center" on Broadway.

Most of Cleveland's nineteenth-century Polish businessmen, leaders, and politicians originated from the Prussian sector of Poland. These included Stanisław Koniarski, Franciszek Orlikowski, Teodor Olsztyński, Stanisław Twarogowski, Matt Dłużyński, Józef Sawicki, C. J. Bentkowski, M. Konkolewski, and Michael P. Kniola. For many years Kniola was the most important figure among Cleveland Poles.[96] A businessman and civic leader, he lived in Warszawa, but his influence and importance extended beyond the neighborhood.

Kniola had come to America from Prussian Poland as a fourteen-year-old boy in 1873. He arrived in Cleveland in 1880, worked in the Cleveland

Rolling Mills, saved his money, and in 1886 opened his own grocery store in Warszawa. Gradually this shop came to serve as a something of a financial institution, where Kniola sold ship tickets and issued foreign money orders; by 1890 it had evolved to become primarily a travel agency and insurance office. (There were three Polish-owned travel agencies in Cleveland: Stanisław Lewandowski ran one in Poznań, and Józef Tetlak another in Kantowo.) Kniola served not only Poles, but Hungarians and Czechs as well. He also dealt in real estate, selling lots in both Warszawa and Kraków, and ran an employment agency. His stature in the Polish community was such that people turned to him for all sorts of advice and help. A typical request might, for example, relate to problems at work: "Now, I would like to ask you to request my boss to pay me these few dollars which are remaining, and for your trouble you can charge as much as you think is proper."[97]

As early as the 1890s immigrants started to publish ethnic newspapers in Cleveland. *Polonia w Ameryce* was the first local Polish-language publication to last more than a few issues. A weekly newspaper, it was launched in 1892 by Kniola, Olsztyńki, Dłużynski, and Joseph Śledź. It began daily publication in 1918, had its name changed to *Monitor Clevelandski* in 1922, and existed until 1938. Before World War I six Polish-language newspapers were published in Cleveland. New titles appeared during and after World War I, among them *Wiadomości Codzienne*. The editor of *Wiadomości Codzienne* was Thomas Siemiradzki, formerly a well known activist of PNA from Chicago, during the was the treasurer of Committee of National Defence. In Cleveland, at least until 1932, he continued pro-Pilsudski's activity.[98]

Socialism

In counterpoint to the growing middle class was the small cadre of Polish socialists. Many immigrant socialist leaders had started their activities in Europe, and drew on the traditions of European socialism, while also participating in and influencing the socialist movement in America. For immigrants, support of socialism was complicated by questions of nationalism during the pre-war years. Some socialists rejected the drive for independent national states as contrary to the international goals of the class struggle. More commonly, immigrant leftists, by calling for new states in which social and economic justice would prevail, mingled strains from both ideologies. Still others subordinated economic to national goals. Conflict among these viewpoints helped to fragment the left, among Poles as among other groups.[99]

The first Polish socialist circles originated among the New York intelligentsia in the late 1880s. By 1893 there was a socialist presence in Cleveland, as evidenced by the publication of the journal *Przegląd Tygodniowy* by Józef Zawisza, who had started similar publications in other American cities. Journalist and playwright Alfred Chrostowski, who founded *Jutrzenka* in Pittsburgh in 1893, subsequently moved the weekly to Cleveland. It became the press organ of Kolaszewski's independent parish, and was also involved in the founding of the Alliance of Polish Workers (Związek Robotników Polskich) in Cleveland. Eight hundred people attended the organizational meeting, and three hundred actually joined the group, which was affiliated with the ephemeral Alliance of Polish Workers in America. In 1894 Chrostowski and his staff, along with Kolaszewski and others, greeted and assisted Coxey's Army when it came through Cleveland (particularly "General" Jan Rybakowski's unit, which included about 130 Poles).[100]

In the same year, Polish socialist groups in the United States allied with the Socialist Labor Party (SLP) to form the Alliance of Polish Locals (APL SLP). In 1896, a socialist organizer from Poland visited Cleveland and helped to found a group known as Siła (Society of Polish Workers Strength) in the Warszawa neighborhood. Siła had thirty-five to forty-five members in the period around the turn of the century. Leon Czołgosz, who in 1901 assassinated President McKinley, was a Warszawa resident and a member of Siła (as well as of a more radical anarchist group). Poles nationwide sought to distance themselves from Czołgosz's act. In Cleveland, south side Poles organized an "indignation meeting ... for the purpose of denouncing Czołgosz's crime and taking some action to show that he is not of Polish blood or Polish nativity."[101]

The SLP's opposition to immigrants' participation in ethnic organizations and nationalist activities contributed to its low popularity among the various Slavic groups, including Poles. When the Alliance of Polish Locals separated into two factions in 1900, Siła went with the less radical Alliance of Polish Socialists (APS). The APS advocated cooperation with labor unions, and the creation of an independent Polish state. In 1908 another schism within the Polish socialist movement in America resulted in the creation of the Polish Section of the Socialist Party (PSSP, with 134 locals and 2,500 members, or two to three percent of total SP membership), which supported Polish independence but considered advancing the workers' struggle in the United States its primary goal. The less numerous APS (67 locals, 1,600 members) focused on promoting the creation of a democratic, independent Poland. Cleveland had four PSSP branches. An APS group continued to exist in Warszawa, but the most active Cleveland APS affiliate was Kantowo's "Proletariat" group. Other leftist groups active in Cleveland's Polish community during the 1910s were the Polish People's University, the Committee for the Defense of Political Prisoners in Poland, and the socialist fraternal benefit organizations People's Sick Fund (PSSP), with two locals, and the Polish Workers Sick Mutual Aid, with one local in Warszawa.[102]

In 1916 a small internationalist faction seized control of the PSSP, resulting in the departure from the SP of the many Poles who supported the Polish national forces, and their realignment with the APS. In Cleveland, the APS and former PSSP groups cooperated with each other. Kantowo remained the center of Polish socialist activity in Cleveland. Polish socialists had ties to the Polish Library Home in the neighborhood. There, "Proletariat" and the Polish People's University had their meetings. Next door on West 14th Street the Ukrainian socialists had their headquarters, and Slovak socialists also had a local nearby. However, the socialist presence in the Library met with strong opposition in 1918, as pro-National Democratic sentiments strengthened within the Polish community, as did fears that the Library could be persecuted for harboring socialist gatherings, and "Proletariat" had to move out.[103]

Although the immigrant left did not disappear after the war, it was increasingly marginalized. On May 1, 1919, a riot broke out in downtown Cleveland when socialists and some trade unionists attempted to march to Public Square. The five thousand demonstrators, representing many nationalities, clashed with bystanders and police; two people were killed, forty injured, and 116 arrested. Nearly all of the detainees were of foreign birth, and all of the Poles among them lived in Kantowo. In December 1919, some of Cleveland's Polish socialists were arrested during the Palmer raids.[104]

Polish Ethnic Organizations

There were many Polish societies organized on the local level, often within parishes, in Cleveland. These societies had economic functions, providing mutual benefit insurance and other financial assistance, and also served as administrative, educational, and social organizations. They held meetings, sponsored charities, arranged picnics and other outings, and prepared celebrations to mark national anniversaries.

Two supralocal Polish ethnic organizations, the Polish Roman Catholic Union (PRCU), founded in Chicago in 1873, and the Polish National Alliance (PNA), founded in 1880 and also headquartered in Chicago, were both active in Cleveland. Over time, they incorporated smaller local societies into their structures. As the secular and nationalistically oriented PNA was sometimes barred from meeting in parish halls, lay meeting places were built, including White Eagle Hall in Poznań, the Polish National Hall in Warszawa, and the Polish Library Home in Kantowo. In Kantowo, a neighborhood known (like the Tremont settlements of other ethnic groups) for its secularist, populist bent, the PNA had greater influence than the PRCU.[105]

The personal ambitions and rivalries of some members, as well as controversial policies promulgated at the national level, caused arguments and splits within the local branches of these organizations. During the eleventh PNA convention in 1895 (which was held in Cleveland), it was decided, after heated debate, to allow socialists to join the organization. This caused a certain number of Cleveland Poles to withdraw and create their own organization, the Alliance of Poles in Ohio (APO). During the organizational meeting, Stanisław Lewandowski "explained why we are establishing the Alliance of Poles in Ohio and . . . mentioned that the PNA cares only about Chicago and nothing else." By 1917 the APO also operated in Pennsylvania and Michigan, and became the Alliance of Poles in America (APA). In 1932 the APA numbered 133 locals and about 20,000 members.[106]

Alliance of Poles members had accepted Ludwik Dewoyno's motion that the APO's goal should be "To unite Poles and Americans of Polish extraction, including also under the same heading Lithuanians, Ruthenians, and Slovaks." In 1903, nineteen Lithuanians founded the APO's group No. 26. Nor were other societies necessarily made up exclusively of Poles; in 1891, fifty Poles and Lithuanians had formed the Sons of Poland and Lithuania, registered as PNA group No. 171.[107]

Cleveland's Polish community also founded some other local insurance societies. In Rev. Kolaszewski's independent Immaculate Heart of Mary parish, the Polish Roman Catholic Union of the Immaculate Heart of the Blessed Virgin Mary was organized in 1894, and registered with the state of Ohio as an insurance society in 1915. It accepted members from other parishes and from other nationalities, specifically "Lithuanians, Carpatho-Russins, and the other Slav groups." Another organization, the Polish Roman Catholic Union of Our Lady of Czestochowa, was founded in 1898 in affiliation with St. Stanislaus parish. It endeavored "to unite the Polish and Slovenian Catholics in one large organization." Both of these organizations attained memberships in the thousands, with numerous Cleveland branches. In 1939 they merged to form the Union of Poles in America (UPA), the majority of whose members resided in Cleveland or elsewhere in Ohio.[108]

Most of these organizations conducted both cultural and social activity, in addition to providing insurance. The Society of Sons of Free Poland (APO group No. 87) was created for the purpose of "spreading education, patriotism," and "also provided a social setting for discussion and camaraderie." Although most groups centered their recreational programs on celebrations, anniversaries, and dances, some societies, mainly singing and dramatic groups, which focused exclusively on more serious cultural activities also existed, often in affiliation with parishes or other broader organizations. In 1907, at the corner of Broadway and 71st Avenue, the city's first theater dedicated to Polish-language performances was built. Finally, quasi-military groups, athletic clubs, and gymnastic societies also operated. Poles, like Czechs, Slovaks, and Croatians, had active Sokol, or Falcon, groups.[109]

From the very beginning of the formation of the various Polish neighborhoods, their inhabitants interacted with each other. In spite of the distances separating their districts, Warszawa, Kantowo, Kraków, and Poznań community members celebrated together. In 1891, they joined to commemorate the anniversary of the Polish uprising in 1830; in 1892, they met to lay the cornerstone for the church of St. Casimir; in 1893, they celebrated the promulgation of the Polish Constitution on May 3, 1791.[110]

One major instance, however, showed not only the extent, but also the limitations of intracommunity cooperation. This was the erection of Cleveland's monument to Tadeusz Kościuszko, the Polish nationalist hero who had also fought in the American Revolutionary War. Because the initiator of the project was none other than Antoni Kolaszewski, controversy was inevitable. Rev. Kolaszewski had been impressed by the construction of a Kosciuszko monument in Chicago and by a statue of Lajos Kossuth in Cleveland, and spearheaded a drive to create a Kościuszko monument in Cleveland. After funds were raised, a sculpture was commissioned from a source in Italy and completed in 1903. However, complaints to Cleveland's city council that those promoting the project were not truly representative of the city's entire Polish community threatened to derail the entire enterprise. In the spring of 1904 the Committee for the Building of the Monument to Thaddeus Kościuszko in Cleveland was substantially enlarged, making it possible for plans to erect the monument in the city's Wade Park to proceed. Sufficient harmony was achieved to enable all Polish organizations and their leaders to participate in the parade marking the statue's unveiling on May 7, 1905. It should be noted that the protests and controversies did not (as in the case of the Kossuth monument) concern the person of Kościuszko himself, and what he represented. They were reflections of controversies between the church and lay groups, and of the ostracism directed against the Rev. Kolaszewski's independent parish. The supporters of the monument had protested the intrusion of these extraneous issues: "It is not a church problem but a purely national [matter]." Later, at the time of the monument's unveiling, the unifying rather than the divisive nature of the event was again stressed: "It was not by any means a church undertaking but a Polish national one, and every Pole could take part in it without any reservations."[111]

Polish ethnic communities during World War I

War and the Independence Movement

Before, during, and shortly after World War I, one could observe in Polish communities in the United States two coexisting and mutually dependent tendencies. In the first place, there had evolved a growing unity within the group, a development of "common institutions," and an "intensified collective awareness." The links among Polish communities and neighborhoods were then strengthened by frequent appeals to Polish patriotism. Patriotic fervor reached its height during the war years, kindled by the hope that an independent Polish state would arise out of the wartime chaos. The regaining of Polish independence would mean heightened prestige for Polish ethnic groups in the United States, and a stronger position in the broader American society.[112]

Perhaps the most notable feature of the support for the Polish independence movement within Polish-American communities was its crystallization into two political camps between 1912 and 1914. The first, the Committee of National Defense (CND) supported the political coalition existing in Poland (particularly in Galicia), headed by Józef Piłsudski and allied with the Central Powers, as the best means of achieving a Polish state. The second, known, as of 1916, as the Polish National Department (PND), cooperated with the Polish National Democrats. Its adherents believed that joint action with the Allied Powers would lead to the re-establishment of Polish independence. In 1914 all major Polish ethnic organizations in the United States (including the PNA and the PRCU) entered this faction. Newspapers entered into the rivalry between the two camps. Adherents of one side referred in print to their opponents as "filomoscovites," or "puppets in German hands," as "socialist bugs," "parish activists from the camp of boor," and the like. The average Polish immigrant, liable to become lost in these disputes, which also often reflected local rivalries and personal quarrels, generally followed the views of whichever community leader he most trusted.[113]

Alignment with the PND found its greatest support in Warszawa, led by Sawicki, and also in Poznań, led by Lewandowski, Rev. Soliński of St. Casimir, and J. Orzechowski. The APO and *Jutrzenka* also solidly supported this orientation. PND supporters cooperated with representatives of other ethnic groups representing similar political views, such as V. Svarc of the Czech community.[114]

The president of Cleveland's PNA group No. 671 became the main local supporter of the CND, and in January 1913 he organized its Cleveland affiliate. Inhabitants of Kantowo followed his lead. As the CND later lost, for the most part, whatever adherents it had in other parts of the city, Kantowo remained its base, with *Wiadomości Codzienne* and PNA District Council 88 remaining steadfast in their support.[115]

Following the proclamation of an independent Poland in 1918, Polish groups from all political camps continued to promote the Polish cause and to collect money to that end, as they had done during the war. The dangers the country faced (such as in August 1920, when Bolsheviks occupied huge parts of Poland) served as a catalyst for unanimous activity. "Let us display solidarity . . ., particularly now, when Poland's enemies want to ruin her economically," J. Sawicki urged during a rally in Gray's Armory.[116]

Return Migration

Patriotic sentiment might have been expected to inspire return migration to Poland from America. Indeed, such migration started as early as 1919. Along with a longing for the homeland, hopes of gaining personal material success while contributing new-found skills and knowledge to invigorate the Polish economy caused many individuals to think about returning. At the same time, they had doubts: "If not for this war I would have been at home a long time ago; but now, after this war a man doesn't know what to do."[117]

Of course, Polish immigrants were not the only ones who thought about returning to the homeland. A federal official projected that thirty-five thousand foreigners would leave Cleveland in 1919. A representative of the city's Chamber of Commerce warned of an impending scarcity of labor, predicting that about a third each of Rusyns, Slovaks, Ukrainians, and Yugoslavs would return to Europe. United States authorities found it necessary to make some attempts to regulate the post-war return movement.[118]

Before the war "conservative returns" and "returns of failure" by immigrants disillusioned with life in America had predominated. After the war
"returns of innovation," or "group returns," which were promoted in Cleveland's Polish-American community by some ethnic leaders and journalists,
grew in importance. The Alliance of Polish Farmers (*Związek Rolników Polskich*) offered to assist those willing to return and revivify the war-damaged
Polish agricultural economy. More commonly, however, return migration
was promoted for the sake of reconstructing and expanding the industrial
sector. Cooperatives and corporations were organized to raise capital in the
United States for transfer to Poland, now regarded as "a promised land,"
destroyed by war and deprived of industry, awaiting the emigrants' initiative. Return to the Polish homeland was viewed as a pioneering venture,
a crusade for progress in which patriotism and self-interest meshed: "You
will help Poland industrially, but you won't do yourself wrong, either."[119]

In Cleveland's Warszawa and Poznań neighborhoods, the Polish Commerce Corporation organized classes on the mechanisms of trade. Local
community leaders such as Olsztyński and Sawicki supported the Chicago-
based Union Liberty Co., a trade and export corporation; the Polish American Navigation Corporation; Polus, a shoe factory; and the Ursus Motor
Co., which manufactured agricultural machines. In Cleveland, S. A. Titus,
F. J. Kowalczyk, and A. Turajski organized the "Commercial Corporation,"
headquartered on Broadway Ave. Most such enterprises, however, soon went
bankrupt and disappeared.[120]

Conditions in Poland itself also had a dampening effect on the return
migration movement. Unstable borders and political chaos and crises made
for uncertainty. The tales related by disappointed returnees, of theft, swin-
dling, stupidity, poverty, and filth, served to discourage others. The rampant
bureaucracy obstructed their efforts, despotic priests irritated them. At the
personal level, the worn and lined faces of their relatives, on which the story
of years of hardship was clearly written, sobered them.[121]

'Emigrants for Themselves'

Concurrently, excitement about Polish independence diminished in Cleveland's Polish community. As early as August 1917, some APA groups had protested against contributing to the Polish National Fund. At the beginning of
1919 some APO lodges asked the organization's directors "to cancel the 5%
taxation for the national cause." The St. Stanislaus pastor declared from the

pulpit: "Nobody can force you to pay the [Polish] national tax." In 1923 the UPA decided to sell the Polish bonds it held and replace them with American ones.[122]

Immediately after the war, during the Diet of the Polish National Department, exhortations like "Everything for Poland" and "Let's help Poland first of all" had been heard everywhere. Two years later, such sentiments were replaced by a more pragmatic watchword, "Emigrants for Emigrants," that is, "emigrants for themselves." A program based on ethnic ideology, and focused on solving the group's own internal problems, protecting Polish ethnic culture, and promoting active participation in American social and political life, won acceptance.[123]

In 1923 Judge Sawicki, presiding at the Fourth Emigration Diet in Cleveland, recalled that in 1918 "we generously forgot about ourselves. We were altruists and patriots. A Free Poland was our dream. The relief for Polish people was our duty. . . . Now, it's high time to think about ourselves. We have a lot to do. All of us, our youth, and clergy need our united and immediate help. Polish people must be defended against the attacks of chauvinists and pseudo-Americans. Polish youth must be educated and saved from national destruction." A speaker at the 1925 Emigration Congress declared that Poles, as American citizens, should "participate in American life equally with the other groups," an ideal that was in fact becoming the real situation.[124]

One index of this was the growing number of Poles that were being naturalized as American citizens. In Cleveland, naturalization and Americanization pressures had been manifested earlier. For instance, the Schauffler Missionary Training School and other missions worked in ethnic neighborhoods to convert immigrants away from Catholicism, still regarded as a "foreign" religion by some Protestants. Organizations like the Cleveland Immigrant League and the City Immigration Bureau provided services to immigrants, more or less overtly aiming at the eventual goals of Americanization and citizenship. They offered English language classes, and classes in preparation for naturalization.[125]

Acculturation during the 1920s

Polish Roots, American Citizens

During the war, in Cleveland as elsewhere, members of immigrant groups had found it expedient to demonstrate their loyalty to America. Sawicki,

Kniola, and Lewandowski all participated in the efforts of the Mayor's Advisory War Committee. Sawicki was especially zealous in the campaign for the purchase of Liberty Loan Bonds, addressing Poles in their own language at their workplaces. Other community members and groups also participated in the Liberty Bond drive. Kniola was the first president of the county's Savings Committee. Eleonora Wasilewska promoted the buying of bonds among employees of companies like the Cleveland Worsted Mills where many women were employed. Polish ethnic organizations bought and distributed bonds. The campaign led to an unofficial race among ethnic groups to pledge and collect the largest amount of money. This became a question of national prestige. "Poles are in the first place," *Wiadomości Codzienne* proudly announced on April 16, 1918. Three days later, boasting that Cleveland's Poles had "pushed Germans out from first to second place," a writer urged that "Poles in Otis, Wait, and other factories should acknowledge their Polish origins; it is necessary that Poles show their nationality, which is different from Austro-Hungarian or German." (On April 21 the news was not so good: "The Czechs pushed us back!")[126]

In addition to bond campaigns, Polish ethnic leaders had also supported wartime Americanization efforts. Sawicki was a member of the Cleveland Americanization Council's executive committee. The Council coordinated the work of the numerous local organizations that offered English and naturalization classes, including evening classes in factories. Leaders of the Polish community stressed the need for participation in American political life, realizing that their own positions and influence in the city depended on their status as representatives of Cleveland's substantial Polish population.[127]

By the postwar period, members of the Polish community increasing identified themselves as Polish-American. Ideally, loyalty to the adopted homeland and loyalty to ethnic roots would go hand in hand. One could become a naturalized citizen without relinquishing Polish culture and language. Unfortunately, however, the teaching of Polish, and teaching in Polish, in the schools did at times cause tensions between members of the Cleveland Polish community on one side and city and diocesan authorities on the other.[128] It was argued that preservation of Polish culture would stimulate feelings of greater security, freedom, and pride. At the same time, familiarity with English and at least "partial acceptance of the spirit of American culture" was necessary. "Those who cut off their mustaches, and who want in their appearance to be identical to surrounding Americans, have not broken with Polishness." Polish organizations aimed to preserve the Polish language, religion, and culture within the community, while promoting participation in the broader spectrum of American social and political life. In the mid-1920s, there were attempts within the PNA, APW, and other organizations to reserve full membership rights for American citizens only.[129]

In 1918, Poles had taken part in Cleveland's Fourth of July celebrations. In 1921 the city's own 125th anniversary celebration provided "an unusual opportunity to show our strength and power as Poles. . . . All nationalities will participate in these celebrations, and we can't be at the back!" Polish participation proved worthwhile, with members of Polish societies, dressed in colorful national costumes, drawing admiration for their striking appearance. If celebration of civic and national holidays was an indicator of where loyalties lay, by 1936 there were no doubts. Polish ethnic organizations and their representatives voted against celebrating May 3, the Polish national holiday. In so doing, Polish Americans declared that they had become Americans of Polish descent.[130]

While holiday celebrations symbolized Poles' acculturation, involvement in Cleveland politics indicated the reality of their commitment to their new home city. Initially, only members of the middle class were politically active, largely to further their own influence, ambition, or financial interests, and during the nineteenth century, Cleveland Poles seemed to favor the Republican party. In about 1889, a Polish Jew, William Welfeld, established the Polish Republican Club in Warszawa. Michael Kniola, who would be the party's most active and influential supporter in the Polish community, soon became the club's president. In the early 1890s, the club had about 140 members. In subsequent years Czechs, Germans, and Irish were also members. The less numerous politically active Poles who identified themselves as Democrats finally succeeded in forming a Polish Democratic Club in 1899.[131]

During the 1890s, presidential candidate William McKinley (an Ohioan) and his supporters, notably Cleveland business magnate Mark Hanna, attempted to make the Republican party more attractive to Catholics. Although their attentions focused on the Irish, they also included the newer immigrant groups in their political machine, meshing with the ambitions of Polish leaders such as Kniola. Kniola, whose principal contact was U.S. Representative (and later Senator) Theodore Burton, was invited to dinner at McKinley's Canton residence and, later, served as a delegate to the Republican national convention.[132]

Polish supporters of the Republican Party sometimes exploited the animosity between Poles and the Irish to turn Poles away from the Democrats, where, claimed the *Kurier Clevelandski,* "they were perceived as tools in the hands of the Irish party." Nonetheless, by the turn of the century it was clear that Democrats were gaining strength among Cleveland Poles. Although Kniola and other Polish leaders such as Lewandowski organized support for Burton's 1900 campaign, in the Poznań neighborhood Democrat rallies attracted twice as many attendees as Republican ones. (According to Lewandowski, most of those at one such gathering were actually Republicans who "went there because one saloon keeper Karpiński was elected president and beer was free.") In the Cleveland mayoral elections of 1899, the Republican candidate outpolled Democrats in Polish precincts, but in 1905 Democrat Tom Johnson defeated his Republican rival in those precincts by a two-to-one margin.[133]

At this point, the number of Poles in the electorate was still small, since most Polish immigrants were not yet citizens, and even among those who were, a large number did not register to vote. In 1900, of the 235 Polish immigrants in Cleveland eligible to vote, 131 had registered. By 1905, there were still only 493 naturalized Poles in Cleveland.[134]

Political issues with direct connections to the neighborhoods, such as municipal improvements and services, had the most interest for Poles, who focused their attention on races at the local, as opposed to the state, level. "We are not interested in state senators," wrote *Wiadomości Codzienne.* The exception to this was when a Pole ran for state office. Poles began achieving elected office in Cleveland early in the twentieth century. During the nineteenth century, Poles, initially having no candidates of their own, had often supported "our brother" Czechs who ran for seats on the city council.[135]

The first Polish councilman was Joseph Śledź, a saloon owner and Democrat from Ward 17, which comprised much of the Warszawa district. Śledz was instrumental in getting a bridge constructed over Morgana Ravine, which considerably shortened the trip to downtown Cleveland. He served from 1902–1907 and from 1914–1917; another Polish Democrat held the seat from 1908–1913. Republican Stanley Dembowski was elected for a single term in 1918, after which Democrat Bernard Orlikowski represented Warszawa for four terms, 1920–1927. (November 18 was designated Thaddeus Kościuszko Day in Cleveland due to Orlikowski's efforts.) A Republican Pole was elected for the 1930–1931 term. From 1902 on, the concentration of Poles in Warszawa guaranteed the election of a Polish councilman from the area (even during 1923–1931 when larger electoral districts temporarily replaced small wards), except in 1927 when two Poles split the vote, allowing an Irish candidate to win.[136]

Polish councilmen were not elected in Ward 7, which included Kantowo, until the 1930s. This ward, being in Tremont, had a mixed population, and

Czech candidates received Polish support during the 1910s and 20s. Jerry Zmunt, a Czech Republican councilman from Ward 7 who later ran for the state and national legislatures, helped maintain ties with his Polish constituents by attending Polish ethnic celebrations and meetings.[137]

By this time a new generation of Polish political leaders, including Śledź, Orlikowski, Kurdziel, Dangel, and Józef Sawicki, had taken over from the aging Kniola and his contemporaries. Sawicki was born in Poland but brought to the United States as a small child, and educated at St. Stanislaus School and Cleveland public schools. He worked his way through college and law school and began his political career almost immediately following his admittance to the bar in 1904. At the age of twenty-four, he was elected to the Ohio legislature in 1905, where he served until 1908, and again in 1911–1912. Initially, he must have received support from the numerous Irish residents of the district, since the number of Polish voters was still quite small. However, the growth of the Polish population, combined with redistricting, made the seat something of a Polish sinecure in subsequent years; incumbents included Sawicki's son Edwin.[138]

Sawicki was appointed a judge in Cleveland's municipal court in 1919, and was the elected twice, serving in the position until 1932, when financial problems and ethics questions forced his retirement from the bench. He returned to private practice but remained a leader in the Polish community, involved in politics and ethnic organizations and activities. He had founded the Kraków Political Club in 1923, which grew to a membership of five hundred men and four hundred women by 1928.[139]

Other Polish clubs active in the 1920s included the Polish Democratic, Republican, and Women's Republican Clubs, and the Warsaw Political Club. The Polish American Chamber of Commerce and Industry in Cleveland, established in 1908, also had political aims. It functioned as a lobby, demanding municipal improvements for the Polish neighborhoods and government jobs for Poles, and sometimes endorsing candidates. There were also a few short-lived attempts to create an umbrella organization to unite Poles irrespective of party or neighborhood, such as the Polish Political League, organized in 1919, and the Polish Political Club, active from 1925 until about 1928.[140]

Consumerism, Acculturation and the Second Generation

Although ethnic leaders, newspapers, and businessmen had always attempted to persuade people to buy Polish products from Polish hands, in the 1920s the "each one for his own [ethnic group]" mentality was promoted more widely and aggressively. The ethnic press wrote: "We carry our money, which we toiled so hard to earn, to foreign financial institutions, alien to our nationality; we are convinced that the foreign financier will take care of our savings and won't betray our interests." "This is a national crime; it is the suppurating ulcer on the body, which must be cut away."[141]

People were urged to use instead the financial institutions which existed within Cleveland's Polish community. As the community had prospered, growing in stability and wealth, relatively small steamship ticketing and money transfer agencies had grown into banks and savings and loan associations. Cleveland's first Polish bank had its start in 1913, when Stanley Klonowski opened a private business which offered banking, foreign exchange, real estate, insurance, and ticketing services. Officially incorporated as the Klonowski Savings Bank in 1920, the enterprise was soon reorganized and renamed the Bank of Cleveland, operating under federal charter. In 1916 Kniola and S. Orlikowski incorporated the Warsaw Savings and Loan Association. Other examples included S. Olsztyński's state-chartered Washington Savings Bank; St. Hyacinth's Savings and Loan Association, established by the parish of that name; and the Polish American Savings and Loan Company, as well as several other institutions in which Polish capital predominated.[142]

During the 1920s Poles did in the main use such local, private financial institutions, which were not controlled by either state or federal authorities. These institutions were hard hit during the Great Depression, although the Bank of Cleveland, Warsaw Savings and Loan, and others did in the end survive the crisis. However, almost thirty per cent of Polish trade, industrial, and financial enterprises were forced to close. As work became scarce, people had less money to save, and less to spend, hurting the shops and other small business of the Polish neighborhoods.[143]

Before the Depression, in the 1920s, chain grocery stores with cheaper and sometimes better goods were already endangering small independent shops. In Cleveland, the first efforts to unite against the danger were made in the late 1920s. The Polish American Chamber of Commerce and Industry tried to bring bankers, grocers, and other shopkeepers together. The Polish Grocery Association, organized in 1928, quickly gained 250 members. The Association imported goods from Poland, and tried to help its members sell groceries at competitive prices. However, membership plummeted to 65 in 1934, recovering only slightly to 82 by 1937. Other business associations active during the late 1930s included the Association of Polish Merchants, the Association of Restauranteurs, the Polish Importing Company, and the Association of Polish Bakers.[144]

Although employees lost struggles for control of their on-the-job lives when trade unions were defeated in the early 1920s, from 1922 workers' real incomes generally grew. Now, workers could spend more for pleasure and search for satisfaction outside the workplace. They could convert their wages into consumption, and into prestige within their group. Although the Polish ethnic press often complained about materialism in the American settlements, it was to an extent a natural outgrowth of the work ethos and the desire to make good that immigrants had brought with them from Europe.[145]

Ownership of real property was still of primary importance in conferring status, and provided a sense of security as well. In 1900, 17 percent of Cleveland's Polish immigrants owned houses, although as late as 1909, in the relatively poor Kantowo area, only 13.5 percent of the Polish residents were homeowners. By 1914, 89 percent of the houses in Polish and Czech blocks of Warszawa were wholly or partly owner-occupied. In the post-war years properties were purchased in even larger numbers. Increasingly, Poles bought lots with borrowed money, a phenomenon supportive of the thesis that immigrants were by this time acculturating. Polish ethnic banks and loan associations profited from the trend.[146]

Polish dwelling habits were also now conforming to American norms. Workers' families lived in larger, more spacious apartments. The average occupancy rate was one person per room. Houses and apartments became increasingly more comfortable and better furnished. More and more, emigrants' lifestyles indicated that they were in the United States not on a temporary basis, but rather as permanent residents.[147]

People were attracted by the new mass-produced consumer goods: clothing, sewing machines, washing machines, vacuum cleaners, phonographs, radios, and especially automobiles. Car ownership brought prestige and enhanced leisure; on Sundays the automobile offered escape from the monotony of work. With cars relatively affordable by the 1920s, it was not unusual for Polish families to have one.[148]

After the war advertisements swamped the Polish ethnic press, opening up a new world of consumption. This world not only offered the factory worker a sense of autonomy and satisfaction in his personal life through the purchase of consumer goods, in counterpoint to the machine-driven routine of the shop floor; the new appliances and conveniences also had a significant impact on domestic economy and the roles of family members. Conveniences like hot plates, gas rings, canned foods, vacuum cleaners, and washing machines had a significant effect on women's household tasks. The diets of immigrant families changed, albeit slowly. The home was no longer a place of production, or, in most cases, a source of income. Boarders and lodgers disappeared as new immigration restrictions went into effect in the mid-1920s.[149]

The economic and social position of women in the Polish community changed, as did that of women in society at large. Some changes had occurred earlier. In 1900, the PNA began accepting women into its ranks. Delegates attending the organization's national convention were persuaded by numerous women's voices to abolish regulations "which humiliated [women] by accepting only men." The women's victory did not come easily. "We have met various obstacles, particularly the lack of understanding from some Alliancers, who criticized us openly saying that 'crones' should organize the kitchen, house and children and not . . . women's lodges."[150]

Cleveland women also formed their own local organizations. In 1913 some Cleveland members of the Polish Women's Alliance, which was headquartered in Chicago, founded the Association of Polish Women as a fraternal benefit society. These women preferred that their dues "stay right here in Cleveland" rather than going to "other cities." They wanted to devote all their attention to local matters, and not only established an insurance fund, but also undertook charitable, educational, and cultural projects. Incorporated in Ohio in 1917, the Association established a weekly newspaper, *Jedność Polek* [*Unity of Polish Women*], in 1924. Another local women's organization was the Polish Women's Club, founded by Katarzyna Radomska and approximately one hundred other women in 1922 for the purposes of study and community service. The club participated in promoting Americanization and naturalization activities, including the improvement of English language skills and citizenship education.[151]

For Polish organizations in general, the changing social contexts of the war and post-war years brought new needs and new challenges. The continued existence of some older organizations was threatened; new groups were founded in response to contemporary needs. For instance, local veterans of General Haller's "army" of Polish volunteers, returning to the United States after World War I, formed the Polish Army Veterans' Association in America, with headquarters in Cleveland. The Association's goals were to provide assistance to invalids and the unemployed among its membership. In 1923 the Association affiliated with the American Legion. The Polish Sport League was established in response to the growing interest in sports like baseball and basketball among the city's Polish-American youth in the 1920s, an interest which diminished the appeal of traditional Sokol groups like the Polish Falcons.[152]

The second generation also formed new professional and cultural asso-
ciations in Cleveland. The city's Polish Medical and Dental Association
(which became part of the national Polish Medical and Dental Association)
was founded in 1916. Seventy percent of its members had been born in the
United States. During the first meeting they decided to accept as members any
Polish-speaking Rusyn or Slovak physicians and dentists who wished to join.
In 1923 the Cleveland Society of Poles was established. It brought together
Polish professionals and businessmen, and sponsored cultural events.[153]

Cultural activities flourished in the 1920s and 1930s, as the Polish and
other ethnic communities made efforts to reach beyond their own groups
and attain recognition in the city as a whole. In the 1920s a Polish group
opened a new theater. Musical organizations, including the Halka, Harmo-
nia, and Chopin Singing Societies were also quite active. The Polish community participated in multicultural projects such as the Theater of Nations
and the Cultural Gardens. The Theater of Nations featured a Series of plays
presented by various nationality groups in Cleveland's Public Hall over a
three-year period beginning in 1930. The city's Cultural Gardens similarly
attempted to foster a sense of "one community, many nations." Beginning
in the 1920s and 1930s, areas within a city park were set aside for the creation
of landscaped gardens with statuary, each garden honoring a different ethnic group. The Polish Garden, with busts of Fryderyk Chopin and other cultural icons, opened in 1935.[154]

Perhaps more than any other activity, education, and particularly education in English, served to integrate Poles with other ethnic groups and into
the community at large. The original impetus to learn English and send children to school came not, however, from high-flown ideals of brotherhood
and communality, but from practical necessity and the desire for economic
betterment. Significant numbers of Polish children attended Cleveland public schools, which tended to further acculturate themselves and their families. In 1921, they made up six percent of the total enrollment in Cleveland
public schools. As the Polish-American community grew wealthier in the
1920s, it put more money into education. The Polish Educational Society,
formed in 1920, organized English language classes and lectures on politics and history. Settlement houses in Polish and other neighborhoods conducted educational activities that also expanded contacts and cooperation
among ethnic groups. The Broadway Mothers Club had both Polish and
Ukrainian women as members. Poles, Germans, and Italians met at the
Harvard Community Club, and the University Settlement House brought
together Slovenes, Irish, Italians, and Poles. Even St. Stanislaus's pastor came

to appreciate the benefits of the American social settlement: "The church has learned that recreational programs provide a means of keeping the people in the parish and securing their active participation in parish programs, at the same time providing healthy interests for each person." Michael Kniola and other members of the Polish community served on the University Settlement's advisory board, demonstrating Poles' willingness to cooperate in a multi-ethnic endeavor.[155]

Conclusion

Thus, the 1920s brought economic stabilization and development of cultural and social life to the Polish communities of Cleveland. The higher standard of living, increased emphasis on education, and the growth and changing character of Polish organizations reflect this. The first and second generations by this time appeared fairly well acculturated to their American surroundings. Wanting to play a more significant role in Cleveland, and in their adopted country, Polish-Americans increasingly cooperated with representatives of other nationality groups as well as the society at large.

The Great Depression hit ethnic neighborhoods hard in the 1930s. People tended to seek help within their own ethnic groups. Polish charities active in Cleveland during this period included the Holy Ghost Orphanage for Polish Children, and the Polish Welfare Federation, established in 1928 to assist unemployed workers. Parishes and ethnic organizations seconded the Federation in its relief efforts; for instance, businessmen from St. Stanislaus parish funded support for widows and orphans. However, the very severity of the economic difficulties meant that intracommunal resources were not always adequate to meet the Polish-American community's needs. Like their fellow Clevelanders, the city's Poles and their children also turned to broader-based organizations, and especially to government agencies and programs like the WPA and the CCC to tide them over the difficult years and set them back on course to prosperity, a course ultimately made possible by the economic swell of the Second World War. Again, circumstances tended ultimately to break down communal barriers and strengthen ties with American society at large.[156]

Although the vicissitudes of the Depression temporarily halted the movement of Poles into the middle class, those difficulties did not retard their integration into American culture and life. The restriction of immigration as of the early 1920s and the return of some migrants to Poland allowed little replenishment of the first generation community in Cleveland. While that community stabilized in number and then, through reimmigration and death, began to shrink, it was supplanted by an American-born generation that confronted the challenges of Depression-era Cleveland in ways that were both Polish and American. The experiences of this generation in the coming world war would eventually change forever the way Cleveland Polonia viewed itself and its relations to its surrounding community.

Notes

1. Florian Znaniecki, "Wychodźstwo a położenie ludności wiejskiej zarobkującej w Królestwie Polskim," *Wychodźca Polski*, no. 3 (1911, December), quoted after Zygmunt Dulczewski, *Florian Znaniecki, redaktor Wychodźcy Polskiego* (Warszawa, 1982), 125; Lack of space makes any discussion about the complexity of causes of migration impossible. Apart from the traditional push/pull interpretation, "Recent studies of international population movements have reconceptualized this problem, recasting the unit(s) of analysis from separate nation-states, linked by one-way transfer of migrants between two unequally developed economies, to a comprehensive economic system composed of a dominant core and dependent periphery—a world system that forms a complex network of supranational exchanges of technology, capital, and labor," Ewa Morawska, "Labor Migrations of Poles in the Atlantic World Economy, 1880–1914," *Comparative Studies in Society and History*, 31 (1989, no 3), 237–272; on Polish history, see Norman Davies, *God's Playground. A History of Poland* (New York: Columbia University Press, 1982), 2 volumes; on reasons for migration, see *Emigracja z ziem polskich w czasach nowożytnych i najnowszych*, ed. Andrzej Pilch (Warszawa, 1984); also Ewa Morawska, "For Bread with Butter: Life-Words of Peasant Immigrants from East Central Europe 1880–1914," *Journal of Social History*, 17 (1984), 388–389; Adam Walaszek, "Preserving of Transforming Role? Migrants and Polish Territories in the Era of Mass Migrations," *People in Transit. German Migrations in Comparative Perspective, 1820–1930*, ed. Dirk Hoerder, Jörg Nagler. Cambridge: Cambridge University Press, 1995, 101–126.

2. Jerzy Fierich, *Przeszłość wsi powiatu ropczyckiego w ustach ich mieszkańców* (Ropczyce, 1936), 58.

3. Marian Czuła, "W niewoli życia i polityki. Pamiętnik," mss. 12400 II, Biblioteka Zakładu Narodowego im. Ossolińskich, Wrocław, 65; Zjazd 12-ty XX Dziekanów w 1907 r., Archiwum Kurii Metropolitalnej, Kraków, file Wychodźstwo, 25.

4. Cis-049, vol. 1–2, 17, 20–22, Oral History Archives of Chicago Polonia, Chicago Historical Society, Chicago.

5. Władysław Bronikowski, *Drogi postępu chłopa polskiego* (Warszawa: Biblioteka Puławska, Vol. 41, 1934), 150–153; Morawska, "For Bread," 390; Morawska, "Labor," 262–266; Walaszek, "Preserving of Transforming Role? Migrants and Polish

Territories," 101–126; Adam Walaszek, *Reemigracja ze Stanów Zjednoczonych do Polski po I wojnie światowej, 1919–1924* (Warszawa-Kraków: PWN, 1984). 5–14, 149–154; about the termimology, see Frank Bovenkerk, *The Sociology of Return Migration: A Bibliographic Essay* (The Hague: Martinus Nijhof, 1974), 9–10.

   6. Witold Kula, Nina Assorodobraj-Kula, *Writing Home: Immigrants in Brazil and the United States 1890–1891* (hereafter cited as *Writing*), (Boulder, Colo.: East European Monographs, 1986), 354 265, 328–329, 365, 391; Cf. family and friends' correspondence, Kniola Travel Bureau, Cleveland, Records 1894–1950 (hereafter cited as KTB), Series I, cont. 1, 2, 3, Western Reserve Historical Society (hereafter cited as WRHS); also see John Bodnar, *The Transplanted: A History of Immigrants in Urban America* (Bloomington: Indiana University Press, 1985), 57; Dorota Praszałowicz, "Wokół mechanizmów migracji łańcuchowych," in *Przegląd Polonijny 25* (1999), no 1, 55–66.

   7. Witold Kula, Nina Assorodobraj-Kula, and Marcin Kula, *Listy emigrantów z Brazylii i Stanów Zjednoczonych, 1890–1891* (Warszawa: LSW, 1973), 424; *Writing*, 264, 355, 365; also T. Olstyn to his sister, 26 February 1910, Olstyn v.f., WRHS; M. P. Kniola to A. Nowicki, 8 June 1893, KTB, Series I, cont. 1, fold. 1; see also fold. 22.

   8. Cf. F. Pachulski to J. Nasielewski, 12 September 1912, KTB, Series I, cont. 1, fold. 22.

   9. Interview with S. Radzymiński, Immigrant Experience Project (hereafter cited as IEP), Greater Cleveland Ethnographic Museum , Cuyahoga Community College (hereafter cited as GCE), 2, 8.

   10. Emil H. Dunikowski, *Wśród Polonii w Ameryce. Druga seria 'Listów z Ameryki'* (Lwów: P. Starzyk, 1893), 41; John Gallka Collection, vol. 1, 18, WRHS.

   11. Dunikowski, *Wśród*, 103, 53.

   12. Poles first came to Cleveland in 1846 (6 persons); and the 1870 census registered 77 Poles, cf. John J. Grabowski, *Polish Americans and Their Communities of Cleveland* (Cleveland: Cleveland State University, 1976), 151–156; Cf. Justin B. Galford, *The Foreign Born and Urban Growth in the Great Lakes, 1850–1950: A Study of Chicago, Cleveland, Detroit and Milwaukee* (New York University, 1957), 108–110; in 1865, a group of Poles worked in sandstone quarries of Berea, southwest of Cleveland; and in 1873 they created a Catholic parish of St. Adalbert; cf. Wacław Kruszka, *Historya polska w Ameryce. Początek, wzrost i rozwój dziejowy osad polskich w Północnej Ameryce (w Stanach Zjednoczonych i Kanadzie)* (Milwaukee: Kurier Polski, 1908), vol. 12: 36.

   13. Kruszka, *Historya*, 45–46; Grabowski, *Polish*, 157–158; Church and School Reports, 1878–1903, St. Stanislaus Parish Records (hereafter cited as SS), Archive Diocese Cleveland, Cleveland (hereafter cited as ADC).

   14. SS, Liber Copulatorum.

   15. SS, Liber Natorum.

   16. KTB, Series II, Cont.2, fold. 2, 3.

   17. *Writing*, 354, 328; Jeanne Kish, "A Demographic Study of Warszawa 1900" (paper, Cleveland State University, June 1988), 7–8, 11–12; William J. Galush, "Form-

ing Polonia: A Study of Four Polish American Communities 1890–1940" (Ph.D. dissertation, University of Minnesota, 1975), 110; *Atlas of Cuyahoga County and the City of Cleveland, Ohio* (Chicago, 1892), parts 35, 37, 47, 49.

18. The 1892 map records only 77 buildings in the area between Molden Street, Clair Street and Superior Avenue; *Atlas of Cuyahoga (1892)*, plate 29.

19. A. Kolaszewski to Bishop Gilmour, n.d. [1891], SS, file 1872–1891.

20. "Historical sketch" (typescript), St. Casimir Parish Records, (hereafter cited as SC), ADC, file 1892–1908.

21. *Kurier Clevelandski*, 16, 9, 22 July 1891; also *Polonia w Ameryce*, 12 May 1892, 2.

22. Dunikowski, *Wśród*, 104; also Ludwik Grzebień, SJ, ed., *Burzliwe lata Polonii amerykańskiej. Wspomnienia i listy misjonarzy jezuickich 1864–1913* (Kraków: WAM, 1983), 139; interview with S. Radzymiński, 10–11, interview with C. Radzymiński, 10, IEP, GCE); S. Lewandowski to T. Burton, 20 September 1900, Theodore E. Burton Papers (hereafter cited as TBP), box 6, folder 4, WRHS.

23. Dunikowski, *Wśród*, 108; Galush, "Forming," 84–86, 107–111; Out of 24 marriages which had taken place in the years 1898–1899, one-third of the newlyweds came from neighboring villages. See St. John Cantius Church (hereafter cited St. JC), Liber Matrimonis 1898–1907; US Immigration Commission, *Reports* (Washington, D.C.: Government Printing Office, 1911) (hereafter cited as RIC), vol. 26, 530–531.

24. Grabowski, *Polish*, 160–1; Ohio Historical Records Survey Project, Service Division WPA, *Parishes of the Catholic Church Diocese of Cleveland. History and Records* (Cleveland, 1942), 123; *Pamiętnik srebrnego jubileuszu Parafii św. Jadwigi w Lakewood, Ohio i zarazem pamiątka zmniejszenia długu parafialnego 1938* (Cleveland, 1938), n.p.

25. Grabowski, *Polish*, 161; *1891–1941. Księga wspomnień wydana z okazji Złotego Jubileuszu Parafii Najsłodszego Serca Jezus w Cleveland, Ohio* (Cleveland, 1941), 55; *Atlas of the Cuyahoga (1892)*, part 38; "Sacred Heart of Jesus Polish, Cleveland 1889–1898," Sacred Heart of Jesus Papers, 1892–1908, ADC.

26. Grabowski, *Polish*, 161–2; *75th Diamond Jubilee St. Hyacinth Parish. 1906–1981* (Cleveland, 1981), 22.

27. Grabowski, *Polish*, 164–5; Church and School Reports for the Year 1915, cont. 1, bd. vol. 1, St. Stanislaus Parish Papers (hereafter cited as St. S.) WRHS; Rough Census of the St. Stanislaus Parish, Cleveland, January 31, 1913, *ibid.*, cont. 2, fold. 6; Canonical Visitation of St. Stanislaus Church, 1913, *ibid.*; Sprawozdanie roczne [1915], SS, 1913–1916, ADC.

28. Grabowski, *Polish*, 165–166; *Parishes*, 64; Cf. Our Lady of Czestochowa Parish File, 1914–1920, 1923, ADC.

29. Grabowski, *Polish*, 166–7.

30. *Ibid*, 166.

31. *Ibid.*, 165, 168.

32. *Ibid.*, 254.

33. Dan W. Gallagher, "Different Nationalities in Cleveland: The Poles of Cleveland," *Cleveland News*, 23 December 1927.

34. "Success through Hard Work: A Biography, 1 May 1945," 1, mss v.f. Ratajczak, WRHS.

35. *1891–1941. Księga*, 55; Minutes of the Society No. 171 PNA, 18 August 1895, Polish Library Home Collection, WRHS; *The City Record*, 22V1918, 686; 1922, 609; *Polonia w Ameryce*, 12 May 1912, 3; interview with S. Radzyminski, 10, IEP, GCE.

36. *The City Record*, 1921, 1043; 1922, 664; Coroner File, cases 2090, 2500, 3575, 37267, Cuyahoga County Archives Cleveland (hereafter cited CCA).

37. *The City Record*, 1921, 1606; *Monitor Clevelandski*, 31 October 1923, 8.

38. A. Kolaszewski to Bishop Gilmour, 4 November 1890, SS, file 1873–1892; *Polonia w Ameryce*, 1 December 1898; interview with Józef Szostek, 5, IEP, GCE; Grabowski, *Polish*, 166.

39. Mildred Chadsey, *An Investigation of Housing Conditions of Cleveland's Workingmen* (Cleveland: Department of Public Welfare of the City of Cleveland, Monograph Series, No. 1, April 1914), 9, 13, 22; Cleveland Chamber of Commerce, *Housing Conditions in Cleveland, 1904* (Cleveland, 1904), 19; James B. Whipple, "Cleveland in Conflict: A Study of Urban Adolescence, 1876–1900," (Ph.D. Western Reserve University, Cleveland, 1951), 234; Galush, "Forming," 84; Dunikowski, *Wsród*, 104.

40. Chadsey, *An Investigation*, 7–8, 14–15.

41. *Ibid.*, 14–16, 18–22; RIC, vol. 26, part 1, 557–565; Cleveland Chamber of Commerce, *Housing Conditions in Cleveland, 1904* (Cleveland, 1904), 19, 40.

42. Bureau of Statistics of Labor of the State of New York, *Third Annual Report for the Year 1885* (Albany: The Argus Co. Printers, 1886), 511; Krzysztof Groniowski, *Robotnicy rolni w Królestwie Polskim* (Warszawa: LSW, 1977), 184; Fierich, *Przeszłość*, 26–28.

43. John Modell, Tamara Hareven, "Urbanization and the Malleable Household: An Examination of Boarding and Lodging in American Families," *Journal of Marriage and Family*, 35 (August 1973): 467–472; Groniowski, *Robotnicy*, 67; Chadsey, *An Investigation*, 22–25; RIC, vol. 26, part 1, 526, 539–552; "Chronica 1922," 17, St. S., cont. 1, fold. 1, WRHS; Rough Census of the St. Stanislaus Parish, January 31, 1913, cont. 2, fold. 6, St. S., WRHS.

44. RIC, vol. 26, part 1, 587; *Pamiętniki emigrantów. Stanach Zjednoczone* (Warszawa: Książka i Wiedza, 1977), vol. 2, 54–55; Chadsey, *An Investigation*, 23–25.

45. Galush, "Forming," 111; *Pamiętniki emigrantów*, vol. 2, 54–55; John Bodnar, "Immigration, Kinship, and the Rise of Working Class Realism in Industrial America," *Journal of Social History*, 14 (Fall, 1980): 56. Cf. Robert Slyton, *Back of the Yards. The Making of Local Democracy* (Chicago/London: University of Chicago Press, 1986), 33–34.

46. John Bodnar, "Schooling and the Slavic-American Family 1900–1940," in *American Education and the European Immigrant: 1840–1940*, ed. B. J. Weiss (Urbana/Chicago: University of Illinois Press, 1982), 80.

47. RIC, vol. 26, Part 1, 571–2; Edna Brynner, *Dressmaking and Millinery*, (Cleveland: Cleveland Foundation, 1916), 12, 19; Charles W. Coulter, *The Poles of Cleveland*,

(Cleveland, 1919) 10; Raymond Boryczka, Cary Lorin Lee, *No Strength Without Union. An Illustrated History of Ohio Workers, 1803–1980*, (Columbus: Ohio Historical Society, 1982), 115.

48. Witold Nowosz, "Gospodarka rolna w Klonowej," in *Klonowa i okolice, pow, Sieradz, Prace i Materiały Muzeum Archeologicznego i Etnograficznego w Łodzi. Seria Etnograficzna* (Łódz, 1960), 91; Stanisława Matczakowa, "Dziecko w rodzinie wiejskiej. Materiały z powiatu radomszczańskigo," in *Łódzkie Studia Etnograficzna*, 5/1963: 154–5, 169–73; Dan W. Gallagher, "Different Nationalities in Cleveland. The Poles of Cleveland," Cleveland *News*, 23 December 1927.

49. Jeffrey E. Mirel, David J. Angus, "From Spellers to Spindles: Work-Force Entry by the Children of Textile Workers, 1888–1890," *Social Science History*, 9/1985, No. 2: 139; Boryczka, *No Strength*, 114–5.

50. Henry B. Leonard, "Ethnic Cleavage and Industrial Conflict in Late 19th Century America: The Cleveland Rolling Mill Company Strikes of 1882 and 1885," *Labor History* 20, Fall 1979: 527; Kish, "A Demographic," 3, 9; interview with Sylvia Dykes, IEP, GCE, 2; *Polonia w Ameryce*, 12 May 1892, 4.

51. Boryczka, *No Strength*, 119; A. Kolaszewski to Bishop Gilmour, 1 November 1890, 4, SS 1872–1891, ADC; M. Kniola to Duczyński, 9 February 1904, KTB, Series I, Cont. 1, folder 2, 598; M. Kniola to Z. Jankowski, 16 August 1904, KTB, Series I, cont. 1, folder 12, 505; John J. Grabowski, "Michal P. Kniola, Polish Entrepreneur," *Western Reserve Historical Society News*, May/June 1977: 27–8; *Polonia w Ameryce*, 13 May 1898, 4; 20 May 1898, 4; 15 July 1898, 4; 1 June 1899, 8; 13 July 1899, 8; 30 November 1899, 8; 7 December 1899, 8; 7 September 1905, 8; W. Williams to J. H. Foster, 1 April 1919, Williams Whiting papers, cont. 1, folder 1, Record Group 3580, WRHS.

52. Leonard, "Ethnic," 525–526; W. Glazier, *Peculiarities of American Cities* (Philadelphia, 1886), 148–149, quoted in Joseph J. Barton, *Peasants and Strangers: Italians, Rumanians, and Slovaks in an American City, 1890–1950* (Cambridge: Harvard University Press, 1975), 12; Leopold Caro, *Emigracja i polityka emigracyjne ze szczególnym uwzględnieniem ziem polskich* (Poznań: Ksiegarnia sw. Wojciecha, 1914), 149–150; Seweryn Skulski, *Od Cleveland do Lipna* (Warszawa: PIW, 1953), 27.

53. Kish, "A Demographic," 9; David Brody, *Steelworkers in America; the Nonunion Era*, (Harvard University Press 1960), 101; Coroner files, Nos. 3436, 3477, 5473, CCA; *Echo*, 29 October 1903, 1; *Wiadomości Codzienne*, 16 April 1919, 6.

54. RIC, vol. 26, Part 1, 575–585; Adam Walaszek, "'For in America Poles Work Like Cattle': Polish Immigrants and Work in America, 1890–1891," in *In the Shadow of the Statue of Liberty: Immigrants, Workers, and Citizens in the American Republic, 1880–1920*, ed. Marianne Debouzy (St. Denis: Presses Universitaires de Vincennes, 1988), 95–105.

55. Walaszek, "For in America," 95–105; Skulski, *Od Cleveland*, 27; Leonard, "Ethnic," 527, 536; Kish, "A Demographic," 3, 9; interview with Sylvia Dykes, IEP, GCE, 2; *Polonia w Ameryce*, 12 May 1892, 2; Walaszek, *Reemigracja*, 10; Adam Walaszek, *Polscy robotnicy, praca i szwiązki zawodowe w Stanach Zjednoczonych Ameryki, 1880–1922*, (Wrocław: Ossolineum, 1988), 78–84.

56. Leonard, "Ethnic," 526–536; Richard L. Ehrlich, "Immigrant Strikebreaking Activity: A Sampling of Opinion Expressed in the *National Labor Tribune, 1878–1885*," *Labor History*, 15 (Winter 1974), 540–541; John J. Bukowczyk, "The Transfornation of Working Class Ethnicity: Corporate Control, Americanization, and the Polish Immigrant Middle Class in Bayonne, New Jersey, 1915–1925," *Labor History*, 25 (Winter 1984); Van Tassel and Grabowski, eds., *Encyclopedia of Cleveland History* (here after cited as ECH), (Bloomington: Indiana University Press, 1987), 270.

57. ECH, 270–1; Leonard, "Ethnic," 531, 536–41, 546–7; *Cleveland Leader and Morning Herald*, 4, 6–9, 11, 15–17, 20 July 1885.

58. *Plain Dealer*, 17 August 1898, 10; *Polonia w Ameryce*, 29 September 1898; 6, 20, 27 July, 3, 10 August 1899; *Gazeta Polska w Chicago*, 22 June 1899; M. Kniola to Kwiatkowski, KTB, Series I, Cont. 1, folder 4, 544; "Cleveland Boycott," *Outlook*, 12 August 1899, 1.

59. *Ameryka*, 20 June 1896, 1; A. T. Lane, "American Labor and European Immigrants in the Late Nineteenth Century," *Journal of American Studies*, 11 (1977): 241–260; Idem., "American Trade Unions, Mass Immigration, and the Literacy Test: 1900–1917," *Labor History*, 25 (Winter, 1984): 5–25; Leonard, "Ethnic," 529, 543–544; Jesse S. Robinson, *The Amalgamated Association of Iron, Steel and Tin Workers*, (Baltimore: The Johns Hopkins Press, 1920), 44, 47; *Dziennik Chicagoski*, 5 July 1892, 2; *Zgoda*, 6 December 1893; *Ameryce*, 30 May 1896, 1; *Wiadomości Codzienne*, 13 February 1919, 4; Central Labor Union, Building Trades Council, *Labor Day Souvenir, 1901* (Cleveland: Cleveland Citizen, 1901), 27, 31, 45; and 1902 edition, 94; United Trades and Labor Council, Cuyahoga County, *Year Book*, 1906, 95–97; 1908, 93–4; 1909, 84, 88, 92; 1910, 71; *The Cleveland Federation of Labor Year Book, Labor Day Souvenir Program* (Cleveland, 1913); *Cleveland Citizen*, 10 July 1911, 3; *Official Year Book of the Cleveland Federation of Labor, 1915* (Cleveland, 1916), 105, 107; *Official Year Book and Directory of the Cleveland Federation of Labor, 1923* (Cleveland), 87.

60. David Montgomery, *Workers' Control in America. Studies in the History of Work, Technology, and Labor Struggles* (Cambridge-London, 1979). 32–47, 101–4; 114–127; James R. Barrett, "Unity and Fragmentation, Class, Race, and Ethnicity on Chicago's South Side, 1900–1922," *Journal of Social History*, 18 (Fall 1984), 44; Brody, *Steelworkers*, 89, 109, 267; Stephen Meyer, "Adapting the Immigrant to the Line: Americanization in the Ford Factory, 1914–1921," *Journal of Social History*, 14 (Fall 1980), 69; Boryczka, Lee, *No Strength Without Union*, 121–126, 145; Daniel Brody, *Workers in Industrial America: Essays on the 20th Century Struggle*, (New York: Oxford University Press, 1980), 10–12, 49–57; Daniel Nelson, *Managers and Workers. Origins of the New Factory System in the United States, 1880–1920*, (Madison: University of Wisconsin Press, 1975), 57–75; Otis Steel Co. vs. International Molders Union, November 1913, National War Labor Board Records, Record Group 2, National Archives, (hereafter cited NA), case 881a; Vacation Pay Notice, 17 July 1918, TRW Inc. papers, Record Group 3942, WRHS, Box 27; Cleveland Americanization Committee, Mayor's Advisory War Board, *Americanization of Cleveland* (Cleveland,

1918), 3, 4; Tyler Co. Card File, WRHS; *Wiadomości Codzienne,* 12 April, 21 August, 2 December 1918; John Gallka Collection, vol. 1, 19, WRHS; Skulski, *Od Cleveland do Lipna,* 27; Gerald G. Eggert, *Steelmasters and Labor Reform, 1886–1923* (Pittsburgh: University of Pittsburgh Press, 1981), 41–47, 93–96; David Montgomery, "Immigrant Workers and Managerial Reform," in *Immigrants in Industrial America,* ed. Richard L. Ehrlich, (Charlottesville, 1977) 96–98; James R. Green, *The World of the Worker. Labor in Twentieth Century America: Essays on the 20th Century Struggle,* (New York: Hill and Wang, 1980), 103–104; *Employees' Incentive Plans in Cleveland Industries,* Reports of the Committee on Labor Relations, approved by the Board of Directors, January 12, 1921 (Cleveland, 1921), 3–4; Otis Steel Company Records, uncatalogued, WRHS; Raymond E. Cole, *A Handbook on Industrial Americanization* (Cleveland, 1919), 5, 13; *Wiadomości Codzienne,* 2 July 1919; *Jutrzenka,* 8 May 1919, 6.

    61. Montgomery, "Immigrant Workers and Managerial Reform," ed. Ehrlich, (Charlottesville, 1977), 91–112; Brody, *Steelworkers,* 82–88; idem, *Workers,* 4–7; David Montgomery, "New Tendencies in Union Struggles and Strategies in Europe and the United States, 1916–1922," in James E. Cronin and Carmen Sirianni, eds., *Work, Community, and Power: The Experience of Labor in Europe and America, 1900–1925* (Philadelphia: Temple University Press, 1983), passim; Boryczka, *No Strength,* 160; Adam Walaszek, "Was the Polish Worker Asleep? Immigrants, Unions, and Workers' Control in America, 1900–1922," *Polish American Studies,* 46 (1989), 74–961; Adam Walaszek, "Stubborn Newcomers: Polish Immigrants, Unions, and Workers' Control in America, 1900–1922," *Migracijske Teme,* 4 (1988), 167–175; *Official Yearbook and Directory of the Cleveland Federation of Labor, 1915,* 105, 109; *1916,* 127; *1918; 1919; 1920,* 87; *1921,* 73, 77; *1922,* 33, 91; *1923,* 87; *1924,* 99; *1925,* 91; *Plain Dealer,* 26 September 1919, 4; *Wiadomości Codzienne,* 19 July 1919, 11 March 1920, 4.

    62. Cleveland manufacturers struck during the 1914–1918 period included Otis Steel, the Drop Forge Co., the School and Product Co., the Cleveland Worsted Mills Co., and the Semet Solvay Co.

    63. Robert K. Murray, "Communism and the Great Steel Strike of 1919," *Mississippi Valley Historical Review,* 38 (1951) 447–449; Brody, *Steelworkers,* 120–121, 219, 222, 224, 246, 260; Barrett, "Unity," 44–45; *Wiadomości Codzienne,* 4 October 1918, 4; Pilawski Antoni, Petition, Declaration of Intentions no. 4269, Justice Court, Court of Common Pleas, CCA; Agent J. P. Sawicki, 13, 19 October 1919, Agent Morton, 5 November 1920, A. Pilawski, 17 October 1919, Investigative Case Files of the Bureau of Investigation, 1908–1922, NA, Old German Files, case 376477; *Wiadomości Codzienne,* 30 January 1918, 4, 23 August 1920, 4, 25 October 1920, 27 November 1920, 1–2, 21 September 1920, 4; *Plain Dealer,* 23 September 1919, 2.

    64. *Wiadomości Codzienne,* 5 March 1918, 4 October 1918, 4; 29 March 1919, 1; 7 April 1919, 4; 29 April 1919, 1; 9 June 1919, 4; 12 July 1919, 4; 14 July 1919, 4; 22 July 1919, 1; 30 July 1919, 2; 2 August 1919, 2; 8 September 1919, 4; 23 September 1919, 2; 25 October 1919, 2; *Plain Dealer,* 6 October 1919, 15.

65. *Jutrzenka*, 25 September 1919, 6; 9 October 1919, 1; 16 October 1919, 8 September 1921, 1; *Wiadomości Codzienne*, 10 October 1919, 3; 17 October 1919, 3; 2 December 1919, 2; 10 January 1920, 4.

66. Brody, *Steelworkers*, 253–262; *Wiadomości Codzienne*, 12 January 1920, 1; 29 April 1920, 2; 17 July 1920, 4; 14 December 1920; *Jutrzenka*, 20 May 1920, 3 June 1920, 12 February 1920, 13 January, 31 March, 1921, 2 September 1921; Brody, *Labor*, 134–136, 162; Walaszek, *Polscy robotnicy*, 203–4, 229–30; Union of Poles in America, Board of Directors, Minutes, 1 April 1928, Union of Poles in America Records, WRHS (hereafter UPA); James R. Barrett, "Americanization from the Bottom Up: Immigration and the Remaking of the Working Class in the United States, 1880–1930," *The Journal of American History*, 79 (1992) 27–37.

67. *Polonia w Ameryce*, 12 May 1892, 3; *Kurier Clevelandski*, 9 July 1891.

68. Interview with Stanley Radzimiński, 11–12.

69. Interview with S. Radzymiński, 11–12, J. Szostek, 5, S. Dykes, 4, IEP, GCE; Galush, "Forming Polonia," 123; Leon Fink, *Workingmen's Democracy, The Knights of Labor and American Politics* (Urbana-Chicago: University of Illinois Press, 1983), 193–4; E. C. Moore, "The Social Value of the Saloon," *The American Journal of Sociology*, 3 (July 1897), 3–8; John Bodnar, *Anthracite People: Families, Unions and Work, 1900–1940* (Harrisburg: Pennsylvania Historical and Museum Commission, 1983), 48; John T. Cumbler, *Working-Class Community in Industrial America: Work, Leisure and Struggle in Two Industrial Cities, 1880–1930*, (Westport: Greenwood Press, 1979), 149–150; Slayton, *Back of the Yards*, 100–101; *Plain Dealer*, 6 July 1885.

70. John Gallka Collection, vol. 1, 19, WRHS.

71. *Polonia w Ameryce*, 2 February 1905; Gallagher, "Different," WRHS, 52.

72. Grabowski, *Polish*, 156–162; Galush, "Forming," 86; 75. *Diamond Jubilee St. Hyacinth Parish, 1906–1981* (Cleveland, 1981), 22; *1914–1939. Pamiętnik srebrnego jubileuszu Parafii św. Jadwigi*; Grzebień, *Burzliwe*, 193, 207.

73. *Kurier Clevelandski*, 16–23 July 1891; *Jutrzenka*, 20, 27 June, 1894; *Echo*, 3 December 1890, 8; *Polonia w Ameryce*, 25 March 1898, 22 June 1899; *Wiadomości Codzienne*, 4 and 6 November 1924.

74. *Jutrzenka*, 4, 11 April 1894; *Polonia w Ameryce*, 1 July 1898, 4; leaflet of the Slavic Alliance, 12 August 1904, KTB, Series I, cont. 1, fold. 20; letter to A. Gradowski, 4 February 1904, *Ibid.*, fold. 11; Slavic Alliance to T. H. Burton, 14 April 1903, TBP, cont. 4, fold. 2; *Charities*, no. 14 (1 July 1905), 875–881.

75. Andrzej Brożek, *Polish Americans 1854–1939* (Warsaw: Interpress, 1985), 43–59; 97–99; Bodnar, *The Transplanted*, 152–156; Anthony J. Kuzniewski, *Faith and Fatherland: The Polish Church War in Wisconsin, 1896–1918* (Notre Dame: University of Notre Dame Press, 1980), 158; Hieronim Kubiak, *Polski Narodowy Kosciół Katolicki w Stanach Zjednoczonych. Jego społeczne uwarunkowania i społeczne funkcje* (Wrocław-Warszawa: Ossolineum, 1970), 99–101; John J. Bukowczyk, "Mary the Messiah: Polish Immigrant Heresy and the Malleable Ideology of the Roman Catholic Church, 1880–1930," *Journal of American Ethnic History*, 4 (Spring, 1985), 11–12,

28–29; *1891–1941, Księga wspomnień* 53; Publicanda, January 23, 1916, St. S., Cont. 1, bound vol.

76. *Księga protokołowa Zarządu Parafialnego Parafii św. Stanisława B.M.*, 9 October 1909, 26; 16 October 1907, 17; St. S., cont. 1, fold. 2; *Roczne sprawozdanie*, 1912, St. S. cont. 2, fold. 16; *Polonia w Ameryce*, 7 December 1899.

77. Also see note 75 above.

78. Kolaszewski to Bishop Gilmour, 4 November 1890, 1–6, ss, 1872–1892. The most recent analysis of "Kolaszewski's Affair" is Charles R. Kaczynski's, "What Mean Ya By These Stones? Cleveland's Immaculate Heart of Mary Parish and the Construction of a Polish American Rhetoric," *Polish American Studies* lv, (1998), no. 2, 25–54.

79. Bishop R. Gilmour to A. Kolaszewski, 25 August 1886, 544, 11 October 1886, 659, Bishop Gilmour Letter Books, adc (hereafter cited as bglb), vol. F; Kruszka, *Historya*, vol. 12, 34–46; *Kurier Clevelandski*, 9 July 1891, 2; *Polak w Ameryce*, 27 May, 14 June 1887; Dunikowski, *Wśród*, 104; Joseph H. Lackner, "Bishop Ignatius F. Horstmann and the Americanization of the Roman Catholic Church in the United States" (Ph.D. dissertation, St. Louis University, 1977), 65.

80. *Wykaz długów ciążących na parafii św. Stanisława B.M. w Cleveland na dniu 8 czerwca 1892* (Cleveland, 1893), 1–3; F. Motulewski to Bp. F. Horstmann, 16 April 1892, S. Lewandowski to Bp. Horstmann, 25 March 1892, ss, 1892, adc; Henry A. Schauffler, *Work Among the Slavs, An Address Delivered at the Anniversary of the American Home Mission Society* (New York: The Christian Union Co., 1889), 8–9; Chronica, St. S., Cont 1, Bound vol. 1; *Wiara i Ojczyzna*, 21 January 1891, 43; 18 June 1890, 393–4. Lackner, "Bishop," 70.

81. Lackner, "Bishop," 70–80; A. Kolaszewski to Bishop F. Horstmann, 24 May 1892, Bp. Horstmann to Kolaszewski, 28 May 1892, ss 1892.

82. *Jutrzenka*, 10 May 1894, 1–2.

83. *Jutrzenka*, 23 May, 4; 13 June, 4; 27 June, 1; 25 July, 8; 15 August 1894; Lackner, "Bishop," 90; *Constitution and Regulations of the Polish Catholic Congregation Known as the Congregation of the Immaculate Heart of the Blessed Virgin Mary of Cleveland, Ohio* (Cleveland: Jutrzenka Print, 1894), 10; Kruszka, *Historya*, vol. 12, 53.

84. *Jutrzenka*, 25 July; 27 June 1894, Grabowski, *Polish*, 181; Minutes of the Towarzystwo Synowie Polski i Litwy, Group 171, pna, 10 February 1895, Polish Library Home Collection, wrhs (hereafter quoted plh), cont. 2, fold. 28; cf. Bukowczyk, "Mary," 12.

85. A. Kolaszewski to F. M. Boff, September 1908, Immaculate Heart of Mary Parish Papers, adc (hereafter cited as ihm), 1892–1908; Lackner, "Bishop," 102–104; *Polonia w Ameryce*, 25 August 1894; Grabowski, *Polish*, 181.

86. Bukowczyk, "Mary the Messiah," no. 2, 11.

87. Galush, "Forming," 86–7, 219.

88. Galush, "Forming," 220, 222; Parishioners to Bishop J. Farrelly, 20 December 1912, St. John Cantius Parish Papers, adc (hereafter cited as sjc), fold. 1910–1918;

"Parafia Polsko- Katolicka Narodowa w Cleveland, Ohio," *Kalendarz Narodowy na roky 1916*, (Scranton: PNCC, 1915), 152.

89. Galush, "Forming," 84–6, 139–40, 203–205; "Historia Gminy 88 ZNP," in *Pamiętnik z okazji trzydziesto-pięciolecia Gminy 88-ej Związku Narodowego Polskiego* (Cleveland, 1940).

90. Frank Nowak Papers, WRHS (hereafter cited as FNP), cont. 3, bound vol. 2, 51; letter to Bishop Koudelka, 12 June 1908, SJC, 1892–1908; "Historia Gminy 88-ej ZNP, w: *Pamiętnik z okazji trydziestopięcio lecia Gminy 88-ej Związku Narodowego Polskiego*, (Cleveland 1940), b.p."; Galush, "Forming," 223–224; Stanislaw Dangel, file 10059, Military Intelligence Division (hereafter cited as MID), NA.

91. Bishop F. Horstmann to H. Orłowski, 24 January 1903, quoted after Galush, "Forming," 87; Bishop J. Schrembs to Paul Marella, 9 April 1925, SJC.

92. Galush, "Forming," 223–6, 228; "Parafia Polsko," 153; *Księga Pamiątkowa '33' w trzydziestą rocznice powstania Polsko-Narodowego Kościoła w Ameryce 1897–1930 i dwudziestą rocznicę Pierwszego Sejmu Polsko Narodowej Spójni 1909–1929 (kalendarz na rok 1930)*, (Scranton: PNCC, 1930), 421; *Wiadomości Codzienne*, 7 January 1918, 4.

93. Historical Sketch of St. Casimir (Polish) Church, 2–3; Rev. Cerveny to Bishop F. Horstmann, 14 September 1894, J. Woźny, and T. Rumiński to Bishop F. Horstmann, 14 January 1895, J. Urbanowicz and the Committee to Bishop F. Horstmann, 31 July 1903, SC, 1892–1908; *Jutrzenka*, 17 January 1894; 4, 7 November 1894, 1; I. Hoffman and I. Kaczmarek to Bishop J. Farrelly, 15 August 1910, SC, 1909–1920; Ignacy Piotrowski to Bishop J. Farrelly, 3 October 1910, 22 May 1911, Chancellor to I. Piotrowski, 7 October 1910 Ibidem.

94. I. Hoffman and J. Kopczyński to Bishop J. Farrelly, 18 April 1911, SC, file 1908–1920; Parish Committee to Bishop J. Farrelly, July 1911, 16 February 1912, also other correspondence, SC, file 1909–1920.

95. *Polonia w Ameryce*, 18 May 1899; Galush, "Forming," 122.

96. *Polonia w Ameryce*, 1898, 1899, 1905; *The Cleveland City Directory for the Year Ending July 1883* (Cleveland, 1882), passim; *Cleveland Press*, 6 March 1934, 27 February 1934; *Jutrzenka*, 3 October 1894; *Kurier Clevelandski*, 27 August 1891; Stanley Olstyn Papers, WRHS, fold. 3; Gallagher, "Different," WRHS, 54, 57; Francis Bolek, *Who's Who in Polish America* (New York: Harbinger House, 1943), 399; Twarogowski and Zielinski Papers, fold. 1, 3, WRHS.

97. John J. Grabowski, "Michael M. Kniola," 26–28; Kniola's correspondence in KTB, Series I and II.

98. Henryk Nagiel, *Dziennikarstwo polskie w Ameryce i jego 30-letnie dzieje* (Chicago 1894), 111, 118, 121–122, 126; *Polak w Ameryce*, 23 March 1888, *Polonia w Ameryce*, 27 April 1899, 8; A skech of T. Siemiradzki biography, cf. A Andrzej. Zięba, "Siemiradzki Tomasz," in: *Polski Słownik Biograficzny*, no. 152, (Kraków: Ossolineum, 1996): 55–58.

99. Cf. Mary Cygan, "Political and Cultural Leadership in an Immigrant Community: Polish American Socialism, 1880–1950," (Ph.D. dissertation, Northwestern University, 1989).

100. Krzysztof Groniowski, "Socjalistyczna emigracja polska w Stanach Zjednoczonych (1883–1914)," *Z Pola Walki*, 20 (No. 1, 1977), 1–7; Nagiel, *Dziennikarstwo*, 89, 118–20, 126; Bolek, *Who's*, 71; *Jutrzenka*, 24 January 1894, 1–2; 21 February 1894, 4; 4 April 1894, 1; 25 July 1894, 4; 8 August 1894, 4; Lysle E. Meyer, "Radical Responses to Capitalism in Ohio Before 1913," *Ohio History*, 79 (No. 3–4, 1970), 200.

101. Groniowski, "Socjalistyczna," 10–12; *Ameryka*, 28 March 1896, 20 June 1896, 1, 22 August 1896; *Polonia w Ameryce*, 5 October 1899, 8; *Cleveland Leader*, 8 September 1901, 1–2; 10 September 1901, 12; 12 September 1901, 4; 18 September 1901, 7.

102. *Polonia w Ameryce*, 25 May 1899, 8; Feliks Cienciara, "Wspomnienia. 35 lat temu," typescript, 4–5, Polish Museum and Archive in America, Polish Roman Catholic Union, Chicago; Groniowski, "Socjalistyczna," 14–17, 20; *Robotnik*, 1 May 1903, 6; *Zgoda*, 10 March 1904, 5; Danuta Piątkowska, "Polscy socjaliści w USA wobec rewolucji 1905 roku," *Przegląd Polonijny*, 12 (No. 2, 1986), 44; Zygmunt Piotrowski, "Polski ruch socjalistyczny w Ameryce," *W trzydziestą rocznicę. Księga pamiątkowa PPS* (Warszawa, 1923), 258; Mirosław Frančić, *Komitet Obrony Narodowej w Ameryce, 1912–1918* (Wrocław-Warszawa: Ossolineum, 1983), 22; Groniowski, "Socjalistyczna," 26, 30–32; Brożek, *Polonia*, 118–9; United Trades and Labor Council, Cuyahoga County, *Year Book, 1908* (Cleveland, 1908), 95, *Year Book, 1910* (Cleveland, 1910), 77; *Cleveland Citizen*, 10 July 1911; "Polish Societies," typescript, Mayor's Advisory War Committee Collection, WRHS, (hereafter quoted MAWC, Cont. 33, folder 1; *Wiadomości Codzienne*, 11 January 1918, 8 February 1918, 1 March 1918, 3 June 1918, 2, 3 December 1918, 1, 19 December 1919; *Dziennik Ludowy*, 29 January 1916, 16 February 1916, 20 April 1916, 3 May 19116, 5, 25 July 1916, 5, 22 August 1916; Polish Library Home Minutes, PLH, Cont. 1, folder 1, 68, 75–6; *Ameryka Echo*, 29 March 1913, 4; Józef Miąso, *Dzieje oświaty polonijnej w Stanach Zjednocznych* (Warszawa: Państwowe Wydawnictwo Naukowe, 1970), 215; H. J. Weikart, "Organizations in a Polish Community, Their Description and Analysis," (M.A. Thesis, School of Applied Social Sciences, Western Reserve University, Cleveland, 1929), 16.

103. *Dziennik Ludowy*, 29 January 1916, 16 February 1916, 25 July 1916, 5; 27 July 1916, 5; 28 July 1916, 5; 21 August 1916, 3; *Wiadomości Codzienne*, 9 June 1918, 4; 29 November 1918, 4; 3 December 1918, 1; 10 December 1918, 4; Polish Library Home Minutes, PLH, Cont. 1, folder 1, 21, 76–7, 93; Cont. 1, folder 2, 3, 6–7; Towarzystwo Synowie Polski i Litwy, Group 171 PNA, Minutes, PLH, Cont. 2, folder 31, 108; Polish National Alliance, Group 229, Minutes, 9 September 1918, 29–30, Polish National Alliance Group 229 Records, WRHS.

104. Letter to Major T. B. Crockett, 13 May 1919, and leaflet, "The Socialist Challenger," April 1919, no. 3, 1, NA, MID, file 10110–804, 64; *Wiadomości Codzienne*, 2 May 1919, 1, 10 May 1919, 2; *Plain Dealer*, 2 May 1919, 1, 4 May 1919, 6b; *Jutrzenka*, 8 May 1919, 2, 6.

105. Brożek, *Polish*, 47–49, 60–84; Bodnar, *The Transplanted*, 148–150 Galush, "Forming," 84–86; *Pamietnik 35 lecia założenia Związku Polaków w Ameryce. 1895–1930* (Cleveland, 1930); on the activities and functions of the organizations see the ethnic press, also e. g., *Pamiętnik obchodu 100-letniej rocznicy powstania*

listopadowego 1830–1930, urządzonego pod egidą Ligii Organizacji w Cleveland dnia 30-go listopada 1930 roku (Cleveland: Monitor, 1930); St. Stanislaus Parish Committee, Minutes, 4 February 1913, 19; 4 August 1914, 45; 17 January 1915, 53, St. S. cont. 1, fold. 3.

106. Alliance of Poles in the State of Ohio, Board of Directors, Minutes, 22 September 1895, 6 October 1895, 20 October 1895; Protokół Sejmu I, Alliance of Poles in America, Cleveland Records, WRHS, (hereafter cited as APA), cont. 1.

107. Protokół Sejmu II, APA, cont. 1, vol. 1, 38–42; *Konstytucja i prawa, przepisy i reguły Związku Polaków w Ameryce oraz prawa, przepisy i reguły Wydziału Małoletnich opracowane przez Prezesa Zarządu Centralnego Komisji Konstytucji* (Cleveland: Monitor, n.d.); Minutes of the Towarzystwo Synowie Polski i Litwy, Group 171, PNA, 25 October 1891, 1 November 1891, 15 November 1891, PLH, cont. 2, fold. 28.

108. *Jutrzenka,* 19 May 1921, 6 January 1921; "Polish Societies," typescript, MAWC, cont. 33, fold. 1; Weikart, "Organizations," 9–13.

109. *Konstytucja Towarzystwa Synowie Wolnej Polski Grupa 87 Związku Polaków w Ameryce, założone dnia 12go marca 1916* (Cleveland, n.d.); Cf. ethnic press; also *Pamiętnik 23 Zjazdu Związku Spiewaków Polskich w Ameryce 1889–1929 w rocznicę czterdziestolecia istnienia Związku dnia 12, 13, 14 Maja 1929* (Cleveland: Monitor, 1929), 52; *65th Anniversary of the Polish Falcons of America Nest 141, Cleveland, Ohio, Souvenir Book, September 7, 1974* (Cleveland, 1974).

110. Galush, "Forming," 195; *50 letni jubileusz Towarzystwa Synowie Polski, Grupy 143 ZNP w niedziele dnia 6 października 1940, 1890–1940* (Cleveland, 1940); Historical Sketch of St. Casimir's Polish Church, Cleveland, 1892–1898, SC, 1892–1908; *Jutrzenka,* 12 February 1920.

111. "Historia Komisji Budowy Pomnika T. Kościuszki," 9 May 1915, KTB, Series II, cont. 3, fold. 20; A. Kolaszewski to T. E. Burton, 4 December 1902; leaflet The Board of Directors of Kosciuszko Monument, TBP, cont. 9, fold. 2; *Polonia w Ameryce,* 11 May 1905. See below, chapters by Puskás and Kopanic, for an account of the Kossuth statue controversy.

112. Cf. Mirosław Frančić, *Komitet Obrony Narodowej w Ameryce, 1912–1918* (Wrocław-Warszawa: Ossolineum, 1983), 11–36, 136; Galush, "Forming," 199.

113. Frančić, *Komitet,* 33–36, *Jutrzenka,* 12 May, 29 September 1921; *Wiadomości Codzienne,* 25 February, 16 February 1918; *Pamiętniki emigrantów,* vol. 2, 59–60.

114. Alliance of Poles in America, Minutes, no. 21, 28 March 1915, 9, No. 27, 27 September 1915, 21, APA, vol. 3; *Wiadomości Codzienne,* 16 February, 9 May, 13 May 1918; *Jutrzenka* i.e 12 May 1921, 2 March 1922.

115. Galush, "Forming," 139–141, 203–213; NA, MID, file 10059-2(37), 10059-26(1); *Wiadomości Codzienne,* year 1918; Towarzystwo Synów Polski i Litwy, Minutes, 11 and 25 March, 13 May 1915, PLH, cont. 2, fold. 31; Polish Library Home Minutes, 3 October 1919, 24–25, PLH, cont. 1, fold. 2.

116. *Wiadomości Codzienne,* 16 August 1920; *Jutrzenka,* 9 September 1921.

117. A. S. Swiątkowski to wife, 11 June 1923, KTB, Series I, cont. 3, fold. 23.

118. R. Hartt, "Emigration from America," *Outlook*, 29 January 1919, 186–187; "Trend of Events," *Cleveland Citizen*, 2 August 1919, 1; cf. Walaszek, *Reemigracja*, chapter 2.

119. Walaszek, *Reemigracja*, 54–58, 82–93; *Wiadomości Codzienne*, 4 January, 13 February, 15 April, 12 August, 1919, 9 January, 26 March, 9 April, 10, 15, 22 July, 13 November, 2, 16 December 1920, 10 July 1922.

120. Walaszek, *Reemigracja*, 84; *Wiadomości Codzienne*, 11, 22 July 1919, 13 December 1919, 22, 24, 27 January, 23 February, 2 March 1920; *Jutrzenka*, 13 May, 10, 24 June 1920, 10 February 1921.

121. Walaszek, *Reemigracja*, 53–64, 91–93, 128–148; *Wiadomości Codzienne*, 21 October 1919, 15 January, 2, 28 February, 6, 8, 13 March, 13 November, 16, 17 December 1920, 30 June, 15 December 1921, 6, 10 July, 6 September, 18 November 1922.

122. Alliance of Poles in America, Minutes, 23 March 1919, 99; 26 August 1917, 63, vol. 3, APA; *Miesięcznik Parafii św. Stanislawa B.M. w Cleveland, Ohio*, no 5, 1918.

123. *Protokół urzędowy z obrad Drugiego Sejmu Wychodźstwa Polskiego w Buffalo odbytego w dniach od 10 do 13 listopada 1919* (Chicago, 1921), 21; *Urzędowy Protokół Sejmu XXIII. Związku Narodowego Polskiego odbytego w dniach 26 września - 1 października 1921 w Toledo, Ohio* (Chicago, 1922), 165.

124. *Protokół Sejmu IV Wychodźstwa Polskiego w Ameryce, odbytego w dniach 16, 17, 18 kwietnia 1923 w Cleveland, Ohio* (Chicago: Wydział Narodowy Polski, 1923), 3–4, 44–45; *Kongres Wychodźstwa Polskiego w Ameryce. Odezwy, mowy, referaty, rezolucje, uchwaly oraz urzędowy protokol odbyty w dniach 21–23 V 1925 w Detroit, Mich.* (Chicago, 1925), 16; *Urzędowy Protokoł Sejmu XXIV Zwiazku Narodowego Polskiego, odbytego w dniach 25-go do 30-go sierpnia 1924 w Lulu Temple w mieście Philadelphia, Pa.* (Chicago, 1925), 3–25.

125. Schauffler, *Work*, 8–9; [John Prucka], *The Churches and the Foreign Situation in Greate Cleveland. Based on the 1920 US Census and Reports of Churches for that Year* (n.d.), 5, 10; Cleveland Bureau of Immigration, *Why Cleveland Needs the City Immigration Bureau* (Cleveland, 1916), 1.

126. Names and addresses of Four Minute Men, Cleveland Committee on Patriotism and Minute Men Speakers, MAWC, cont. 6, fold. 4; four minute men speech cards, MAWC, cont. 6, fold. 4; *Wiadomości Codzienne*, April–May, 12 August 1918; Union of Poles in America, Board of Directors, Minutes, 3 September 1923, UPA.

127. Cleveland Americanization Committee of the Mayor's War Board, *Americanization in Cleveland: An Account of the Work Which Has Been Done in Cleveland to Develop and Maintain a City Morale* (n.d.); Cleveland Americanization Committee, Mayor's Advisory War Board, *Americanization of Cleveland* (Cleveland, 1918), 2–3; Bukowczyk, "The Transformation of Working Class Ethnicity," *Labor History*, 25 (1984), 77–80.

128. Jan Czyżak, *Rozdzial kościelny wśród Polaków w Ameryce* (Rochester 1927), 29–32, 41–49; correspondence from 1922, 1923, Nationality and Race File, Joseph Schrembs Papers, ADC; *Jutrzenka*, 28 December 1922; L. L. Sommerfeld, "An

Historical Descriptive Study of the Circumstances that Led to the Elimination of German from the Cleveland Schools, 1860–1918" (Ph.D. dissertation, Kent State University, 1986), 233–252.

129. *Miesięcznik Parafii św. Stanisława*, no. 12, 1922, 375–376; *Jutrzenka*, 28 August 1919; *Wiadomości Codzienne*, 21 March 1919, 10 May 1919, 20 September 1922.

130. *Wiadomości Codzienne*, 3 July, 1918; *Jutrzenka*, 4 July, 27 June 1918, 14 July, 4 August 1921; Board of Directors of the Alliance of Poles in the State of Ohio, 28 July, 1918, Alliance of Poles in America Minutes, vol. 3, 85, WRHS.

131. Republican Committee to Kniola, 30 October 1895, KTB, Series I, Cont. 1, folder 15; *Polonia w Ameryce*, 25 March 1898, 12 January, 20,27 April, 5, 12 October 1899, 3 August, 7 September 1905, 8 March 1920; Weikart, "Organizations," 36; *Jutrzenka*, 20 September 1893.

132. Gwendolyn Mink, *Old Labor and New Immigrants in American Political Development, Union, Party, and State, 1875–1920* (Ithaca-London: Cornell University Press, 1986), 135–7; Grabowski, *Polish*, 213; idem, "Michael," 28; Law Offices, Second National Building, to M. Kniola, 24 May 1916, KTB, Series II, Cont. 1, folder 2.

133. *Kurier Clevelandzki*, 30 July 1891; S. Lewandowski to T. E. Burton, 20, 24, 25 September and 3 October 1900, Box 6, folder 4, TBP; *Echo*, 24 October 1903; *Polonia w Ameryce*, 6 April 1899, 9 November 1905.

134. Grabowski, *Polish*, 212; Kish, "A Demographic," 14.

135. *Wiadomości Codzienne*, 8 December 1922, 10 November 1924, 2 October, 1, 3 November 1926; Slayton, *Back*, 160; *Jutrzenka*, 20 September 1893; *Polonia w Ameryce*, 9, 16 February 1899. At the end of the nineteenth century, Ward 17 was represented by Czech councilmen. City Council, List of Councilmen and Mayors, typescript, WRHS.

136. Grabowski, *Polish*, 213–4, 256; *Monitor*, 9, 12, 16 November 1927.

137. Grabowski, *Polish*, 256; *Wiadomości Codzienne*, 7 January, 20 April, 15 May, 30 October, 4 November, 6 December 1918, 3 September 1919, 5 August, 1 November 1920, 3 November 1926, *Monitor*, 28 October, 1 November 1926.

138. *Polonia w Ameryce*, 28 September 1905; Bolek, *Who's*, 399; Grabowski, *Polish*, 215–6; Van Tassel and Grabowski, eds., ECH, 870.

139. Grabowski, *Polish*, 215; Van Tassel and Grabowski, eds., ECH, 870; Weikert, "Organizations," 34–7; *Wiadomości Codzienne*, 28 June 1928.

140. Weikert, "Organizations," 34–7, 621; E. P. Lewandowski Scrapbook, No. 123, vol. 1, Scrapbook No. 124, Joseph Trinastic Papers, WRHS; *Wiadomości Codzienne*, 28 October 1919; 21 October 1922, 5 November 1927, 28 June 1928; *Jutrzenka*, 15 September, 13, 26 October 1921; *Monitor*, 27 October 1926, 29 October, 5 November 1928.

141. *Jutrzenka*, 13 October 1921, 1; 10 February 1921, 1.

142. Polish Consul in Detroit to Polish Embassy in Washington, 7 July 1930, Polish Embassy in Washington, D.C. Collection, Archive of New Files, Warsaw, (hereafter PEW) Collection, Archiwum Akt Nowych (hereafter AAN), Warsaw, file 1095, 48–9; Organizacje kredytowe Polaków zamiaszkałych w stanach Michigan i Ohio,

6 September 1929, typescript, file 175, 21–9; Polish Consulate in Pittsburgh to Polish Embassy in Washington, 7 July 1934, (Światowy Związek Polaków z Zagranicy Collection, AAN, file 186, 85–9; Warsaw Savings and Loan Association of Cleveland Records, Cont. 1, Folder 1, Record Group 3775, WRHS; *Miesięcznik Parafii sw. Stanislawa B. M. w Cleveland, Ohio*, 4 (1921, no. 5); *Jutrzenka*, 29 July 1920; *Ameryka Echo*, 15 March 1913; *Wiadomości Codzienne*, 4, 8 March 1918.

143. Polish Consulate in Pittsburgh to Polish Embassy in Washington, 12 May 1934, Polish Consulate in Detroit to Polish Consulate in Pittsburgh, 7 July 1934, PEW, file 1095, 48, 58–61; Polish Consulate in Pittsburgh to the Ministry of Foreign Affairs, 31 August 1936, PEW, file 1079, 313–5; Bukowczyk, "The Transfornation of Working Class Ethnicity" *Labor History*, 25 (Winter 1984), 77–81.

144. Podbipięta, *Przyszłość wychodźstwa polskiego w Stanach Zjednocczonych* (Warszawa, 1927), 38; *Wiadomości Codzienne*, 21 March 1931, 7; Sprawozdanie delegata Krajowego Zrzeszeń Gospodarczych, 19–21 April 1936, Ministry of Foreign Affairs Collection, AAN, file 7220, 79; "Krótki zarys historii Stowarzyszenia Polskich Grosernikόw," *Pamiętnik pierwszego Zjazdu Kupiectwa Polskiego w Ohio i Pόłnocnej Pensylwanii, niedziela 28 IV 1935* (Cleveland: Monitor, 1935), n p.; Polish Consulate in Pittsburgh to the Ministry of Foreign Affairs, 24 February 1934, PEW, file 1079, 3; K. Herse to Światowy Związek Polaków z Zagranicy, 18 May 1937, Polish Consulate General in New York Collection, AAN, file 135, 95–9; *Wiadomości Codzienne*, 9, 30 March, 27 April 1931; Polish Consulate in Pittsburgh to the Ministry of Foreign Affairs, 31 August 1936, PEW, file 1079, 312.

145. Green, *The World*, 111; Brody, *Workers*, 62–66.

146. Kish, op. cit., 15; RIC, vol. 26, Part 1, 561; M. Chadsey, *An Investigation*, 25; Polish Consulate in Buffalo, Report, 21 June 1924, Polish Consulate in Buffalo Collection (hereafter PCB), AAN, file 67, 85–86; Lucille D. Grames, "An Investigation of Existing Data on Economic Conditions in the Area of the University Neighborhood Centers and an Interpretation of the Data as they Apply to Community Organization" (M.A. thesis, Western Reserve University, 1932), 44, 47, 95.

147. Charles N. Glaab, "Metropolis and Suburb: The Changing American City," in *Change and Continuity in Twentieth Century America, The 1920s*, eds. J. Braeman, R. H. Bremner, D. Brody (Columbus: Ohio State University Press, 1968), 405, 411, 430.

148. Brody, *Workers*, 63; Irving Bernstein, *The Lean Years. A History of the American Worker 1920–1933* (Baltimore, 1966), 65; *Pamiętniki emigrantόw*, vol. 2, 437.

149. Green, *The World*, 112–113; Mieczyslaw Szawleski, *Wychodźtwo polskie w Stanach Zjednoczonych Ameryki Pόłnocnej* (Lwόw-Warszawa: Ossolineum, 1924), 57; *11th Annual Report of the Secretary of Labor for the Fiscal Year ended June 30, 1923* (Washington, D.C.: Government Printing Office, 1923), 80–83.

150. *Pamiętnik jubileuszowy na 25 lecie rόwnouprawnienia kobiet w Związku Narodowym Polskim i na pamiątkę wręczenia nowego sztandaru* (Chicago, 1925), 5, 41; Wspomnienia uczestniczki Pierwszego Zjazdu Wydzialu Kobiet ZNP," *Dziennik Związkowy*, December 1956, (clipping), Polonia Research Institute, Jagiellonian University, Cracow.

151. Teodore Andrica, "Association of Polish Women Grows," *Cleveland Press*, 4 February 1935; Grabowski, *Polish*, 189; Weikert, "Organizations," 12–15; Polish Women's Club History, Salomea Nowak Schmidt Papers, Cont. 3, folder 25, Manuscript Collection 3970, WRHS.

152. L. Adamczak, "W piódziesiątą rocznicę Stowarzyszenia Weteranó w Armii Polskiej w Ameryce," *Weteran*, no. 600, June 1971, 44–45; Grabowski, *Polish*, 195.

153. Minutes of the Medical and Dental Arts Club, 30 February 1916, 2–3, 13 April 1916, 10; Dr. Ignatius Jarzynowski Papers, cont. 1, fold. 4, WRHS; *Wiadomości Codzienne*, 17 January 1931, 5; Grabowski, *Polish*, 191–2.

154. Grabowski, *Polish*, 190–191; Herbert R. Mansfield, "Theater," in Van Tassel and Grabowski, ECH, 964; Department of Public Properties, City of Cleveland, *Cleveland Cultural Gardens* (Cleveland, n.d.), 4; ECH, 226–7.

155. Chronica, Report from the St. Stanislaus Church and Residence—Cleveland, 1914, St. S., cont. 1, vol. 1; Division of Research, Cleveland Board of Education, *A Census of Nationalities Represented in the Cleveland Public Schools* (Cleveland, November 1922), 3–6; Lois B. Blanchard, "Report of Adult Work in the University Neighborhood Center for the Year 1926–1927" (typescript), and University Settlement History and Purpose, 1, University Settlement Records, WRHS, cont. 15, folders 1 and 2; Mary Ellen Finley, "The Relationship between St. Stanislaus Parish and University Settlement" (M.A. thesis, Western Reserve University, 1938), 1, 6.

156. *Jutrzenka*, 9 March 1922; Weikart, "Organizations," 31–33; Polish Welfare Association, leaflet, Frank J. Olbrys Papers, Manuscript Collection 4139, WRHS, oversize container.

The Slovaks in Cleveland, 1870–1930

MICHAEL KOPANIC

During the early twentieth century, Cleveland was host to one of the largest settlements of Slovaks in the United States and was for a time said to have had the largest Slovak population of any city in the world.[1] The Slovak neighborhoods that developed in Cleveland were anchored by churches, with religion serving to bind the immigrants together and ease their cultural transition. Religion also, however, created divisions within the community, between and within the various confessions as well as between secular and religiously based organizations. When Cleveland's Slovak community perceived itself as under threat from the outside, it united, both within itself and with other groups regarded as allies. Such outside threats usually had to do with interethnic conflict, most often stemming from the group's troubled relationship with the Magyars, or ethnic Hungarians, who also had a large settlement in Cleveland.

Americans, not bothering to distinguish among the various East European immigrant groups, frequently referred to Slovaks as "Hunkies." Most Slovak immigrants came to America from the *northern part* of pre-World War I Hungary, an area slightly smaller than the state of South Carolina. The Slovak homeland, or Slovakia, never constituted a separate administrative unit within Hungary and had no clearly defined borders until after World War I. Despite its small size, Slovakia did not exhibit complete social, cultural, or linguistic uniformity. Western Slovak differed considerably from eastern Slovak dialects. The western region was the most economically developed, and a smaller percentage of its population emigrated. In the south, in the pre-World War I era, most people worked as peasants on large estates owned by Magyar nobles. In central and eastern Slovakia, forestry and mining were the leading economic activities. A tradition of working in the mines or the iron and steel industry helped Slovaks to find similar occupations in America. Until the twentieth century Slovaks identified themselves according to their local origins, especially their home counties. In Cleveland, Slovak migrants often settled in neighborhoods inhabited by others from the same counties.[3]

Outside of "Slovakia" per se, Slovaks were scattered throughout Hungary, with significant numbers living in the capital and industrial hub, Budapest. In 1910, according to official records, there were 1,987,910 Slovaks in all of Hungary (about 9.4 per cent of its population).[4] In the Slovak counties, Magyar nobles dominated the upper classes. A small, weak middle class, ethnically mostly Jewish and German, developed in some Slovak towns. Of the 546,936 Slovak immigrants who registered their occupational status upon arriving in America between 1899 and 1930, only 830 were listed as professionals. The largest number were common laborers (150,017) and farm laborers (149,996). Most possessed at least some education: of the 377,527 registered as entering to the United States between 1899 and 1910, only about a fifth (82,216) were illiterate. A sample from the Cleveland census of 1910 indicated that 87.2 percent of Slovaks knew how to write. Most had attended a few years of grammar school.[5]

Reasons for Migration

Although there were a few cases of political persecution and a significant number of Slovaks fled to avoid being drafted into the Austro-Hungarian army, the great majority emigrated for economic reasons. Even with the official abolition of feudalism following the 1848 revolution, a society of peasants and de facto lords persisted. One percent of the population owned over half of the land. Most Slovak peasants had to make do with small, non-contiguous lots which scarcely sufficed to sustain a living.[6] Industrialization in the late nineteenth century, mainly in the western and central parts of the region, was not extensive enough to absorb the ever-larger unemployed and underemployed pool of workers and peasants, many of whom lived in eastern Slovakia.[7] One-third of all pre-World War I emigrants from Hungary came from the poorer eastern counties of Slovakia, mainly Šariš, Spiš, and Zemplín.[8]

The large number of Slovak emigrants attests to the poverty of the region. Nearly one-quarter of the approximately two million Slovaks in Austria-Hungary left their homeland, with most going to the United States. Slovakia was second only to Ireland in the percentage of population which it lost due to emigration. However, as many as one-third of Slovak emigrants returned home, for most originally had no intention of staying in the New World. In many cases it was those who decided to remain who had changed their minds.[8]

Immigration to America began during the late 1860s. The number of immigrants, initially insignificant, grew substantially during the following decades. A cholera epidemic in eastern Slovakia in 1873, increasing mechanization in agriculture, and a crisis in the mining industry coincided with industrial expansion in the United States. Between 1870 and 1913 emigration from Šariš county—which had a total population of 174,470 in 1900—numbered 78,000. A Slovak newspaper wrote of a district (*okres*) where "only the old were staying behind," with 6,000 people leaving yearly.[10] From 1899 through 1914, 477,276 Slovaks immigrated to the United States, with the greatest number, 52,368, arriving in 1905. Of these immigrants, 4,664 stated that they intended to settle in Ohio.[11]

The earliest Slovak immigrants settled mainly in the anthracite coal-mining districts of eastern Pennsylvania. Only later in the 1880s did a significant number begin to filter west to Cleveland, where they found work in steel mills, oil refineries, machine shops, and other industrial concerns. Although some came directly from Slovakia on the word of relatives and friends, many others had first worked in the mines or factories of Pennsylvania, New Jersey, West Virginia, or other parts of Ohio. This migration to Cleveland from within the United States and Canada would continue through World War II, although immigration from Europe was severely curtailed during World War I and after 1921 by restrictive quotas.[12] Slovak immigration from Hungary peaked in the years 1905–1907. Of the 210 Slovak immigrants in a sample of those who had arrived in Cleveland by 1910, sixty-one percent had arrived after 1901.[13]

The United States census enumerated 12,790 foreign-born Slovaks living in Cleveland in 1910 and 13,430 in 1920. Including the American-born children of immigrants, the 1920 census counted 28,224 Slovaks living in Cleveland: 3.5 percent of the total population, 5.1 percent of white foreign stock, or 15.1 percent of the city's Slavs, and the third largest Slavic group after Poles and Czechs. By 1920 Cleveland had the largest Slovak population of any city in the United States. By that time the inner-ring suburb of Lakewood had an even greater concentration of Slovaks, with 3,983 individuals making up 9.5 percent of its population. Its residents constituted an integral part of the Cleveland Slovak community, so that a total of 32,207 first- and second-generation Slovaks lived in the combined Cleveland-Lakewood settlement. In 1930, 14,584 first-generation Slovaks lived in Cleveland proper, and 2,526 in Lakewood.[14]

Early Impressions

Like other European immigrants, Slovaks began their journey to the New World by traveling from their hometown to a port of embarkation, usually Bremen or Hamburg, less frequently Fiume. After the transatlantic voyage, they would arrive at a port of entry, usually New York, where company agents or, later, government officials would direct them to their destination, or suggest one to immigrants who had none.[15] Many of the earliest Slovak immigrants who came to Cleveland did not intend to settle there, for it was not yet a well-known destination. For instance, in 1880 Jakub Gross, an immigrant from Lipovec in Šariš County, sought work in New York City. The head of an employment bureau suggested that Gruss make his way to the anthracite coal regions in Pennsylvania where many of his compatriots lived and worked. When Gruss objected to the idea of being a miner, the bureau chief reportedly answered: "If you feel that way about it I advise you to go to Cleveland. I have been informed that work in that city is plentiful." Gruss, although not the first Slovak in Cleveland, was later credited with founding the Slovak colony in Cleveland because of his active role in forming some of the city's first Slovak associations. His letters to friends in the old country spread the word about the abundant demand for labor and were an important factor in attracting Slovaks to Cleveland.[16]

Pavel Misenčík, another early settler, arrived in New York in 1884 and headed to eastern Pennsylvania. The seventeen-year-old, willing to work at whatever opportunity presented itself, soon found employment in the mines. For ten months he worked ten hours daily at the rate of eleven cents per hour. Finding that he could not save anything, he made his way on foot to Wilkes-Barre and Scranton, where "I heard about the city of Cleveland, that there are many Slovaks there already. I thought to myself, what should I do? Everything I owned I had on my person, only $3.00 and I did not even know how far away Cleveland was. So I left blindly. I set out on foot, and in some places I hopped on railroad cars, and after wandering for a long time I luckily made it to Cleveland in the spring of 1886."[17]

Neighborhood Development

Slovaks first settled in Cleveland beginning in the 1870s. When Jakub Gruss arrived in 1880, he found several Slovaks already living there. Among them was Ján Roskoš, the city's first known Slovak settler, who had come in 1874, bringing his family with him. According to Gruss, Roskoš was from Hermanovce, in Zemplín county, and another Slovak resident, Ján Leheta, "came from the same village, or from a neighboring one. Roskoš lived on Berg Street [in the Haymarket]. . . . Leheta lived in the so-called 'Heights.' Roskoš collected rags and scrap iron and Leheta worked in a gun powder factory, which stood in the valley of the Cuyahoga River below Lincoln Heights. . . . At that time it was considered far from the city."[18]

The first Slovak neighborhood in Cleveland formed in the city's "Haymarket District," in the area around Hill, Berg, Commercial, and Fourth Streets. Other groups living nearby included Poles, Czechs, some Russian Jews, and a few Germans and African Americans. The district's houses were small, and residents' incomes were low. Most worked in the factories of the adjacent Cuyahoga Valley industrial basin, or maintained small businesses in the area.[19]

During the 1880s the number of Slovak immigrants to Cleveland began to rise steadily, and additional neighborhoods developed. By 1888 there were about 800 immigrants from Hungary in Cleveland, and about ninety-five percent of them came from northeastern Hungary, i.e., the eastern Slovak counties. Twenty percent of these were reported to "prefer" the Magyar language, but most also understood Slovak. Only a few spoke Magyar exclusively. About 150 were German-speaking, most of whom resided on the city's west side. Approximately 400 of the immigrants lived in the Haymarket area. Most of the remaining 250 resided in the Buckeye Road area in the vicinity of Corwin, Bismarck, Holton, and Frederick Streets.[20]

The lower Buckeye Road settlement expanded quickly, partly due to Štefan Furdek, a prominent Slovak priest and community leader, encouraging his compatriots to move there, where land was cheap and plentiful. In the years after 1885, the neighborhood, which reached from East 78th Street to Woodhill Road, became one of the largest Central European ethnic centers in the United States. Its ethnic composition mirrored that of many regions of Slovakia, the immigrant population being a mixture of Slovaks, Magyars, and some Jews. Large industrial firms—the Eberhard Manufacturing Co., the National Screw and Tack Co., and the Mechanical Rubber Co.—provided ample employment nearby.[21] The rapid growth of the Slovak population in the area can be gauged from the records of St. Ladislas parish, founded jointly by Slovaks and Magyars, but it became an exclusively Slovak church after 1891.[22]

Baptisms at St. Ladislas Parish 1888–1935[23]

Years	Total number of baptisms
1888–1890	258
1891–1895	791
1896–1900	393
1901–1905	581
1906–1910	545
1911–1915	778
1916–1920	928
1921–1925	918
1926–1930	603
1931–1935	197*

*The fall in baptisms was due to the establishment in 1928 of a new Slovak parish, St. Benedict's. See pp. 20–21.

The Buckeye Road neighborhood continued to expand, so that even before World War I a large number of Slovaks were starting to move eastward and across Woodland Avenue into an area just west of East Boulevard, near the newly developing suburb of Shaker Heights. In contrast to the flourishing Buckeye neighborhood, the old Haymarket settlement disappeared as commercial development swallowed up the district. However, by the late 1880s, Slovaks had begun to settle to the east of the Haymarket, on Central Avenue and adjacent streets, so that a sizable Slovak community developed near East 25th Street and Scovill Avenue, still within walking distance of the Cuyahoga Valley's factories.[24]

Meanwhile, Slovaks were founding additional settlements as well. Indeed, compared to some other nationalities, Slovaks in Cleveland had a relatively dispersed pattern of settlement. They lived in neighborhoods scattered across greater Cleveland, resulting in a more fragmented ethnic community. After the decline of the Haymarket as a residential district, Slovaks lived in nine principal areas: Central, Buckeye, Newburgh, the near west side, Tremont, St. Clair, Lakewood, Riverside, and Broadway. The first seven of these Slovak neighborhoods were anchored around Catholic and in some cases Protestant Slovak parishes.[25]

Slovaks started to settle in Newburgh, in the southeast, around 1887. Many resided on Sawyer (E. 91st) and Way Streets and Cambridge Avenue

and worked in the nearby American Steel and Wire Company plant. Originally members of St. Ladislas parish, they eventually created a new, more
conveniently located parish—The Nativity of the Blessed Virgin Mary.[26]

By 1888 Slovak immigrants were moving to an area in the northeast part
of the city near the Lake Erie shoreline, between St. Clair and Payne Avenues
from E. 40th to E. 55th Street. Large employers in the area included the Pittsburgh Paint and Glass Co., the Otis Steel Company, the Cleveland Stamp-
ing and Tool Company, and another American Steel and Wire Company
plant. In this district, which was populated predominantly by Slovenes along
with a significant number of Croatians, a Slovak settlement also evolved
as of the late 1890s. In 1906 the area's Slovaks built their own Catholic church,
St. Andrew Svorad.[27]

Another fast-growing Slovak area emerged on the ethnically mixed near
west side. As more Slovaks found jobs in the Cuyahoga Valley steel mills,
some settled in the area between West 19th and West 38th Streets, Columbus
Road, and Lorain Avenue. In 1903 Roman Catholic Slovaks established St.
Wendelin's parish there, which in a short time grew to be one of the largest
Slovak parishes in the city. In the second decade of the twentieth century,
Slovaks also moved to the adjacent Tremont neighborhood, living between
West 5th and West 18th Streets and along Literary and Broyton Streets. This
polyglot community, with a population including Poles, Ukrainians, Rusyns,
Russians, Greeks, and Syrians, acquired the reputation of being a rough
blue-collar district where the youth of the various groups defended their
own turf, and where many groups challenged both political and religious
orthodoxy. Slovak Roman Catholics, Greek Catholics, Lutherans, and (in
associations with Czechs, Baptists) all organized their own churches in
Tremont.[28]

Lakewood, the first Cleveland suburb to develop a Slovak neighborhood,
grew from a largely rural community of 450 people in 1890 to a city with a
population of 15,000 by 1910. One of the key factors in this growth was the
establishment in 1892 of the National Carbon Company factory complex on
Madison Avenue and the Lake Shore and Southern Michigan railroad tracks
at East 117th Street, and the consequent influx of laborers, many of them Slovak immigrants. Through a subsidiary, the Pleasant Hill Land Company,
National Carbon fostered the development of inexpensive housing on streets
adjacent to the plant. These streets, given names like Plover, Robin, Lark,
and Thrush, earned the neighborhood its popular name, the "Bird's Nest,"
or, "Birdtown." Land along these streets was divided into small lots, many
of which were purchased by the company's employees. (Plover Street,

nearest the factory, had the cheapest lots.) A Slovak settlement developed, centered itself in the Bird's Nest and spilled over onto nearby streets. As in Tremont, Slovaks from various denominations established their own churches in Lakewood.[29]

In the twentieth century two additional, small Slovak neighborhoods formed: one on Cleveland's southwest side below Riverside Park, north of Brooklyn, where Slovaks lived interspersed with Poles; the other on the southeast side, in the northern part of the Czech Broadway neighborhood. In neither of these did Slovaks build their own churches. In the Broadway neighborhood they could attend Our Lady of Lourdes, the Czech church where Rev. Štefan Furdek, a Slovak priest and community leader, was pastor. Some Slovak freethinkers, who were a small minority compared to religiously affiliated Slovaks, also settled here among the Czechs with whom they felt more comfortable.[30]

Settling In: Home and Work

For Cleveland's immigrant laborers, transportation was mostly on foot, which cost only shoe leather. Less frequently, they traveled by streetcar. Most Slovak social, religious, and political life took place in the churches and halls and along the streets of their various neighborhoods. People in Tremont or Birdtown, on Buckeye or St. Clair, socialized with their own countrymen in their own part of town. To Slovaks, living in Cleveland meant living in their neighborhood.

Linguistic and cultural similarities, as well as proximity to the workplace and affordability, determined where people decided to live. In order to live inexpensively, newcomers, usually bachelors or men whose wives were still in Slovakia, often lived in boardinghouses. This situation was typically short-lived. Once they had saved some money, they either returned home or found a place of their own to rent or buy, where they could bring a wife and raise a family. They would then live out of one room and the kitchen, renting the remaining rooms (usually to other Slovaks) to meet expenses and save money. Such an arrangement might continue until a family had paid for its own house.[31]

The first Slovak neighborhood was hardly in the best part of town. By 1911, the Immigration Commission report described the Haymarket area as "a locality with a bad reputation of long standing." At this time, foreign-born residents made up 176 of the district's households, compared to only 3 households of native-born Americans. Of the former, 117 were Slovak. Most of the dwellings in the neighborhood had originally been one- to two-story frame single-family houses and stood very close to the street. As immigrants began settling there, the houses were divided and subdivided, and additions or new stories were added. Those places with small backyards even built additional houses in order to accommodate more people.[32]

The Lakewood Slovak neighborhood presented a somewhat different picture. There, too, immigrant factory workers lived in small houses on tiny plots of land. These houses, however, were new. As the settlement grew beyond the company-sponsored development, immigrants built multi-family dwellings and rented out the extra units, or opened shops. They lived upstairs or in the back rooms. Residents cultivated flower and vegetable gardens, and raised poultry, giving the area a village atmosphere. At the surrounding small shops, people could do business with friends and neighbors in their own language.[33]

By the time of the Immigration Commission's 1910 survey, a sizable number of Slovaks were living in Cleveland, many of them in a family setting, others as boarders. The Commission's data showed that of a sample of 1,198 Cleveland Slovaks, 133 (11.1 percent) were boarders or lodgers. A related sample recorded that the largest percentage of those keeping boarders had been in the United States from 5 to 9 years. Those who stayed longer were less likely to be keeping borders. (The data also indicated that other nationalities from East Central Europe had greater percentages of individuals living as boarders: for Magyars the percentage was 33.9, for Slovenes 24.6, and for Poles 14.4.) Sixty-five percent of the Slovaks sampled lived in single-family households without boarders. Fewer than a third of households kept boarders, with the number of boarders averaging 1.77 per household.[34]

In the above-mentioned sample of 1,198 Slovak individuals, 54.1 percent were male, 45.9 percent female. Another sample, of 245 Slovak households, found 226 to be headed by males, 85.4 percent of whom were in the 20–44 age group. The higher overall percentage of males substantiates the commonly-held notion that more males were coming to America with the intention of marrying later, or sending over for their spouses at a later date. By 1910, however, there was less of a gender imbalance than there would have been in previous years. In the years 1900–1910 Slovak immigration to Cleveland was at its height. Many women were making the trek overseas which their husbands or fiancés had made earlier.[35]

The early immigrants typically married within their own nationality group, oftentimes with someone from their original locality, even if it meant going overseas to find a spouse. One study found that among 74 of 94 couples married at St. Ladislas, both partners originated in the same district of Šariš County. Likewise, St. Wendelin's records showed 66 percent of marriage partners originating from a 15-square-kilometer triangle in Slovakia.[36]

When Slovak immigrants first arrived, with no funds and no English proficiency, they had to take whatever jobs might be available. A Slovak railroad worker, who came to America with a friend in 1880, started off as a railroad worker in West Virginia, but the pay was so low that the pair decided to move on (on foot) to Baltimore. Eventually they ended up in Cleveland, where they had heard wages were better. Living in a Polish boardinghouse, where they shared a bed in shifts with three other immigrants, they worked at various jobs: construction, chopping ice on Lake Erie, and finally in the oil refineries where they could earn $1.50 a day. Jakub Gruss found work as a mason, "truly here one of the worst jobs, but I was glad that I had it. I received a wage of $1.25 . . . for a ten-hour day. I was satisfied to have a secure living."[37]

Most immigrants had arrived with the intention of saving enough money to return to Slovakia and buy land. Low as wages were, they were much higher than those in Hungary, and Slovak laborers were willing to do difficult, often menial jobs in unpleasant and even dangerous working conditions in order to achieve their goal. Gruss worked his way up in the unceasing din and scorching heat of a Cleveland steel mill, from stoker to the more skilled position of molder, and then to a foreman's job. Paul Misenčik, still in his teens, obtained work "by a furnace" in the City Forge and Iron Company at the wage of $1.25 for a ten-hour day upon his arrival in Cleveland in 1886. "In 1887 I married and I worked still in the Cleveland City Forge factory. But the work made me ill, and for this reason they fired me from my job, and I . . . went to work as a bricklayer on the newly constructed buildings. This work was also very difficult, but the pay was a little better. . . . I was satisfied, because it was necessary to work hard, and at least I was working in the fresh air and I wasn't burning myself by a furnace all day and [coming] home in the evening like I was cooked." Life could be precarious as well as toilsome. Fraternals' records cite many instances of payouts due to railroad accidents, for example.[38]

Slovaks earning their livings in the skilled trades were a small minority. Most Slovak immigrants were farm workers or common laborers. Early pastors reported that ninety percent of their parishioners worked in factories, with eighty percent doing low-paid unskilled labor. Skilled workers and even professionals often worked as laborers when they came to America. "A teacher will only obtain work with a shovel," observed Rev. Furdek.[39] Ján Pankuch, the son of a skilled cabinet-maker and Slovak nationalist who brought his family to the United States in the 1880s, resorted to various means of making a living while trying to establish a Slovak newspaper in Cleveland. He worked as a blacksmith, a factory hand, and a streetcar motorman.[40]

A few Slovaks set up small businesses in Cleveland. Initially, saloons were the most numerous, serving as social and information centers for the fledgling Slovak community, which in the early years had no newspapers, churches, or fraternal groups. Ján Matis, who arrived in New York in 1888 and moved on to Cleveland, worked as a night watchman, a sailor, and then, after his marriage, for a short time as a factory laborer before starting up his own business, a saloon. Matis chose his location well, establishing one of the first saloons in the growing Buckeye neighborhood. His saloon quickly became a favorite gathering place.[41]

Besides saloons, early Slovak settlers opened dairy and small general stores. They were slow to start other kinds of businesses because they lacked sufficient capital and experience. Not until after 1900 did Slovaks venture into areas such as dry goods and furniture. In the meantime, Slovaks shopped for such items at Jewish-owned stores in their neighborhoods.[42]

Religion and the Churches

More than businesses, however, the church was the keystone in the building of a Slovak neighborhood. Between 1888 and 1930 Slovaks in Cleveland and its immediate suburbs founded eight Roman Catholic, four Greek Catholic, four Lutheran, one Congregational, one Baptist, and one Calvinist church. Slovaks, once established in an area, built a church, which served to attract more residents. In a sample of parishioners from St. Wendelin church, one study found that most resided less than six blocks from St. Wendelin's Catholic Church, and another twenty-five percent were no more than ten blocks away. The pastor of St. Benedict's church reported that three-quarters of the parish's families lived within four or five blocks of the church. About eighty percent of Nativity of the Blessed Virgin Mary Church parishioners lived no more than two blocks away. Well into the 1930s, Slovaks continued to live close to their churches.[43]

Built with their money and often with their own labor, the local nationality church was a building which immigrants could truly claim as their own. Churches became centers of social life as well as places of worship. Singing society practices, fraternal organizations meetings, drama performances, celebrations, and club meetings frequently took place in the church basement or hall. Priests and ministers provided pastoral leadership which went beyond religious duties. The clergy, better educated than most immigrants, served as intermediaries between members of their ethnic group and the community at large, easing the transition into American life. The pastor of the Greek Catholic Holy Ghost Church, for example, personally helped new arrivals who could not speak English and did not know their way around the city. He would take them to factories to apply for jobs, helping them to fill out forms and using his influence with employers to get a job-seeker accepted.[44]

Churches also brought Slovaks into close contact with other nationalities. Before 1888 most attended either German or Czech churches. Since the Catholic liturgy was in Latin, only the sermon and songs were in the vernacular. Slovaks were fortunate in that the young Rev. Furdek, although pastor of a Czech parish, as of 1885 also conducted Slovak-language services at the German Franciscan Monastery Chapel of St. Joseph on Woodland Avenue, a twenty-minute walk from the Haymarket area. Both Slovaks and Magyars attended these services. Slovak Lutherans at first attended German services. Czech and Slovak Baptists and Calvinists worshipped together. In 1890s Slovak, Magyar, and Rusyn Greek Catholics all attended the Hungarian parish of St. John the Baptist. This fellowship grew out of necessity, however. Slovaks founded their own churches as soon as their numbers were sufficient to do so.[45]

Roman Catholics

Rev. Furdek's mixed Slovak-Magyar worshippers formed, in effect, a congregation without an ethnic church. The rapidly increasing settlement of those nationalities in the Buckeye neighborhood made possible the founding of Cleveland's first Slovak church, St. Ladislas. Planning started in 1887, with considerable assistance from Rev. Furdek. The church building was constructed and consecrated in 1889. Initially, St. Ladislas, named after the saint-king of Hungary, was a mixed Slovak-Magyar parish intended for immigrants from Hungary. Rev. Furdek, as pastor of Our Lady of Lourdes, could not assume the pastorate at St. Ladislas as well, but he did recruit the new church's first regular priest, Ján Martvoň, during a trip to Slovakia. Although Rev. Martvoň, a Slovak, spoke both languages, and conducted both Slovak and Magyar services every week, he could not quell the disputes that soon arose between the two nationalities. During 1891 it became clear that the two groups could not peacefully co-exist within the confines of St. Ladislas Church. A banner-blessing ceremony during Sunday worship touched off a violent confrontation, due to an altercation over which group could use the church at what time, a disagreement rooted in language differences and ethnic enmity.[46]

The diocese had decided long before that the Magyar service would be at 8 A.M., and the Slovak at 10 A.M. On this occasion, one of the nationality-based societies that had been organized within the church, the Magyar St. Imre Society, had arranged that their banner be blessed during the 10 o'clock mass. Slovak lay leaders had consented on the condition that the sermon still be given in Slovak. Rev. Martvoň agreed to this but did not inform the Magyars (who were also hoping to obtain the more convenient 10 o'clock mass time on a permanent basis). That Sunday, parishioners of both nationalities crowded into the church (according to a Slovak source, Magyars from outside also attended). When Rev. Martvoň began his sermon in Slovak, pandemonium broke out. A Slovak's letter to the diocese charged that "The wild Huns jumped on the pews, hissed, cursed, swore . . . and desecrated the house of the Lord." According to the Plain Dealer, "the infuriated Magyars" then "armed themselves with clubs and stones and threatened to kill the priest." Jakub Gruss, serving as a church alderman, ran to his nearby home to fetch his gun, and then stood beside Rev. Martvoň while his brother went for the police. "As long as the priest remained in the sanctuary," continued the Plain Dealer story, "it appeared that the wrathy Huns would lay siege to the edifice." Once the police arrived, however, they had no trouble escorting the pastor out of his church to safety. Meanwhile, the Slovaks, "who were in a hopeless minority . . . pursued a wise course in leaving as soon as the tumult began."[47]

Ultimately, it was the Magyars who left St. Ladislas. It was obvious that the parish had to be split, and each group, wishing to claim St. Ladislas as their own, declared a willingness to reimburse the other for the loss of the church. According to a church history and to Ján Pankuch, Furdek's wit saved St. Ladislas for the Slovaks. A meeting with the diocesan administrator, Monsignor J. M. Boff, over the fate of the church (allegedly kept secret from Slovaks until the last moment) was attended by an overwhelmingly Magyar audience. Only a few Slovaks, including Rev. Furdek, were present. At Furdek's sotto voce suggestion, the administrator asked Magyars to sit on one side of the hall and Slovaks on the other. This pleased the majority of the crowd, which thought that the church would now surely go to the Magyars. Furdek then again whispered to Rev. Boff: "Tell them that the church is too small for the Hungarians and therefore, it should remain a Slovak church." Rev. Boff concurred, and Rev. Furdek announced the decision in both Slovak and Magyar. The crowd protested, but the decision remained. St. Ladislas became a Slovak church and the Magyar parishioners received $1,000 in compensation to establish their own church, St. Elizabeth.[48]

Controversy, it seemed, had become a way of life at St. Ladislas, for Rev. Martvoň left the parish in 1892, victim not of "wrathy Huns" but of one of the clerical-lay altercations so common in ethnic churches in the United States. In this case, parishioners claimed that Rev. Martvoň was managing the church and its finances poorly and neglecting the sacraments.[49] The fact that ordinary parishioners, rather than the diocese or the nobility as in Europe, were now funding their own churches, along with the freer atmosphere in America, led to schisms unheard of in the old country. Former peasants took the purse strings, and the accompanying power, into their own hands.

The pastorate of St. Ladislas continued to change hands frequently until 1907, due in part to continuing controversies and in part to the shortage of Slovak priests in the United States. Meanwhile, parish life went on. There had been a St. Ladislas school from the very beginning, taught first by a lay teacher and, beginning in 1898, by Ursuline nuns (succeeded in 1907 by Notre Dame sisters). In 1899 the 150 families of the parish celebrated its tenth anniversary, by which time the school's enrollment had grown from 40 to 150 pupils.[50]

By this time, additional Slovak parishes had been founded within the diocese of Cleveland. In 1892 Ignatius Horstmann, an American of ethnic German descent, was installed as bishop of the diocese. This marked a new phase in the history of church-immigrant relations. Although Bishop Horstmann, like Bishop Richard Gilmour before him, could not avoid becoming entangled in the controversies and schisms that beset his frequently unruly flock, his devotion to the cause of preserving the Roman Catholic faith among the city's new immigrants led to particular consideration of their religious needs. During his sixteen-year tenure, twenty-two new ethnic parishes (out of a total of thirty new parishes) were created to serve Cleveland's various nationality groups; five of these were Slovak.[51]

Soon after his installment, he granted permission for the formation of a parish for Slovaks living in the Haymarket area, who otherwise had to walk four miles to attend St. Ladislas. The new parish, St. Martin of Tours, was officially established in 1893, due in part to the efforts of a lay fraternal group, the Sts. Peter and Paul Society. Rev. V. Panuška, pastor of St. Ladislas at the time, helped the new parish get started, despite objections from his own parishioners, who knew that a new church would hurt St. Ladislas financially by drawing away some of its members and their contributions. St. Martin's parish purchased a former Lutheran church on Henry (East 25th) Street near Woodland Avenue. In 1894, Rev. Panuška, left St. Ladislas to assume the pastorate at St. Martin's. St. Martin's fourth pastor, Václav Horák, who arrived in 1899, led the parish until his death in 1946.[52]

As Slovak immigrants continued to stream into Cleveland, both of these churches grew in membership and financial stability. St. Ladislas School had 473 students and four teachers by 1905. Parishioners came under strong pressure from peers and priest alike to send their children there. In 1903 the priest attributed the attendance of five children at public schools to the "carelessness of parents"; in 1905 Rev. Ján Svozil, with more understanding, noted that fourteen parish children went to public school due to "the distance being too great or they are unable to pay the monthly tuition." Under Rev. Svozil's leadership, the parish raised funds and built a church capable of holding three to four hundred families. His successor, Ladislas Necid, a Moravian Czech, served a pastor of St. Ladislas from 1907 to 1942.[53]

As at St. Ladislas, the many young couples at St. Martin produced large numbers of children, as evidenced by the school enrollment and the number of baptisms: 126 in 1894, and 248 in 1902. The school, which started in the mid-1890s with a single schoolroom, one lay teacher, and 83 pupils, by 1907 had four Sisters of St. Joseph teaching 205 pupils. At one point St. Martin's had as many as 2,500 families in its parish, and 1,200 pupils in its school, and was one of the largest parishes in the Cleveland diocese, until the creation of additional Slovak parishes eventually resulted in a decrease in numbers.[54] In the first decade of the twentieth century, three new neighborhood parishes branched off from the centrally located St. Martin's: SS. Cyril and Methodius, St. Wendelin, and St. Andrew Svorad.

The Slovaks of Lakewood, especially, needed their own church, since this western suburb was nowhere near either of the existing Slovak parishes. A group of laymen, including Paul Misenčik, met in 1902 and decided to found a parish in Lakewood to serve Catholics who worked at the National Carbon Company. Bishop Horstmann, believing that the small number of Catholic families in Lakewood (about sixty) did not really warrant a separate parish, "grudgingly" gave his permission, and the new parish received the name of SS. Cyril and Methodius. Priests from other churches at first conducted services in a private residence, and catechism instruction was provided for the children until in 1905 a church, with a school on the second floor, was built. In 1907 Adalbert Masat began his nineteen-year tenure as priest of SS. Cyril and Methodius. The parish's eighty-five families included sixty Slovak, fourteen Polish, four Magyar, three Croatian, two German, and one Bohemian (Czech) family. The Poles later founded their own church, but nonetheless, SS. Cyril and Methodius had grown to 450 families, or 1,100 parishioners, by 1914. The parish by now had a separate schoolhouse where three Notre Dame sisters conducted classes for 326 pupils in seven grades.[55]

Another Slovak parish, St. Wendelin's, was founded in the near west side neighborhood in 1903, with two hundred families. The parish immediately proceeded to build a frame church on Columbus Road near West 25th Street. Rev. Joseph Koudelka, a Czech Moravian pastor at the nearby German parish of St. Michael, who assisted the Slovak community on many occasions, had helped to found St. Wendelin's and offered mass there until the arrival of the parish's first permanent pastor in 1904. In 1908 Rev. Augustus Tomašek became priest of St. Wendelin's, serving there until his retirement in 1957.[56]

Here, too, a school was one of the first concerns. It started with two nuns and one hundred pupils. The enrollment increased so rapidly in subsequent years that finding enough space became an ongoing problem for the parish. In 1915, with five hundred families in the parish, the school had six hundred pupils, who received instruction from ten sisters and one lay teacher. Five years later there were more than a thousand pupils enrolled. By 1930 St. Wendelin's was one of the largest Slovak parishes in Cleveland, with 3,800 members.[57]

In 1906, a group of Slovak laymen, with assistance from Revs. Furdek, Koudelka, and Svozil, established the parish of St. Andrew Svorad in the St. Clair neighborhood in northeast Cleveland. At first the parishioners met in the school hall of a nearby Slovene church, St. Vitus, but in 1907 moved to their own new brick church at Superior Avenue and East 51st Street. The first pastor was a Czech, but a young Slovak nationalist priest, John Liš-činský, took over the pastorship in 1908. Although it never attained the size of St. Wendelin's or St. Martin's, this parish also grew quickly, as did its school. In 1922 the Benedictine order assumed the administration of the parish. A Catholic boys' high school, Benedictine High School, opened at St. Andrew's in 1927, but it moved to the Buckeye area in 1929, along with the order's monastery.[58]

One other Slovak parish, the Nativity of the Blessed Virgin Mary, was also founded in the first decade of the twentieth century, for Roman Catholics residing in the Newburgh area. Up to this time, Newburgh Slovaks wishing to attend a Slovak church had had to make the four-mile trek to St. Ladislas. In 1902 they received permission to found their own parish. Although a priest was appointed in 1903, there was rapid turnover in the post until Václav Chaloupka, a Czech priest, began his long tenure at Nativity in 1909. Rev. Chaloupka, Bohemian-born but a resident of the United States from the age of eight, was one of those multilingual priests able to communicate equally well with immigrant parishioners and with the broader American community. Moreover, having served under Rev. Furdek at Our Lady of Lourdes, he was able to absorb from his mentor some of the diplomatic skills needed in dealing with a congregation of a different nationality.[59]

Unlike other Slovak parishes in Cleveland, Nativity grew rather slowly at first, but by the 1920s was expanding rapidly. There were 640 parishioners in 1910, 2,013 in 1920, and 3,180 in 1930. As of 1909, the Sisters of St. Dominic from Adrian, Michigan, served as teachers in Nativity school. Whatever funds the parish could afford for construction projects were generally spent on the school facilities. During the steel strike of 1919, strikers assisted in constructing a frame addition to the large brick school building that had gone up less than a decade before. In 1922, six hundred children from the parish's five hundred families attended the school. In the 1920s "the old church bulged with schoolchildren and even the portable buildings . . . could not contain them."[60]

In the 1920s two additional Slovak Roman Catholic parishes, Our Lady of Mercy and St. Benedict, were created. The former, which became a parish of the Cleveland Diocese in 1921, had in fact begun its existence as the schismatic St. John the Baptist Slavish Catholic Church in 1916 (Slavish was another name commonly used to designate Slovaks at the time). Perhaps not surprisingly, this was the parish of the Tremont Slovaks, who, true to the neighborhood's reputation for heterodoxy and independent thinking, clung stubbornly to the idea of having their own church, with or without the approval of the authorities. Although St. Wendelin's was not especially far from Tremont, railroad tracks and the Abbey Street bridge made the walk difficult and dangerous, especially for children. The parish was also becoming very crowded. Thus, Tremont residents petitioned Bishop John Farrelly for a church of their own. Rev. Tomašek of St. Wendelin contended that a separate parish was unnecessary, and the bishop concurred with his judgment, noting also the difficulty of finding Slovak priests.[61]

The residents, who had already purchased land, consulted with the pastor of the schismatic Polish National Catholic Church parish on 14th Street. He suggested that they place themselves under the jurisdiction of his Church's Scranton-based bishopric. The Slovaks, at least some of whom apparently did not understand that this would remove them from the Roman Catholic Church, chose what seemed to be a way to obtain their own church despite

Bishop Farrelly's veto. A young Slovak-American priest was sent to take charge of the new parish, St. John the Baptist. Three hundred families joined the congregation, and three frame houses on West 11th Street served as the church, rectory, and school. However, as St. John, parishioners realized that they had, in fact, left the Roman Catholic Church, they began to drift back to St. Wendelin's. As early as 1916 they had offered to return to the diocese with their church, but were rebuffed. By 1921 only sixty families remained at St. John's, struggling to maintain their church and two-room school, and burdened by a $35,000 debt. The newly installed bishop of the Cleveland Diocese, Joseph Schrembs, gave the parishioners a sympathetic hearing when they again petitioned to return to the diocese. The schismatic parish was reborn as Our Lady of Mercy parish in December 1921. Again, Tremont Slovaks deserted St. Wendelin's for their own parish, and membership in the formerly schismatic parish went back up, to 321 families.[62]

As Slovaks began to settle beyond the confines of the original Buckeye neighborhood, in the area around East Boulevard, and the Slovak population of the entire Buckeye neighborhood continued to grow, the need for an additional church also grew. In contrast to the situation in Tremont, the pastor of St. Ladislas, Rev. Necid, provided considerable assistance and support, especially in the planning of the new school, which became the largest and best of the Slovak schools. Following construction of the school, the new parish itself, St. Benedict, was established in 1928 by the Benedictine order. Rev. Stanislaus Gmuca, a Benedictine priest who had served at St. Andrew's parish since 1922, became the first pastor. The parish began with 4,500 members; 1,100 children attended the school, which soon had a faculty of twelve nuns and six lay teachers.[63]

Next to St. Benedict, the Slovak Benedictines located their monastery, St. Andrew's, and also Benedictine High School, which had previously been started at St. Andrew's church in the St. Clair neighborhood. The monastery was declared an independent abbey in 1934, with Rev. Gmuca as its first abbot. The high school, although at first attended mainly by Slovak boys, was open to others as well, and eventually became one of Cleveland's best-known high schools, attracting boys from diverse backgrounds through its reputation for excellence in academics and, especially, athletics. Slovak girls also gained the opportunity to pursue Catholic studies beyond the elementary level when in 1928 the Vincentian Sisters founded a convent in nearby Bedford with the intent of training Slovak nuns and teachers for the Cleveland diocese. Over the next few decades, the convent became a source of teachers for the Slovak parochial schools in Cleveland.[64]

Greek Catholics

Four of the churches founded by Greek, or Byzantine Rite, Catholics in Cleveland included mixed congregations of Slovaks and Rusyns, and in some instances also Ukrainians, Magyars, and Croatians. Most members of these churches originated from eastern Slovakia, Sub-Carpathian Ukraine, western Ukraine, and southern Poland. Slovak and Rusyn nationalities had lived together in the Old World, spoken similar dialects, and attended the same churches. Their association in America was a natural extension of their earlier living patterns. Although their Uniate Church had reunited with Rome in the 16th and 17th centuries, their different Old Slavonic liturgy and traditions made Greek Catholics a people apart. Clerical marriage, in particular, while accepted in Europe as a long-standing custom of the Byzantines, led to conflict with the American Roman Catholic hierarchy, which would have preferred to abolish the tradition. Greek Catholics tended to identify themselves more by religion than by nationality, and Slovak Greek Catholics were less nationally conscious than most Lutherans and Roman Catholics. Although there were no real conflicts between Greek Catholics and other Slovaks, Roman Catholics tended to treat Greek Catholics condescendingly, as members of a minority rite practiced mostly in the poorest mountain regions of Slovakia. Nonetheless, Slovaks of all confessions, including Greek Catholics, lived in the same Cleveland neighborhoods, and joined in some of the same organizations, causes, and public events.[65]

In the Greek Catholic churches, Slovaks were most closely associated with Rusyns, a small group that did not have a national homeland in the sense that Slovaks or Poles did. They acquired a sense of national identity only after living for some time in America. Thus, Slovaks and Rusyns, who had similar surnames and often intermarried, mingled freely in their churches, to the extent that it is difficult to determine the precise ethnic composition of a parish. The Cleveland Rusyn-Slovak churches appear to have been predominantly Rusyn.

The first Greek Catholic Slovaks and Rusyns in Cleveland attended a Hungarian Greek Catholic church, St. John the Baptist, founded in 1892. The first Greek Catholic church in the city founded primarily by Rusyns was also named St. John the Baptist, and was established in 1898 in the east central part of the city. In 1909 west side parishioners branched off from St. John's to form their own parish, and built Holy Ghost Church at W. 14th Street and Kenilworth in Tremont. Holy Ghost had more Slovak parishioners than did St. John's. Earlier, in 1905, Rusyns and Slovaks had founded St. Gregory's

Greek Catholic Church in Lakewood. The parishioners purchased two lots on Quail and Thrush Streets and built a small frame church in 1906.[66]

In 1912, members of a fraternal group in Newburgh, St. Joseph's Lodge No. 537 of the Greek Catholic Union (*Sojedinenije*), began to organize a new parish, which built St. Joseph's Greek Catholic Church on Orleans Avenue. The records indicate that St. Joseph's had perhaps as many as 250 parishioners during its first years. Evidence on nationality is inconclusive, but it appears that the majority were Rusyn, with about a quarter or possibly more being Slovak.[67]

Protestant Churches

After the Roman Catholics, the Lutherans were the second largest Slovak religious denomination in the Cleveland area, and by far the largest of the Protestant denominations among the Slovaks. The Lutheran church had a long history in Slovakia, dating back to the 16th century when German and Slovak students brought Martin Luther's ideas to the towns of Slovakia. The Czech and Slovak Lutheran churches were very close; Slovak Lutherans used the Kralice Bible and Czech songs during their services, but Lutheran services were held in the vernacular language, so there was a real drive to found Slovak Lutheran churches.[68]

Lutheran churches experienced divisiveness sometimes even greater than that in the Roman Catholic parishes, where a clearly defined diocesan hierarchy could most often resolve conflicts in the end, however much the laity reveled in the new degree of power they had in their American parishes. In Protestant churches, the "priesthood of all believers" gave the laity an even greater role. When disputes arose over religious doctrine, fraternal organizations, or personalities, the Slovak Lutheran Church had great difficulty in containing the centrifugal forces that tended to pull its congregations apart.

One reason for the disunity was the fact that Lutheran congregations in America had no single united church but rather belonged to non-Slovak Lutheran synods that competed to attract Protestant immigrants. Slovak Lutherans organized their own synod in 1902 (officially called the Slovak Evangelical Lutheran Church, but known as the Slovak Synod). The American church's conservative Missouri Synod had discarded some customary practices and added some new ones, creating dissension. The Slovak Synod acted as an independent body, thus Slovaks could belong to two Synods, their own Slovak Synod, or the Missouri Synod, with which it later affiliated in August 1908.

The relationship of fraternals and other lay organizations with the church was a particularly divisive issue, and eventually led to a split between the synod and the first Slovak Lutheran fraternal society, the Slovak Evangelical Union (SEU). The SEU, organized in 1893 to provide insurance and aid immigrants, was also instrumental in founding Slovak Lutheran churches across the country. It later split with the Slovak Synod after 1908 because of a bitter dispute over lay interference in church affairs. The SEU thought that only Lutherans could join its fraternal; the clergy thought the church should decide who was Lutheran. Clergy affiliated with the Slovak Synod also disapproved of dancing and social occasions held on Sundays, and wished to keep the SEU clear of church matters. The Slovak Synod claimed the SEU was interfering with its leadership role; the SEU countered that the Slovak Synod was changing long established customs and teachings of the Lutheran Church of Hungary. Cleveland-area Slovak Lutherans formed eight branches of the SEU, six branches of the Evangelical Ladies Society, and, during the pre-World War II period, four churches.[69]

The first of these, Holy Trinity Evangelical Lutheran Church, was founded in 1892, by the First Slovak Lutheran Church Society of Holy Trinity, which became a lodge of the SEU after 1893. All but one of the founders were from Šariš county; Ján Pankuch was a member of the group. Holy Trinity joined the Missouri Synod, and received considerable help from Cleveland's German Lutherans. However, like many of the Catholic parishes, the church had great difficulty in obtaining a permanent minister. The strong role of the lay leadership caused disagreements over control of the parish and contributed to the high turnover of pastors. Under the leadership of its third minister, Daniel Bella, who arrived in 1899, Holy Trinity purchased a house on Woodland Avenue in the Central neighborhood and remodeled it to serve as a church.[70]

Rev. Bella worked very closely with Ján Pankuch, and in 1900 Cleveland Lutherans began publishing the national newspaper *Luterán* (*The Lutheran*) under Pankuch's editorship. The two also played an active role in the founding of the Slovak Synod, formally the Slovak Evangelical Lutheran Church. Rev. Bella left Holy Trinity in 1905, leading to another unsettled period. Pankuch, as president of the congregation, helped to hold the parish organization together, while Holy Trinity's organist-teacher, Michal Brucháč, took over some of the pastor's duties. Meanwhile, membership had continued to grow, and a new brick church was built on East 20th Street.[71]

In 1907, L. A. Jaroši, a strict orthodox preacher, arrived from St. Louis. He served as minister of Holy Trinity for twenty-nine years, perhaps because he was strong-willed enough to meet the similarly strong-willed lay leadership on equal terms. Among the accomplishments of his pastorate was the opening of a Lutheran day school at Holy Trinity. During the late 1890s, the congregation's children had begun attending classes in religion and Slovak language and culture after public school hours. Rev. Jaroši found this system incomplete, and in 1915 Holy Trinity opened its school. At first, only three grades were offered, but in 1925 Holy Trinity School became the first eight-grade parochial school in the Slovak Synod.[72]

Despite the many controversies, Cleveland remained an important center of Slovak Lutheranism in America. Besides the Lutheran periodicals *Cirkevné listy* (*Church Letters*, 1894–1899) and *Luterán* (1900–1902) the Slovak Synod's periodical *Svedok* (*Witness*) was also published in Cleveland from 1908–1910. Holy Trinity also played a role as a missionary base for other Slovak colonies in Ohio and surrounding states. The pastor traveled across the state and held services at one of the mission stations he had organized. In time, these efforts led to the founding of Slovak Lutheran churches in Akron, Lorain, Massillon, and Pleasant City, as well as Detroit, Michigan.[73]

Slovak Lutherans in Lakewood, like their Catholic neighbors, soon decided they needed a church in their own neighborhood. SS. Peter and Paul was formed as an offshoot of Holy Trinity in 1901. Dissension with the mother church arose, with the Lakewood Lutherans willing to share a pastor but not control over their church. Holy Trinity refused to accept the idea of a church independent from itself, the battle went to court, and Rev. Bella, disgusted with the fighting, left Cleveland.[74]

The dissension between the two churches continued in the following years, as did SS. Peter and Paul's efforts to obtain a minister. One young clergyman who took the pastorship for a brief period came into conflict with the lay leaders, who had become accustomed to running the church as they saw fit. At one point, he and a church member came to blows. The next minister, Andrej Olšavský, became embroiled in the hostilities with Holy Trinity. In 1916, young people at Holy Trinity had organized a youth circle. Rev. Jaroši claimed that youth circles were part of the Evangelical Slovak Union (ESU), a lay fraternal which had split off from the SEU, and threatened to expel anyone who would not leave the circle. This controversy led a number of members to leave Holy Trinity and join SS. Peter and Paul. Rev. Jaroši and other ministers of Slovak Synod churches in Ohio then accused the Lakewood church of accepting unsuitable members into its congregation.[75]

After two years of dissension, SS. Peter and Paul left the Slovak and Missouri Synods. The president of the Slovak Synod, not satisfied with the outcome, came to Lakewood to discuss the matter after services. With him came Ján Vojtko, pastor of Akron's Slovak Lutheran church—the same young minister who had briefly served as pastor of SS. Peter and Paul and gotten into a fist fight with one of the church members. The "discussion" became so heated, with Rev. Vojtko jumping up on a bench to address the meeting while the congregation shouted him down, that the police (who had been warned ahead of time by the visiting ministers) entered the church to stop the commotion.[76]

SS. Peter and Paul did in fact leave the Synod, but some members holding views in line with those of the Slovak Synod disagreed with the move and split off to form their own church, Pentecost Evangelical Lutheran Church. In 1921 Pentecost built a school and church building on Madison Avenue at Clarence Street. Meanwhile, at SS. Peter and Paul, stability had returned. For it, as for most Slovak churches, the 1920s were good years, as the Slovak community matured and shared in the general prosperity of the decade. In 1927, a new SS. Peter and Paul church and school was dedicated, located on Grace and Madison, just across the street from Pentecost.[77]

The controversy that led to the splits in the Lakewood church was actually part of the broader controversy (beginning in about 1909) within the Slovak Synod regarding control of church-related lay organizations, particularly the SEU. The synod had ruled to limit membership in church-based fraternal organizations to those people it defined as Lutherans. It objected to the lay members of the SEU making this decision for themselves, and also to the SEU's sponsorship of secular activities such as dances, club meetings, gymnastic practices, and other social events. When the SEU refused to refrain from endorsing such activities, the Synod ruled that members of its churches could not belong to the organization.[78]

The issue of membership in lay organizations also figured in the founding of the city's third Slovak Lutheran church, Dr. Martin Luther Evangelical. When some members of Holy Trinity Church appeared at a funeral wearing the lapel badges of their lodge and carrying its flag, the pastor refused to let them enter the sanctuary unless they divested themselves of these symbols. The aggrieved mourners departed for the cemetery, where they held their own services. A number of Slovaks from the Tremont area, in part because of the controversy and in part because of the distance, stopped attending Holy Trinity. Initially, the Slovak-speaking minister of a nearby German Lutheran church conducted services for them. In 1910 they decided to form their own church, Dr. Martin Luther Evangelical, which began with about fifty members. The church prospered, becoming one of the largest Slovak Lutheran congregations in the country, with over six hundred families and 2,700 individual members. Although the parish never opened a day school, it employed a teacher to give instruction in religion and Slovak language.[79]

Slovaks also founded Congregational, Calvinist, and Baptist churches in Cleveland and Lakewood. The small number and consequently limited resources of Slovaks of these denominations often led to close association with co-religionists of other ethnic backgrounds, although they founded their own churches when practicable. The members of these denominations also tended to assimilate into the American church more quickly, fulfilling the hopes of missionary preachers.[80]

American Congregationalists through their missionary activities laid the foundations of what became Cleveland's only Slovak Congregational church. Adhering to religious doctrines similar to those of the Calvinist or Reformed churches of central Europe, Congregationalists hoped to win converts among immigrants from the region. The Bethlehem Chapel, founded in the Czech Broadway neighborhood, was active among Slovaks as well as Czechs. A woman volunteer from the chapel would go from house to house on Saturdays and Sundays to convert and minister to Slovaks. In 1888 Czechs started a mission of the chapel on Cyril Street on the west side, which became a self-supporting church in 1901. Over the next decade, Slovaks attending the Cyril Chapel came to outnumber Czechs, and eventually the name was changed to Cyril Slovak Congregational Church.[81]

Like the Lutheran church, the Baptist church had existed in Slovakia beginning in the early Reformation years, although numbers of adherents were very small following the Counter-Reformation. In the late nineteenth century Czech Baptists began winning over Slovak converts, and the pattern duplicated itself among Slovak immigrants in America.[82]

In Cleveland, members of Cyril Congregational Church assisted Baptists in founding a Czech and a Slovak congregation on the west side. Rev. Rade Pesut, a Croatian Baptist, and Rev. Paul Bednár, a Slovak, also helped to generate interest in the Baptist church among Slovaks, Czechs, and other Slavs, and to set up the First Slovak Baptist Church in 1907, with Rev. Bednár serving as its first pastor. The Czechs began their own church in 1916. In 1921 the two churches merged as the Czecho-Slovak Baptist Church (later known as the West Side Czecho-Slovak Baptist Church), which by the 1930s had 45 families and 185 members. The first pastor was Czech; in 1926 a Slovak minister, Paul Kubik, assumed the pastorate. In 1925 some of the Czech members established a mission on Corlett Avenue at East 127th Street, which became known as the East Side Czecho-Slovak Baptist Church.[83]

The number of Slovak Calvinists in the Cleveland area was also small. At first they belonged to one of the three Hungarian Reformed churches. Slovaks had also attended church with Magyars in Europe, where there were likewise relatively few Slovak Calvinists. Most Cleveland Slovak Calvinist lodge members belonged to Magyar lodges until 1917, when some Lakewood Slovaks, caught up in the nationalistic fervor of the World War I years, formed Lodge No. 33 of the national Slovak Calvinistic Presbyterian Union. Although they began organizing services with the assistance of the Lakewood United Presbyterian Church and various visiting ministers in 1921, the Slovak Calvinist Presbyterian Church was officially founded in 1928, with forty-five charter members. Because of its small size, the church had difficulty obtaining ministers, but the elders and other lay leaders took an active role in running the church and provided some continuity.[84]

Slovak Fraternal Societies

Along with the churches, fraternal benefit societies served as important social organizations for Cleveland's Slovaks. At least in the Catholic parishes, the two institutions often worked hand-in-hand to ease the transition to a new environment. Fraternal benefit societies were not entirely new institutions to the Slovaks. In the Middle Ages, craft guilds and religious brotherhoods of unskilled workers had existed, and workers in mining towns of Slovakia later established self-help societies. However, Hungarian officials had outlawed any Slovak fraternal organizations during the 1880s, fearing that they would become centers of nationalist agitation, as they in fact did during subsequent years in Cleveland and the United States.[85]

Of the 15,000 Slovaks estimated to be in Cleveland in 1912, about one-third belonged to one of the fraternal societies. In 1918 all of the twelve large national Slovak fraternals had branches in the city. By 1930 there were over one hundred lodges in the area. Besides being important providers of insurance, fraternals gave considerable support to Slovak churches, and also served as centers of social life. Before World War I lodge members routinely paraded around church and neighborhood on religious and other holidays, garbed in special uniforms or wearing large cloth and metal badges. Fraternals also provided practical experience in developing leadership and organizational skills. Almost every Slovak politician in Cleveland also served as a fraternal officer. Fraternals kept extensive written records and conducted meetings in Slovak, which indirectly promoted literacy and proper use of the Slovak language. On the negative side, although fraternals might have hoped to create unity and cooperation in Cleveland's Slovak community, such hopes proved ill-founded. The large number of different fraternal societies both reflected and exacerbated the many divisions in the community.[86]

Cleveland Slovaks at first joined Czech fraternal organizations, especially the Czech Catholic Union branch at Our Lady of Lourdes. A few even joined the German gymnastic organizations, the Turnverein. These, along with the self-help societies of Slovakia, served as prototypes for Slovak fraternals. The earliest local Slovak society in Cleveland was the Slovak Roman Catholic Society of St. Stephen, founded under the direction of Rev. Furdek in 1885. Four years later, Rev. Furdek engineered the establishment of the Society of St. Joseph. The first officers, besides the priest, included an ironworker, a grocer, a cabinetmaker, and three manual laborers. The Society evolved into the founding lodge of the First Catholic Slovak Union (Prvá Katolícka Slovenská Jednota, or simply Jednota). Jednota's founding convention, attended by twelve members of Slovak societies in Cleveland, Pennsylvania, and Illinois, took place at the home of Jakub Gruss in 1890. Jednota became the most influential Slovak fraternal in Cleveland, the home of its national headquarters and of the bi-weekly *Jednota,* one of the earliest and most widely read Slovak newspapers in America. Over twenty branches formed in Cleveland and 51,000 members would join nationwide by 1918. Slovak and Rusyn Greek Catholics, as well as Roman Catholics, also initially belonged to Jednota, and the Greek Catholic Union, founded in 1892, patterned itself after Jednota.[87]

Besides providing insurance, Jednota served first as a religious society, and secondarily to promote Slovak nationality and heritage, as the word order in its slogan *Za Boha a národ* (For God and Nation) made clear.[88] Members of Jednota lodges were instrumental in the founding of Slovak parishes in Cleveland, and in raising funds for the construction of churches, schools, and other parish buildings. Jednota lodges even checked on members' attendance at Sunday mass and required them to receive the sacraments. Lodges fined members who neglected their religious duties and could oust habitual offenders.[89]

When Jednota first formed, it accepted both nationality-conscious Slovaks and "Magyarones," that is, Slovaks linguistically and otherwise assimilated with the Magyars. To Rev. Furdek, fellow Catholics, even Magyarones, were preferable to Protestants and freethinkers. After the split of St. Ladislaus parish, national sentiment heightened and Jednota became less tolerant of Magyarone sympathies. In the meantime, Slovaks who considered Jednota as being too soft on the Magyarone question joined the Pennsylvania Slovak Roman and Greek Catholic Union, which established four branches in Cleveland.[90]

A national non-sectarian fraternal and cultural organization, the National Slovak Society (NSS), was founded in Pittsburgh in 1890. In Cleveland, the First National Slovak Benefit Society (Prvý Národný Slovenský Podporjúci Spolok), founded in 1889, was incorporated as Branch No. 4, "Garfield," of the NSS after the latter's founding. The group polarized the local community with its suggestion that Slovaks need not follow the dictates of their priests because this was "a free country," and everyone could do as he pleased. Slovaks from Spiš County and Protestants showed a propensity to join the NSS. St. Ladislaus parishioners, many of whom were from Šariš County, belonged to Jednota, evidence of continuing local identification. The secular NSS came into conflict with both Catholic Jednota and conservative Lutherans of the Missouri Synod.[91] A local fraternal benefit organization founded in 1899, the Cleveland Slovak Union (Clevelandská Slovenská Jednota, SCU), also was non-sectarian, open to all Cleveland Slovaks. Despite the good intentions of its founders, it failed to become a true unifying force, as few Catholics joined. Consequently the organization grew slowly, but eventually had thirty-one branches and twenty youth circles in Cleveland and Lakewood, with membership reaching over two thousand in the 1930s.[92]

The secular-religious split extended to the Slovak Sokols (Falcons), which as ethnic-gymnastic organizations appealed mainly to youth. The secular Slovak Gymnastic Union (Telocvičná Slovenská Jednota), also known as the National Sokols, had two branches in Cleveland. After 1905, a national Slovak Catholic Sokol emerged in reaction to anti-clericalism among the leaders of the National Sokols, and in 1910 Jednota formed a Sokol group. The relations among the Sokols were not amicable, with the Sokol Gymnastic Union refusing to allow Jednota Sokols to participate in their Cleveland meeting (Slet) in 1913.[93]

The importance which most Slovaks accorded to their faith boosted membership in religious fraternals. Protestants, too, founded their own fraternals, notably the Slovak Evangelical Union (SEU). An alternative Lutheran organization, the Evangelical Slovak Union, founded by dissident members of the SEU in Cleveland in 1909, completely rejected clerical control of church-related lay organizations. The SEU had five lodges in Cleveland, two in Lakewood, and seven in other parts of the country. Ján Pankuch served as its president. Calvinists also formed their own fraternal, which was one of the smallest Slovak lodges in the Cleveland area.[94]

In addition to the sectarian and mainstream secular organizations, there also existed a socialist-oriented fraternal, the Slovak Workers Society (Slovenský robotnícky spolok, SRS), founded in Newark, New Jersey, in 1915.

Slovaks from the Cleveland suburb of Lakewood participate in a 1939
municipal parade. WRHS

Its first Cleveland branch, No. 6, formed on the west side in 1916 with 28
members, and had 110 members by 1925. Branch No. 37 was organized on
the east side in 1918, and Branch No. 63 in Lakewood in 1919. The SRS, which
attracted anti-clerical and leftist Slovaks, provided insurance benefits at the
lowest cost possible and also promoted socialist and general Slovak culture.
Branch No. 6 started an evening school to teach Slovak language and history, as well as socialist principles, and also formed a youth group. However,
the SRS remained outside the mainstream Slovak community, as evidenced
by its low membership figures.[95]

The first Slovak fraternals had male-only memberships, since it was considered that men, who provided the family income (often in hazardous
occupations), had more need for insurance. However, many women died
young, especially during childbirth, which might result in children being
sent to an orphanage so that the father could continue to work. Women

therefore began establishing their own mutual-benefit organizations on a national basis in the 1890s, which gave them opportunity to participate in Slovak cultural and social life, as well as to obtain insurance. After the first Slovak women's society, Živena (Giver of Life), was founded in New York in 1891, Branch No. 4 was established in Cleveland. Živena, a non-sectarian organization, worked closely with the NSS in promoting Slovak nationalism and sponsoring fund-raising events. Two more Živena branches were subsequently founded in Cleveland and Lakewood.[96]

Women, like men, also founded sectarian organizations. The first national mutual-benefit society for Catholic women—the First Catholic Slovak Ladies Union (Prvá Katolícka Slovenská Ženská Jednota), commonly referred to as the Ženská Jednota—was organized in Cleveland in 1892 by twelve women from across the country, under the leadership of a Cleveland woman, Anna Hurban. Its first branch was founded in St. Ladislaus parish. By the 1940s the organization counted over five hundred branches for adults, of which twenty-five were in Cleveland. Ženská Jednota became a sister organization of the men's Catholic Jednota, but the two had a falling out when the men's society began to accept female members, and Ženská Jednota, in turn, began to recruit men.[97] Lutheran women also established their own society, the Women's Evangelical Union (Ženska Evanjelická Jednota). The first unit, the "Evangelical Sisters," was formed at Holy Trinity Church, and several additional branches in Cleveland and Lakewood soon followed.[98]

Women and Family

Although men were the principal wage-earners, Slovak women, who followed their spouses or fiancés to America, often had to contribute to the family economy immediately upon arrival. Many families, even those still without children, could not exist on the husband's wages alone, especially during the first few years in America. Later, teen-aged daughters also took jobs to supplement the family income. Some women, mostly young and unmarried, worked in light industry, or as maids. In 1902, the N. J. Rich & Co. advertised in *Jednota* for fifty girls who would be trained to make gloves. The American Cigar Co. placed an ad in *Hlas* for women and girls in 1913. In the post-war period, the Theodore Kundtz Co. advertised in *Denný Hlas* for girls to perform light factory work. Married women could earn money at home by taking in laundry or running boardinghouses. Women's work was considered a temporary expedient. Slovak men did not want their wives to work any longer than necessary and took a certain pride in being able to say their wives did not have to work outside the home.[99]

Being able to stay home allowed Slovak women to work as homemakers and mothers, taking care of their large families, which averaged five children, according to parish records (although having as many as ten children was not highly unusual). One author has noted that even upwardly mobile immigrants "did not sacrifice family values through the limitation of births." These cultural values limited Slovak women's activities largely to the confines of the home. Besides looking after the children, cooking, and cleaning, women did tasks that made what income there was go farther: making the family's clothing, raising vegetables and poultry, and preserving and canning food. (Making sausage and curing bacon, however, were men's jobs.) Much of the social life of a Slovak immigrant woman involved doing everyday tasks with friends and relatives.[100]

The world of Slovak immigrant children was also defined by the family's economic needs. Both girls and boys had household chores to perform. As they grew older, boys usually left school in their early or mid-teens to take jobs; girls took on more responsibility in the home, or, like their brothers, went out to work. Typically, after a few years' work in a clothing or other factory, a girl would marry at an early age, and enter into the life of a homemaker, scrimping and saving and perhaps opening her home to boarders, meanwhile bearing and raising her children. A few of the most enterprising women ran or helped to run family businesses.[101]

Mary Lesčak Sčerba's father was one of northern Ohio's early Slovak immigrants. A year after he immigrated to America, he sent for his wife and daughter to join him on Kelley's Island in Lake Erie, where he worked in a quarry. Less than three weeks after the family's reunification, he was killed in an accident. Mrs. Lesčak first supported herself by cooking for twenty to thirty workingmen on the island, but soon moved to Cleveland, where she married again. Mary attended school until age twelve, and then went to work in a cigar factory, but was dismissed when her employer learned she was underage. At thirteen she found employment in a knitting factory, where she earned $1.75 to $2.00 a week, which she considered a fair wage at the time. She stayed there until her marriage to Adam Sčerba, a Slovak factory worker employed by the National Carbon Co. They settled on Lark Street in the Bird's Nest, and kept boarders to supplement their income. With the money they saved they were able to open a small grocery store, and later, Adam Sčerba started an undertaking business.[102]

Anna Balogh Ondrej had a similar story. In Europe she worked as nursemaid for a merchant family, and accompanied them when they immigrated to Cleveland. She then went to work in a knitting factory, and apparently also in the Grasselli chemical works, where she met Ján Ondrej. They married and settled in the Haymarket, where they raised ten children. Like the Sčerbas, they improved their fortunes first by keeping a boardinghouse, and then by opening a grocery store near Buckeye Road. The store doubled as a central forwarding address for the many Slovak immigrants who wished to correspond with their relatives. Mrs. Ondrej expanded the business further by writing letters for customers who were not literate.[103]

Labor, Unions and Socialism

The overwhelming majority of Slovak men who came to Cleveland during the great migration were manual laborers. Some had previously worked in the mines in their homeland; in Cleveland and other cities, a large number found work in the steel mills. Other large manufacturing concerns in Cleveland employing many Slovaks included the Grasselli Chemical Co. and the Standard Oil Co. refinery in the Cuyahoga Valley, as well the National Carbon works in Lakewood. Slovaks also found jobs in smaller machine shops and at construction sites. Although the pay was low, it was much more than they could earn in the old country. Workers changed employment often, partly because jobs were not secure, and partly because they were always in search of better-paid work at another factory.[104]

There is little evidence of Slovak involvement in trade unions and other labor activities during their earlier years in Cleveland. Most were of peasant origin and had little experience with organized labor. In addition, Slovak immigration began relatively late, so that most members of the Slovak community had not witnessed the Cleveland Rolling Mill strikes of 1882 and 1885, the first major event in Cleveland labor history that involved a large number of immigrants. However, the Lattimer Massacre of 1898, in which a number of Slovak and other Slavic miners were shot during a strike in eastern Pennsylvania, roused indignation in Slovak communities across America, including Cleveland. In the following years, *Jednota*, and Rev. Furdek, expressed sympathy for strikers and unions in Cleveland and elsewhere, but also urged workers to be cautious and to refrain from using or provoking violence.[105] By the time of the Worsted Mill strike of 1911 and the great steel strike of 1919, Slovaks were well integrated into Cleveland's labor force, and took part in these and other actions. Increasingly, not to be a union man was to be an outsider, both in the workplace and in the saloons where men gathered after work. Unions and strikes also served to bring Slovaks into common cause with other nationalities. Hence, information about

Slovak participation in Cleveland strikes is difficult to come by because they were overshadowed by the larger numbers of Poles and Czechs.[106]

When the Akron rubber factories went on strike in 1913, workers at Cleveland's Mechanical Rubber Works did the same, demanding higher wages and shorter hours. The plant employed many Magyars, Poles, Slovaks, and Czechs, and organization meetings were held in Szabo Hall on Buckeye Road in three languages—English, Magyar, and Slovak. The strike, which was unsuccessful, was denounced by Pankuch in the pages of *Hlas*. Later, *Denný Hlas* printed both a request for workers to stay away from the factory, and a notice from the employer calling on them to return, during the strike against Kundtz and Co. in 1919. (In the days before telephones were commonplace, the immigrant press served an important function in relaying such information.) In 1916 a Slovak, Julius Bayer, helped organize a section of the Czecho-Slovak branch of the Amalgamated Clothing Workers of America in Cleveland, where a number of Slovaks worked as tailors in the garment industry.[107]

Although unions appealed to Cleveland's Slovaks, socialism, for the most part, did not. In the first place, they had no real tradition of Slovak socialism in Europe on which to draw—a Slovak segment of the Social Democratic Party was not formed until 1904. Secondly, although the United States was far from a workers' paradise, it did seem to most Slovaks in America that hard work could in fact lead to a better life for themselves and their children, a state of mind hardly conducive to revolutionary fervor. Finally, the strong influence of religious belief in the Slovak community militated against acceptance of socialist doctrine. The small Slovak socialist movement was bitterly anti-clerical. Especially in Cleveland, the birthplace of the men's and women's national Slovak Catholic unions, this was hardly a popular position. One Slovak socialist from Buffalo referred to Cleveland as "a town with religious fanatics." Although Rev. Furdek and other priests might support unions—Rev. Chaloupka of Nativity parish offered workers jobs around the parish so they could earn a bit of money during the steel strike of 1919—they drew the line at socialism. Most secular leaders also uncompromisingly opposed radical doctrines.[108]

Initially, Cleveland's few Slovak socialists had ties with German- or Czech-dominated organizations, and also with the IWW. At the national level, Slovaks were organized as a sub-section of the Czech section of the American Socialist Party until 1911. In that year, Slovak socialist leaders from around the country gathered in Cleveland to found a Slovak section of the Socialist Party. (Chicago, where the Slovak socialist newspaper *Rovnost' l'udu* was published, became a more important center for Slovak socialism, however.) Slovak Branch No. 1 of the Socialist Party, also organized in 1911 in Cleveland, had its monthly meetings in Tremont. In 1918 two additional branches were organized on the east side, both of which met at the Czech Sokol hall on Buckeye Road, and in 1919 a Lakewood branch was founded. Socialist Party Slovak section branches, and branches of the Slovak socialist fraternal benefit society Slovak Worker's Society tended to form in tandem in Cleveland.[109]

Total Cleveland-area Socialist Party membership among Slovaks probably numbered no more than a few hundred. During the campaign for the creation of a Czecho-Slovak Republic, Cleveland's Slovak socialists joined forces with their Catholic and Protestant co-nationals, and with Czechs, to work for an independent state. Following the accomplishment of this goal, the alliance evaporated.[110] In 1919 Slovak socialists participated in the May 1 demonstration in Cleveland. Regarded, unfavorably, as "communists" by most Slovaks, their isolation increased in 1920 following the split in the international socialist movement. While the national organization, now known as the Slovak Socialist Federation, did in fact incline towards communism, choosing to ally with the more radical doctrines of the Third International, the Czech section supported the American Socialist Party's reformist approach. The Slovak socialists subsequently made various attempts to work with other radicals. At a "common meeting" of Slovak socialists from the various local branches in 1922, held at Finn Hall on the west side, representatives of the Czech Marxist Federation and the iww featured in the program.[111]

Business, Social Mobility and Education

Professionals and business owners, also a small minority, had a more prominent place in the Slovak community, and were apparently more numerous in Cleveland than in other cities in the United States. Most local Slovak entrepreneurial activity occurred after 1900, for it took years, if not decades, for the earlier immigrants to build the necessary capital base for starting a business. By 1915, Slovaks were doing about twenty-five percent of their business with Slovak proprietors; an article listed 331 Cleveland Slovaks as owners of businesses or professional offices in that year. Slovaks had by this time ventured into more diverse types of businesses, but grocers, butchers, and saloon-keepers still predominated. The list also included seven building contractors, five funeral parlors, three steamship ticket agencies, and a factory, as well as shoe and tailor shops, fabric and clothing stores, and other small retail businesses, plus two attorneys, one physician, and one journalist.[112] Almost all Slovak entrepreneurs set up small, family-run concerns involved in sales and services, rather than production. In the prosperous 1920s several Slovak individuals tried their luck at founding bigger companies, but they failed to remain solvent.[113]

Like other immigrant groups, Slovaks did successfully establish savings and loan associations and similar financial institutions. One of the first such was the First Slavonian Mutual Building and Loan Association (Prvá Slovenská Sporitečna), established in Cleveland in 1906. Its beginnings were typical of such endeavors. The founders started the company in the home of a steamship ticket agent, Michal N. Soboslay. Only when its capital assets increased substantially did it move to offices in the Buckeye neighborhood.[114] The Slovak financial institutions openly courted Slovak customers, urging them to "buy Slovak" (*svoj k svojmu*, to each his own) and lending money at competitive rates of interest. The Tatra Saving and Loan Company, which eventually became the largest of the city's Slovak savings institutions, was founded in 1909 by Ján A. Sotak in his home on Scovill Avenue. The company maintained a conservative financial stance while at the same time offering a five percent interest rate, one percent higher than most large Cleveland banks. Tatra prospered under the management of the Sotak family, and moved to a new building in the early 1920s. (The sculptural decorations on the neo-classical facade featured an eagle and a monumental "5%.") Tatra, and also the Orol Savings and Loan Co. (Slovenská Sporujúca a Požiavajúca Spoločnost'; later State Savings and Loan), each had main offices on one side of town, and a branch on the other. The greatest growth of these institutions took place in the 1920s when increased prosperity led to a surge in home building and buying. While successful during their early years, some of them, including First Slavonian, failed to survive the Depression, when customers were unable to make payments on their mortgages.[115]

A few Cleveland Slovaks ventured into real estate development and met with little success. Even schemes to help the homeland failed. For example, following World War I, Slovak businessmen joined in founding a million-dollar company, the Czechoslovak Commercial Corporation, to inject capital into the new country's economy. It lasted only a few years.[116]

Those individuals who did manage to move into the middle class accomplished this by continually advancing to better paying jobs until they could save enough to make a small investment. Paul Misenčik, who had worked as a laborer at a forge, a construction site, then the National Carbon Company, and later another Lakewood factory, finally saved enough to start his own business, undertaking. In some families, such as the Sčerbas and the Ondrejs, husband and wife worked together to make the business a success.[117]

Ján Pankuch built his successful printing, publishing, and travel business only after saving the wages he earned by working for others. His first newspaper, *Americký Slovák* (1892–94) was intended for a national readership, but failed. After a stint of publishing Slovak Lutheran newspapers, in 1907 Pankuch began publishing *Hlas* (*The Voice*), a weekly that served Cleveland's growing Slovak community at a time when events in the homeland were heightening national consciousness. It remained in publication until 1947. From 1915 to 1925, the years leading up to and following the establishment of Czechoslovakia, he published a daily, *Denný Hlas* (*Daily Voice*). Pankuch, along with Rev. Furdek, was acknowledged as a leader of Cleveland's Slovak community, active as a member and officer of numerous local and national organizations.[118]

Previous studies have indicated that Slovaks were less socially mobile than some other immigrant groups in America. Joseph Barton, in his comparative study of Slovaks, Romanians, and Italians in Cleveland, found that first and second generation Slovaks were economically, educationally, and socially less mobile than members of the other two groups. From 1930 to 1950, only twenty percent of Slovaks moved into a class different from that of their fathers.[119]

Another tabulation, based on a survey of Slovak parishes, showed that in 1930 over eighty percent of Slovak Roman Catholics still worked in factories, two-thirds of them as laborers and about fourteen percent as skilled workers.

Occupations of Cleveland Slovaks in Roman Catholic Parishes, 1930[120]

	Number	Percentage of total
Professionals	29	
Store owners	147	
Skilled workers	678	14.37
Laborers	66.88	
Farming families	12	

Slovaks were reputedly more interested in owning a house and a piece of land than moving into white-collar jobs. Compared to other first-generation immigrants, they had a high percentage of home ownership. Home ownership conferred its own status within the community, and resulted in neighborhood stability. Given the high rate of home ownership and the lack of aspiration to improved personal status among many of the property owners, Slovak neighborhoods retained their character longer than those of groups like the Czechs, whose more rapid mobility resulted in geographic dispersion.[121]

A small number of Slovaks entered the professions and became physicians, lawyers, or members of the clergy. The latter was the most popular and prestigious choice, at least among Roman Catholics. For example, while St. Benedict's parish counted nine professionals among its membership in 1930, six parishioners were studying for the priesthood. St. Andrew's had four professionals, but six candidates for the priesthood. St. Ladislaus counted only three professionals, but twenty-five of its female members would become nuns. Given the importance of religion to the Slovak community, such statistics were to be expected. Priests and nuns functioned as managers of the not inconsiderable infrastructure of the Catholic Church, as well as counselors, teachers, and community leaders.[122]

As for the secular professions, a list of Cleveland Slovaks active in law and medicine during the 1930s counted twenty-two lawyers and six physicians. Most had been born, or at least raised and educated in the United States; several of the lawyers went on to hold political offices at the state and local level. Even those who aspired to leadership in secular roles, however, needed and valued religious connections, and were usually active in church-based fraternal groups and in the church itself.[123]

These middle-class Slovaks, like their working-class counterparts, were likely to have been educated by the church as well. Early Slovak leaders in America had valued education not so much for its economic value, as for the moral training it provided, and for its role in preserving the Slovak language and Slovak culture. This, in part, represented a reaction to conditions in the homeland, where the government had used the schools to impose the Magyar language and culture. Given the importance of religion in Slovak tradition, distrust of state-sponsored education, and pressure from pastors and peers alike, most families sent their children to parochial schools.[124]

By 1915 there were five Slovak Catholic schools with an enrollment of 2,377. The remaining 1,558 Slovak children attended public elementary schools. The parochial schools reached their peaks of attendance in the mid-twenties and attendance at the Catholic schools remained high into the 1930s. Until the founding of Benedictine High School in 1928, Slovak students had no choice but to attend public high schools. As many as seventy-five percent of Slovak children entered public high schools during the twenties, but few received diplomas. Most left school for work.[125]

The Politics of Nationalism

Slovaks, like other immigrant groups, carried with them as cultural baggage the traditional attachments and antipathies of their homelands. Initially, whatever interest they had in politics was directed toward the situation in Europe, rather than American domestic affairs. Indeed, to begin with, it was not in the field of politics per se, but in everyday interaction with co-workers, neighbors, and fellow church or club members, that these friendships and hostilities were played out.

In the pre-World War I period, generally speaking, Slovak immigrants cooperated most closely with Czechs. Many instances of this cooperation in Cleveland, notably the sharing of clergy and church buildings, have already been mentioned. The connection between the two groups was a natural outgrowth of their proximity in Europe, and the fact that they spoke closely related languages. Prior to the establishment of Slovak neighborhoods, Slovaks in Cleveland had often settled in or near Czech neighborhoods, where they could find some cultural security and familiarity. Slovaks joined Czech benefit societies and singing groups, and held events in Czech halls. Czech writers in Cleveland, like their counterparts in Europe, spoke out against perceived Magyar oppression and supported the movement for Slovak rights in Hungary.[126]

Slovak and Czech interests did not, however, always perfectly mesh (as became obvious following the creation of the Czechoslovak state), nor were the two communities always in perfect harmony, however amicable the relationship appeared on the surface. Increasing national self-awareness made Slovaks very sensitive to anything they perceived as threatening to their identity. An underlying tension characterized some aspects of Slovak-Czech relations even before the First World War. Slovaks, who came largely from poor rural districts, felt, with some justification, that Czechs considered them ignorant and backward, and treated them in a patronizing manner. Moreover, the natural antipathy between freethinkers, an important part of the Czech community, and Roman Catholic and other religious loyalists, so influential among the Slovaks, formed a significant point of divergence.

As in so many other instances concerning the Slovak and other ethnic communities, however, it was often within the religious institutions (rather than between the church and those outside it) that the balance between harmony and hostility in Slovak-Czech relations tended to be upset. As has been mentioned, there was a shortage of qualified clergymen for the growing number of immigrant churches, with the result that the nationality of pastor and parishioner might differ, depending on whomever was available to fill the post. Ironically, the most prominent Slovak in the Cleveland community, Štefan Furdek, served in a Czech parish.

Born in Trstena, Slovakia, in 1855, Furdek studied for the priesthood in Prague, in part because seminaries in Slovakia were under Magyar control. He came to Cleveland in 1882, following Bishop Gilmour's request to the Prague seminary for a priest fluent in both Czech and Slovak. At this point, the number of Slovaks in Cleveland was still too small to warrant a separate parish. Rev. Furdek was first assigned to St. Wenceslaus, and then organized a new Czech parish, Our Lady of Lourdes. He was briefly assigned to another parish, but his Czech parishioners at Our Lady of Lourdes insisted on his return. He remained there for thirty-two years, until his death in 1915. His successor at Our Lady of Lourdes, the Czech cleric Oldřich Zlámal, eulogized him as "By birth Slovak . . . by education Czech and by conviction Pan-slav." He played an important role in fostering Slovak-Czech cooperation and was an active national officer of the First Czech-Roman Catholic Central Union. For all this, however, the welfare of his fellow Slovaks and the cause of Slovak nationalism, along with the upholding of the Roman Catholic faith, remained the causes nearest his heart. More than anyone else, he was responsible for promoting the word "Slovak," rather than "Slavish" or "Slavonian," as accepted English usage in the United States.[127]

The shortage of Slovak priests meant that Slovaks often had to accept Czech priests as their parish pastors. Most of these were Moravian, whose traditions and dialect resembled those of the Slovaks more closely than did those of Bohemian Czechs.[128] The predominance of Moravian and some Bohemian priests in Slovak parishes was so widespread that in the years before World War I, only one Slovak parish priest who remained at a church for any length of time, John Liščinský at St. Andrew Svorad, was of Slovak origin. In August 1908, a "Slovak Committee" at St. Wendelin accused the "Bohemians" of deliberately excluding Slovak priests from Slovak parishes and "conspiring" against Rev. Koudelka (a Moravian whom the Slovaks considered one of their own). Most Slovak parishioners, however, got along well with their Czech clergymen, barring the occasional disputes over finances or personalities that plagued parishes and congregations of all ethnicities, no matter what the national origins of the pastor. Rev. Necid, a Bohemian, was well-respected and admired in the Slovak community, as was Rev. Chaloupka of Nativity.[129]

Stefan Furdek's leadership set the tone for the generally amicable Slovak-Czech relations in Cleveland. It should be noted, however, that he had little love for the freethinking segment of the Czech community, and frequently denounced socialists and freethinkers in articles he wrote for the Cleveland Czech Catholic press. Jozef Hušek, a Cleveland Slovak and editor of *Jednota,* also attacked "Czech free-thinking democracy," and went further, promoting a separate Slovak identity: "Brothers, do not force on us your Czecho-Slovak mutuality. We do not care for your love. We are not giving you our own to taste. . . . We are not chauvinists but we wish to remain a nation of Slovaks with Czechs as our brothers."[130]

Nonetheless, at least until the postwar period, Slovaks and Czechs lived and worked together in reasonable harmony. Relationships with some other groups could be far less amicable. At work, Slovaks encountered problems with fellow employees. The culprits most often were other immigrants. "The Irish, Germans and other older immigrants incited their children . . . to make life unpleasant for the hated Slovak immigrant."[131]

By far more problematic than the contempt of old for new immigrant, however, was the uneasy relationship between Cleveland's Slovaks and Magyars, often vituperative and occasionally violent. Both nationalities had one of their largest settlements in America in Cleveland. The two groups often lived co-mingled (in the large Buckeye neighborhood, for example), as they had in the northern counties of Hungary, and culturally had much in common. The relationship in the homeland had been an unequal one, however, with Magyars in the ascendant, and prejudices and resentments were carried to the New World.

A particular grievance of the Slovaks was the Hungarian government's program of Magyarization, an attempt to meld the various nationality groups living in Hungary into a single cultural identity through use of the Magyar language in the schools, and similar measures. Slovak nationalism, which developed partly in reaction to this, was able to flourish in the freer atmosphere of the New World. One result was that once Slovak communities in American cities grew large enough to sustain their own institutions, churches and fraternal groups with mixed Slovak-Magyar membership became flashpoints for inter-ethnic conflict. In Cleveland, the controversy at St. Ladislas church set the tone for subsequent confrontations between the two groups.

The growth of Slovak national consciousness also brought those Slovaks identified as Magyarone in for a share of the anti-Magyar sentiment. During the 1890s, Cleveland's "Garfield" branch of the National Slovak Society expelled its Magyarone members—including a number of its officers—as a result of a disagreement over which flag, Slovak or Hungarian, would be used by the lodge.[132]

But the issue which received the greatest attention in the Cleveland mainstream press, as well as in ethnic newspapers both locally and nationally, was a conflict in 1902 over the erection of a statue of Hungarian leader Louis

Kossuth, considered by Slovaks as an oppressor, on the city's Public Square. Cleveland Slovaks banded together in vehement opposition to the proposed statue. The issue united Catholics and Protestants, and also created a working alliance of various Slavic groups, which foreshadowed the inter-ethnic cooperation of the World War I period. Slovaks, in their effort to halt the project, invited "every brother Slav, Czech, Pole, Russian, Croatian and Slovenian" to join them. In the course of lobbying Cleveland city officials and conducting a publicity campaign, they made an appeal to the broader community as well, by suggesting that only statues of *American* patriots should have a place on the city's central square.[133]

Since the city government eventually rescinded permission to erect the statue on Public Square, the anti-Kossuth faction claimed victory. (So did the Magyars, since they received permission to raise the statue at an alternative site.) Slovaks across America hailed the final verdict as a decisive triumph: "Praise to Our Brother Czechs and All Slavs," read a headline in a Pittsburgh Slovak paper. In Cleveland, a protest rally was turned into a victory celebration, with leaders of several ethnic groups taking turns denouncing Kossuth in speeches received with "most vociferous" ovations. The incident served to boost political self-confidence among Slovaks, encouraging them to take a more active role in debating issues that concerned them. It also resulted in the foundation of the Cleveland Slavic Alliance, a relatively short-lived umbrella organization intended to represent the interests of the city's Slavic immigrants.[134]

At Černová, Slovakia in 1907, Hungarian gendarmes fired into a crowd, killing a number of Slovak civilians, and provoking a storm of indignation and national fervor among Slovaks in America. In Cleveland, Slovaks united to form a Slovak National Committee (Slovenský Národný Výbor, later known as the Cleveland Slovak Alliance, Sdruženia Clevelandských Slovákov) under the presidency of Ján Pankuch. The Committee raised funds to aid the victims and to help elect Slovak delegates to the Hungarian parliament, and in 1907 authorized Pankuch to publish *Hlas*. Also in 1907, Cleveland hosted the National Slovak Congress, which led to the founding of the Slovak League of America. The congress, attended by over seven thousand people, was reportedly the largest gathering of Slovaks in the United States up to that time.

Not all Slovak-Magyar conflicts had political content. At weddings and other neighborhood gatherings where alcohol was freely served, "free-for-all fights which sent half the guests to hospitals with broken heads and landed the rest into police stations" sometimes broke out. In fact, declared one American observer, the feud between Slovaks and Magyars had been "explained so many times in police court that he [knew] the explanation by heart."[135]

In the period leading up to World War I, two additional public events, both visits of Hungarian leaders to the United States, gave Slovak and other immigrant groups a chance to attack the policies of the Hungarian government regarding national minorities and bring them to the attention of the American public. In 1911, Count Albert Apponyi delivered a speech on the subject of international peace in Cleveland. Opposition groups prepared their strategy for weeks beforehand. Were it not for Štefan Furdek's counsel, a direct and possibly violent confrontation might have occurred during Apponyi's visit. Instead, at Rev. Furdek's suggestion, Slovaks and their allies held a mass protest meeting at a separate location, thereby avoiding the type of ugly scene that took place in Chicago, the next stop on Apponyi's tour. There, police had to protect Apponyi from bodily harm when hecklers mobbed the stage during his speech; after the crowd was cleared out to prevent a riot, two bombs were discovered on the floor.[136] In 1914 Count Michael Károlyi, on a similar tour, also provided a focus for anti-Magyar sentiments among Cleveland's immigrant groups. He was presented with an open letter (as Apponyi had been) protesting the treatment of non-Magyar nationalities, but the visit passed off peacefully.[137]

World War I and the Creation of the Czecho-Slovak State

During the World War I years, the nationalities of the Austro-Hungarian Empire began first to hope, and then to plan, for their liberation and the creation of new, independent states following the end of the conflict. Again, issues which divided Magyars and Slovaks brought non-Magyar immigrant groups from the empire closer together. The Cleveland Slovak Alliance, which had reorganized as Branch No. 50 of the national organization, the Slovak League (founded in 1907), played an active role in mobilizing area Slovaks in support of the war.[138]

In 1915, the Bohemian National Alliance invited the Slovak League to attend a meeting at Cleveland's Bohemian National Hall to discuss the situation in Europe. Representatives of Czech and Slovak communities from across the United States gathered in Cleveland, where they announced their intention to work for the dissolution of Austria-Hungary and the creation of an independent, democratic state in the Czech and Slovak lands, with full autonomy and equality for both peoples. This group of Slovaks and Czechs was self-appointed, and had no authorization from people in the homeland or from the Czecho-Slovak National Council which later formed in Paris under the leadership of Thomas Garrigue Masaryk. Nonetheless, the Cleveland Agreement of October 25, 1915 preceded by three weeks the

Paris group's declaration of war on the Hapsburg Empire and intention to create a Czecho-Slovak state.[139]

In the American Slovak community, some disagreement existed over the degree of autonomy necessary for Slovakia. Cleveland became the center for those favoring autonomy, while a New York-based faction advocated a fully integrated "Czechoslovak" identity. *Denný Hlas* and the *New Yorkský Denník* carried on an embittered rivalry for the next decade.[140]

Despite differences between and within the Slovak and Czech communities, with the vision of an independent state as a unifying force, Slovak-Czech relations in Cleveland were, over the next four years, at their best since the early days of immigration. Both groups went to work collecting funds for the new state and later for the United States' war effort. They also set up a war committee and recruited ninety-six soldiers for the Czecho-Slovak Legion. (The relative number of Slovak and Czech men joining became a matter of contention; according to Ján Pankuch, the majority were Slovak.) A women's organization, *Včelky,* did needlework, held bazaars, and collected supplies, which went to the American Red Cross or the Slovak Legion.[141]

The great symbolic event of the war years was the visit of Thomas Masaryk to Cleveland in June 1918. But although the city's English-language newspapers painted a picture of perfect harmony between Slovaks and Czechs on the occasion, one of Masaryk's tasks while in the city was in fact to mediate between the two. Slovak members of a "revolutionary committee" organized by Cleveland Czechs and Slovaks to support the creation of an independent state expressed to Masaryk their fear that Czechs would dominate Slovaks in a common state, just as the Czech members, in their view, dominated the joint committee. Masaryk reassured them, as he had reassured Slovaks in Pittsburgh and elsewhere, that Slovaks would receive complete equality in the proposed nation.[142]

Masaryk's visit created a lingering atmosphere of good will between the two groups, as well as a favorable impression on the American public in general. But eventually, many Slovak-Americans came to consider his words as just another of the promises that was to be broken after the formation of the new state. In 1920, a centralist constitution changed the spelling of the republic's name from Czecho-Slovakia to Czechoslovakia. To many Slovaks, this orthography—with the two components merged into a single word, and Slovakia coming second and in lower case—aptly represented the place of Slovaks within the union.[143]

The developments in the homeland soured Slovak-Czech relations in Cleveland during the early post-war period, as evidenced by the recriminations that the two groups continually traded in the pages of their news-

papers. But overall, relations between the two groups were never uncompromisingly hostile, and tended to improve in subsequent years. As for Slovak-Magyar relations, while issues in the homeland, such as the treatment
of the Slovak minority in Hungary, and fears of Hungarian revanchism,
continued to create ill-will, the extreme hostility of the earlier period abated.
More than anything else, perhaps, the passage of time, and the coming of
age of the immigrants' children, and grandchildren, whose identity and
interests lay in America, marginalized the relevance of old-world hostilities
in everyday life.

Domestic Politics

Another indicator of Slovak acculturation into the broader community was
their increased involvement in local politics during the 1920s and 1930s. In
the early years of settlement, the relatively low numbers of Slovaks, their
status as "birds of passage," and their inability to communicate in English
meant that they had almost no political power, and no particular interest in
gaining it. In the post-war period, however, by which time many Slovaks
had decided to make the United States their home, become citizens, and
gained the right to vote, the situation changed. American politics began to
supersede international politics in relevance to their lives, and their greater
numbers gave them greater influence, particularly when they could be persuaded to vote as a part of a Slovak or Slavic bloc. Initially, their involvement
was limited to the role of voter, but in the 1920s several Slovaks, most of
them relatively young, American-educated lawyers, entered the political
arena as candidates.

As early as 1893, Cleveland Slovaks had formed a small political organization, the Slovak Republican Club. In addition to providing a forum for
political discussion, it took on the character of a fraternal self-help group.
As dues money accumulated in its treasury, it was able to use the funds to
help members in need. Also like the fraternal societies, the club promoted
camaraderie, since meetings ended with a one-hour "beer social." Eventually the club dropped its political functions, changed its name to the Cleveland Slovak Union, and became a purely fraternal organization, as did
another Republican club founded in Newburgh in 1899, which evolved into
a Jednota lodge. A Slovak Democratic Club also existed, founded at some
point before 1909.[144]

By the turn of the century, Slovak newspapers were endorsing candidates, usually based on issues or ethnicity rather than on party affiliation.
Democrat Tom Johnson, reformist mayor and champion of the three-cent

streetcar fare, drew accolades from the Slovak press, which had also endorsed Republican Theodore Burton's candidacy for the U.S. House of Representatives because of his support for public works projects. Slovaks were
also encouraged to vote for various Slavic candidates for local office.[145]

Although some Slovak leaders, notably Pankuch, were staunch Republicans, most Slovaks aligned themselves with the Democratic Party. As early
as 1906, Slovak neighborhoods showed a heavily Democratic voting pattern.
By 1930, one survey indicated that about two-thirds of Roman Catholic Slovaks voted Democratic, while a Republican source opined that eighty-five
percent of all Slovaks were Democrats.[146] However, Democrats could by no
means count on the Slovak vote as a given, particularly in the post-World
War I years. Candidates perceived as anti-immigrant could lose Slovak support, while those who ran on issues with a populist appeal gained Slovak
votes, regardless of party affiliation.[147] The Slovak Progressive Club, a non-
partisan organization founded in 1926, became the largest Slovak political
club in Cleveland, with five hundred members in 1927. It assisted Slovaks in
obtaining citizenship papers and sponsored recreational activities as well as
representing the interests of the Slovak community to Cleveland politicians
and government officials.[148]

The first Slovak to run for Cleveland city council, in 1913, was unsuccessful. Although a few other Slovaks ran for various state and local offices
during the 1910s, Slovaks did not attain any significant successes until the
1920s and 1930s. Lawyer Ján Smolka, a Democrat, was elected to Lakewood's
city council in 1925, and to the Ohio State Legislature in 1930. He received
support from the Slovak Republican League as well as from fellow Democrats.[149] Other Slovaks who entered politics in the 1920s included George
Tenesy, a Democrat, and Frank Soták, a Republican. Both men were lawyers,
who had attended law school in the evenings while working at other jobs
during the day. In the 1930s, Tenesy was named a municipal judge, becoming Cleveland's first Slovak judge. Soták was appointed to a position in
the Ohio attorney general's office. His wife, Mary Soták, also had an active
political career, becoming a member of the Ohio Republican Committee,
executive secretary of the Cuyahoga County Republican League, and a member of city council. In 1934, Štefan Zona was elected to the state legislature,
and served in Columbus for twenty years. He later served as mayor and then
judge in the Cleveland suburb of Parma.[150] In 1930, George Matovitz, a vet-
eran member of the Cleveland police force, and another graduate of evening
law school, was appointed Cleveland's chief of police, a position he held
for the next quarter-century.[151]

Despite success stories such as these, the overall number of Slovaks holding elected office or major government appointments during this period remained small, far from proportionately representative of their numbers in the Cleveland area. Nonetheless, the image of the Slovak community, and its position vis-à-vis the broader Cleveland community, had certainly changed over the preceding half century. The "Hunkie" boarder and itinerant laborer, who had come to Cleveland to work, earn money, and return to the Slovak homeland, soon became the householder, churchgoer, and American citizen.

As the character of the individual immigrant changed, so did that of the settlement. An institutional framework of church, school, and lodge anchored Cleveland's several self-contained Slovak neighborhoods, with residents focused upon building stable and prosperous lives for themselves and their families. The events of the World War I period brought the Slovak community out of isolation, and into conflict or alliance with other nationality groups, as well as before the attention of the American public. For those Americans observing the campaign for an independent Czecho-Slovak state, it seemed a wonderful example of two oppressed nationalities working together to create a new democratic state out of the ruins of an old world monarchy. Slovaks and Czechs, who were up to that point viewed as part of the undefined immigrant masses, now had an identity.

What the American public did not see was the divisive matter of ethnic identity that lay just below the surface. This juxtaposition of need and national aspiration which bound Cleveland's Czechs and Slovaks together and which, at the same time, contained the seeds of their division, epitomized the continuum of conflict and cooperation that existed among the city's ethnic groups. This and other such conflicts were, if not resolved, at least smoothed over by the process of acculturation and assimilation. Slovaks' valuing of economic security over social mobility tended to delay their entrance into the professions and other white-collar activities, and consequently into political leadership as well. Nonetheless, during the 1920s and 1930s, while still living, for the most part, in stable, identifiable Slovak neighborhoods, the immigrants and, especially, their children and grandchildren participated in the common economic and civic life shared by all Clevelanders.

Notes

1. For some histories of Cleveland Slovaks the most useful works for establishing a general framework were: Eleanor Ledbetter, *The Slovaks in Cleveland* (Cleveland:

Americanization Committee, 1919); Dan W. Gallager, "The Slovaks in Cleveland," *Cleveland News*, 16 January 1928; John Mihal, "Czechoslovakia—the Slovaks," *Cleveland News*, 9 January 1935; Ján Pankuch, *Dejiny Clevelandských a Lakewoodských Slovákov* (Cleveland: Pankuch Printing, 1930); Július Badzik, "Predmluva k dejinám slovenských osád v Cleveland, Ohio," *Furdek*, 15 July 1926, 17; W. G. Fordyce, "The Immigrant Groups of Cleveland, Ohio" (Columbus: Ohio State University, M.A. thesis, 1933); Works Progress Administration, *The Peoples of Cleveland* (Cleveland, 1942). More recent attempts to summarize the Slovaks in Cleveland are Susan Megles, Mark M. Stolarik, and Martina Tybor, *Slovak Americans and their Communities of Cleveland* (Cleveland: Cleveland State University, 1979); Joseph Barton, *Peasants and Strangers: Italians, Rumanians and Slovaks in an American City, 1890–1950* (Cambridge, Mass: Harvard University Press, 1975). Concerning the claim that Cleveland had the largest Slovak population of any city in the world, in 1900 Budapest had a Slovak population of 24,191, and thus it would definitely rank higher at the beginning of the twentieth century. By 1920, however, if one includes children born in America, the Cleveland-Lakewood Slovak community numbered over 32,000, which could rank it as the largest Slovak city. See the U.S. Bureau of the Census, *Fourteenth Census of the U.S.*, (1920), vol. II, 1008–1011, 1030–1037. For the Budapest data, see Vladislav Zápletal, *Slovenské socialné demokratické dělnické hnuti v Budapešti*, Olomouc, 1969, 3; Slovak Research Institute of America, *The Unconquerable Slovaks*, (Lakewood, 1989), 1.

2. Although "Slovakia" was not a defined political entity until after the war, the term is used in this study for the earlier time period as well, as an alternative to the somewhat awkward "the Slovak homeland," or "Slovakland," a term that the immigrants themselves frequently used to identify their country.

3. *Slovensko: Priroda* (Bratislava: Obzor, 1972), 11; Václav Beneš, "Czechoslovak Democracy and Its Problems," *A History of the Czechoslovak Republic 1918–1948*, eds. V. Mamatey, R. Luža (Princeton, 1973), 40; Emily Green Balch, *Our Slavic Fellow Citizens* (New York, 1910), 97–98.

4. See map "Die Nationalitaetenvestennisse in Königreich Ungarn 1910," *Anapkelet Lexikona* (Budapest, 1927).

5. Balch, *Our Slavic*, 96. Data compiled from *the Annual Reports of the Commissioner General of Immigration, 1899–1910*, and Baska Papers, Slovak Institute (hereafter cited SI). 1910 Census data compiled by Matjaž Klemenčič, University of Maribor. On education cf. Owen Johnson, *Slovakia: Education and the Making of a Nation, 1918–1938* (Boulder: East European Monographs, 1983).

6. František Bielik et. al., *Slováci vo svete*, (Martin: Matica Slovenska, 1980), vol. 2, 13–14; P. Slabey, "Prehl'ad dejín Slovákov v Amerike," *Kalendár N.S.S., 1926, 42*.

7. J. A. Ferienčik, a leading Slovak journalist in Cleveland, assigned the Jews as primarily responsible for Slovaks' emigration to America. He claimed that Jews from Galicia came south to Slovakia and established saloons and took advantage of the poor Slovak peasant who was weak-willed when it came to alcohol. Cf. his "Načrtok dejín prist'ahovalectva slovenského do Ameriky," *Sborník Národného Sloven-*

ského Spolku, 1(1915), no 2–3, 9–10; also Slabey, "Prehl'ad," 42. Migration from Slovakia for seasonal work began as early as in the late 17th century, and increased during the 18th and 19th centuries. Slovaks journeyed to the Hungarian and Austrian lowlands for seasonal work, and in the nineteenth century increasingly headed south and westward to work in the large construction projects and expanding industries in Budapest and Vienna. Smaller numbers ventured farther away, to German factories and mines, mainly in Westphalia and Porynia. Cf. Jozef M. Rydlo, *Slováci v europskom zahraniči včera a dnes* (Lausanne: Liber, 1976), 26–27, 41–44; also Michael J. Kopanic, "Industrial Trade Unions in Slovakia, 1918–1929" (Ph.D. diss., University of Pittsburgh, 1986), 35–41; Bielik, *Slováci,* vol. 2, 16–17.

8. *Slovenské vyst'ahovalectvo. Dokumenty,* ed. F. Bielik (Martin: Matica Slovenská, 1978), vol. 3, 14; Tajtak, "Slovak," 55–63; Barton, *Peasants,* 32–33, 57.

9. Bodnar, *The Transplanted,* 2.

10. *Katolícke Noviny,* no. 76, 1900, as quoted by K. Čulen. Also Mark Stolarik, "Slovak Migration from Europe to North America, 1870–1918," *Slovak Studies* XX (Cleveland-Rome, 1980), 5–24.

11. Based on *Annual Report of the Commissoner General of Immigration,* 1899–1914.

12. Harold C. Livesay, "From Steeples to Smokestacks: The Birth of the Modern Corporation in Cleveland," *The Birth of Modern Cleveland, 1865–1930,* ed. Thomas F. Campbell and Edward M. Miggins (Cleveland: Western Reserve Historical Society, 1988), 54–70; Joseph S. Roucek, *The Czechs and Slovaks in America* (Minneapolis: Lerner Publ., 1967), 46; Jozef Stasko, *Slovaks in the United States of America* (Cambridge, Ontario: Dobrá Kniha, 1974), 25–27; Jozef Stasko, "Distinctive Characteristics of Slovak Immigration to America," *Czechoslovak and Central European Journal* 9 (1990, nos. 1–2), 91–94.

13. Sample from Klemenčič census survey. In detail the figures for the sample are: before the year 1890—16.2%, 1891–1895—12.9%, 1896–1900—9.5%, 1901–1905—25.7%, 1906–1910—35.2%.

14. U.S. Bureau of Census, *Thirteenth Census of the U.S.* (Washington, D.C., 1910*); Fourteenth Census of the U.S.* (Washington, D.C., 1920), vol. 2, 1008–1011, 1030–1037; *Jednota,* 29 May 1912, 5; Howard Whipple Green, *Population Characteristics by Census Tracts: Cleveland, Ohio, 1930* (Cleveland: The *Plain Dealer,* 1931), 29. In 1918 Ledbetter used parish and congregation data to arrive at an estimate of 35,000 Slovaks—cf. Ledbetter, *The Slovaks,* 16, 25.

15. A.P. Slabey, "When Rovnianek Came to the U.S.A.," *Národný Kalendár N.S.S.* 1967, 191–196; J.A. Ferienčik, "Slovenské prist'ahovalectvo a slovenská spisba v Amerike," *Pamätník Národného Slovenskeho Spolku v S.S.A.,* 22–26. One of the best and most descriptive accounts of the Slovak immigrants' first experiences in America is Mark Stolarik, *Growing Up on the South Side* (1988), chapter 1; Ferienčik, "Náčrtok dejín," 9–19; Balch, *Our Slavic,* 106–107.

16. Dan Gallagher, "The Slovaks in Cleveland," *Cleveland News,* Jan. 16, 1928; Pankuch, *Dejiny,* 6–7.

17. Pankuch, *Dejiny,* 18–19.

18. Pankuch, *Dejiny,* 5–7, 203; *Cleveland Press,* 18 January 1941; Barton, *Peasant,* 71. Roskoš related his early experiences to Pankuch, the journalist, fraternal leader, and political activist who gathered considerable information and interviewed some of the first Slovak immigrants in the city for *A History of the Cleveland and Lakewood Slovaks.* Although he was not a historian by profession, Pankuch's book remains the best single source for Slovak history in the area. The Western Reserve Historical Society has published a translation of Pankuch's history.

19. Gallagher, "The Slovaks"; John Mihal, "Czechoslovakia—the Slovaks," *Cleveland News,* Jan. 9, 1935; Pankuch, 5–6. According to the Dillingham (officially, Immigration) Commission, out of 176 foreign-born individuals living on Commercial Road, 117 were Slovaks. *Reports of the Immigration Commission* (hereafter cited as RIC), vol. 26, *Immigrants in Cities,* vol. 26, Part VI, *Cleveland. Statistics* (Washington, 1911), 513–520; Megles et al, *Slovak Americans,* 110.

20. Church and School Report for the year Ending December 31, 1888, St. Ladislaus Parish Papers (hereafter LPP), ADC. Some sources also spell St. Ladislas as St. Ladislaus.

21. *Parishes,* 136; "History of the Slovak Parish of St. Ladislaus," typescript, 3–5, LPP; Historical Data of St. Ladislaus, 1888, 1889. LPP *75th Anniversary St. Ladislaus Church* (Cleveland, 1961); *Pamätný Program Oslavy 50. Ročného Jubilea Zlate Jubileim Osady Sv. Ladislava* (Cleveland, 1939); *1889–1914. Pamatník Dvatsat pät rokov v osade sv. Ladislava* (Cleveland, 1914); *Cleveland News,* 18 January 1941; Julius Badzik, "Predmluva k dejinám slovenských osád v Cleveland, Ohio," *Furdek,* 15 July 1926, 17.

22. Historical Data of St. Ladislaus Parish, LPP; St. Ladislas Church, Cleveland, O. 1885–1899, mss, Lazur Papers, SI.

23. Baptismal registers, St. Ladislas Parish, Westlake, Ohio; Lazur Papers, SI.

24. Baska Papers, 716; Megles, 135–7; Badzik, *Furdek,* July 15, 1926, 18.

25. Ledbetter, *The Slovaks,* map, 11. For the overall picture of immigrant settlement the Immigration Bureau map, dating from 1915, in the Cleveland Public Library, is among the best sources; also Howard Whipple Green's maps (1930) in the Cleveland Public Library's City Hall collection. Cf. also Donald Levy, *A Report on the Location of Ethnic Groups in Greater Cleveland* (Cleveland, 1972), for more recent data.

26. Pankuch, *Dejiny,* 28, 212; Petition to Bishop Horstmann, 14 February 1902; Chancellor to John Hedegetz, 22 August 1902; Second Petition, 1 September 1902; Financial Report 1903; Historical Data of St. Mary Nativity Church, 1904, Nativity B.V.M. Parish Papers, ADC; John Sobol, *Nativity Memories, 1903–1984,* (Cleveland, 1984); Baska papers, 712.

27. *Pamätník posviacky nového kostola Sv. Andreja Svorada* (Cleveland, 1926); Ledbetter, 23; Megles et al, 135; Pankuch, 218–219; DOC Archives, Historical Reports of the Parish of St. Andrew, 1945; Baska papers, 715.

28. Megles et al, *Slovak Americans,* 129, 135, 151; Pankuch, *Dejiny,* 214–217, 220–222; Ledbetter, 21; *Strieborný jubilium osady sv. Vendelina, Cleveland, Ohio,*

1903–1928 (Cleveland, 1928); Historical Report of the Parish of St. Wendelin, type-script, 1945, St. Wendelin Parish Papers, ADC; *Dedication of Our Lady of Mercy Church* (Cleveland, 1949); interviews with Joe Hornack, Joe Labuda, April–May 1988; *Plain Dealer,* 22 February 1987, G1, 4.

29. James and Susan Borchert, *Lakewood: The First Hundred Years* (Norfolk-Virginia Beach, Virginia: The Donning Company Publishers, 1989), 40–41; James and Susan Borchert, "The Bird's Nest: Making of an Ethnic Urban Village," *The Gamut,* no 2 (Summer, 1987); James and Susan Borchert, "Migrant Responses to the City: The Neighborhood, Case Studies in Black and White, 1870–1940," *Slovakia,* 31(1984), 8–45; Ledbetter, 23; Megles et al, 132–3, 135; Pankuch, *Dejiny,* 19, 22–33, 218–9, 235–40.

30. Interview with Joseph Hornack, April 1988; Immigration Commission Map, 1915, Cleveland Public Library.

31. Megles et al, *Slovak Americans,* 110.

32. *RIC,* vol. 26, Part 6, 513–514.

33. Borchert and Borchert, *Lakewood,* 60–61. Also see other Borchert works cited in note 29.

34. *RIC,* vol. 26, Part 6, 521–25, 538–45.

35. *Ibid.,* 525–28, 530.

36. Stolarik, *Immigration and Urbanization: The Slovak Experience, 1870–1918* (New York, AMS Press, Inc., 1989), 41–42. Stolarik disproved Barton's claim that Slo-vaks did not migrate in chains by his intricate study of county and village origins. The pattern also held true for the Catholic church marriage records examined for the present study. In St. Martin parish, all but a small number of the children bap-tized in the early years had both parents from Slovakia. Lazur papers, Baptismal Registry, St. Martin of Tours Parish, Maple Heights, Ohio.

37. "V novej zemi," *Kalendár Jednota,* 1911, 75–89; Megles et al, *Slovak Americans,* 110; Pankuch, 7.

38. Pankuch, *Dejiny,* 7, 18–9.

39. Baska Papers, SI; Štefan Furdek, "Z Ameriky," *Tovaryšstvo* (Ruzomberok), vol. 1 (1893), 233. The *Annual Reports of the Commissioner General of Immigration, 1899–1910,* also list given occupation upon U.S. entry.

40. Interview with Jewel Muffler, July 1988; Jozef Paučo, *Slovenskí Priekopníci v Amerike* (Cleveland, 1972), 299–301; K.B., "Večnek na pamiatku Jána Pankucha," *Národný Kalendár NSS* (1969), 66–67; Andrej Rolnik, "Ján Pankuch st.—Ako som ho poznal," *Kalendár NSS* (1976), 16 ff; *Národné noviny,* 5 March 1952, 6.

41. Pankuch, *Dejiny,* 21–2; "Zo starého slovenského Clevelandu," Cleveland folder, SI.

42. Pankuch, *Dejiny,* 22.

43. Interview with Joe Labuda, 26 June 1988; Megles et al, *Slovak Americans,* 149; Stolarik, *Immigration,* 26–28; Baska survey, SI; Alec Lazur Papers, SI.

44. Susan Mandzak, unpublished manuscript, 1984, 3.

45. Julius Badzik, "Predmluva k dejinám slovenských osád v Cleveland, Ohio," *Furdek,* 15 July 1926, 17; Pankuch, *Dejiny,* 227; Historical Data of St. Ladislaus Church, 1888, LPP, ADC; Works Projects Administration, *Parishes of the Catholic Church Diocese of Cleveland: History and Records* (Cleveland, 1942), 136–8.

46. St. Ladislas was the first Slovak church to be built in Ohio and the seventh oldest Slovak church in the United States. See Joseph Hornack, Cleveland, Ohio and Cuyahoga County 1880 to the Present and its Slovak Identification, http://www.iarelative.com/krakovany/cleveland.htm; Pankuch, *Dejiny,* 15, 203; Badzik, "Predmluva," 17; WPA, *Parishes,* 136; "History of the Slovak Parish of St. Ladislas," 3–5, ADC; *75th Anniversary of St. Ladislas Church* (Cleveland, 1961); *Pamätný Program, Oslavy 50. Ročného Jubilea Zlaté Jubileum Osady Sv. Ladislava* (Cleveland, 1939); *1899–1914 Pamätnik Dvatsat pät rokov v osade sv. Ladislava* (Cleveland, 1914); Historical Data of St. Ladislas, 1888, 1889, ADC; "St. Ladislas Church, Cleveland, O., 1885–1899"; Baska, 706, SI. Also see chapter by Puskás regarding the Magyar community and St. Ladislas.

47. Pankuch, *Dejiny,* 12–13; *Plain Dealer,* 3 August 1891, 2; letter to the Diocese, ADC.

48. Pankuch, *Dejiny,* 13–14; "History of the Slovak Parish of St. Ladislas," ADC.

49. Correspondence between the bishop and Revs. Martvoň and Panuška, 1892–1894, Horstmann Letters, v. J, Box 1, ADC.

50. WPA, *Parishes;* "History of the Slovak Slovak Parish of St. Ladislas," 9–11; "St. Ladislas Church, Cleveland, O., 1885–1899."

51. Van Tassel and Grabowski, eds., *ECH,* 519.

52. Pankuch, *Dejiny,* 204; Badzik, "Predmluva," 17; Baska Papers, 704, SI; WPA, *Parishes,* 136; "History of the Slovak Parish of St. Ladislas," 9–11; "St. Ladislas Church, Cleveland, O., 1885–1899"; Church and School Report, 1894, St. Martin's Parish Memo, 9 September 1960, 2–3, and St. Martin's Parish [1948?], ADC.

53. Church and School Reports, St. Ladislas, 1903, 1905; "History of the Slovak Parish of St. Ladislas," 9–11; "Historical Report of the Parish of St. Ladislas, Cleveland, Ohio, from the Time of Its Erection to December 1945," ADC; Baska Papers, 704, SI. Rev. Svozil was also a Moravian.

54. Baptismal Registry, St. Martin of Tours Parish, Maple Heights, Ohio; Church and School Report, 1894, St. Martin's Parish Memo, 9 September 1960, 2–3, St. Martin's Parish [1948?], and St. Martin's church history, n.d., ADC.

55. "Historical Report of the Parish of SS. Cyril and Methodius," 1945, ADC; Baska Papers, 705, 710, SI; Pankuch, *Dejiny,* 210; *Nový Kostol SSV. Cyrilla a Metoda Budovany, 1929, 1930, 1931* (Cleveland, 1931); SS. Cyril and Methodius parish records, Status animarum, 1914, 1918, ADC; Lazur Papers, SI.

56. *Pamätník Strieborný jubilium osady sv. Vendelina, Cleveland, Ohio, 1903–1928* (Cleveland, 1928), *Rubinové Jubileum Osady Sv. Vendelina* (Cleveland, 1943), *Sixtieth Anniversary St. Wendelin Church* (Cleveland, 1964), and Historical Report of the Parish of St. Wendelin, typescript, 1945, ADC; Pankuch, *Dejiny,* 214–5. It will be noted that all of the first group of Slovak parishes founded followed a similar pattern: after

an initial period of high turnover in their pastorates, at some point before 1910, a priest arrived at each parish who would remain there at least into the 1920s, and in several cases well beyond that. The same thing occurred at Holy Trinity Lutheran Church.

57. Historical Report of the Parish of St. Wendelin, typescript, 1945, ADC; *Pamätník z príležitosti otvorenia novej siene v Osade Sv. Vendelina* (Cleveland, 1937).

58. Historical Report of the Parish of St. Andrew, 1945, ADC; *75th Anniversary St. Andrews Church* (Cleveland, 1981); Baska Papers, 715, SI; Pankuch, *Dejiny,* 218–9; *Pamätník Posviacky Nového Kostola Sv. Andrej Svorad* (Cleveland, 1926), 8–9, 20–22; St. Andrew's Church records, SI.

59. Petition to Bishop Horstmann, 14 February 1902, and other correspondence, 1902, ADC; Financial Report, B.V.M. Parish, 1903, ADC; Historical Data of St. Mary Nativity Church, 1904, ADC; John Sabol, *Nativity Memories, 1903–1984* (Cleveland, 1984), 2; Pankuch, *Dejiny,* 212–3; Baska Papers, 712, SI; *Ruby Jubilee 1909–1949, Rev. Vaclav A. Chaloupka, Nativity of B.V.M. Church* (Cleveland, 1949).

60. Nativity of the Blessed Virgin Mary parish records (1903–1939), Lazur Papers, SI; Sabol, *Nativity Memories,* 3; Historical Data of St. Mary Nativity Church, 1909, and Status Animarum, ADC.

61. *Dedication of Our Lady of Mercy Parish* (Cleveland, 1949), 13; Baska Papers, 714, SI; letter, 6 October 1921, ADC.

62. *Dedication of Our Lady of Mercy Parish,* 13–14; Baska Papers, 714, SI; Historical Data, Our Lady of Mercy Church, 1921, Letter to Rev. Farrelly, February 1916, Letters to Rev. Schrembs, 6 October and 3 November 1921, ADC; Ledbetter, 21; Megles et al, 135.

63. Baska Papers, 716–7, and Baska survey, 171, SI; Megles et al, 135–7; Joseph Cincik, *The Church of St. Benedict* (Cleveland, 1953), 3; Pankuch, *Dejiny,* 223–4; "Osada sv. Benedikta, Cleveland, O.," *Pamätník, Program Slavnosti Slovenského Dňa* (Cleveland, 1929).

64. It might be added that an "Association of Cleveland Slovaks," which included both Catholic and Protestant representatives, originally in 1916 discussed the possibility of opening a Slovak national high school; the project collapsed duri to opposition from the priests. Stolarik, "Slovak Migration," 96–97; "Rt. Rev. Abbot Stanislaus F. Gmuca, O.S.B.," *Furdek,* 1968, 132–6; Megles et al, 137; Stolarik, 94–97; Pankuch, *Dejiny,* 224–5; Baska Papers, 718–9, SI; "Benedictine High School for Boys, Cleveland, Ohio," *Furdek,* 1967, 112–4; *Slovenská Vyššia Škola a Slovenskí Benediktini, Pamätník* (1929); Fr. Andrew V. Pier, O.S.B., "Six Decades of Slovak Apostolate by Benedictines in Cleveland," *Furdek,* 1982, 119–121.

65. Paul R. Magocsi, *Our People* (Toronto, 1984), 9; Paul Magocsi, *The Shaping of a National Identity: Sub-carpathian Rus', 1848–1948* (Cambridge, Mass., 1978); Morawska, *For Bread,* 377, n. 51; interviews with Slovak and Rusyn Greek Catholic church members in Cleveland, June–July, 1988; Susan Mandzak, unpublished manuscript, 2, ADC; Megles et al, *Slovak Americans,* 138; Ledbetter, *The Slovaks,* 23–24;

Jednota, 28 September 1898, 1; Pankuch, *Dejiny,* 62; Baska Papers, SI, 717. Many Ukrainians claim that the Rusyns are not a separate nationality but simply a branch of Ukrainian. Nicholas Zentos has estimated that as many as 30,000 "Carpatho-Russians" lived in Cleveland during the 1930s (Van Tassel and Grabowski, eds., ECH, 154–155). The figure includes not only Rusyns, but Lemkos from Polish areas as well. Rusyns, however, do have some different traditions and have historically been closer with the Slovaks and Magyars since they lived in Hungary.

66. *Dedication Album. Saint John's Hungarian Greek Catholic Church* (Cleveland, 1954); *85 Years, St. John the Baptist Hungarian Byzantine Church, Cleveland, Ohio* (Cleveland, 1977); *Byzantine Catholic Cathedral of St. John the Baptist* (Parma, 1971); *Plain Dealer,* 8 November 1948; Van Tassel and Grabowski, eds., ECH, 145; *Solemn Blessing and Dedication of the Holy Ghost Parochial School* (Cleveland, 1958); *Golden Jubilee of Holy Ghost Greek Catholic Church, Cleveland, Ohio, 1909–1059; Holy Ghost Greek Catholic Church, Cleveland, Ohio, 1909–1984, Diamond Jubilee;* Mandzak, manuscript; *St. Gregory the Theologian Byzantine Catholic Church, Sept. 1905–Sept. 1980* (Lakewood, 1980); *Golden Jubilee and Re-Dedication of St. Gregory's Greek Catholic Church - Lakewood, Ohio* (Lakewood, 1955).

67. *St. Joseph's Byzantine Catholic Church, 1913–1963* (Cleveland, 1963); Baptismal Register, 1916–1924, St. Joseph's Byzantine Catholic Church; interview with Mary Janacko, June 1988.

68. David P. Daniel, "The Protestant Reformation and Slovak Ethnic Consciousness," *Slovakia,* 28 (1978–1979), 49–64.

69. Ledbetter, 19–20; Pankuch, *Dejiny,* 265–6, 270; George Dolak, *A History of the Slovak Evangelical Lutheran Church in the United States of America, 1902–1927* (St. Louis, 1955), 24–26, 34–45; June Alexander, *The Immigrant Church and Community: Pittsburgh's Slovak Catholics and Lutherans, 1885–1915* (Pittsburgh: University of Pittsburgh Press, 1987), 67–71.

70. Pankuch, *Dejiny,* 226–229; Dolak, *History,* 24, 26; L. A. Jarosi, "Zo života Sv. Trojice, Cleveland, Ohio," *Sion Ev. Kalendár* (1911), 101–102; *Pamätník Evanjelickej Augsburgskeho Vyznania Cirkvi S. Trojci* (Cleveland, 1953?), 3–7, 28–30; The minutes of the church society are found in Prvý *Evanjelický Slovenský Spolok Sv. Trojice založeni dňa 14. Februara roku 1892 v Cleveland, O.;* Baska Papers, 720, SI; Pankuch, *Výťah z Dejín Slovenského Evanjelického Aug. Vyznania Cirkvi Sv. Petra a Pavla v Lakewood, Ohio* (Lakewood, Ohio, 1927), 4–6.

71. Colin F. Moore and Sherri L. Bures, "The Slovak Lutheran People in the City of Cleveland, Ohio" (unpublished seminar paper, Cleveland State University, 1978), 8–9; Dolak, *History,* 42; Pankuch, *Dejiny,* 231–3; Megles et al, 127. Bruhac later served as organist-teacher at Martin Luther Church for thirty-eight years. Organists frequently had a special role in Slovak Lutheran churches.

72. *Pamätník Evanjelickej,* 10–11, 34–5, 38–9; Moore and Bures, "Slovak Lutheran People," 12–13; Baska Papers, 722, SI; Dolak, *History,* 145; Pankuch, *Dejiny,* 233–4.

73. Moore and Bures, "Slovak Lutheran People," 12–13; Baska Papers, 721, SI.

74. Pankuch, *Výťah z Dejín*, 4–8; Pankuch, *Dejiny*, 230–1, 235; *Saints Peter and Paul Lutheran Church, Seventy-Fifth Anniversary* (Lakewood, Ohio, 1976).

75. Pankuch, *Výťah z Dejín*, 12–13; *Hlas*, 13 March 1918, 3.

76. Pankuch, *Výťah z Dejín*, 14–18; *Hlas*, 20 March 1918, 7.

77. Interview with Rev. Robert Matej, 1988; Pankuch, *Dejiny*, 238, 244; Pankuch, *Výťahz Dejín*, 18–42; *Saints Peter and Paul, Seventy-Fifth Anniversary*.

78. Alexander, 69–70.

79. Moore and Bures, "Slovak Lutheran People," 12; *Zlaté jubileum založenia Ev. A.V.V. Cirkev Dr. Martin Luther* (Cleveland, 1960); Rev. M. F. Benko, "Historícky Načrt Cirkvi 'Dr. Martin Luther' na Západ 14. Ulici Cleveland, Ohio," in Pankuch, *Dejiny*, 241–3; *Pamätník Evanjelickej*, 39; Baska Papers, 723, SI; Ledbetter, 23.

80. On the missionary work of Protestants in America see Kenneth D. Miller, *The Czecho-Slovaks in America* (New York: George Doran Co., 1922).

81. A. J. Moncol, "Cyrilská Slovenská Kongregačná cirkev na západnej strane," in Pankuch, *Dejiny*, 247–8; Ledbetter, 25; Baska Papers, 726, SI.

82. Vaclav Vojta, *Czechoslovak Baptists* (Minneapolis: Czechoslovak Baptist Convention in American and Canada, 1941), 16–97.

83. Ohio Baptist Convention, Committee on foreign-speaking people, Columbus Committee Report, 21 October 1912, WPA, box 21, WRHS; Cleveland Baptist Association, *150 years of Mission to Greater Cleveland, 1832–1982*, 7–8, 85–6; Vojta, *Czechoslovak Baptists*, 168–174; Baska Papers, 727; *Cleveland City Directory*, 1912–13, 1484, and 1921, 1503; Moncol in Pankuch, *Dejiny*, 250.

84. *Pamätnica zlatého jubilea Slovenskej Kalvínskej Presbyterianskej Jednoty v Amerike* (1951), 68–99, 214–5, 251; Rev. F. J. Uherka, "Slovenská Kalvínska Cirkev v Lakewood, Ohio," in Pankuch, *Dejiny*, 78–9, 213–4, 251–6; interview with Michael Kovac, June 1988; Megles et al, 170. See also Stephen Szabo, *Thirtieth Anniversary Album of the First Hungarian Reformed Church* (Cleveland, 1979). Most of the church's Slovak members were Magyarized; Slovaks are not mentioned as such in this album.

85. Howard F. Stein, "An Ethnohistory of Slovak American Religious and Fraternal Associations: A Study in Cultural Meaning, Group Identity, and Social Institutions," *Slovakia*, 29 (1980–1981, nos. 53–54), 64. Konštantín Čulen, *Dejiny Slovákov v Amerike*, v. 1 (Bratislava: Nakladateľstvo Slovenskej Ligy), 195; Kopanic, "Industrial Trade," 551–552, notes 4–6; *Slovensko: Dejiny* Jín Tibenský ed. (Bratislava: Obzor, 1978), 248, 276; Stolarik, *Immigration and Urbanization*, 43–44, 69–73; Alexander, 18.

86. *Jednota*, 29 May 1912, 508; 20 September 1989, 4; 20 December 1989, 4; 10 January 1990, 4; Megles, Stolarik, *Slovak Americans*, 118–120; Daniel Tanzone, "Slovak Fraternal Organizations," *Slovakia*, XXV (1975, no 48), 68–71; Stolarik, *Immigration*, 46–48; Anthony X. Suthlerland, "Slovak American Organizations," *Jednota*, 10 January 1990, 4; Sutherland, "A Century," 299–314; *Hlas*, 4 September 1925, 1; 4, September 30, 1925, 2; *Národné Noviny*, 2 November 1927, 6; 11 July 1928.

87. Pankuch, *Dejiny,* 28, 262–6; interview with Joe Kopčo, April 1988; Anthony Sutherland, "A Century of Fraternalism: Jednota—The First Catholic Slovak Union, 1890–1990," unpublished manuscript (1991), 8–10; *Kniha dejín Spolku Sv. Jozefa čislo 1.* Jednoty," *Jednota,* 28 September 1898, 1; *Jednota,* 1 March 1922, 1; Anthony X. Sutherland, "The Twelve Men," *Jednota,* 19 July 1989, 4; *Zoloto-Jubilejnyj Kalendár Grécko Kat. Sojedninenja,* ed. Michael Roman (Munhall, 1942), 35–56, 339–342, 349, 399, 401.

88. Paučo, *75 Rokov,* 10–11.

89. *Ibid.,* 50–51; Sutherland, "Some Reasons for forming a Jednota Branch," *Jednota,* 20 September 1989, 4; Uherka, in Pankuch, *Dejiny,* 78–9; Megles et al, 120.

90. Pankuch, *Dejiny,* 85, 266; Stolarik, *Immigration,* 47, 78; *Pennsylvania Slovak Catholic Union Diamond Jubilee* (Pittston, Pa., 1968).

91. J.A.F. [Ferienčik], "Slovenské pristaholalectvo a slovenská spisba v Amerike," *Pamätnik Národného Slovenského Spolku v S.S.A.,* 22–26; Vladimir Baumgarten and Joseph Stefka, *The National Slovak Society 100 Year History* (1990), 9–11, 28; Čulen, *Dejiny,* 208–209; Pankuch, *Dejiny,* 9, 257–258; Megles et al, *Slovak Americans,* 115; *Souvenir Book. Twenty-first Regular Convention of the National Slovak Society* (Cleveland, 1954), 115.

92. *Slovenská Ozvena,* 7 August 1929, 5; *Denný Hlas,* 20 May 1918, 1; 24 May 1918, 1; Pankuch, *Dejiny,* 26–27, 271–272.

93. "Review of Sokol History," *Souvenir Book, 60th Anniversary* (1965); Stolarik, *Immigration,* 47; Pankuch, *Dejiny,* 270; Sutherland, "A Century," 293–297. For the Sokol movement, also see chapter by Chrislock.

94. Pankuch (and Uherka in Pankuch), *Dejiny,* 78–9, 213–4, 276–277; Ledbetter, *The Slovaks,* 19–20; *Pamätnica zlatého jubilea Slovenskej Kalvínskej Presbyterianskej Jednoty v Amerike* (1951), 68–69, 251.

95. Slovenský robotnícky spolok, *Pamätnik 1915–1925* (Chicago: Rovnost Ludu, 1925), 5–6, 131–2; Miloš Gosiorovský, "Contribution to the History of the Slovak Workers' Society in the United States of America," *Historica, Sborník Filozofickej Fakulty Univerzity Komenského,* XII–XII (1961–1962), 11–12; *Rovnost' L'udu,* 27 March 1918, 3; 11 December 1918, 3; 19 March 1919; 14 May 1919, 2–3.

96. Sutherland, "Slovak Ladies Fraternals," *Jednota,* 21 February 1990, 4; Sutherland, "Century," 141–2; Pankuch, *Dejiny,* 266–269; *Cleveland Press,* 10 January 1935; Stolarik, *Immigration,* 78; Baumgarten and Stefka, 28.

97. Krajsa, 18; Sutherland, "Slovak Ladies"; Pankuch, *Dejiny,* 267–9; Sutherland, "Century," 162–163.

98. Pankuch, *Dejiny,* 270.

99. Jeanette Tuhe interview with Margaret Revacko Henning, March 1987; *Jednota,* 21 May 1902, *Hlas,* 19 March 1913, *Denný Hlas* 4 February 1920, 3; Otis Steel Company employee records, uncatalogued, WRHS.

100. Slovak parish records, ADC; Baska Papers, SI; Jeanette Tuhe interview with Margaret Revacko Henning, and with Ann Kovala Hudak, February 1986; Barton, *Peasants,* 130–133.

101. Barton, *Ibid.*, 120–22, 143.

102. *Cleveland Press,* 5 March 1934.

103. *Cleveland Press,* 21 February 1934.

104. David Brody, *Labor in Crisis: The Steel Strike of 1919* (Philadelphia: J. B. Lippincott Co., 1965), 38–44; Stolarik, *Immigration,* 62; interviews with Mr. Polomsky, George Tomšek, July 1988.

105. *Jednota,* 24 August 1898, 1; 4 November 1903, 1; 14 December 1910, 1; Jozef Paučo, *Stefan Furdek a slovenské prist'ahovalectvo* (Middletown, Penna., 1955), 84–7.

106. Stolarik, "Slovak Immigration," 49; interview with George Tomsek.

107. *Americké dělnícke listy,* 7 March 1913, 1; 14 March 1913, 2; 6 February 1914, 3; *Denný Hlas,* 26 April 1919, 3 May 1919, 4; ADL, 16 July 1916, 2; *Rovnost' L'udu,* 8 September 1920, 6. For these labor actions, see also chapters by [Chrislock, Walaszek, Puskás].

108. Kopanic, "Industrial Trade Unions," 90–1; Pavel Hapak, "Počiatky robotníckeho a socalistického hnutia," *Prehl'ad dejín KSČ na Slovensku,* ed. V. Plevza (Bratislava, 1971), 69–79; Ladislav Tajtak, "Vývov robotníckeho hnutia na Slovensku na začiatku 20. storočia," *Historícky časopsis,* vol. 29, No. 6 (1981), 844; Stolarik, "Slovak Immigration," 50; *Jednota,* 29 January 1908, 2; 19 February 1908, 2; 13 September 1911, 4; 20 September 1911, 4; 10 December 1913, 2; Štefan Furdek, "Socialismus," *Kalendár Jednota* (1910), 190–8; Paučo, 95–6; *Rovnost' l'udu,* 27 September 1922, 5; 22 July 1924, 7; [Baran]; *Denný Hlas,* 28 December 1920.

109. *Slováci vo svete,* 2, 114; *Americké dělnické listy,* 10 September 1909, 8; 3 December 1909, 7; Matlocha, 110–112; Bielik, 114–5; *Cleveland Citizen,* 27 May 1911; *Rovnost' l'udu,* 14 May 1919, 2–3; *Pamätnik 1915–1925,* 131–2.

110. *Rovnost' l'udu,* 20 June 1917, 3; 3 November 1920, 4.

111. *Pamätník 1915–1925,* 41–44, 118–21; interview with George Tomšek, May–June 1988; *Rovnost' l'udu,* 2 June 1920, 1; 16 June 1920, 1; 7 July 1920, 5; 29 September 1920, 2; 8 December 1920; 31 May 1922, 5.

112. Pavel Jamarik, "Život amerických Slovákov dakedy a teraz," *Sborník Národného Slovenského Spolku,* I (No. 2–3, 1915), 102–103; Stolarik, *Immigration,* 68; *Hlas,* 22 June 1925, 4; 14 September 1925; 2 December 1925, 3.

113. *Jednota,* 18 July 1906; Pankuch, *Dejiny,* 286.

114. *Hlas,* 5 June 1925, 1; 19 March 1913; Pankuch, *Dejiny,* 286; *Jednota,* 17 August 1904, 3.

115. *Denný Hlas,* 23 February 1921, 2; 18 February 1922, 4; 2 August 1924, 3; *Slovenská Ozvena,* 3 July 1929; Megles et al, *Slovak Americans,* 164–165; Pankuch, *Dejiny,* 30, 286; *Hlas,* 6 April 1925, 4; *Národné Noviny,* 4 January 1928.

116. Pankuch, *Dejiny,* 163–164; *Denný Hlas,* 6 February 1919, 1; 10, 19–20 February 1919; 7 February 1921, 4. Advertisements for the venture also appeared in issues of *Denný Hlas.* See chapter by Walaszek, regarding similar initiatives among Poles. Some members of Holy Trinity Church purchased land in Florida with the intent to found a Slovak settlement, Slávia. Although the project failed due to lack of interest, one of the settlers from Cleveland, Andrej Dudra founded a celery farm

that became one of the largest in the country and made him a millionaire. Pankuch, 200–1; information from Rev. A. Pier, May 1988.

117. Pankuch, *Dejiny*, 25.

118. K. B., "Večnek na pamiatku Jána Pankucha," *Národný Kalendár NSS* (1969), 66–7; Andrej Rolnik, "Ján Pankuch st. – Ako som ho poznal," *Kalendár NSS* (1976), 16 ff.; *Národné noviny*, 5 March 1952, 6; Van Tassel and Grabowski, eds., *Dictionary of Cleveland Biography*, 344.

119. Barton, *Peasants*, 99, 106.

120. Questionnaire on Slovaks in the U.S. by Parishes, 1930, Baska Papers, SI.

121. Barton, 102–3.

122. Baska survey, SI; Mark Stolarik, "Immigration, Education, and the Social Mobility of Slovaks, 1870–1930," *Immigrants and Religion in Urban America*, ed. Randall M. Miller and Thomas D. Marzik (Philadelphia, 1977), 103–109.

123. The list was compiled by Pankuch. Pankuch, *Dejiny*, 285.

124. Stolarik, *Immigration*, 81–97.

125. Herbert Adolphus Miller, *The School and the Immigrant* (Cleveland, 1916), 24–25, 30, 50, 69; Baska Papers, 716–9, 722, SI; Baska survey, 171; *Cleveland Press*, 18 January 1941; Pankuch, *Dejiny*, 223–224, 233–4; Dolak, *History*, 145; "Osada sv. Benedikta, Cleveland, O.," *Pamätnik. Program Slavnosti Slovenského Dňa* (Cleveland, 1929); Barton, *Peasants*, 150; Stolarik, *Immigration*, 94–97; Megles et al, *Slovak Americans*, 137; A.P., "Benedictine High School for Boys, Cleveland, Ohio," *Furdek*, 1967, 112–114; *Slovenská Vyššia Škola a Slovenskí Benediktini, Pamätník* (1929); Fr. Andrew V. Pier, "Six Decades of Slovak Apostolate by Benedictines in Cleveland," *Furdek*, 1982, 119–121.

126. On the situation in Europe, see Edita Bosak, "The Slovak National Movement," *Reflections on Slovak History*, ed. Stanislav J. Kirschbaum and Anne C. R. Roman (Toronto: Slovak World Congress, 1987), 66–72; Bosak, "Czecho-Slovak Relations and the Student Organization Detvan, 1882–1914," *Slovak Politics*, ed. S. J. Kirschbaum (Cleveland-Rome: Slovak Institute, 1983), 6–41. On cooperation in America see for example *Americké dělnické listy*, 23 July 1909; 20 August 1909, 7; 29 September 1911, 2.

127. Paučo, *Štefan Furdek*, 158; *Kalendár Jednota* I (1896), 22, 28, 31, 36; *Cleveland Press*, 9 December 1933; *Američan*, 19 January 1915; Maria Leocadia Stefan, SS C.M., "The Role of Reverend Stephen Furdek in Education Among the Slovaks in America from 1882 to 1915," (M.A., Catholic University of America, Washington, D.C., 1952); Oldřich Zlámal he noted, as a young priest served briefly in St. Wendelin parish and helped to organize SS. Cyril and Methodius; he succeeded Rev. Furdek at Our Lady of Lourdes in 1915.

128. Zlámal, *Povidka mého*, 32. Historians have documented that the Hungarian government was subsidizing the installation of pro-Magyar clerics in Slovak churches in America. Even Slovak Calvinists in Cleveland had to contend with such a problem. The guidance of Furdek prevented the installation of "Magyarones" at

any Roman Catholic Slovak parishes in the city. See Paula K. Benkart, "The Hungarian Government, the Magyar Churches, and Immigrant Ties to the Homeland, 1903–1917," *Church History,* vol. 52 (September 1983, No. 3), 312–321; Stolarik, *Immigration,* 46–47; Bodnar, 157. Rev. Zlámal commented that a Moravian could learn Slovak in just a few hours of study, but he overestimated the similarities. See his *Povidka,* 32. Moravians did not see themselves as "Czechs" through much of the 19th century ("Czechs" were from Bohemia). Both groups used the same literary language, but retained a sense of distinction much more acute than that which developed after World War I. Cf paper by Barbara Reinfeld, presented during Czechoslovak Society of Arts and Sciences World Congress, Toronto, October 1984.

129. St. Wendelin Parish Papers, ADC; Sr. Karen M. Baran, *The History of a Slovak Community in Cleveland, Ohio* (M.A., John Carroll University, 1979), 23–27.

130. Sutherland, "Century," 103; *Jednota,* 20 September 1911, 4.

131. Pankuch, *Dejiny,* 6–7.

132. Pankuch, *Dejiny,* 34.

133. *Souvenir Book, Twenty-first Regular Convention of the National Slovak Society* (Cleveland, 1954), 66–8; Pankuch, *Dejiny,* 53. See also chapter by Puskás.

134. *Plain Dealer,* 9 August 1902; Pankuch, *Dejiny,* 53.

135. *Plain Dealer,* 19 February 1911, 1.

136. "Apponyi" (Slovak Institute, Cleveland); Stolarik, *Slovak Migration from Europe to North America, 1870–1918,* 109–10; *Kalendár Jednota,* 1905, 100–5; Pankuch, *Dejiny,* 92–5, 98–103; *Plain Dealer,* 14 Feburary 1911, 2; 20 February 1911, 1–2; 24 February 1911, 1; *Jednota,* 16 and 22 February 1911, 1; Paučo, 95. See also chapter by Puskás.

137. *Cleveland Leader* and *Plain Dealer,* 16 April 1914.

138. Elena Jakešová, "Americi Slováci, zahraničný odboj a Československá štatnost (1914–1918)," *Historický časopis,* (1989) vol. 37, no. 5, 691; Pankuch, *Dejiny,* 111–2; Stolarik, *Slovak Migration,* 22–3.

139. Stolarik, "The Role of American Slovaks in the Creation of Czecho-Slovakia, 1914–1918," *Slovak Studies,* VII, 1968, 7, 26–26, 55; Jakešová, "Americi Slováci," 693; Pankuch, *Dejiny,* 113–9; Gilbert Oddo, *Slovakia and its People* (New York: Speller & Sons, 1960), 162; Megles et al, 172–3; *Národné noviny,* 23 October 1915, 1; Betty Miller Unterberger, *The United States, Revolutionary Russia, and the rise of Czechoslovakia* (Chapel Hill: University of North Carolina, 1989), 10. See also chapter by Chrislock.

140. Stolarik, "The Role," 27; Pankuch, *Dejiny,* 127.

141. Pankuch, *Dejiny,* 121–2, 132–3; Michael J. Kopanic, "70th Anniversary of the Death of General Milan Rastislav Štefánik," *Jednota,* 7 June 1989, 1, 6; Stolarik, "The Role," 36–40; *Hlas,* 19 December 1917, 8; 2 January 1918, 4.

142. Pankuch, *Dejiny,* 152–6; correspondence between J. A. Ferienčik and Albert Mamatey, January–February 1918 (Slovak Institute); *Denný Hlas,* 17 June 1918, 1; 18 June 1918, 2. See also chapter by Chrislock.

143. *Denný Hlas,* 26 June 1918; 5 October 1920, 2; 29 November 1920, 4; 5 August 1921, 2.

144. Pankuch, *Dejiny,* 24–6, 28–9; *Jednota,* 24 March 1909, 5.

145. Wellington G. Fordyce, "Nationality Groups in Cleveland Politics," *The Ohio State Archaeological and Historical Quarterly,* vol. 46 (1937), 125; *Jednota,* 26 October 1898, 1; 2 November 1904, 8; 20 February 1908, 1; 28 July 1909, 1; Pankuch, *Dejiny,* 144.

146. Board of Elections, Abstracts of Votes, 1906; Cuyahoga County Archives; Baska survey, SI; *Národné Noviny,* 29 October 1930, 6.

147. Abstracts of Votes, 1916, 1919, 1924.

148. *Národné Noviny,* 8 August 1927, 4; 4 January 1928.

149. *Národné Noviny,* 11 July 1928, 8 August 1928, 2, 29 October 1930, 6, 19 November 1930, 2; Pankuch, *Dejiny,* 282.

150. *Slovenská Ozvena,* 6 February 1928, 1; 5 June 1929, 2; *Národné Noviny,* 27 June 1928, 1; 23 July 1930, 2; 8 August 1930, 8; 27 August 1930, 3; Rev. A. V. Pier, "Early Slovak Immigrants in Cleveland, Ohio," *Jednota Annual Furdek,* XII (1973), 115–116; Pankuch, *Dejiny,* 282–3; Anna Sotak Papers, WRHS; Megles et al, 165.

151. *Furdek,* IX (2), November 1930; Pankuch, *Dejiny,* 283; Megles et al, 165.

Slovenes in Cleveland

MATJAŽ KLEMENČIČ

Background

Cleveland's Slovene community originated with a handful of settlers
in the early 1880s. Its most vigorous period of growth occurred in
the 1890s and early 1900s when the city's expanding need for industrial
workers coincided with the mass movement of Slovenes from their traditional homelands.

Slovenes began immigrating to the United States in large numbers during the late nineteenth century. At this time, most Slovenes were subjects of
the Habsburg Empire. They inhabited an area comprised of six provinces—
Carinthia, Styria, Carniola, Gorizia, Trieste, and Istria—in the western, or
Austrian part of the Empire; and of two *comitats* (counties)—Zala and
Vas—in the eastern, or Hungarian part. Slovenes in Vas and Zala comitats
(the most Western Hungarian comitats) in what is today Prekmurje were
known as Hungarian Slovenes. Slovenes were not an ethnic majority in any
of these administrative units except Carniola. However, they had demonstrated some sense of ethnic identity as early as the sixteenth century, when
Slovene peasants, together with Croatians, rebelled against feudal exploitation. In the more modern period, ethnic awareness crystallized in 1848, when
Slovene nationalists proposed that all Slovene-inhabited lands be united
into a single administrative unit. Following the example set by Czech nationalists, they popularized their "United Slovenia" program among peasants, townspeople, and workers during open-air meetings and in reading
clubs. After the expansion of voting rights in the year 1907, Slovene delegates to the Austrian parliament (Reichsrath) in Vienna allied with their
Czech counterparts to work for social and national rights within the Habsburg Empire. After World War I part of the Slovene-inhabited territory went
to the newly established Yugoslav Kingdom of Serbs, Croats, and Slovenes
which was later renamed Yugoslavia. The remainder was divided among
Italy—this portion often being referred to as the Littoral—Austria, and
Hungary.[1]

At the period when significant Slovene immigration to America was beginning, industrialization of the area in which Slovenes lived in Europe was still in its initial phase, with the great majority of the population working in agriculture. As was the case with various other ethnic groups, many people who emigrated from Slovenia were the younger sons or the daughters of peasants. Others leaving the country included Slovene coal miners working in the Austrian province of Styria, and migrant workers from the industrial basin of the Hapsburg monarchy. Farm-owners and professionals comprised only a small number of the emigrants.

Slovenes arriving in the United States settled in the iron range in northern Minnesota, and in the industrial and mining centers of Colorado, Michigan, Pennsylvania, Illinois, and California. But it was Cleveland which eventually became the largest Slovene settlement in the United States; some claimed it to be the largest Slovene city in the world.[2]

Slovene Migration to Cleveland

John Pintar, the first Slovene known to have come through Cleveland, spent only a few months there. The first permanent Slovene resident, Jožef Turk, arrived in Cleveland in 1882. In the initial decades of settlement, people from Lower and Upper Carniola predominated among Slovene immigrants to Cleveland; after World War I, migrants from the Italian Littoral joined them.[3]

During the first phase of Slovene immigration to Cleveland, immigrants from the Upper Carniola region arrived and settled in the Newburgh area on Cleveland's southeast side, where the Cleveland Rolling Mill Company (later part of the U.S. Steel Corporation) provided employment. Next, Slovenes settled around St. Clair Avenue, establishing what would become the city's major Slovene neighborhood in the area reaching from East 24th to East 87th Street. The Otis Iron and Steel Company plant on the lakeshore at East 33rd Street was a major source of employment in the area. Immigrants from the Ribnica area (in Lower Carniola) settled west of St. Clair's intersection with East 55th Street; people from Žužemberk (also in Lower Carniola) settled east of that point. In the westernmost part of the St. Clair neighborhood, Slovene immigrants from Bela krajina mixed with Croatians. Immigrants from the Littoral, who arrived later (particularly after fascism came to power in Italy), settled in Cleveland's Collinwood district, also home to an Italian settlement. As of the turn of century a small Slovene community had formed in Maple Heights, southeast of Cleveland's city limits. Another neighborhood existed on the west side of Cleveland, where a Slovene national home was built, and a number of Slovene businesses were established. In the 1920s many second generation Slovene-Americans moved east to Euclid, a community adjacent to Cleveland, creating yet another neighborhood with a discernible Slovene identity.[4]

Some of the early immigrants arrived in Cleveland more or less by chance. Frank Javh-Kern, who would become a leader of the city's Slovene community, was a teenage seminary student in Ljubljana when J. M. Solnce, a parish priest from St. Paul, Minnesota, visited Slovenia shortly after the turn of the century. Kern and a schoolmate were among those persuaded by Rev. Solnce to come to the United States and minister to Slovene immigrants. The young men left Austria-Hungary in 1903, and despite having no passports, encountered no difficulties on the way. They departed Europe via Hamburg, and after twelve days at sea landed in New York. Kern traveled to Minnesota with Rev. Solnce and enrolled in the St. Paul Seminary. While there, he became familiar with Janez Evangelist Krek's Slovene Christian Socialist movement; Marxism also formed part of the seminary's curriculum.

Kern's acquaintance with Cleveland came about in 1904, when the seminary students were promised an excursion to any destination within the United States, with half of their expenses paid, during summer vacation. Kern chose to travel to East Palestine in Ohio, 70 miles southeast of Cleveland, where he had relatives. In August 1906, without having completed his studies, he decided to move to Cleveland, where he went to work for the Slovene newspaper *Nova Domovina*. In 1908 Kern enrolled in the Western Reserve University School of Medicine, and after graduation and internship opened a practice on St. Clair Avenue. Meanwhile, true to the ideas he had absorbed while in St. Paul, he joined the Socialist Party in 1910.[5]

Vatroslav Grill, another future leader of Cleveland's Slovene community, followed a more direct route to the city. Grill's father had spent time in America during the first decade of the twentieth century. The elder Grill again left Europe for America in June 1913, saying, "There's going to be a war here. Let's go, while there's still time and while we still possess something." His family followed him a few weeks later, sailing from Bremen, Germany, to Ellis Island, and then immediately proceeding by train to meet him in Cleveland. A guidebook written by a Cleveland Slovene advised immigrants what to expect upon arrival there: "In the center of the city, on Public Square, stop and wait until the carriage of the street train with 'St. Clair Ave.' written on it comes by. Get in and ride the street train until you hear the sound of an accordion: Then you shall have arrived among Slovenes." Young Vatroslav was disappointed by his first impression of Cleveland: "One huge, gray village.... Even the houses and cottages on both sides of the main street were mostly built of wood—one broad board on top of another and all of them painted gray." But his disappointment turned to surprise when he saw that the "cottages" were "comfortable . . . and even pleasant" inside, and then to positive enjoyment when he found that food was plentiful and inexpensive.[6]

Demographic Characteristics of Cleveland's Slovenes

Estimates of the number of Cleveland Slovenes differ. The census data for the year 1910 showed slightly fewer than 20,000 Slovenes in the city. The figure for 1920 was 24,804. Parish records offer another source for population statistics. There were 8,230 people registered as parishioners in Slovene churches in 1910; 13,200 in 1915; 17,250 in 1920; 15,888 in 1925; and 16,808 in 1930. In the 1920s about 18,500 Slovenes of all generations were living in the vicinity of their churches in Cleveland, and about 6,000 more were scattered throughout the Cleveland area, especially in Maple Heights and West Park.[7]

Number of Parishioners in Cleveland Slovene Parishes[8]

Year	1910	1915	1920	1925	1930
Parish					
St. Vitus	6,000	8,500	8,250	7,582	7,150a
St. Lawrence	1,500	2,500	3,000	3,800	4,413
St. Mary	730	2,200	6,000b	3,200	3,610
St. Christine	—	—	—	1,306c	1,635d
Total	8,230	13,200	17,250	15,888	16,808

a—data for 1930 are missing; the figure for 1929 has been used
b—data for 1920 are missing; the figure for 1922 has been used
c—data for 1925 are missing; the figure for 1926 has been used
d—data for 1930 are missing; the figure for 1933 has been used

Additional sources give more detailed information on Cleveland's Slovene population. These include: for 1907, the U.S. government's Immigration Commission report; for 1910, a sample of census originals giving details on 1,034 members of the community living in the St. Clair neighborhood; and, for 1930, an analysis giving data according to census tracts.[9]

    Of those Cleveland Slovenes surveyed in 1907 for the Immigration Commission report, 426 (64.5 percent) had been born abroad, and 234 (35.5 percent) in the United States. Among those born abroad, 18.1 percent had come to the U.S. before 1890; slightly less than half had arrived in the first decade of the twentieth century. The report's category "Head of the family" showed 61.1 percent of household heads to be 30–44 years old; 28.4 percent were 20–29 years of age. Already, a relatively high proportion of the children under 10 years of age had been born in America.

The 1907 sample also provided information on employment, which affected Cleveland Slovenes' financial status. Among the 107 heads of families represented in the sample, 33.6 percent were laborers and 17.8 percent factory employees. These were mainly unskilled and semi-skilled persons employed in the metal industry. Salesmen and firemen each numbered 5 persons (4.7 percent). Some individuals were employed in commerce, in occupations such as innkeeping that yielded relatively quick profits with little capital outlay. Of those persons above 14 years of age, 95 percent could read and write.[10]

Among the Cleveland Slovenes in the 1910 sample, 41.2 percent were female. Married men and women comprised 46 percent of the total, while 53 percent (including children) were unmarried, and 1 percent were widowed. Children 10 and under made up 30.7 percent of the total, teenagers 13.5 percent, and 21–30 year olds 31.6 percent. As categorized by status within the household, 19 percent were heads of families, 18.1 percent wives, 36.8 percent children, 1.3 percent brothers, 22.7 percent boarders, and 2.1 percent others. The great majority lived in rented apartments. Only 4 percent of those surveyed were naturalized, while 36 percent had filed the first papers for citizenship. The illiteracy rate within this sample was 15 percent.[11]

By the 1920s and 1930s the early Slovene settlements had coalesced into distinguishable neighborhoods. According to the 1930 data, census tracts in the St. Clair Avenue and East 55th Street areas had the highest percentages of Slovenes, followed by Newburgh and Euclid. These neighborhoods were able to support ethnically based cultural, economic, and religious establishments during the first three decades of twentieth century. Within the Cleveland census tracts, Slovenes were still in the process of establishing their families in 1930, as evidenced by the fact that men outnumbered women by approximately 20 percent.

Although most Slovene immigrants to Cleveland came from a rural background, 99.7 percent of employed Slovenes living in the St. Clair census tract in 1930 worked outside the primary sector (agriculture). Only 6 persons (0.3 percent) were employed in the primary sector. The secondary sector (industry) employed 1,302 persons (67.2 percent), and the tertiary (commerce and the professions), 629 (32.5 percent).[12]

Development of Slovene Private Enterprise

Vatroslav Grill's first impressions of Cleveland Slovenes' educational attainments had not been positive. He observed that although they already spoke "a distorted Slovene," they knew only a few phrases of English. Nor, according to him, did they give much thought to schooling and the available opportunities for educating themselves. They were indifferent or even hostile to the idea. "Nonsense schooling! Here in America we work," was the prevalent attitude.[13] Nonetheless, Cleveland Slovenes in fact attained a high literacy rate. The labors of the uneducated and unsophisticated first generation of immigrants created a socio-economic base that enabled the second generation to pursue a higher level of education and gain yet greater economic strength. The capital accumulated by the early Slovene entrepreneurs also helped make it possible for Cleveland Slovenes to establish community institutions, such as fraternal benefit societies, national homes, and parishes, and eventually to run successful political campaigns. Small-scale retail trade was the first step in this accumulation of capital, eventually leading to the founding of larger enterprises as well as Slovene banks and savings and loans.

The desire of neighborhood residents to shop in stores where merchants spoke their own language spurred the creation and growth of the first Slovene retail businesses. Initially, Cleveland's Slovene residents, who were more likely to speak German than English, tended to patronize the city's numerous German and German Jewish shopkeepers and tradesmen. For instance, halls owned by Germans were rented and used for various Slovene celebrations and parties. However, within a decade after the Slovene community was established in Cleveland, its members were starting their own businesses.

One of the earliest Slovene entrepreneurs in Cleveland was Jožef Turk. Turk managed to save enough of the wages he earned in the Newburgh steel mills during the 1880s to set up in business for himself. He soon owned a grocery store and three boardinghouses. He also opened a saloon to serve Slovene laborers in the developing St. Clair neighborhood near the Otis Iron and Steel Company's lakeshore plant. Turk was for a time the only Slovene businessman in the area, and his saloon prospered. He gave it to his daughter as a wedding gift, and also bought saloons for his two sons. His own businesses grew to include another saloon, a restaurant, and a general store. Turk was so well known that, when new Slovene settlers arrived at the city's railroad station, the police directed them to his establishment. When necessary, he lent money to his co-nationals and sometimes assisted those who ran afoul of the law. The depression of 1893 hit Turk hard. He lost almost every-thing, but eventually recovered sufficient prosperity to move to suburban Euclid. There he grew grapes, made and sold wine, and established a new saloon in Nottingham (a Euclid township village annexed to Cleveland in 1911–1912).[14]

As was the case with many other nationality groups, saloons were among the first businesses organized by Slovenes. Even on a small scale, saloon-keeping could be profitable, and also politically advantageous. According to Grill, "Nothing [was] easier for people with initiative. These men signed a contract with a brewery to sell only that company's beer. The remaining responsibilities were taken care of by the brewery—from renting the prem-ises to obtaining the liquor license and all the other formalities. The saloon-owners who were also bankers were usually the first individuals to be contacted by the local politicians. . . . These politicians . . . issued legitimate certificates of American citizenship to new Slovene arrivals in these saloons on the evenings before the local elections. The proprietors were the ones who explained to their compatriots how to vote and for whom they should vote." In point of fact, Grill was himself a saloon-owner. His establishment was one of several in operation on St. Clair Avenue when Frank Javh-Kern first came to Cleveland. Kern noted that in another tavern, owned by the Lausche family, a man named Jože Svete (who would later become a notary) had a business office, thus attesting to the multi-purpose role of the saloon in the early years of community-building.[15]

Ethnic newspapers also contributed to give the settlement a sense of cohesion and identity, providing a more formal venue than the saloon for the exchange of information. In later years, Vatroslav Grill would serve for many years as the editor of *Enakopravnost* (Equality), a newspaper with a free-thinking liberal orientation that began daily publication in 1918. Cleve-land's first Slovene newspaper was *Nova domovina* (*New Home*), published from 1899 to 1908, when it was replaced by *Clevelandska Amerika,* founded by Louis Pirc, who had also been among the owners of *Nova domovina.* The name was changed to *Ameriška Domovina* (*American Home*) following World War I. Although this newspaper had a Catholic orientation, it was independent of the church and in fact came into conflict with the religious establishment upon occasion.[16] Later, in 1923, another Catholic publica-tion came to Cleveland when *Glasilo KSKJ,* the newspaper of the main na-tional Slovene Catholic fraternal, moved its offices to the city.[17]

As additional Slovene-run businesses, shops, and drinking places began to appear in the St. Clair neighborhood, Slovene and German business interests began to clash, as reported by *Clevelandska Amerika*. For example, after Slovene clubs and societies stopped renting German-owned halls for parties and dances, some German businessmen, concerned about the loss of Slovene clientele in their shops as well, retaliated. They allegedly disturbed the peace and then blamed the trouble on the Slovenes, suggesting to the city authorities that the latter should not be given permits for their parties.[18]

Clevelandska Amerika adopted a pro-active stance on the subject of Slovene commerce, campaigning for the establishment of a Slovene retail tradesmen's organization. An article published in 1910 suggested that Slovene tradesmen organize and unite, following the example set by other ethnic groups in the city. These groups had their own associations, providing effective support for the development and sustenance of their businesses. A Slovene association would be able to persuade fellow immigrants to patronize Slovene-owned stores, in accordance with the slogan, "Each to his own." *Clevelandska Amerika* regarded the growth of the new Slovene businesses as a demonstration of Slovene ethnic consciousness. It noted that the amount of Slovene-owned property was growing rapidly, and that non-Slovene enterprises were leaving the St. Clair neighborhood while Slovene businesses were expanding.[19]

In response to the newspaper's suggestion, the Slovene Tradesmen's Association was founded. *Clevelandska Amerika* and the association soon parted ways, however, when the priests of two Slovene parishes accused the newspaper of printing stories offensive to the Catholic church. The association, which had offices in a parish school, sided with the clerics. Association members put pressure on the newspaper by demanding repayment of debts owed to their businesses, and by withdrawing their advertisements from *Clevelandska Amerika*. The newspaper, which refused to change its editorial policy, came near to financial collapse as a result, and the two sides were not able to put aside their differences until World War I.[20]

The Slovene Tradesmen's Association was not the only organization created by Cleveland's Slovene businessmen. As early as 1910, the St. Clair Merchants' Improvement Association, whose membership also included laborers and craftsmen, worked to implement community improvements in the neighborhood. Industry-specific groups, such as the Club of Slovene Green-Grocers and Butchers, also existed. Later, in 1935, the Progressive Tradesmen's Association was founded as a non-political organization dedicated to solidifying the economic position of area South Slav merchants and craftsmen, for instance by helping them to sell products at competitive prices.[21]

In 1910 Slovene-owned businesses in the St. Clair neighborhood included twenty-nine saloons, twelve shoe shops, nine grocery stores, four tailor shops, three butcher shops, two confectioners, two hardware stores, two furniture stores, a barber shop, and a bicycle shop. In the same period there were also about twenty Croatian-owned enterprises there. A Slovene soft drink bottler and distributor, the Double Eagle Bottling Company, was also located in the St. Clair district. Founded in 1908 by John Potokar, the family-owned firm continued to flourish through both World Wars and beyond. By the post-World War I years, Slovenes had established about three hundred small businesses in Cleveland, mostly in the retail and service sectors. Collectively, they were able to amass sufficient capital to start a manufacturing company, the Euclid Foundry, in 1921. Initially, the foundry's investors and managers were Slovene, but by 1928 Croatians had also assumed positions on the board of directors. The company had 259 shareholders, and was valued at almost two hundred thousand dollars.[22]

The leading entrepreneur among Cleveland Slovenes was a man named Anton Grdina. Grdina had grown up in Ljubljana, where he received an elementary school education. He arrived in Cleveland at the age of 23 in 1897, joining a brother who already lived there. After working at various unskilled laboring jobs, in 1903 he founded a retail hardware and furniture store, Grdina & Pucelj, and ten years later expanded into the wholesale furniture market as well, in an attempt to consolidate his position vis-à-vis competitive pressure from Jewish-owned retail businesses. In 1910 Grdina established a highly successful funeral parlor, and in 1928 incorporated his business holdings as Anton Grdina & Sons. By the late 1930s the company was opening new branches of its main St. Clair Avenue furniture store in the Collinwood, Nottingham, and Euclid neighborhoods, and renovating its funeral parlor. Anton Grdina became known as the "father" of Cleveland's Slovene community, and was also regarded as a leader by Cleveland's ethnic middle class members in general, as well as by Slovenes across the country.[23]

Grdina was foremost among the founders of the first Slovene bank in America, the North American Banking & Savings Company, incorporated in 1920 and later known as the North American Bank. The bank's assets grew from less than two hundred thousand dollars at the outset to four million by the end of 1925. Most of the bank's officers and board members, including two other members of the Grdina family, were active in Slovene fraternal, religious, and cultural organizations. The future U.S. Senator Frank Lausche served as legal counsel (as he also did for the Euclid Foundry). Although North American experienced considerable difficulties during the

1929 to 1933 period and was forced to close during the bank holiday of 1933, it soon reorganized and reopened. It remained in operation, under the presidency of Anton Grdina from 1939 until his death in 1957, until acquired by a larger Cleveland bank in 1959.[24]

Grdina also helped to organize the Slovene Building and Loan Association, later known as the St. Clair Savings Association, in 1916–1917. This organization went bankrupt in the 1930s. Another savings and loan, the Slovene Loan and Savings Company, founded in the Nottingham neighborhood in 1928, was able, with difficulty, to survive the Depression.[25]

Slovene Workers, Strikes, and Socialism

If the amount of copy given to Slovene participation in strikes and labor issues in Cleveland's Slovene press is any indication, Slovenes, who had a relatively large number of middle class members compared to some other immigrant groups, likewise had comparatively little interest in the workers' movement. In the pre-Depression era, *Clevelandska Amerika* and *Ameriška domovina* took specific note of Slovene participation in only two strikes. In the first, against the Chisholm and Moore Foundry Company in 1913, although most of the strikers were Slovenes they were not organized along ethnic lines. During the nationwide steel strike of 1919, the eighteen thousand workers who struck sixteen Cleveland mills, of which Otis Steel was one, included a significant number of Slovenes: as many as two thousand, according to the local Slovene press.[26] Although Slovenes did join mainstream labor unions, they had no workers' organization of their own apart from the Slovene socialist clubs active within the national Yugoslav Socialist Federation-Socialist Party (YSF-SP).

The Yugoslav Socialist Federation, founded in 1905, had Slovene, Croatian, and Serb branches. Each published a newspaper, *Proletarec* being the Slovene title. A schism soon developed within the organization, resulting in the creation of the YSF-SP, a section of the American Socialist Party, and the YSF-SLP, a section of the Socialist Labor Party.[27] Until 1910, Cleveland Slovenes had belonged to a German socialist club. In that year Slovenes formed their own club in the St. Clair neighborhood. In 1911 the group became Slovene Socialist Club No. 27 of the YSF-SP. The other two Slovene Socialist clubs later formed in the city, Nos. 28 and 49, were in fact offshoots of No. 27. In 1913 No. 27 began renting a house in which they and Croatian socialists held meetings, and established a reading room where Slovene-, Croatian-, English-, and German-language workers' newspapers were available. A Croatian choral society, *Crveni Barjak* (The Red Flag), rehearsed there. *Sloga* (Harmony) and then *Zarja* (Dawn) served as the Slovene club's own choral section. No. 27 kept in touch with other socialist groups in Cleveland, sending delegates to meetings of the Socialist Party's Central Municipal Committee.[28]

Like other socialist organizations whose members came from the Austro-Hungarian Empire, the YSF-SP experienced turmoil in the World War I era, temporarily seceding from the Socialist Party over the question of America's entry into the war. In the post-war period a few Cleveland Slovenes joined the more radical Socialist Labor Party, but most remained members of the YSF-SP. In 1921, *Proletarec* had 824 subscribers in Cleveland, eleven percent of its total circulation.[29]

Some socialists and leftists were members of the middle class, as evidenced by the activities of individuals like Frank Javh-Kern. Moreover, a significant amount of leftist sentiment existed within Cleveland's Slovene community, but more or less outside of the socialist party organizations per se. The Cleveland newspaper *Enakopravnost,* for example, was among the Slovene leftist publications criticized by the YSF-SP for their lack of doctrinaire socialist orientation.[30]

One of the several national homes built by Cleveland Slovenes to house meetings and other social and cultural activities was the Slovene Workmen's Home in Collinwood. Fifteen cultural, veterans', and fraternal groups joined forces in 1916 to raise funds for the home's construction, which was not completed until 1926. The first board of directors represented groups on the political left, thus the choice of name, and the eventual selection of *Enakopravnost* as the home's newspaper.[31] Overall, Cleveland Slovenes most frequently developed and expressed leftist sentiments within the context of free-thought fraternal societies, particularly the Slovene National Benefit Society.[32]

Slovene Benefit Societies and Associations

The original motivation behind the foundation of Slovene fraternal benefit societies had little to do with politics. The fraternals were founded by immigrants in order to provide mutual support in the event of a member's illness, injury, or death. Their function went far beyond that of an insurance company, however. They did in fact quickly become cultural and political focal points for their communities, and can be considered the basic form of organization for Slovenes in the United States. The early local lodges grew

Members of Cleveland's Slovenian community attend the cornerstone ceremony

for the Slovenian National Home on St. Clair Avenue in the 1920s. WRHS

to become national associations which in turn spawned the creation of additional local branches. Some locals remained independent, preferring to concentrate on the needs of the local membership; others withdrew from the national organizations following disagreements over finances or policies, sometimes founding new associations. Slovenes had founded eight supralocal fraternal benefit organizations by the end of World War I, in part due to the various political orientations that existed within the community at the national and local levels. Only one of these fraternals was based in Cleveland; despite Cleveland's status as the largest Slovene settlement in the United States, very few Slovene organizations of any sort located their national headquarters there.[33]

Slovenes modeled their fraternal benefit societies after similar organizations created by other Slavic groups. In the 1880s and 1890s Slovenes, relatively few in number, relied on the aid of Czech associations in particular. They founded their own societies, which were often known collectively as *jednotas* after the Czech word for union, under the aegis of preexisting Czech organizations. Slovenes looked to the Czechs in part because of their previous association in Europe. Both nationalities formed part of the western half of the Hapsburg Empire, had representatives in the parliament in Vienna, and were united by a common desire to resist domination by the German Austrians.[34] However, in Cleveland the determining factor in the relationship was the advanced economic and cultural development of the already well-established Czech community.

In 1884, with about thirty Slovene immigrants resident in Cleveland, the creation of an independent Slovene organization was not a realistic venture. In that year, however, the accidental death of a Slovene laborer at his workplace brought home the need for some form of insurance. There being no money to pay for the funeral, Jožef Turk stepped in and arranged for the burial and covered all expenses. Turk, who rented rooms to bachelor laborers and often assisted new arrivals, and whose saloon served as a natural meeting place for Slovenes in Cleveland, realized that a more formal mechanism of social insurance was needed. He began to investigate the idea of creating a Slovene mutual benefit society. The first such society in Cleveland was not actually formed until 1890, with help from the Slovak priest Stefan Furdek, pastor of the Czech church attended by many Newburgh Slovenes. Rev. Furdek's experience as a member of a Czech benefit society, and a founder of similar Slovak groups, helped guide the organization of the Marijin Spolek (Mary's Society). The group's name bespoke Czech influence, *spolek* being the Czech word for society. Turk served as the organization's first president and treasurer. Five years later Marijin Spolek joined the national Carniolian Slovenian Catholic Union (Kranjsko Slovenska Ka-toliška Jednota, or KSKJ), and changed its name to the St. Vitus Lodge.[35]

Since Cleveland had the largest concentration of Slovenes in the United States, various mutual aid and fraternal societies headquartered as far away as Denver, Colorado, subsequently tried to attract membership from the city. Differences among these organizations reflected their ideological ori-entations, and affected their membership rules. The KSKJ, established in 1894 in Joliet, Illinois, required that members be religious Catholics. Each lodge had its own priest. At first the KSKJ accepted only Slovene Catholics as mem-bers. Later, Catholics from other Slavic groups (Croatians, in particular) with Slovene spouses were also accepted. By the 1920s, there were 13 KSKJ lodges in Cleveland, with about a quarter of the organization's membership residing in Ohio, primarily in Cleveland.[36]

The Slovene National Benefit Society (Slovenska Narodna Podporna Jed-nota, or SNPJ), established in Chicago in 1904, had a secular orientation and accepted members without regard to religious affiliation.[37] It also accepted members from other Slavic and even non-Slavic ethnic groups. The SNPJ attracted a large following among Cleveland Slovenes. Lodge Naprej was one of the founding lodges of SNPJ. The politically active stance adopted by Naprej can be attributed to the lodge's president, socialist Jože Zavertnik, who was also a founder and editor of *Proletarec* and later served as editor of the SNPJ's national newspaper, *Glasilo SNPJ* and later *Prosveta* (Enlight-enment).[38]

The lodge became a driving force behind every progressive movement among Cleveland Slovenes. Its members were among the founders of So-cialist Club No. 27, and also worked toward the creation of Cleveland's chapter of Yugoslav Republican Alliance during World War I. The Naprej lodge was subjected to considerable criticism from the more conservatively oriented Cleveland lodges and groups, especially those belonging to the KSKJ.[39] The Naprej Lodge's delegates played an influential role during SNPJ conventions. Upon their initiative, the SNPJ passed a number of resolutions objecting to German and Italian participation in the Spanish Civil War and sent support to the Spanish Republican government. The lodge was also critical of the conditions prevailing in interwar Yugoslavia and condemned King Alexandar's rule as a dictatorship. By the 1920s twenty-five additional SNPJ lodges had been founded in Cleveland, but Naprej remained the largest and most politically active.[40]

Cleveland Slovenes formed lodges of other national organizations as well. The South Slavic Catholic Union (Jugoslovanska Katoliška Jednota, or JSKJ), established in Ely, Minnesota, in 1898, eventually had five branches active in

Cleveland. The Slovene Progressive Benefit Union (Slovenska Svobodo-miselna Podporna Zvera, or sspz), another Chicago-based free-thinking association with a political alignment similar to that of the snpj (with which it later merged), also had five Cleveland lodges by the 1920s. The first of these grew out of the Lunder-Adamic Society, founded in 1908 as a dramatic club and named after two students killed in a demonstration against the Austrian authorities in Ljubljana.[41] Cleveland Slovenes also founded one of the easternmost branches of the Western Slavonic Association (Zapadna Slovanska Zveza, or zsz), established in Denver, Colorado, in 1908.[42]

The Slovene Mutual Life Association (Slovenska Dobrodelna Zveza, or sdz), established in Cleveland in 1910, was the only national fraternal benefit society with its main offices in Cleveland. Its founders had originally belonged to *Postaja* (station, or lodge) No. 6 of the St. Barbara Society, headquartered in Forest City, Pennsylvania. In 1910, after a disagreement about the society's financial policies, No. 6 decided to build its own organization, initially in Ohio only. The sdz immediately adopted a policy of accepting members irrespective of their religious or political views. By the middle of 1911 the organization had 317 members and was continuing to grow. New lodges, often named after places in the old country, or sometimes after saints (indicative of the ideologically neutral outlook of the sdz), were organized in Cleveland's various Slovene neighborhoods. The sdz concentrated primarily on providing financial support for deceased members' survivors and for victims of illnesses or workplace injuries. In 1919, the sdz also introduced an old-age pension plan. During the Depression, the organization dipped into its treasury to pay the premiums of members temporarily unable to do so themselves. *Clevelandska Amerika* and later *Ameriška domovina* served as the sdz's official newspaper from 1911 until 1939.[43]

The sdz made special efforts to attract the community's youth. As early as 1911, the society had in place a youth section for those under the age of sixteen. It also sponsored sporting activities and established English-speaking lodges, of which the first was the Slovenian Young Men's Lodge No. 36, founded in January 1926. The next, founded three months later, was the first English-speaking lodge in Cleveland for Slovene women. Identification with America was evidenced by the name its members chose: the Martha Washington Lodge. Many of the lodges founded in the 1920s emphasized typically American sports like basketball, responding to and at the same time promoting the process of acculturation already taking place within the younger generation. Lodges also offered gymnastic programs more in keeping with their members' European roots. In 1934 the sdz became a member organization of the National Fraternal Congress, a Yugoslav fraternal federation, and also at that point began to accept Croatian members. By 1940 the sDZ had 61 different lodges and 12,000 members.[44]

Cleveland's Slovene women also joined, and in some cases founded, national women's mutual benefit organizations, some of which later merged with men's fraternals of similar political orientation. The first Slovene women's lodge in Cleveland was the Srce Marije, founded in 1897 and initially housed in the St. Vitus parish school, as was the Marijin Spolek. Later, Catholic Slovene women had the option of joining the Slovene Women's Union (Slovenska Ženska Zveza, sžz), founded in Chicago in the late 1920s. By the 1930s, the sžz had ten lodges in Cleveland. An early independent non-sectarian women's group, the Free-thinking Slovene Women's Society (Svodobomiselne Slovenke), merged with the sDZ in 1911. In 1934, Cleveland women founded a national organization, the Progressive Slovene Women of America, to advance democratic and cultural values.[45]

Cleveland, as one of the largest Slovene settlements in the United States, took its turn in hosting national *jednota* conventions; likewise, a number of Cleveland Slovenes served as officers of the national organizations. The conventions provided an opportunity for area Slovenes to express pride in their culture, and to raise their own community's profile within the broader Cleveland community, not least with local politicians and other notables, who were often invited to participate as guests in the ceremonial events accompanying the meetings. The first such national gathering in Cleveland was the KSKJ's seventh convention in 1902. The SNPJ held its fourth convention in Cleveland in 1909. In 1919 a joint convention of the SNPJ and the SSPZ took place in Cleveland. These and other fraternals continued to hold national meetings in the city at intervals over the following decades. The Slovene national fraternal organizations also kept considering moving their headquarters to Cleveland, since it provided them with a large percentage of the membership. Cleveland Slovenes holding national offices included Anton Grdina, who served as president of the KSKJ, and Vatroslav Grill, who was president of the SSPZ. A number of Clevelanders were SNPJ officers or supervisory committee members, in addition to Jože Zavertnik's position as editor of the organization's newspaper.[46]

Development of Slovene Parishes

Between the 1880s and 1930s Cleveland Slovenes established four Roman Catholic parishes. In this as in so many areas, Jožef Turk was a pioneer, playing a key role in the formation of the community's first parish. The first Slovenes who settled in Newburgh attended mass in a Czech Catholic church, Our Lady of Lourdes. Its pastor, Rev. Furdek, even learned some Slovene, but not enough to perform duties like hearing confession. (A Slovene priest from distant St. Paul, Minnesota, made several trips to Cleveland to accomplish that task.) Turk worked with Rev. Furdek and Bishop Richard Gilmour to obtain a Slovene priest for the Cleveland diocese. The bishop turned down Turk's suggestion that ordained clerics be brought over from Slovene lands, but was willing to have Slovene students recruited for study in American seminaries. Rev. Furdek visited Slovene lands while traveling in Europe and brought back with him a young man, Vitus Hribar, who would soon become the first priest of Cleveland's first Slovene parish.[47]

The parish was established in 1893. It numbered sixty-five families and a large number of single men. Rev. Hribar at first celebrated masses at Our Lady of Lourdes, and then in the school chapel of a German Catholic church. In the meantime, Turk, following the bishop's advice, had started to raise funds for construction a church. The process was a slow one. Turk's son later recalled: "It took such a long time that they thought there would never be a Slovenian church in Cleveland. You would commonly hear comments such as: 'Two years ago I gave twenty-five cents for the Slovenian Church, but the church still isn't built.' My father's reply was, 'My dear countryman, for 25 cents we cannot buy a church, so here is your quarter back.'" Finally the fund-raising committee accumulated two thousand dollars, and purchased a lot on the corner of Norwood and Glass Avenues in the St. Clair neighborhood. The new church building, completed in 1894, was dedicated to St. Vitus.[48]

In 1905 a dispute similar to those which occurred in other ethnic parishes in Cleveland and elsewhere broke out in St. Vitus parish. Some parishioners disagreed with Rev. Hribar regarding financial support for the church. A member of the Grdina family later observed that: "The parishes of the old country and of America differed immensely. In the old country . . . [the parishioners] did not need to pay for the maintenance of the school, since the state and the priests cared for the schools. In the United States, things were different. The maintenance costs for churches, schools, and even the livelihood of the parish priest had to be covered by the parishioners. This demanded great sacrifices—something the people did not understand straight away." In the view of the dissident parishioners, Fr. Hribar's demands went too far. A Slovene priest new to Cleveland, Kazimir Zakrajšek, became Rev. Hribar's rival, favored by the dissidents to replace the latter at

St. Vitus. At one point, protesters demonstrated in front of the priest's residence, and at that of Bishop Ignatius Horstmann.[49]

In 1906 Bishop Horstmann decided to solve the problem by dividing the parish into two. The part west of East 55th Street became the new parish of Our Lady of Sorrows, with Rev. Zakrajšek as its pastor. It existed only seven months, during which the rivalry between the priests and the protests and demonstrations by the parishioners continued, attracting notice in the mainstream press. Eventually, in 1907, Bishop Horstmann transferred Rev. Hribar to a Slovene parish in Barberton, Ohio, and Rev. Zakrajšek to a parish in Lorain, Ohio. The two Cleveland parishes merged. Although some parishioners continued to demand the appointment of Rev. Zakrajšek as priest of the reunited St. Vitus parish, pressure from the superior of Slovene Franciscans in the United States caused Rev. Zakrajšek to request the parishioners to accept and obey their newly appointed pastor, Jernej Ponikvar.[50]

Rev. Ponikvar, another Slovene student recruited to study for the priesthood in the United States, assumed his duties at St. Vitus at the age of thirty. His tenure, which lasted until 1952, brought peace and stability to the parish. During this period the construction of a new church building took place. Completed in 1932, St. Vitus was to be one of the largest Slovene churches in the country. Rev. Ponikvar was attentive to the material as well as the spiritual needs of his parishioners, organizing numerous charitable activities and, during the Depression, personally requesting Slovene farmers to donate produce to be distributed among households where there were neither jobs nor food. In 1936 he was elevated to the rank of Monsignor in recognition of his accomplishments.[51]

Since St. Vitus church and parish was relatively distant from the Slovene settlement in Newburgh, residents there continued to attend mass at Our Lady of Lourdes. An assistant priest from St. Vitus, Frančišek Kerže, together with a lay committee, in 1901 obtained permission from the diocese to organize a parish and build a church, St. Lawrence, in the Newburgh neighborhood. A church was built in 1902; Rev. Kerže served as the parish's first priest, until he was transferred in 1909 (in part because he had been involved in the schism at St. Vitus) and replaced by Joseph Lavrič.[52]

The parish continued to grow. In 1915 John Oman, who had spent the previous four years as assistant pastor at St. Vitus, was appointed priest at St. Lawrence a short time after Rev. Lavrič's death. Rev. Oman had been born in Brockway, Minnesota, home to one of the oldest Slovene settlements in the country. Both of his parents were from Kranjska gora in Slovenia. Rev. Oman himself, as a member of the second generation, could not speak

Slovene well although he took pride in his Slovene heritage.[53] Also, his Gorenjska accent did not sit well with his parishioners, most of whom were from Lower Carniola (with "a handful" from Carinthia and "quite a few" from the coastal and Karst areas, according to Rev. Oman).[54] To help obviate this problem, the priest tried to have Slovene assistants assigned to his parish, eventually visiting Slovenia to recruit an assistant from Lower Carniola. Through this and other efforts Rev. Oman succeeded in winning over his parishioners. He successfully guided the parish through the 1920s, a decade of expansion accompanied by financial difficulties partly due to the considerable expense of running a large parish school. In 1926 the parish numbered 750 families, with 650 children attending St. Lawrence school the following year.[55]

Many of the Carniolian Slovenes who began settling in the Collinwood neighborhood in about 1900 had previously attended St. Vitus church. Since St. Vitus was now too far away, they began attending Collinwood's only Catholic church, St. Joseph, where English was the vernacular used. The parish priest also spoke some German, which many Carniolians understood. Despite this, they soon decided to organize a congregation of their own, and began holding separate services at St. Joseph in 1905. Controversy immediately arose over the question of whether the church should be sited on the north or south side of the Collinwood railroad tracks. At a parish meeting in 1906 a slight majority voted for the southern location. Bishop Horstmann approved the decision, and Marko Pakiž was appointed the first priest of the new parish, St. Mary's. Enough funds were collected to build the church, with the first services held there in late 1906.[56]

Some of those who had favored the northern location, including Croats, Slovaks, and Magyars as well as Slovenes, joined an independent parish organized by a cleric described as "a renegade Bohemian priest." The parish, which built its church of Sts. Peter and Paul north of the railroad tracks, turned out not to be financially viable, and within a few years the mortgage on the church property was foreclosed by the bank holding it. Many of its members then joined St. Mary's. In 1913 Paul Hribar became priest at St. Mary's. Formerly assistant at St. Joseph, and clergyman in charge of the Slovene mission of Our Lady of Perpetual Help in Euclid, Rev. Hribar was already familiar to his new parishioners. In 1909 the mission had become attached to St. Mary's, with the Euclid Slovenes becoming regular members of the parish, although the mission church remained separate.[57]

The next priest at St. Mary's, Joseph Škur, had been born in Venetian Slovenia and thus spoke Italian as well as Slovene, an advantage in communicating with the Italian community in Collinwood. However, like so many of his colleagues, he too became a magnet for dissatisfaction and complaints on the part of his parishioners. At their request, the bishop appointed the former priest of St. Vitus, Rev. Vitus Hribar, to the post at St. Mary's.[58]

In the parish, Rev. Hribar was confronted with rising Slovene-Italian tensions. In 1923 he wrote to the bishop: "The greatest need in St. Mary's congregation is to delegate the Italians a parish of their own. The reasons are: 1. The Slovenians despise the Italians who they see as their natural enemies. 2. There is no room even for Slovenes. 3. The Italians do not understand Slovene. We hold only Slovene sermons though quite a few understand English. 4. Therefore, the Italians will not get the proper care, because it is impossible." The estrangement between the two groups was evidenced by the fact that no marriages took place between Slovenes and Italians in St. Mary's church until the 1950s.[59]

In 1925 the Slovene mission in Euclid became an independent parish and church, St. Christine's, which served the growing Slovene population in the suburb. The Edwards Land Company, a major land developer in Euclid, donated property on East 222nd Street for the building of the church. The first priest designated by the diocese was of Polish-American background, and, predictably, soon ran into opposition within the parish, with parishioners petitioning the bishop for a Slovene priest. Eventually, in June 1928, Bishop Joseph Schrembs appointed a newly arrived Croatian priest, Venčeslav Vukonić, as pastor of St. Christine's, since there were no Slovene priests available at the time. Although Rev. Vukonić was popular with his parishioners, in part due to the fact that he spoke good Slovene, and was considered by them "a true spiritual father," the diocese in 1931 appointed a priest of Slovene background, Anthony Bombach, to lead the parish. Needs were changing, since by this time most parishioners came from the second generation. Rev. Bombach was in favor of making St. Christine's a geographically rather than an ethnically based parish, especially since many of the Slovenes in the vicinity were active in other parishes. Although St. Christine's remained a Slovene parish, with Rev. Bombach as pastor until his death in 1962, opposition to the very concept of a non-ethnic church during the 1930s led some Slovene families to stop attending St. Christine's and sending their children to its school.[60]

Slovene parochial education had begun in Cleveland in 1902, when the parish of St. Vitus enlarged its church and built the first Slovene parish primary school. Initially, Slovene was the principal language of instruction in the Slovene parish schools. The teachers were nuns, brought from the Maribor diocese in Slovenia. Later, Notre Dame sisters, as well as nuns from Lemont, the Slovene Franciscan monastery in Illinois, also taught in Cleveland's Slovene parish schools.[61]

By 1910, 730 pupils were enrolled in the St. Vitus and St. Lawrence parish schools, whereas only 72 of the parishes' children attended public schools. St. Vitus school was badly overcrowded by this time, and the campaign to raise funds for a new school brought all of the parish societies and factions into genuine harmony for the first time since the rift in 1905–06. The new school, completed in 1914, was among the largest parish schools in Cleveland. It had eighteen classrooms, nine grade levels, and conducted classes in both English and Slovene for its 1,063 students. By 1915, Cleveland's three Slovene parishes (now including St. Mary's) had 1,551 pupils enrolled in their schools, while 265 pupils attended public school. In 1922 the three parochial schools had 2,660 pupils, with 300 of the parishes' children attending public schools.[62]

By 1930, however, the situation had begun to change. Even though the total enrollment in the city's four Slovene parochial schools (by this time including St. Christine's), 2,575, was twice the public school number of 1,209, the proportion of children attending public school had increased significantly. Parish ethnic schools continued to play an important role in preserving Slovene ethnic identity among members of the second generation, but did not enjoy the near-monopoly they had had in educating the community's children in earlier years. The community's perceptions of its children's educational needs had changed with the passage of time. By the 1930s, Slovene was taught only as an extra subject in the parish schools, although it was frequently used as the language of instruction in religion and music.[63]

As early as 1909 Slovenes in one parish had complained about only Slovene- and not English-language catechism instruction being available to their children.[64] Most pastors, however, accommodated or even promoted the use of English among their parishioners, realizing that adults, as well as children, had to be able to speak the language of America. Thus, for example, Rev. Oman encouraged and helped St. Lawrence parishioners to learn English, although he was also keenly aware of the immigrants' need for Slovene-speaking clergy. "All the older people make their confessions in their own language, they will simply stop coming if they lose the opportunity to communicate in their mother tongue." While the American-born Rev. Oman went to Slovenia in search of an assistant fluent in Slovene, those senior clergymen less comfortable in English preferred to have as assistants younger priests who spoke both Slovene and English.[65]

In terms of its cultural functions, the church did not serve only as an institution in which Cleveland Slovenes could attempt to define their position with respect to the host society. It was also at times a venue for interaction with other immigrant groups. At the most personal level, this came about through inter-ethnic marriages. Although the overall rate of inter-ethnic marriage involving Slovenes was low in Cleveland, marriages between Slovenes and Croatians were relatively common.

When the bride and groom came from different parishes, or when the priest of one parish married a couple who belonged to another parish, both priests had to give their approval. Failure to follow this procedure could cause personal friction between clergymen, despite the inter-ethnic harmony that the marriage of a Croatian groom to a Slovene bride, or vice versa, seemed to indicate. In 1912 and in subsequent years Rev. Ponkivar of St. Vitus complained to the diocese about Rev. Niko Gršković of the Croatian parish of St. Paul's, saying that he was marrying St. Vitus parishioners without asking permission. Rev. Gršković responded that he regarded the numerous Slovenes who attended St. Paul's church on a regular basis as members of his own congregation.[66]

In point of fact, both St. Paul's and St. Vitus had members of both nationalities. The St. Clair neighborhood had overlapping Slovene and Croatian parishes due to the practice of creating ethnically-based churches within the diocese. The apparent inter-ethnic conflict over where marriages should take place stemmed mainly from clerical jealousies, and from geographic factors, rather than Slovene-Croatian animosity. A number of Prekmurje Slovenes lived in the St. Clair area. In Europe, the Prekmurci had always had more contacts with Croatians than they had with other Slovenes. When the Prekmurci settled in the United States, they preferred to locate in or near Croatian neighborhoods, or, in cities lacking these, near Magyar or Slovak neighborhoods, since they had lived in the Hungarian part of the Hapsburg Empire. A number of Prekmurje Slovenes lived in the mixed Slovene-Croatian St. Clair neighborhood in Cleveland, and many chose to attend St. Paul's rather than St. Vitus, with only two families from Prekmurje registered as parishioners of the Slovene church before 1925. The first documented Prekmurian wedding in Cleveland took place in St. Paul's in 1907, and in subsequent years as well, most Prekmurci married in the Croatian parish.[67]

The Impact of World War I

In counterpoise to the private expression of interaction between Slovenes and other nationalities as symbolized by intermarriage, ethnic alliances and rivalries assumed their most public aspect during World War I. The national aspirations of central and eastern European peoples became the focus for political activity among immigrants from those lands residing in the United States.

In July 1917 a unit of Slovene, Croatian, and Serbian volunteers left Cleveland, bound for the Salonika front. The contingent, which included twenty-six Slovenes, marched down St. Clair Avenue to the cheers of thousands of Clevelanders of south Slav origin. They had their photographs taken in the South Slav Sokol Gardens, attended a farewell luncheon in Grdina Hall, and then marched to the railway station where they boarded cars decorated with banners proclaiming their status as the "first group to go with the glorious flag for free Yugoslavia." A similar contingent departed in the summer of 1918. Slovene soldiers who left for service in the U.S. Army in 1917 were also honored at a farewell banquet held in Grdina Hall, and marched in a parade of departing American soldiers witnessed by hundreds of thousands of Clevelanders of all backgrounds.[68]

Slovenes were by no means united in their reaction to the events of World War I. Many American Slovenes held pro-Austrian sentiments, although these sentiments either changed or had to be kept secret following the entry of the United States into the war. While this faction never developed a formal structure, Slovenes favoring separation of their homeland from the Hapsburg Empire were active in various organizations with somewhat different visions of the post-war order.

The Slovene League was founded in February 1915, and headquartered in Chicago. The formation of a Cleveland branch immediately followed, at a rally attended by two thousand people. Rev. Grškovič, as president of the Croatian League, addressed the rally, comparing Austria to a mother with six children who cared for only two of them. "Only the Germans and the Hungarians have human rights and the rights of the Slavs are trampled underfoot." Edward Kalish, who served as secretary of Cleveland's Slovene League branch, was also elected secretary of the national organization. Louis Pirc, the owner of *Clevelandska Amerika*, was president of the Cleveland branch. Initially, his newspaper published an article which envisioned Slovenes working together with Czechs and Croatians, whose homelands were also under Austrian domination, rather than forming a south Slav union with the Serbs, who already had an independent state. "But," continued the writer, "by no means shall we unite into one conglomerate league with these other nations. There shall still exist three separate leagues: the Slovene, the Croat and the Czech league, who shall each be engaged in activities for the good of its own nation."[69]

Nonetheless, at a meeting in Chicago in March, attended by representatives of all of the south Slav immigrant groups, including two delegates
from the Cleveland Slovene League, a resolution affirming Yugoslav unity was
passed, thus in effect giving up the Slovene nation's claim to a separate sov-
ereignty. In subsequent months, Cleveland Slovenes organized a number of
meetings featuring speeches by various proponents of Yugoslav unity and
liberation, including Dr. Niko Zupanič a Slovene envoy from the Yugoslav
Committee in London. The Slovene League had chosen to support the
Yugoslav Committee's goal of a Yugoslav state of Serbs, Croatians, and
Slovenes headed by the Serbian royal dynasty. When the League disbanded
in 1917 due to dissension among its leadership, the Slovene National Union
(Slovenska narodna zveza) was founded, with headquarters in Cleveland.
The Union also favored a monarchic Yugoslav state.[70]

In opposition to the monarchists, other south Slavic immigrants organized in support of a Yugoslav Republic. Liberal and socialist-oriented Slovenes were instrumental in promoting the "Chicago Declaration" of 1917,
which led to the formation of the Yugoslav Republican Alliance. The declaration, written by the leaders of the YSF, called for unification of the south
Slav nationalities into a republic, with each group on an equal basis. The
Slovenes in Cleveland organized a Slovene lodge of the Yugoslav Republican Alliance (Jugoslovansko Republičansko Združenje) in 1918. In April of
that year the Slovene National Union met, producing a "Cleveland Declaration" in counterpoint to the Chicago document. This declaration also called
for equality among the Serb, Croatian, and Slovene components of the Yugoslav nation, but stressed the importance of a unified nation, noting that
Slovenes could not exist alone.[71]

Immediately following the war, the peace settlement gave Italy, as one
of the victorious allies, land belonging to the defeated Hapsburg Empire that
Slovenes regarded as their own. This tended to exacerbate ill-will between
the Slovenes and Italians who had settled side by side in the Collinwood
neighborhood. In post-war and later years, events in Yugoslavia would also
create tensions that were reflected among and even within the south Slav
groups in Cleveland. South Slav participation in the Cleveland Cultural
Gardens, a civic project intended to celebrate the national cultures of the
city's ethnic groups and promote harmony among those groups, was a prime
example of the way national and political loyalties could affect seemingly
innocuous undertakings. By the time the South Slavs were ready to plan their
garden in the early 1930s, events within Yugoslavia had caused a strongly
anti-Yugoslav sentiment to develop among American Croatians. Slovenes'
primary quarrel was internal, as conservative-Catholic and progressive

factions argued over the statue representing Slovene culture (each nationality was to have its own) to be placed in the garden. Although a compromise—the setting up of two statues, one of Bishop Baraga and the other of
writer Ivan Cankar—was reached, it did not restore total harmony. Socialists and progressives had begun mocking the entire project, and the Cankar
statue was stolen even before it could be placed in the garden.[72]

Slovene Political Activity in Cleveland

Old world affinities and antipathies also affected Slovenes' participation in
local Cleveland politics. Slavic solidarity, particularly with Croatians, came
into play, as did rivalry with Italians. And the interracial tensions that were
part of the political landscape in America had increasing significance as time
went on.

Cleveland Slovenes were politically organized at a relatively early point
in the settlement's existence. The Slovene Political Club, for instance, was
founded in 1912. During the early period, as later, Democratic Party candidates received more support among Slovenes than did Republicans. The
Slovene press took a leading role in promoting Slovene participation in the
American political process. In later years this meant promoting the candidacy of Slovene politicians. Initially, however, *Nova domovina* and then
Clevelandska Amerika focused largely on the issues of citizenship and voter
registration, recognizing their importance as prerequisites for political power.
In 1912, according to *Clevelandska Amerika,* there were only three thousand
voters among Cleveland's twenty-five thousand Slovenes, since most were
not United States citizens and therefore did not have voting rights. The
paper criticized this situation and not only encouraged but also actively
assisted Slovene immigrants to become citizens and voters. It worked in tandem with the Slovene Political Club, which held citizenship classes, offered
information about voting procedures, endorsed candidates, and generally
organized the Slovene vote. Also in 1912, following a change in state law
which affected Cleveland's voting procedures, ethnic newspapers including
Clevelandska Amerika received governmental subsidies to publish information on the new system.[73]

At the time of the United States entry into World War I, *Clevelandska
Amerika* reported that more than half of the eligible Slovenes in the city's
wards had not yet registered as voters. The paper warned its readers: "If you
do not register to vote, you deserve to have your certificate of citizenship
taken away from you, and you can be sure that this will happen, if you do

not vote."[74] Nonetheless, the number of Slovene naturalized citizens and registered voters had increased and was continuing to do so. Already, they frequently held the balance of power within the electoral districts where they resided, and thus gained some political leverage, although Slovene candidates had no success even at the level of city council until the 1920s.[75]

The city's mayoral elections had attracted interest within Cleveland's Slovene community early on, as mayoral candidates began to court the burgeoning ethnic vote. In 1907 Slovenes supported incumbent Democrat Tom L. Johnson against the Republican candidate Theodore Burton. *Nova domovina* also favored Johnson, although it did not endorse either candidate on its editorial pages, and accepted paid advertisements from both sides. Burton's advertisements attempted to appeal to Catholic sentiments, accusing Johnson of defying the pope because he allowed saloons to be open on Sundays. However, the civic improvements credited to Johnson, and especially his advocacy of low streetcar fares, ensured his reelection. For immigrant as well as native-born voters, the focus of this contest was on city problems.[76] During some later campaigns, European issues took on increased significance, particularly among Slovenes and other nationality groups. Such was the case in 1915, when *Clevelandska Amerika* did not support Democratic candidate Peter Witt, who had declared "that he would rather try his luck with the German Emperor than with the ignorant Russians."[77]

In 1919 European politics and local issues combined to affect the way Slovenes voted in the mayoral election. *Clevelandska Amerika* expressed opposition to incumbent Harry L. Davis on three counts: first, as a Republican, he was to be mistrusted because his party was pro-Italian and anti-Yugoslav, while Woodrow Wilson and the Democrats had always backed Slavic interests; second, Davis had increased the city's debts by $2.5 million during his second term, resulting in a bankrupt municipal treasury, with high taxes inevitably to come; and finally, it was claimed that criminals had prospered during Davis's administration.[78]

In subsequent elections, Slovenes showed less interest in mayoral politics, focusing instead on getting one of their own elected as councilman of Cleveland's 23rd ward, which included the St. Clair neighborhood. Eventually, their interest in the mayor's race was rekindled by rumors that a second-generation Slovene, Democrat Frank Lausche, was going to run as a candidate for mayor in the 1937 election. Lausche, born in Cleveland to immigrant parents in 1895, graduated from Cleveland Marshall Law School and entered practice in 1925. He was appointed to a municipal court judgeship in 1932 and elected to the common pleas court in 1936. Lausche did not actually run for mayor until 1941. His election as Cleveland's first mayor of eastern European descent signaled a victory for the Slavic proliberal movement, and the greatest success to that date for Slovenes in Cleveland politics.[79]

Although the mayor's office had a higher profile, ward councilmen were equally if not more important to the people in the neighborhoods. Members of each eastern and central European ethnic group in Cleveland believed that a councilman of their own nationality could best represent their interests. Thus, council races were especially important to these groups, including the Slovenes. During the 1912 elections, Slovenes for the first time had their own candidate on the ballot in the 23rd ward: Frank Kern, who was running on the ticket of the Socialist Party. Although Slovenes supported him (despite rather than because of his political orientation), he ultimately lost to an opponent from the Democratic Party.[80]

Slovene candidates ran in the council elections of 1917, 1919, and 1921, but with no success. John Julič, who ran in 1917, was president of the large KSKJ St. Vitus lodge. The election attracted national attention among Slovene Catholics since the KSKJ's newspaper strongly supported Julič's candidacy. With misgivings about his qualifications, *Clevelandska Amerika* endorsed Julič purely on the basis of his ethnicity, but to no avail. Although more Slovenes were becoming citizens, their numbers were still not large enough to elect candidates without support from other ethnic groups, and they were as yet failing to gain this.[81]

In 1923 Cleveland held its first city council election according to the proportional representation system, instituted following the adoption of a city manager plan of government in 1921. The city, formerly divided into thirty-three small wards, was reorganized into four large districts, from each of which five to seven council members were elected at large.[82] In 1925, during the second election held under the new system, Clevelanders elected the first Slovene member of city council, John L. Mihelich.

Born in Slovenia in 1891, Mihelich moved to Cleveland with his parents in 1907. He worked as a laborer while continuing his education, and was admitted to the bar in 1917, but soon left for wartime service in France. In 1923 Mihelich launched an unsuccessful campaign for municipal court judge. Two years later, he ran for council in the city's third district, with strong support from Slovene newspapers, the Democratic Party, and Slovaks, who were numerous in the district. Mihelich emphasized his Slavic descent to gain votes from members of all Slavic groups. Like other Democrats, he favored maintaining municipal ownership of the city's electric power plant and increasing its capacity. Not only most ethnic newspapers, but also the mass circulation daily Cleveland *Plain Dealer* supported his candidacy. So did mainstream organizations such as the Citizens League. As the campaign neared its end, meetings were held in the St. Clair Avenue Slovene National Home to rally support for the candidate and encourage a high turnout of Slovene voters. In November 1925 Mihelich was elected to one of the third district's council seats.[83]

In the 1927 election, Slovene voters were again mobilized to help Mihelich gain reelection. On the first day of voter registration that year, *Ameriška domovina* counted 1,123 Slovenes and Croatians as being registered, with 782 added on the next day. There were sixteen candidates in the third district, among them three African Americans. More African Americans than Slovenes had registered to vote in the district, claimed *Ameriška domovina*, in an apparent attempt to use racial tensions to galvanize support for Slovene candidates. The newspaper's attitude was indicative of the two groups' uneasy coexistence in the St. Clair Avenue neighborhood. The election's results did in fact reflect the ethnic and political balance in the district. John Mihelich was reelected, and two African Americans, Forest Gregg and Thomas Fleming, also gained third district seats on city council.[84]

In the fourth district, candidates included two Slovene-Americans, independent Anton Vehovec, a railroad union official, and Democrat James Mally, a dentist; an African American, Clayborne George; and an Italian-American, Alessandro De Maioribus. With Slovene-Italian relations in the district already adversarial, the Slovene press appealed to its readers' ethnic pride: "Will the Slovene candidate win or will the Italian candidate be elected?" The press also urged fourth district Slovene voters to oust incumbent Helene Green from city council, because she favored prohibition and restrictive immigration laws. Taking a more positive approach, Vehovec attempted to gain voter support by endorsing the Nottingham neighborhood's demands for a streetcar line. However, the two Slovene candidates were defeated, while George and De Maioribus won council seats.[85]

In 1929 Mihelich was again re-elected; in the fourth district four Slovene candidates split the vote and went down to defeat. In 1931 Mihelich ran (unsuccessfully) for a municipal judgeship, and Slovene candidates could not garner sufficient votes for election in either the third or fourth district. The 1931 election also saw Clevelanders voting for a return to mayoral system of government and a thirty-three seat council. The return of small wards, many of which were dominated by one or two ethnic settlements, proved a boon for ethnic politicians, providing them with ready-made constituencies. For Slovenes, Wards 23 and now also 32, which included much of Collinwood and Nottingham, were a natural base of power. In the next election, in 1933, three Slovenes and one Croatian (Emil Crown

Gvozdanovič, in Ward 31) were elected to city council. Anton Vehovec, making his fourth run for a council seat, finally succeeded in the new Ward 32, while Ward 23 voters elected Democrat Leopold Kennick. In addition, John Ripic won in Ward 3 on the city's west side. In each of the years 1935, 1937, and 1939, Vehovec (by now affiliated with the Democratic Party) and three other Slovenes were elected as councilmen. With four of its members on council, the Slovene community was now represented far in excess of its proportion of the Cleveland population.[86]

This success can be ascribed at least in part to the very intensive political education campaign undertaken by the Slovene press, especially *Ameriška domovina*. Also, the Slovene community was reasonably prosperous, with sufficient financial resources to support political campaigns. Finally, familiarity with representative institutions in the Hapsburg Empire, and with the balance of conflict and compromise inherent in political activity, formed a basis of experience on which Slovenes could build in the United States.

A Cleveland Slovene also succeeded in gaining election to Ohio's state assembly in the mid-1930s. Lausche and Mihelich had run for the offices of state senator and state representative, respectively, in 1924, but were defeated by Republican opponents. No Slovene candidate won a seat in the state assembly until 1934, when lawyer Joseph J. Ogrin, also a Democrat, was elected a state representative. Two years later, John Mihelich made an attempt to break into politics at the national level, running for the House of Representatives from Ohio's twentieth district. However, he did not win the election, in large part because his campaign focused on Slovenes in his own ward area and neglected to promote his candidacy sufficiently among Slovenes in other parts of the district or among voters of other nationalities.[87]

Cleveland's Slovene community would have to wait until 1944 for one of its members to have significant success beyond the local level in politics. In that year, Frank Lausche won the first of his five terms as Ohio's governor. Following his governorship, he would go on to represent Ohio in the United States Senate for twelve years.[88] Slovene-Americans' political apprenticeship had spanned space and time, moving from the Hapsburg Empire to the industrial cities of America. Lausche's career marked the end of this apprenticeship, and the beginning of Slovene-Americans' full participation in American government at all levels.

Notes

1. Henry Huttenbach, Peter Vodopivec, eds., *Voices from the Slovene Nation 1990–1992, Nationalities Papers, 21, Special Issue,* Spring 1993 (New York: Association

for the Study of the Nationalities of the USSR and Eastern Europe, 1993); Jill Benderly, Evan Kraft eds., *Independent Slovenia. Origins, Movements, Prospects*, (Basingstoke, London: Macmillan Press Ltd., 1997); Janko Prunk, *A Brief History of Slovenia: Historical Background of the Republic of Slovenia* (Ljubljana: Založba Grad, 1996); Jože Pirjevec, *Jugoslavija: Nastanek, razvoj ter razpad Karadjordevićeve in Titove Jugoslavije* (Koper: Založba Lipa, 1995); Leopoldina Plut-Pregelj and Carole Rogel, *Historical Dictionary of Slovenia* (Lanham, Md.: Scarecrow Press, Inc., 1996).

2. Matjaž Klemenčič, *Slovenes of Cleveland: The Creation of a New Nation and a New World Community: Slovenia and the Slovenes of Cleveland, Ohio* (Novo mesto: Dolenjska založba, 1995), 79–89; Matjaž Klemenčič, *Ameriški Slovenci in NOB v Jugoslaviji: naseljevanje zemljepisna razprostranjenost in odnos ameriških Slovencev do stare domovine od sredine 19. stoletja da konca druge svetovne vojne* (Maribor: Založba Obzorja, 1987), 34, 67. According to the census of 1910, there were 50,000 Slovenes in Trieste, just under 20,000 in Cleveland and over 19,000 in the future capital of Slovenia Ljubljana.

3. Jože Grdina, *Spominska knjiga: Izdano ob priliki odkritja spomenika Ireneju Frideriku Baragi v Jugoslovanskem kulturnem vrtu* (Cleveland: *Ameriška domovina*, 1935), 51; Frank J. Turk, *Slovenski pionir, nekaj črtic iz življenja prvih Slovencev v Clevelandu/*History of the First Slovenian Settler in Cleveland (Cleveland, 1955), 5; *St. Vitus Church Diamond Jubilee Book* (South Hackensack: Custombook Inc., 1969), 12.

4. Klemenčič, *Slovenes of Cleveland*, 86–88; Grdina, *Spominska knjiga*, 51.

5. Frank Javh-Kern, *Spomini ob 30-letnici prihoda v Ameriko*, (Ljubljana: Merkur, 1937), 29–44.

6. Vatroslav Grill, *Med dvema svetovoma* (Ljubljana: Mladinska knjiga, 1979), 23, 31–34.

7. *13th U.S. Census of Population 1910*, vol. 2, chapter VII, 781–860; *14th U.S. Census of Population 1920*, vol. 2, chap. VI, 685–736; Annual Parish censuses could be found in the annual parish reports. They are located in Catholic Diocese Archive of Cleveland for each of the Slovene ethnic parishes; Ciril Podgorelec, "Statistična analiza slovenskih far v Clevelandu med 1896 in 1940" (B.A., Department of History, University Maribor: 1988), 7.

8. Podgorelec, "Statistična analiza", 7.

9. The Immigration Commission (also known as the Dillingham Commission after the man who headed it) used sampling techniques to produce its report, *Immigrants in the Cities: A Study of Selected Districts in New York, Chicago, Boston, Cleveland, Buffalo and Milwaukee. 1911 Reports of the Immigration Commission*, vol. 26–7, presented to the 61st Congress, 3rd session, document no.743 (Washington D.C.: Government Printing Office, 1911), (hereafter cited as *IC*). The Commission studied population characteristiques in the year 1907 on the basis of a sample of 666 persons divided in 113 Slovene families in Cleveland; *IC*, 164–212.

The author used sampling techniques also in an attempt to analyze the original U.S. census data for 1910 for the Slovene St. Clair Avenue community. Result was the analysis of the U.S. Census of 1910, computerized sheets, Archives of the Research

Institute, Pedagoška fakulteta, University of Maribor (this analysis includes 1034 members of the community). To analyze the data of the 1930 U.S. census, the author used Howard Whipple Green, "Population Characteristics by Census Tracts: Cleveland, Ohio, 1930" (Cleveland *Plain Dealer*, 1931), 20–35. The census data from which Green compiled information according to census tract combine all persons born on the territory that was comprised in Yugoslavia as of 1930 (it does not, therefore, include Slovenes who came from territories that in 1930 were part of Italy or post-war Austria). The assumption can be made that in Cleveland, a clear majority, likely around three-fourths, of these persons were of Slovene origin, and therefore the population characteristics given by Green can be considered to be true for Slovenes. We do not posses any other demographic statistics that could separate out Slovenes from other Yugoslavs.

10. *IC,* 164–212.

11. U.S. Census of 1910, computerized sheets, Archives of the Research Institute, Pedagoška fakulteta, University of Maribor (this analysis includes 1034 members of the community).

12. Green's (see quote Nr. 10) data were analyzed in Lidija Kropej, "Prebivalci rojeni v Jugoslaviji, Madžarski, Poljski in Češkoslovaški v Clevelandu leta 1930" (Graduate research, Department of History, University of Maribor, 1991), 43–57.

13. Grill, *Med dvema svetovoma,* 34–35.

14. Mary Morgenthaler and Edward M. Miggins, "The Ethnic Mosaic: The Settlement of Cleveland by the New Immigrants and Migrants," in *The Birth of Modern Cleveland, 1865–1930,* eds. Thomas F. Campbell and Edward M. Miggins (Cleveland: Western Reserve Historical Society; London, Cranbury, NJ: Associated University Presses, 1988), 111–112; Turk, *Slovenski pionir,* 5; Turk file, Theodore Andrica Papers, WRHS.

15. Grill, *Med dvema svetovoma,* 23; Javh-Kern, *Spomini,* 45.

16. Matjaž Klemenčič, "Slovenski izseljenski tisk" *in Znanstvena revija: humanistika,* vol. 3, nr. 2. (Maribor: Pedagoška fakulteta, 1991), 303–304.

17. Van Tassel and Grabowski, eds., ECH, 31, 375; *Clevelandska Amerika,* 9 August 1910, 10 March 1914; "K priselitvi 'Glasila' v Cleveland, Ohio," *Glasilo KSKJ,* 9(50):4, 12 December 1923.

18. *Clevelandska Amerika,* 11 October 1910, 1.

19. *Clevelandska Amerika,* 29 April 1910, 1.

20. *Clevelandska Amerika,* 9 August 1910, 10 March 1914.

21. *Ameriška domovina,* 20 January 1931; 21 December 1935; 10 April 1936.

22. *Ameriška domovina,* 20 December 1948 Section 2, 1; Ivan Mladineo, *Narodni adresar,* (New York: John Brankovich, 1937), 526–556; *Ameriška domovina,* 18 March 1927, 23 March 1928, *Clevelandska Amerika,* 25 March 1910; 20 December 1910.

23. Van Tassel and Grabowski, eds., ECH, 467, 721; *Clevelandska Amerika,* 19 December 1913; *Ameriška domovina,* 21 December 1937.

24. *Ameriška domovina,* 21 December 1925, 4 April 1932; Van Tassel and Grabowski, eds., ECH, 467, 721.

25. Ivan Mladineo, *Narodni adresar,* 526–556; *Ameriška domovina,* 29 February 1928, 5 November 1934, 5 June 1937.

26. *Clevelandska Amerika,* 7 March 1913; *Ameriška domovina,* 24 September 1919.

27. See Ivan Čizmić, "Yugoslav Immigrants in the U.S. Labor Movement," in *American Labor and Immigration History, 1877–1920's Recent European Research,* ed. Dirk Hoerder (Urbana, Chicago, London: University of Illinois Press, 1983), 177–190; Joseph Petrovich Stipanovich, "Immigrant Workers and Immigrant Intellectuals in Progressive America: A History of the South Slav Social Democratic Movement, 1900–1908" (Master's thesis, University of Minnesota, 1978), 2–7.

28. Joseph Jauch, "Socialistični klub JSZ, Nekoliko zgodovine o socialističnem gibanju v Clevelandu," *Ameriški Družinski Koledar* (Chicago: Jugoslovanska socialistična zveza, 1923), 177; Mladineo, *Narodni adresar,* 545, 550; "Socialistično gibanje slovenskih delavcev v Ameriki," *Ameriški Družinski Koledar* (Chicago: Jugoslovanska socialistična zveza,1916), 192.

29. Ivan Čizmić, *Hrvati u životu Sjedinjenih američkih država* (Zagreb: Inštitut za hrvatsku povijest, 1975), 125; Files of subscribers to *Proletarec,* Papers of the Yugoslav Socialist Federation, (Immigration History Research Center, University of Minnesota, St.Paul, Minnesota).

30. Igor Žiberna, "Prispevek k zgodovini Proletarca, časopisa ameriških Slovencev" (graduate research, Department of History, University of Maribor, 1986).

31. Louis Kaferle, "Ob štiridesetletnici Slovenskega delavskega doma," *Spominska knjiga* (Cleveland: Slovene Workmen's Home, 1967), 2; Kaferle "Štirideset let Slovenskega delavskega doma v Clevelandu," *Slovenski Izseljenski Koledar (Ljubljana: Slovenska Izseljenska Matica, 1968), vol. 16, 278–285;* Kaferle, "Slovesnosti ob polstoletnici Slovenskega delavskega doma v Clevelandu," *Slovenski Izseljenski Koledar* (Ljubljana: Slovenska Izseljenska Matica, 1977), vol. 25, 234–237; Klemenčič, *Slovenes of Cleveland,* 240–242.

32. snpj societies in Cleveland were members of the Educational Section of the Yugoslav Socialist Federation. Jugoslovanska socialistična zveza, Izkaz prispevkov v "izobraževalno akcijo," Jugoslovanske socialistične zveze za leto, 1927, file, wrhs.

33. Matjaž Klemenčič, "Fraternal Benefit Societies and the Slovene Immigrants in the United States," in Matjaž Klemenčič ed., *Etnični fraternalizem v priseljenskih državah, Ethnic Fraternalism in Immigrant Countries* (Maribor: Pedagoška fakulteta, 1996), 21–32.

34. Toussaint Hočevar, "Češki vpliv pri snovanju slovenskih podpornih jednot," *Časopis za zgodovino in narodopisje* (Maribor; Zgodovinsko društvo Maribor and University of Maribor, 1977), vol. 31, 234–240.

35. *Kranjsko katoliško podporno društvo Sv. Vida, Cleveland, Ohio, Društvene postave,* 29, kskj file, Immigration History Research Center, University of Minnesota; Turk, *Slovenski pionir,* 1–12; *Ameriška domovina,* 19 June 1935, 4. For Štefan Furdek, see chapter by Kopanic.

36. Darko Friš, Bogdan Kolar, Andrej Vovko, *Prvih sto let Kranjsko-Slovenske Katoliške jednote: pregled zgodovine kskj: 1894–1994* (Ljubljana: Ilex, 1997);

Klemenčič, "Fraternal Benefit Societies . . . ," 23; Matjaž Klemenčič, Igor Javernik, "Ustanovitev in razvoj Kranjsko slovenske katoliške jednote - Prve slovenske centralizirane podporne organizacije v Združenih državah Amerike," in *Etnični fraternalizem v priseljenskih državah, Ethnic Fraternalism in Immigrant Countries,* 345–356; Josip Zalar, "Velika jubilejna kampanija," in *Glasilo K.S.K.J.,* 24. September 1924, 3; Mladineo, *Narodni adresar,* 507–10. Following Marijan Spolek, the early Catholic Slovene societies in Cleveland were: Srce Marije (Heart of Mary), the oldest Slovene women's benefit lodge in Cleveland, established in 1897, which met in the school of St. Vitus; Sv. Jožef (St. Joseph), established in 1899, which met in Union Hall on St. Clair Avenue; Presvetega Srca Jezusovega (Sacred Heart of Jesus), established in 1899 by former members of the St. Vitus Society opposed to affiliation with the KSKJ, which met in Gates Hall on E 55th Street; and the Society of St. Aloysius (Društvo Sv. Alojzija), established in 1900 as the first such Slovene association in Newburgh, which met in Stafford Hall. An early non-sectarian independent lodge, "Slovenija", was founded in 1895, which in later years resisted pressure to amalgamate with the SDZ. *Glasilo K.S.K.J.,* 20 May 1927, 1; *Ameriška domovina,* 22 August 1934, 2, 11. August 1939, 3; *Spominska knjiga 35-letnice samostojnega slovenskega podpornega društva Sv. Alojzija* (Cleveland: Slovensko podporno društvo Sv. Alojzija, 1935), 4; "Zapisnik društva Slovenija," Slovenija file, 15, June 7, 1896, Western Reserve Historical Society.

37. Joe Evanish, "SNPJ History: A General Overview," *Etnični fraternalizem v priseljenskih državah, Ethnic Fraternalism in Immigrant Countries* (Maribor: Pedagoška fakulteta, 1996), 69–64.

38. Klemenčič, *Ameriški Slovenci,* 85–87; Zapisnik društva Naprej, 20 March 1904, file, WRHS; Jože Zavertnik, *Ameriški Slovenci—Pregled splošne zgodovine Združenih držav, slovenskega naseljevanja in naselbin ter Slovenske narodne podporne jednote* (Chicago: SNPJ, 1925), 412–414.

39. Zavertnik, *Ameriški Slovenci,* 414; *Ameriška domovina,* 18 May 1937, 1.

40. *Ameriška domovina,* 20 May 1937, 1; Frank Zaitz, "Jugoslovanske podporne organizacije v Zedinjenih Državah," *Ameriški družinski koledar* (Chicago, Jugoslovanska Delavska Tiskovna Družba, 1935), 114; Mladineo, *Narodni adresar,* 516–19.

41. *Slovenec,* (Ljubljana) 21 September 1908, 1.

42. *Ameriška domovina,* 9 September 1936, 1; Mladineo, *Narodni adresar,* 507, 522; *Prosveta,* 15 July 1919; "Zlati jubilej društva 'Lunder-Adamič' iz Clevelanda," *Slovenski izseljenski koledar* (Ljubljana, 1960), 173–177.

43. Simončič Dunja, "Zgodovina Slovenske dobrodelne zveze v Ameriki 1910-1940" (graduate research, Department of History, University of Maribor, 1995); John Gornik, *Zgodovina SDZ Jubilejna knjiga* (Cleveland, 1935), 9; *Ameriška domovina,* 10 September 1919, 15, 17, 21 September 1931.

44. *Clevelandska Amerika,* 29 September 1911, 3; Gornik, *Zgodovina,* 21–22; Margot A. Klima, "The Seventy-Five Year History of the American Mutual Life Association, Diamond Jubilee," souvenir booklet (Cleveland: The American Mutual Life

Association, 1985), 12–23; Rudolph M. Susel, "The American Mutual Life Association 1910-1994," *Etnični fraternalizem v priseljenskih državah, Ethnic Fraternalism in Immigrant Countries* (Maribor: Pedagoška fakulteta, 1996), 101–110.

45. *Glasilo KSKJ*, 20 May 1927; Marie Prisland, *Zgodovina Slovenske ženske zveze* (Sheboygan, Wisconsin, Slovenian Women's Union of America, 1964), 7; Mary Ivanusch, "Ob 30-letnici Progresivnih Slovenk Amerike," *Slovenski izseljenski koledar*, vol. 13 (Ljubljana, Slovenska izseljenska matica, 1965), 216–22; Nataša Cafnik, Bojana Cingerli, "Progresivne Slovenke Amerike (PSWA): 1934-1956," *Etnični fraternalizem v priseljenskih državah, Ethnic Fraternalism in Immigrant Countries*, 379–394.

46. *Glasilo KSKJ*, 11 July 1922, 1; Zavertnik, *Ameriški Slovenci*, 582; *Prosveta*, 15 July 1919, 11; Grill, *Med dvema*, 126–135; *Ameriška domovina*, 18, 20 May 1937; Louis Kaferle, "Društvo Mir ob 60-letnici," *Slovenski izseljenski koledar* (Ljubljana, 1972), 214.

47. Turk, *Slovenski pionir*, 2, 5, 8.

48. *St. Vitus Church, Cleveland, Ohio. Diamond Jubilee Book* (South Hackensack: Custombook Inc., 1969), 12, 33; Turk, *Slovenski pionir*, 4; Frank Česen, "Odlomek iz zgodovine St. Clair Avenue," *Slovenski izseljenski koledar*, vol. 18 (Ljubljana, 1970), 198; Darko Friš: *Ameriški Slovenci in katoliška cerkev 1871–1924* (Celovec-Ljubljana-Dunaj: Mohorjeva založba, 1995); Matjaž Klemenčič, "Razvoj slovenskih far v Cleve-landu," *Celovški zvon*, vol. 9, nr. 32. (Celovec: Društvo Celovški zvon, 1991), 51–60; Edita Husein, "Pregled zgodovine fare sv. Vida", (graduate research, Department of History, University of Maribor, 1990).

49. John J. Grdina, *Spominska knjiga: izdana ob priliki odkritja spomeniku Ireneju Frideriku Baragi v Jugoslovanskem kulturnem vrtu, Cleveland, september 21 and 22, 1935* (Cleveland: *Ameriška domovina*, 1935), 15; *Nova domovina*, 29. April 1907, 1; Česen, "Odlomek," 300.

50. Česen, "Odlomek," 301; *Nova domovina*, 29 April 1907, 1, 2; 5 June 1907, 1; *St. Vitus Church Diamond Jubilee Book*, 34; John Grdina and Ivan Pelan to Rt. Rev. N. Boff, 10 August 1908; Bishop of Cleveland to Rev. Benignus Snoj, 17 January 1908; Rev Snoj to Bishop John P. Farelly, 19 January 1908; Kazimir Zakrajšek to Bishop Farelly, 21 January 1908, St. Vitus File, ADC. In later years, Zakrajšek played an impor-tant role as a spokesman for Catholic Slovenes in America regarding issues con-cerning the Slovene homeland during the First and Second World War years and editor of a Catholic review Ave Maria. See Klemenčič, *Ameriški Slovenci*, 85–129, 214–232; Darko Friš, *Korespondenca Kazimirja Zakrajška, O.F.M., 1907-1928, Viri 6*. (Ljubljana: Arhivsko društvo Slovenije, 1993), 5–35.

51. "Družina John in Lucija Baznik," *Novi svet: Mesečnik za slovenske družine v Ameriki*, vol 4, January 1911, 18; *Ameriška domovina*, 14 November 1962, 2; Klemen-čič, "Razvoj", 55.

52. Ernest Trpin, "Pregled zgodovine cerkve Sv. Lovrenca," *Novi svet*, vol 3., August 1940, 218; *St. Vitus Church, Diamond Jubilee Book*, 42; Secretary of the Bishop to Rev. Joseph Lavrić, 7 January 1913, St. Lawrence Parish file, ADC.

53. Franc Trdan, *Za božjim klicem* (Kranj: Tiskovno društvo Kranj, 1939), 140, 155.

54. *Ibid.*, 155. An analysis of a census sample for the parish confirmed Rev. Omans' statement about his parishioners' origins, cited in Renato Kuzman, "Zgodovina župnije sv. Lovrenca," (Graduate research, Department of History, University of Maribor, 1989), 37.

55. J. Oman to Rev. W. Cullen, 21 March 1921, St. Lawrence Parish File, ADC; Trdan, *Za božjim*, pp 151, 156–7; "Fara sv. Lovrenca, Cleveland O.," *Koledar Ave Maria 1927, Katoliški list za Slovence v Ameriki* (Chicago, Slovenian Franciscan Fathers, 1927), 208–210.

56. Kotnik to Bishop Horstmann, 5 July 1906, St. Mary's Parish File, ADC; *Spominska knjiga župnije Device Marije Vnebovzete v Clevelandu* (Cleveland, Župnija Device Marije Vnebovzete, 1928), 43; Rebol, *History of St. Mary*, 31, 34.

57. Adm. to Most Rev. H. Moeller, 11 January 1909, St. Mary's Parish file, ADC; Anthony Rebol, *History of St. Mary of the Assumption Church and School, Cleveland, Ohio, 1905-1962* (Cleveland: St. Mary of Assumption Parish, 1962), 21–22.

58. *Spominska knjiga župnije*, 25–36; Rebol, *History of St. Mary*, 39; Ernest Trpin, "Kratka zgodovina slovenske župnije Marije Vnebovzete v Collinwoodu," *Novi svet*, vol. 3, September 1940, 244.

59. Rev. Vitus Hribar to Bishop of Cleveland, 27 March 1923; Matrimonial books, St. Mary's Parish, St. Mary's Parish Archive, Cleveland.

60. Vicar General of the Diocese of Cleveland to The Edwards Land Co., 15 April 1925; John Gornk and others to Bishop Schrembs, 12 October 1925; Rev. J. A. McFadden to the future parishioners, 12 November 1925; Chancellor of the Diocese to the Rev. J. Pyan, 12 November 1925; G. J. Coprich to the Bishop, 14 August 1926; Parishioners of St. Christine to Bp. J. Schrembs, n. d.; Chancellor of the Diocese to Rev. V. Vukonič, 1 June 1928; Chancellor of the Diocese to Rev. A. Bombach, 2 February 1931; Rev. A. Bombach to Msgr. V. Balmat, September 1941; Rev. A. Bombach to Rev. J. A. McFadden, 18 October 1936; Rev. A. Bombach to Bishop J. Schrembs, 8 February 1937, St. Christine Parish File, ADC.

61. "Župnija Sv. Vida dobi novega župnika," *Novi svet*, vol. 4, March 1941, 80.

62. Ciril Podgorelec, "Statistična analiza slovenskih far v Clevelandu 1896-1940," (undergraduate research, Department of History, University of Maribor, 1988), 8–11.

63. *Ibid.*; "Odmevi iz slovenskih naselbin," *Koledar Ave Maria 1931, Katoliški list za Slovence v Ameriki* (Chicago, 1931), 180.

64. Rev. Vitus Hribar to Bishop, n.d., St. Mary's Parish File, ADC. The same problem was noted in parishes of other ethnic groups—see for example Francis Bolek, *The Polish American School System* (New York: Columbia Press Co., 1948), 12.

65. J. Oman to Msgr. James Fadden, 15 July 1931 and to Msgr. Joseph Smith, 21 July 1931, St. Lawrence Parish File, ADC; V. Hribar to Bishop, 9 June 1925, St. Mary's Parish file, ADC.

66. Jernej Ponikvar to Bp. John P. Farelly, 18 May 1912, St. Vitus Parish File, ADC; N. Gršković to O'Reilly, 12 June 1912, St. Paul Parish File, ADC. See chapter by Čizmić.

67. Alojz, Janez, and Jože Sraka, *Prekmurci in Prekmurje* (Chicago, Melinci, Rim, 1984), 130–133; Secretary of the Bishop to Rev. Joseph Lavrič, 17 January 1913, St. Lawrence Parish File, ADC.

68. *Clevelandska Amerika*, 16 July 1917, 1; 11 July 1918, 1; 17 September 1917.

69. Matjaž Klemenčič, "Immigrant communities and the establishment of new states in East-Central Europe: the case of the Slovenians in North America," *Srednjeeuropska emigracija i nove demokracije, Društvena istraživanja*, vol, 7, no. 1–2. (Kaliterna Ljiljana, ed.), (Zagreb: Institut društvenih znanosti "Ivo Pilar", 1998), 49; *Clevelandska Amerika*, 23. February 1915, 1.

70. Klemenčič, *Ameriški Slovenci*, 98; *Clevelandska Amerika*, 24 December 1915, 1; 26 April 1916, 1; 16 August 1916, 1; 19 October 1917, 1; January 1918, 1; February 1919, 1.

71. Klemenčič, *Ameriški Slovenci*, 103, 106–116; *Clevelandska Amerika*, 28 February 1919, 1.

72. *Ameriška domovina*, 29 June 1934, 2; 24 August 1934, 2; 8 January 1935, 2; 19 October 1936, 2; 3 December 1937, 2. It was later decided to add a third statue, that of the Slovene poet Simon Gregorčič. The Baraga statue was unveiled in September 1935, and those of Cankar (a replacement) and Gregorčič on Thanksgiving Day, 1936. The Yugoslav Cultural Garden as a whole was not officially opened until 1938; the mayor of Ljubljana attended as a guest of honor; *Ameriška domovina*, 11 and 25 September 1935, 1; 10 February 1936, 1; 28 November 1936, 1; 16 May 1928, 1.

73. *Clevelandska Amerika*, 20 August 1912, 1; Klemenčič Slovenes of Cleveland, 291–334

74. *Clevelandska Amerika*, 15. October 1915, 1.

75. "The distrust of ward politicians supported by the city's foreign-born residents was one of motivating forces behind the demand by good government advocates, including the Citizen League, for a city manager plan. Following on the heels of several incompetent mayoral administrations, Cleveland became the first large city in the country to experiment with the city manager form of government. The new charter approved by voters in 1921, abolished the traditional ward system and provided for a professional manager selected by the city council to administer the city's affairs." Carol Poh Miller, Robert Wheeler, *Cleveland: A Concise History, 1796–1990* (Bloomington: Indiana University Press, 1990), 120–121.

76. *Nova domovina*, 23 March 1907, 1; 8 April 1907, 1; 30 September 1907, 4; 2 October 1907, 4; 8 October 1907, 4; 26 October 1907, 1; 4 November 1907, 1.

77. *Clevelandska Amerika*, 5 November 1915, 1.

78. *Clevelandska Amerika*, 3 November 1919, 1.

79. *Ameriška domovina*, 18 July 1935, 1; 18 November 1935, 2; 30 June 1941, 1; 4 August 1941, 2; 21 August 1941, 1; 22 September 1941, 1; David D. Van Tassel and John J. Grabowski, eds., *Dictionary of Cleveland Biography* (Bloomington and Indianapolis: University of Indiana Press, 1966), 274–5. Cf. also William C. Bitter, *Frank J. Lausche: A Political Biography* (New York: Studia Slovenica, 1975), Edvard Giles

Gobetz, *Frank Lausche, Lincoln of Ohio* (Willoughby Hills, Ohio: Slovenian Research Center, 1987). See Klemenčič article on Lausche in Elliott Robert Barkan, ed., *Making it in America: A Sourcebook on Eminent Ethnic Americans.* (Santa Barbara, CA: ABC-CLIO, 2001) 192–193.

80. *Clevelandska Amerika,* 9 August 1912, 1; 5 November 1912, 1.

81. *Glasilo KSKJ,* 31 October 1917, 5; 5 November 1917, 1, 13; 9 November 1917, 1; *Clevelandska Amerika,* 17 October 1917, 9 November 1917, 1.

82. See Miller and Wheeler, *Cleveland, A Concise History,* 120–121; see also above note 75.

83. *Ameriška domovina,* 31 October 1925, 5; 9 August 1925, 1; 14 September 1925, 1; 5 October 1925, 1; 12 October 1925, 1; 23 October 1925, 1; 9 November 1925, 1; 21 December 1925, 1; *Enakopravnost,* 10 August 1925, 1; 6 October 1925, 1; 10–14 October 1925, 1; 28 October 1925, 1; 31 October 1925, 1; 2 November 1925, 1; 9 November 1925, 2.

84. *Ameriška domovina,* 19 October 1927, 1; 28 October 1927, 2; 7 November 1927, 1.

85. *Ameriška domovina,* 27 May 1927, 1; 2 September 1927, 2; 21 September 1927, 1; 27 October 1931, 1; 7 November 1927, 1.

86. *Ameriška domovina,* 6 September 1929, 1; 6 November 1929, 1; 2 November 1931, 1; 7 November 1931, 1; 10 November 1933, 1; 6 November 1935, 1; 3 November 1937, 1, 8; 9 November, 2 December 1939, 1; Van Tassel and Grabowski, eds. ECH, 186, 210. The successful Slovene candidates, in addition to Vehovec in Ward 32, were: in 1935, George Travnikar (Ward 2), Michael Pucel (Ward 10), and John Novak (Ward 23), and also the Croatian Gvozdanović; in 1937, Travnikar, Pucel, and Novak; in 1939, Pucel, George Kovačič (Ward 23), and Max Traven (Ward 28). A detailed account of Slovene candidates in the City Council elections in Cleveland (1924–1940) and their success is provided in Klemenčič, *Slovenes of Cleveland,* 298–308.

87. *Ameriška domovina,* 24 October 1924, 1; 30 October 1924, 1; 31 October 1924, 1; 8 November 1934, 2; 31 August 1936, 1.

88. *Ameriška domovina,* 8 November 1944, 1; 7 November 1956, 1; Van Tassel and Grabowski, eds., *Dictionary of Cleveland Biography,* 275.

Contributors

DR. C. WINSTON CHRISLOCK is professor of History at the University of St. Thomas in St. Paul, Minnesota, where he has taught since 1972. He received his B.A. in History from the University of Minnesota in 1962, and his M.A. (1964) and his Ph.D. (1971) in History from Indiana University. The focus of his research has been recent Czech and Czechoslovak political and cultural history. More recently, Chrislock has directed his efforts toward Czech immigration to America, contributing a chapter on the Czechs in *They Chose Minnesota* (St. Paul: Minnesota Historical Society, 1981) and *Charles Jonas (1840–1896): Czech National Liberal, Wisconsin Bourbon Democrat* (Philadelphia: The Balch Institute Press and Associated University Presses, 1993). Chrislock was the recipient of a Presidential medal from President Vaclav Havel of the Czech Republic in April 1999 for his contributions to Czech history.

PROFESSOR DR. IVAN ČIZMIĆ is a scientific advisor at the Institute of Social Sciences Ivo Pilar in Zagreb, Croatia. He graduated with degrees in law and history, including his doctorate, from the University of Zagreb. His research focuses on emigration from Croatia. He has written numerous books and article on the subject including four which focus on the Croatian immigrant experience in the United States and one which chronicals the Croatian immigration to New Zealand. His most recent work (written with Ivan Miletic and Dr. George J. Prpic), *From the Adriatic to Lake Erie: A History of Croatians in Greater Cleveland* appeared in 2000.

PROFESSOR DAVID C. HAMMACK is Hiram C. Haydn Professor of History at Case Western Reserve University. His books include *Power and Society: Greater New York at the Turn of the Century* (1982, 1987), *Social Science in the Making: Essays on the Russell Sage Foundation* (with Stanton Wheeler, 1994), *Nonprofit Organizations in a Market Economy* (edited with Dennis R. Young, 1993), and *Making the Nonprofit Sector in the United States* (1998,

2000), and his articles have appeared in *The American Historical Review, The Journal of American History, The Journal of Urban History, Nonprofit and Voluntary Sector Quarterly,* and other journals. He taught at Princeton and the City University of New York before coming to Case Western Reserve University, and he has been a Resident Fellow at the Russell Sage Foundation, a Guggenheim Fellow, and a Visiting Scholar at the Program on Non-Profit Organizations at Yale. He has received the Diekhoff Award for Distinguished Graduate Teaching at Case Western Reserve.

PROFESSOR DR. DIRK HOERDER teaches North American social history and history of migrations at the University of Bremen, Department of Social Sciences. His areas of interest are European labor migration in the Atlantic economies, history of worldwide migration systems, sociology of migrant acculturation. He has been director of the Labor Migration Project and has recently completed a survey of worldwide migration systems. His publications include *Labor Migration in the Atlantic Economies: The European and North American Working Classes during the Period of Industrialization* (Westport, CT: Greenwood, 1985) and, with Leslie Page Moch, *European Migrants: Global and Local Perspectives* (Boston: Northeastern UP, 1996). He has taught at York University, Toronto, Duke University, Durham, NC, and the University of Toronto. He has recently published *Creating Societies: Immigrant Lives in Canada* (Montreal: McGill-Queen's Univ. Press, 1999) and *Cultures in Contact: European and World Migrations, 11th Century to the 1990s* (Durham, NC: Duke University Press, 2002).

PROFESSOR DR. MATJAŽ KLEMENČIČ, a specialist in Slovenian immigrant history, is currently a member of the Department of History at the University of Maribor and also teaches regularly at the University of Ljubljana. He has served as Director of the Research Institute of the University of Maribor's Faculty of Education (1986–1993) and as the Faculty's Associate Dean (1991-1993). He served as Chair of Department of History at the University of Maribor from 1985–1991 and in 1999. He helped to establish a graduate program in American Studies at Faculty of Arts at the University of Ljubljana. Professor Klemenčič is the author of four books: *Ameriški Slovenci in NOB v Jugoslaviji: Naseljevanje, zemljepisna razprostranjenost in odnos ameriških Slovencev do stare domovine od sredine 19. stoletja do konca druge svetovne vojne* (Maribor: Obzorja, 1987); *Slovenes of Cleveland: The Creation of a New Nation and a New World Community: Slovenia and the Slovenes of Cleveland, Ohio* (Novo mesto: Dolenjska založba; Ljubljana: Scientific Institute of the Faculty of Arts, 1995); *Jurij Trunk med Koroško in*

Združenimi državami Amerike ter zgodovina slovenskih naselbin v Leadvillu, Kolorado, in v San Franciscu, Kalifornija (Celovec, Ljubljana, Dunaj: Mohorjeva založba, 1999); and *100 Years of Catholic Faith: St. Joseph's Church, Leadville, Colorado, 1899–1999* (Leadville: The Catholic Community, 2000). He has also contributed a number of entries to Elliot R. Barkan (ed.): *Making It in America: A Sourcebook on Eminent Ethic Americans.* (Santa Barbara, California, Denver, Colorado, Oxford, England: ABC-CLIO, Inc., 2001). He is currently working with Professor Mitja Žagar on a history of the nations of the former Yugoslavia to be published by ABC-CLIO in 2004.

DR. MICHAEL KOPANIC specializes in the history of East Central Europe, Slovakia, and Slovak immigration history in the United States. He writes a column, "Views from the Alleghenies," in the largest circulating Slovak-American newspaper, *Jednota,* and has served as a contributor to the on-line journal, *Central Europe Review* (London-Prague). He has written articles, book reviews, and chapters in numerous other books and journals, including *European Labor Unions, Kosmas, Oost-Europa Verkenningen* (Amsterdam), the National Slovak Society's annual almanac, *Good Shepherd,* and other journals. He contributed entries on Slovak-American sports figures for the *Encyclopedia of Ethnicity and Sports in the United States.* He also is editing and did most of the translating for the new English language version of Anton Špiesz's *Slovak History,* due to be published in 2003. He is also working on an article on the late Andrew Grutka, a prominent Slovak-American bishop. Dr. Kopanic has taught history and/or Slovak language and culture courses at the University of Akron, Lock Haven University, Saint Francis University of Pennsylvania, Teikyo Westmar University, Mount Aloysius College, Cambria County Area Community College, the Pennsylvania State University, Indiana University of Pennsylvania, and Youngstown State University. He is presently a Commonwealth Speaker for the Pennsylvania Humanities Council and a Faculty Consultant for Educational Testing Service. He has also served as a consultant on Slovak broadcasts for Intermedia Survey in Washington, D.C.

JULIANNA PUSKÁS Ph.D., author of several books and many studies on the history of overseas migration from Hungary, worked for nearly thirty years at the Hungarian Academy of Sciences' Institute of History. She began her work by analyzing modernization processes in Hungarian agriculture in the 9th century, then turned to the history of the emigration from Hungary to the United States in the 19th and 20th century. Her name is synonymous with the modernization of the historical analysis of overseas migration from Hungary. As a Fulbright scholar she conducted oral history interviews and collected a variety of sources in a study of three generations whose ancestors migrated from her village. By combining different methodologies of macro- and micro-analyses she is able to give a very colorful picture the complex and many sided social phenomenon of international migration and ethnic life. Two of her major English-language publications are *From Hungary to the United States, 1880–1914*, (Budapest: Akadémiai Kiadó, 1982.) and *Ties That Bind, Ties That Divide: One Hundred Years of Hungarian Experience in the United States*, (New York: Holmes & Meier, 2000.)

PROFESSOR DR. ADAM WALASZEK is a member of the faculty of the Institute of Polish Diaspora and Ethnic Studies of the Jagiellonian University in Cracow, Poland. He specializes in the history of international migrations, and ethnic and social history, particularly of the Polish diaspora. Professor Walaszek has also served as the director (1993–1996) of the Polonia Institute at the Jagiellonian University. He has been the recipient of grants and scholarships from a number of organizations including the Kościuszko Foundation, the Immigration History Research Center, and the American Council of Learned Societies, that have allowed him to research and teach extensively in the United States. He is the author of three books relating the to Polish immigrant experience, *Reemignecja ze Stanów Zjednoczonych ol Polski po I wojnie światowej: 1919–1924, Polscy robotnicy, praca i związki zawodowe w Stanach Zjednoczonych, 1880–1922* (Wroclaw-Warsaw: Ossolineum, 1988), and *Swiaty imigrantow: Tworzenie polonijnego Cleveland, 1880–1930* (Kraków: Nomos, 1994), as well as a number of articles in this subject. Most recently he was the editor of *Polska diaspora* (Kraków, 2001) a synthesis of the history of Polish communities worldwide.

Index